SADLIER-OXFORD

Progress in Mathematics

Authors

Catherine D. LeTourneau

Alfred S. Posamentier

with

Elinor R. Ford

Program Consultants

Madelaine Gallin
Former Math Coordinator
Community School District #6
New York, NY

Frank Lucido
Associate Professor in
Bilingual/Multicultural Education
Texas A&M University
Corpus Christi, TX

Lucy Lugones
Math Coordinator
St. Luke's School
Whitestone, NY

Tim Mason
Title 1 Specialist
Palm Beach County School District
West Palm Beach, FL

R. James Milgram
Professor of Mathematics
Stanford University
Palo Alto, CA

Rosalie Pedalino Porter
Consultant Bilingual/ESL Programs
Amherst, MA

Sadlier-Oxford
A Division of William H. Sadlier, Inc.
www.sadlier-oxford.com

The publisher gratefully acknowledges Rose Anita McDonnell (1905–2003) and her colleagues for the important role they played in the development of *Progress in Mathematics* for more than sixty years.

Reviewers

The publisher wishes to thank the following teachers and administrators, who read portions of the series prior to publication, for their valuable contributions.

Grades 3-6 Reviewers

Madonna Atwood
Teacher
St. Louis, MO

John Palladino
Professor at Eastern Michigan University
Ypsilanti, MI

Debra Wright
Principal
Winter Haven, FL

Judith A. Devine
Educational Consultant
Springfield, PA

Stephanie Garland
Educational Consultant
St. Louis, MO

Grade-Level Reviewers

Marie Bicsak
Math Coordinator
Mt. Clemens, MI

Sara Kobylarz
Grade 3 Teacher
Bronx, NY

Br. Ralph Darmento, F.S.C.
Deputy Superintendent of Schools
Newark, NJ

Suzanne Ryan
Grade 4 Teacher
Orono, MN

Candace Govin
Grades 4–8 Math Teacher/Coordinator
Plantation, FL

Sr. Adriana Cernoch
Grade 6 Teacher
Dallas, TX

Brandy Roth
Grade 3 Teacher
Kissimmee, FL

Elizabeth M. Johnson
Grade 5 Teacher
Bettendorf, IA

Linda Hamby
Grade 5 Teacher
DesPeres, MO

Barbara Murphy
Grade 4 Teacher
Chesterfield, MO

Sr. Martha Carmody, O.P.
Grade 4 Teacher
Springfield, IL

Jacqueline A. Byrd
Grade 5 Teacher
Chesterfield, MO

Sr. Maristella Dunlavy, O.P.
Principal
Springfield, IL

Jeannine Frey
Grade 3 Teacher
Chesterfield, MO

Mary E. Stokes
Grade 5 Teacher
Oak Forest, IL

Dear Family

Progress in Mathematics, now in its sixth decade of user-proven success, is a complete basal mathematics program. Written by experienced teacher-authors, it integrates a traditional course of study and today's academic Standards with the most up-to-date methods of teaching.

Progress in Mathematics is designed to meet the individual needs of all learners. Teachers who use *Progress* come to understand that students may progress as quickly as they can or as slowly as they must.

In Grade 4, multiplication and division will be further developed, and your fourth grader will apply both operations throughout the grade-level, as he or she studies the concepts of measurement, probability and statistics, fractions, geometry, perimeter, area, volume, and decimals. There will also be an increased emphasis on algebraic thinking. Special attention is given to critical thinking, problem solving, mental math, and journalizing.

But overall success in achieving the goals of this program depends on ongoing teacher-family-student interaction. It is important for you to encourage your fourth grader to achieve success in mathematics and to enjoy it as well. You can help your student see math as useful and practical by relating it to everyday situations. It is also helpful to provide a quiet space and time for homework, and to reinforce the idea that by practicing math concepts and skills in your home environment, your student can have fun while learning mathematics.

Throughout the school year, you and your student can access *Math Alive At Home* pages at www.sadlier-oxford.com. These pages include the math vocabulary of each chapter plus fun-filled activities that will help you relate the math your student is learning in school to the real world.

We know that by using **Progress in Mathematics** your fourth grader will not only learn to value math, but become a confident problem solver and learn to reason and communicate mathematically as well.

The Authors

Contents

Algebra Lesson promotes algebraic reasoning.

✱ Develops concept or skill with manipulatives.   Algebra Lesson promotes algebraic reasoning.

✱ Develops concept or skill with manipulatives.   Algebra Lesson promotes algebraic reasoning.

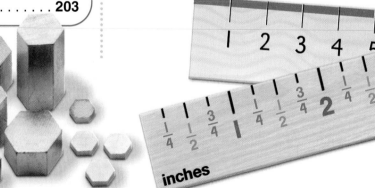

★ Develops concept or skill with manipulatives.　**Algebra** Lesson promotes algebraic reasoning.

*Develops concept or skill with manipulatives.   **Algebra** Lesson promotes algebraic reasoning.

$\dfrac{1}{8}$ $\dfrac{1}{4}$

$\dfrac{1}{5}$ **1** $\dfrac{1}{3}$

*Develops concept or skill with manipulatives.   **Algebra** Lesson promotes algebraic reasoning.

*Develops concept or skill with manipulatives.   Algebra Lesson promotes algebraic reasoning.

*Develops concept or skill with manipulatives.   *Algebra* Lesson promotes algebraic reasoning.

Skills Update

A Review of Mathematical Skills from Grade 3

Progress in Mathematics includes a "handbook" of essential skills, Skills Update, at the beginning of the text. These one-page lessons review skills you learned in previous years. It is important for you to know this content so that you can succeed in math this year.

If you need to review a concept in Skills Update, your teacher can work with you using manipulatives, which will help you understand the concept better.

The Skills Update handbook can be used throughout the year to review skills you may already know. Since many lessons in your textbook refer to pages in the Skills Update, you can use a particular lesson at the beginning of class as a warm-up activity. Or your class may choose to do the Skills Update lessons at the beginning of the year so that you and your teacher can assess your understanding of these previously learned skills.

You may even want to practice specific skills at home. If you need more practice than what is provided on the Skills Update page, you can use the practice pages available online at www.sadlier-oxford.com. These practice pages have an abundance of exercises for each one-page lesson.

Hundreds

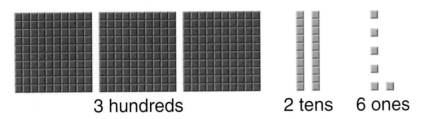

3 hundreds   2 tens   6 ones

Standard Form: 326
Word Name: three hundred twenty-six

HUNDREDS	TENS	ONES
3	2	6

The digit 6 is in the *ones place*.
It has a value of 6 ones, or 6.

The digit 2 is in the *tens place*.
It has a value of 2 tens, or 20.

The digit 3 is in the *hundreds place*.
It has a value of 3 hundreds, or 300.

Write the number in standard form.

1.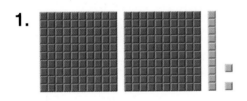

2.

HUNDREDS	TENS	ONES
6	0	7

3. 1 hundred 8 tens 3 ones

4. five hundred sixty-two

Write the place of the red digit. Then write its value.

5. 482   **6.** 369   **7.** 141   **8.** 965   **9.** 174   **10.** 218

11. 522   **12.** 697   **13.** 742   **14.** 831   **15.** 420   **16.** 505

Compare Whole Numbers

> means "is greater than"	< means "is less than"
= means "is equal to"	

To compare numbers:

- Align the digits
  by place value.

  6453
  6459 ↓

- Start at the left. Compare
  the digits in the greatest place.

  6453
  6459

  $6 = 6$

- If these digits are the same,
  compare the next digits.

  6453
  6459

  $4 = 4$

- Keep comparing digits until
  you find two digits that
  are *not* the same.

  6453
  6459

  $5 = 5$
  $9 > 3$

So 6459 > 6453. You could also say 6453 < 6459.

Study this example.

423 __?__ 2423

.Think.........................
There are no
thousands in 423.
....

423
2423 ↓

$0 < 2$ So 423 < 2423   **or**   2423 > 423.

Compare. Write <, =, or >.

1. 57 $=$ 57   **2.** 65 __?__ 62   **3.** 48 __?__ 56   **4.** 82 __?__ 28

5. 325 __?__ 523   **6.** 649 __?__ 841   **7.** 127 __?__ 134   **8.** 525 __?__ 522

9. 6241 __?__ 9246   **10.** 7983 __?__ 7983   **11.** 9015 __?__ 9012

12. 2704 __?__ 2714   **13.** 8619 __?__ 8617   **14.** 1844 __?__ 1846

Recognize and Count Money

ten-dollar bill
$10.00

five-dollar bill
$5.00

one-dollar bill
$1.00

half-dollar
50¢ or $.50

quarter
25¢ or $.25

dime
10¢ or $.10

nickel
5¢ or $.05

penny
1¢ or $.01

To count bills and coins, arrange in order from greatest to least value. Then count on.

| $10.00 | + | $5.00 | + | $.25 | + | $.10 | + | $.01 |

$10.00 ⟶ $15.00 ⟶ $15.25 ⟶ $15.35 ⟶ $15.36

Write each amount. Use the dollar sign and decimal point.

1.

2.

3. 1 five-dollar bill, 3 quarters, 1 dime, 3 nickels, 2 pennies

4. 4 dollars, 1 quarter, 2 nickels

Addition and Subtraction Facts

▶ Add: 5 + 4 = __?__

△ △ △ △ △
△ △ △ △

$$\begin{array}{r} 5 \\ +\ 4 \\ \hline 9 \end{array}$$ ← addends
← sum

or

$$5\ +\ 4\ =\ 9$$
addends   sum

▶ Subtract: 11 − 5 = __?__

□ □ □ □ □
□ ▨ ▨ ▨ ▨
▨

$$\begin{array}{r} 11 \\ -\ 5 \\ \hline 6 \end{array}$$ ← difference

or

$$11\ -\ 5\ =\ 6$$
difference

> **Remember:**
> 5 + 4 = 9 is a number sentence for addition.
> 11 − 5 = 6 is a number sentence for subtraction.

Add or subtract. Watch the signs.

1. $\begin{array}{r}8\\+8\\\hline\end{array}$	**2.** $\begin{array}{r}4\\+9\\\hline\end{array}$	**3.** $\begin{array}{r}16\\-\ 9\\\hline\end{array}$	**4.** $\begin{array}{r}6\\+5\\\hline\end{array}$	**5.** $\begin{array}{r}14¢\\-\ 7¢\\\hline\end{array}$	**6.** $\begin{array}{r}12¢\\-\ 4¢\\\hline\end{array}$
7. $\begin{array}{r}7\\+6\\\hline\end{array}$	**8.** $\begin{array}{r}16\\-\ 7\\\hline\end{array}$	**9.** $\begin{array}{r}0\\+7\\\hline\end{array}$	**10.** $\begin{array}{r}13\\-\ 4\\\hline\end{array}$	**11.** $\begin{array}{r}7¢\\+9¢\\\hline\end{array}$	**12.** $\begin{array}{r}14¢\\-\ 6¢\\\hline\end{array}$
13. $\begin{array}{r}15\\-\ 8\\\hline\end{array}$	**14.** $\begin{array}{r}9\\+9\\\hline\end{array}$	**15.** $\begin{array}{r}11\\-\ 8\\\hline\end{array}$	**16.** $\begin{array}{r}9\\+6\\\hline\end{array}$	**17.** $\begin{array}{r}18¢\\-\ 9¢\\\hline\end{array}$	**18.** $\begin{array}{r}8¢\\+6¢\\\hline\end{array}$

19. 17 − 8　　**20.** 6 + 6　　**21.** 15 − 7　　**22.** 6¢ + 7¢　　**23.** 3¢ + 8¢

Whole Number Operations I

Algebra
Related Facts

These four facts are related facts.
They all use the same numbers.

$$6 + 5 = 11 \qquad 11 - 5 = 6$$
$$5 + 6 = 11 \qquad 11 - 6 = 5$$

Study these examples.

$$12 = 4 + 8$$
$$12 = 8 + 4$$
$$8 = 12 - 4$$
$$4 = 12 - 8$$

$$3 + 3 = 6$$
$$6 - 3 = 3$$

Write the related facts for each pair.

1.

4, 6

2.

2, 7

3.

3, 9

4.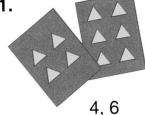

5, 8

5.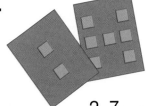

4, 5

6.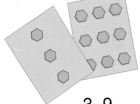

3, 7

7. 9, 5   **8.** 2, 5   **9.** 8, 8   **10.** 6, 7

Complete each addition or subtraction fact.

11. $\underline{\ ?\ } + 7 = 13$ **12.** $\underline{\ ?\ } + 9 = 17$ **13.** $15 = \underline{\ ?\ } + 8$
$\quad\ \ 7 + \underline{\ ?\ } = 13$ $\quad\ \ 9 + \underline{\ ?\ } = 17$ $\quad\ \ 15 = 8 + \underline{\ ?\ }$
$\quad\ \ 13 - 7 = \underline{\ ?\ }$ $\quad\ \ 17 - \underline{\ ?\ } = 9$ $\quad\ \ 8 = 15 - \underline{\ ?\ }$
$\quad\ \ 13 - \underline{\ ?\ } = 7$ $\quad\ \ 17 - 9 = \underline{\ ?\ }$ $\quad\ \ \underline{\ ?\ } = 15 - 8$

Add and Subtract without Regrouping

Add: 2110 + 3022 = ?

Align. Add. Start with the ones.

Add ones.	Add tens.	Add hundreds.	Add thousands.
2110 + 3022 ――― 2	2110 + 3022 ――― 32	2110 + 3022 ――― 132	2110 + 3022 ――― 5132

Subtract: 5867 − 4536 = ?

Align. Subtract. Start with the ones.

Subtract ones.	Subtract tens.	Subtract hundreds.	Subtract thousands.
5867 − 4536 ――― 1	5867 − 4536 ――― 31	5867 − 4536 ――― 331	5867 − 4536 ――― 1331

Find the sum.

1. 42 + 33	2. 128 + 820	3. 173 + 13	4. 8317 + 1222	5. 8117 + 782	6. 6416 + 2103

7. 15 + 22 + 50 + 11   8. 23 + 11 + 34 + 21   9. 300 + 240 + 159

Find the difference.

10. 53 − 21	11. 279 − 151	12. 8576 − 1423	13. 878 − 843	14. 6495 − 3122	15. 5986 − 5082

16. 67 − 5   17. 175 − 25   18. 438 − 16

Whole Number Operations III

Meaning of Multiplication

▶ To find how many, you can add
3 groups of 7: 7 + 7 + 7 = 21

Since you are joining equal groups,
you can multiply:

3 groups of 7
3 sevens
3×7

number of groups	$\times$	number in each group	=	total number
3	$\times$	7	=	21

or

$$7 \longleftarrow \text{factor}$$
$$\times\ 3 \longleftarrow \text{factor}$$
$$\overline{\ \ 21} \longleftarrow \text{product}$$

Remember: $3 \times 7 = 21$ is a multiplication sentence.

▶ Add: 2¢ + 2¢ + 2¢ + 2¢ = 8¢

Or multiply: $4 \times 2¢ =$ _?_

$$\begin{array}{r} 2¢ \\ \times 4 \\ \hline 8¢ \end{array}$$ or $4 \times 2¢ = 8¢$
factors   product

4 groups of 2¢
4 twos
$4 \times 2¢$

**Write an addition sentence and
a multiplication sentence for each.**

1.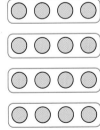

2.

3.

Multiplication Facts

Add:

$$9 + 9 + 9 + 9 + 9 = 45$$

Or multiply:

$$\begin{array}{r} 9 \\ \times 5 \\ \hline 45 \end{array} \quad \text{or} \quad 5 \times 9 = 45$$

5 groups of 9
5 nines
5×9

Find the product.

1. $\begin{array}{r} 8 \\ \times 2 \\ \hline \end{array}$	2. $\begin{array}{r} 7 \\ \times 4 \\ \hline \end{array}$	3. $\begin{array}{r} 6 \\ \times 3 \\ \hline \end{array}$	4. $\begin{array}{r} 5 \\ \times 5 \\ \hline \end{array}$	5. $\begin{array}{r} 9 \\ \times 3 \\ \hline \end{array}$	6. $\begin{array}{r} 7 \\ \times 2 \\ \hline \end{array}$
7. $\begin{array}{r} 2¢ \\ \times 5 \\ \hline \end{array}$	8. $\begin{array}{r} 8¢ \\ \times 3 \\ \hline \end{array}$	9. $\begin{array}{r} 9¢ \\ \times 2 \\ \hline \end{array}$	10. $\begin{array}{r} 5¢ \\ \times 4 \\ \hline \end{array}$	11. $\begin{array}{r} 7¢ \\ \times 3 \\ \hline \end{array}$	12. $\begin{array}{r} 8¢ \\ \times 5 \\ \hline \end{array}$
13. $\begin{array}{r} 7 \\ \times 7 \\ \hline \end{array}$	14. $\begin{array}{r} 4 \\ \times 6 \\ \hline \end{array}$	15. $\begin{array}{r} 7 \\ \times 8 \\ \hline \end{array}$	16. $\begin{array}{r} 8 \\ \times 9 \\ \hline \end{array}$	17. $\begin{array}{r} 7¢ \\ \times 6 \\ \hline \end{array}$	18. $\begin{array}{r} 4¢ \\ \times 9 \\ \hline \end{array}$

19. 4×6 20. 3×4 21. $5 \times 6¢$ 22. $4 \times 4¢$

23. 9×5 24. 7×9 25. $7 \times 4¢$ 26. $9 \times 3¢$

Problem Solving Write a multiplication sentence for each.

27. One factor is 4. The product is 24. What is the other factor?

28. There are 9 mugs. On each mug, students paint 7 flowers and 5 trees. How many flowers are painted in all?

29. The factors are 3 and 7. What is the product?

Whole Number Operations V

Multiply with 10, 11, and 12

Multiply: $3 \times 11 =$ __?__

$$\begin{array}{r} 11 \\ \times 3 \\ \hline 33 \end{array}$$ or $3 \times 11 = 33$

3 groups of 11
3 elevens
3×11

Multiply.

1. $\begin{array}{r} 11 \\ \times\ 6 \\ \hline \end{array}$
2. $\begin{array}{r} 10 \\ \times\ 5 \\ \hline \end{array}$
3. $\begin{array}{r} 12 \\ \times\ 7 \\ \hline \end{array}$
4. $\begin{array}{r} 12 \\ \times\ 4 \\ \hline \end{array}$
5. $\begin{array}{r} 10¢ \\ \times\ 9 \\ \hline \end{array}$
6. $\begin{array}{r} 12¢ \\ \times\ 5 \\ \hline \end{array}$

7. $\begin{array}{r} 11 \\ \times\ 2 \\ \hline \end{array}$
8. $\begin{array}{r} 12 \\ \times\ 3 \\ \hline \end{array}$
9. $\begin{array}{r} 12 \\ \times\ 8 \\ \hline \end{array}$
10. $\begin{array}{r} 10 \\ \times\ 6 \\ \hline \end{array}$
11. $\begin{array}{r} 11¢ \\ \times\ 8 \\ \hline \end{array}$
12. $\begin{array}{r} 10¢ \\ \times\ 7 \\ \hline \end{array}$

13. $\begin{array}{r} 11 \\ \times\ 4 \\ \hline \end{array}$
14. $\begin{array}{r} 12 \\ \times\ 2 \\ \hline \end{array}$
15. $\begin{array}{r} 10 \\ \times\ 4 \\ \hline \end{array}$
16. $\begin{array}{r} 11 \\ \times\ 9 \\ \hline \end{array}$
17. $\begin{array}{r} 12¢ \\ \times\ 6 \\ \hline \end{array}$
18. $\begin{array}{r} 10¢ \\ \times\ 8 \\ \hline \end{array}$

Find the product.

19. 7×12
20. 1×12
21. $1 \times 11¢$
22. $2 \times 10¢$

23. 9×12
24. 3×10
25. $7 \times 11¢$
26. $3 \times 11¢$

27. 1×10
28. 4×10
29. $8 \times 12¢$
30. $5 \times 11¢$

Problem Solving

31. Ms. Black made 11 paper triangles for each of 7 mobiles. How many paper triangles did Ms. Black make in all?

32. Dawn made 4 vests. On each vest she sewed 10 buttons and 12 stars. How many buttons did she sew?

Understand Division

Pablo packs 10 apples into baskets.
He puts 2 apples in each basket.
How many baskets does he pack?

▶ To find how many baskets,
separate 10 into equal groups of 2.
Use repeated subtraction.

..Think.........................
How many groups
of 2 are in 10?
Count back by 2s
until you reach 0.
8, 6, 4, 2, 0

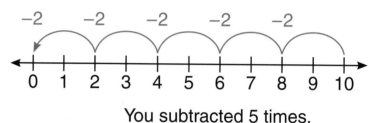

You subtracted 5 times.

Pablo packs 5 baskets.

▶ You can also write a division sentence to show how to
separate 10 into equal groups of 2.

Write: 10　　÷　　2　　=　　5 ◄─ division sentence

number
in all

number in
each group

number of
groups

Read as: "Ten divided by two equals five."

Find how many groups.

1. 16 in all
8 in each group

2. 9 in all
3 in each group

3. 20 in all
5 in each group

4. 14 in all
2 in each group

5. 18 in all
9 in each group

6. 15 in all
5 in each group

7. 36 in all
4 in each group

8. 12 in all
3 in each group

9. 10 in all
2 in each group

Whole Number Operations VII

Division Facts

▶ Divide: 35 ÷ 5 = __?__

Think.........................
> __?__ × 5 = 35
>
> 7 × 5 = 35

So   35   ÷   5   =   7.

   ↑   ↑   ↑

dividend   divisor   quotient

or

        7 ←— quotient
divisor → 5)35 ←— dividend

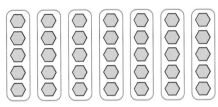

35 in all
5 in each group

Remember: 35 ÷ 5 = 7
is a division sentence.

▶ Find the quotient: 27¢ ÷ 3 = __?__

Think.........................
> 3 × __?__ = 27¢
>
> 3 × 9¢ = 27¢

          9¢
So 27¢ ÷ 3 = 9¢   or   3)27¢.

27¢ in all
3 equal groups

Find the quotient.

     0
1. 2)0   **2.** 4)24   **3.** 5)40   **4.** 3)15   **5.** 2)18¢   **6.** 5)5¢

7. 4)16   **8.** 3)21   **9.** 2)16   **10.** 4)36   **11.** 5)25¢   **12.** 2)12¢

13. 6)6   **14.** 7)28   **15.** 6)54   **16.** 8)48   **17.** 9)63¢   **18.** 9)72¢

19. 45 ÷ 9   **20.** 32 ÷ 8   **21.** 42 ÷ 6   **22.** 64 ÷ 8   **23.** 20 ÷ 5

24. 3¢ ÷ 3   **25.** 14¢ ÷ 2   **26.** 28¢ ÷ 4   **27.** 30¢ ÷ 5

28. 56¢ ÷ 7¢   **29.** 9¢ ÷ 9¢   **30.** 18¢ ÷ 6¢   **31.** 27¢ ÷ 9¢

Relate Multiplication and Division

▶ **Multiply** when you join equal groups to find the total number.

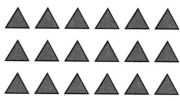

$$3 \quad \times \quad 6 \quad = \quad 18$$

number of groups	number in each group	total number

18 in all
6 in each group
3 equal groups

▶ **Divide** when you want to find:

• the number of equal groups.

$$18 \quad \div \quad 6 \quad = \quad 3$$

total number	number in each group	number of groups

• the number in each equal group.

$$18 \quad \div \quad 3 \quad = \quad 6$$

total number	number of groups	number in each group

▶ A **fact family** uses the same numbers. Use the facts to help you find related facts.

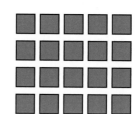

$4 \times 5 = 20$	$20 \div 5 = 4$
$5 \times 4 = 20$	$20 \div 4 = 5$

These four facts make up a fact family for the numbers 4, 5, and 20.

Copy and complete each fact family.

1. $6 \times 5 = 30$
$\underline{?} \times 6 = 30$
$30 \div 5 = \underline{?}$
$30 \div 6 = \underline{?}$

2. $9 \times 7 = 63$
$\underline{?} \times 9 = 63$
$63 \div 7 = \underline{?}$
$63 \div 9 = \underline{?}$

3. $4 \times 4 = 16$
$16 \div 4 = \underline{?}$

Write a fact family for each set of numbers.

4. 2, 4, 8   **5.** 3, 7, 21   **6.** 4, 3, 12   **7.** 5, 7, 35

8. 7, 6, 42   **9.** 9, 1, 9   **10.** 8, 3, 24   **11.** 3, 2, 6

12. 8, 7, 56   **13.** 9, 5, 45   **14.** 5, 8, 40   **15.** 6, 6, 36

Identify Fractions

A fraction can name one or more *equal parts* of a whole or of a set.

▶ $\frac{1}{4}$ of the circle is shaded.

$\frac{3}{4}$ of the circle is *not* shaded.

4 equal parts

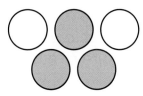

▶ $\frac{3}{5}$ of the set of circles is shaded.

$\frac{2}{5}$ of the set of circles is *not* shaded.

5 equal parts

**Write the fraction for the shaded part of each whole or set.
Then write the fraction for the part that is not shaded.**

1. 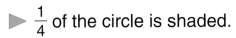   2.   3.   4.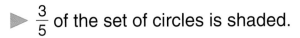

5.   6.   7.   8.

**Write a fraction for the red part of each set.
Then write a fraction for the yellow part.**

9.    10.   11.   12.

Customary Units of Length

The inch (in.) is a customary unit of length.

A quarter is about 1 inch wide. You can use a quarter as a benchmark for 1 inch.

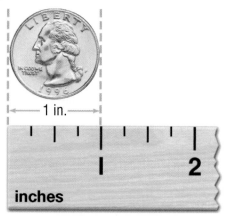

1 in.

inches

> A benchmark is an object of known measure that can be used to estimate the measure of other objects.

The foot (ft) and the yard (yd) are also customary units of length.

> 12 inches (in.) = 1 foot (ft)
> 3 feet (ft) = 1 yard (yd)
> 36 inches (in.) = 1 yard (yd)

1 ft

A license plate is about 1 foot long.

1 yd

A door is about 1 yard wide.

Write the letter of the best estimate.

1. length of a paintbrush   **a.** 9 ft   **b.** 9 yd   **c.** 9 in.

2. length of a bus   **a.** 40 in.   **b.** 40 ft   **c.** 40 yd

3. height of a wall   **a.** 3 in.   **b.** 3 yd   **c.** 3 ft

Cup, Pint, Quart, Gallon

The cup (c), the pint (pt), the quart (qt), and the gallon (gal) are customary units of liquid capacity.

> 2 cups = 1 pint
> 2 pints = 1 quart
> 2 quarts = 1 half gallon
> 4 quarts = 1 gallon

1 cup

1 pint

1 quart

1 half gallon

1 gallon

Write c, pt, qt, or gal for the unit you would use to measure the capacity of each.

1. swimming pool

2. cereal bowl

3. can of soup

4. can of house paint

5. tanker truck

6. small container of frozen yogurt

7. large glass of juice

8. bottle of seltzer

9. family-size jar of mayonnaise

10. car's tank of gasoline

Pound

The pound (lb) is a customary unit of weight.

Three bananas weigh about 1 pound.

Weight is measured on a balance or a scale.

Does each actual object weigh more than 1 pound, less than 1 pound, or about 1 pound?

1.

2.

3.

4.

5.

6.

Centimeter and Meter

The centimeter (cm) and the meter (m) are metric units of length.

100 centimeters (cm) = 1 meter (m)

1 cm

A large paper clip is about
1 centimeter wide.

A full-size baseball bat
is about 1 meter long.

Write the letter of the best estimate.

1. height of a mug   **a.** 2 cm   **b.** 9 cm   **c.** 2 m

2. width of a room   **a.** 4 m   **b.** 20 cm   **c.** 12 m

3. length of a soccer field   **a.** 10 m   **b.** 100 cm   **c.** 100 m

4. height of a cat   **a.** 99 cm   **b.** 1 m   **c.** 30 cm

5. length of a bed   **a.** 2 m   **b.** 20 cm   **c.** 20 m

**Write *cm* or *m* for the unit you would use
to measure each.**

6. width of a dollar bill   **7.** height of a giraffe

Liter

The liter (L) is a metric unit of liquid capacity.

Springwater is sold in bottles that hold 1 L.

Does each actual object hold more than 1 liter, less than 1 liter, or about 1 liter?

1.

2.

3.

4.

5.

6.

7.

8.

9.

Measurement V

Kilogram

The kilogram (kg) is a metric unit of mass.

A small bag of flour has a mass of about 1 kilogram.

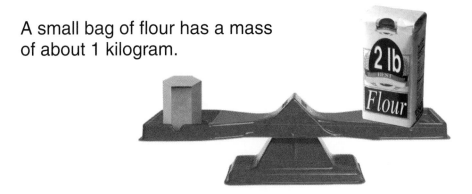

Mass is measured on a balance.

Does each actual object have a mass of more than 1 kilogram, less than 1 kilogram, or about 1 kilogram?

1.

2.

3.

4.

5.

6.

Perimeter

Find the perimeter of the figure below.

> Perimeter is the distance around a figure.

To find the perimeter of a figure, add the lengths of its sides.

100 ft
60 ft
75 ft
+ 50 ft
‾‾‾‾‾‾‾
285 ft

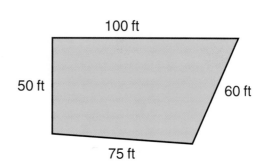

100 ft

50 ft

60 ft

75 ft

Find the perimeter of each figure.

1.

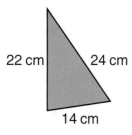

22 cm   24 cm

14 cm

2.

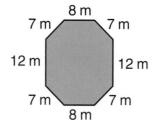

8 m
7 m   7 m
12 m   12 m
7 m   7 m
8 m

3.

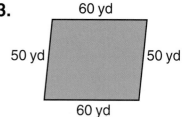

60 yd

50 yd   50 yd

60 yd

4.

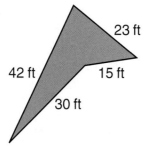

23 ft

42 ft   15 ft

30 ft

5.

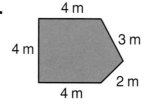

4 m

4 m   3 m

4 m   2 m

6.

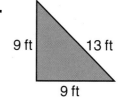

9 ft   13 ft

9 ft

7. a polygon whose sides measure 100 ft, 142 ft, 68 ft, and 127 ft

8. a polygon whose sides measure 92 m, 109 m, and 92 m

Geometry I

Congruent Figures

Each of the patterns below was made
using congruent figures.

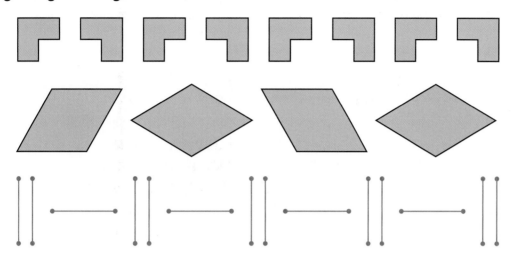

Congruent figures have exactly
the same size and the same shape.

To find whether two figures are congruent:

- Carefully trace one figure onto tracing paper.

- Lay the tracing over the other figure.

If the tracing and the figure match,
the two figures are congruent.

Are the figures congruent? Write *yes* or *no.*
You may use tracing paper.

1.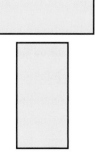

2.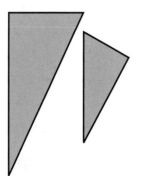

3.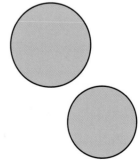

Lines of Symmetry

If you can fold a figure in half so that the two halves exactly match, the figure is symmetrical.

The fold line is a line of symmetry.

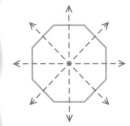 4 lines of symmetry

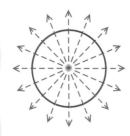 A circle has more lines of symmetry than you can count.

You can also use a reflection to see if the two halves exactly match.

Is each red line a line of symmetry? Write *yes* or *no.*

1.

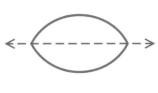

2.

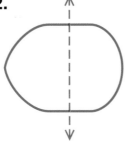

3.

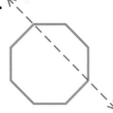

4.

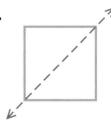

5.

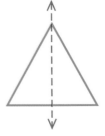

6.

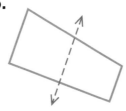

7.

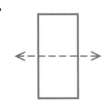

8.

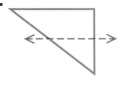

Geometry III

Algebra
Ordered Pairs on a Grid

Ordered pairs locate points on a grid.

▶ Look at the grid. What figure is at point (4,3)?

To find out:

- Begin at 0.

- The first number tells you to move 4 spaces to the right.

- The second number tells you to move 3 spaces up.

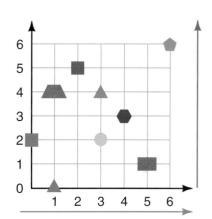

The hexagon is located at point (4,3)

▶ Locate the rectangle. Name the ordered pair for that point.

The rectangle is located at point (5,1)

> The rectangle is 5 spaces to the *right* and 1 space *up*.

**Use the grid for exercises 1–24.
Write the letter for each ordered pair.**

1. (2,3)   2. (3,4)   3. (6,4)

4. (0,6)   5. (4,2)   6. (1,4)

7. (1,1)   8. (5,3)   9. (3,5)

10. (0,0)   11. (4,1)   12. (5,5)

13. (6,0)   14. (0,3)   15. (4,6)

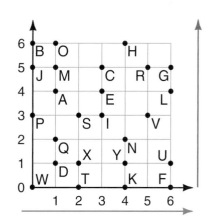

Write the ordered pair for each letter.

16. *K*   17. *I*   18. *M*

19. *U*   20. *T*   21. *G*

22. *O*   23. *X*   24. *Q*

Area

Area is the number of square units
needed to cover a flat surface.

1 square unit

▶ You can find the area of some figures
by counting squares.

9 square units

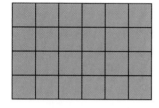

24 square units

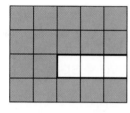

17 square units

▶ Sometimes you need to count half squares
to find the area of a figure.

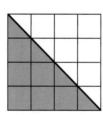

6 whole squares + 4 half squares
6 + 2 = 8
8 square units

.Think...........................
4 half squares =
2 whole squares
....

Find the area of each figure.

1.

2.

3.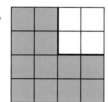

4.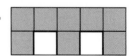

5.

6.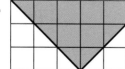

Record and Organize Data

▶ The tally chart at the right shows how many birds of different kinds came to a bird feeder one day.

Kind of Bird	Tally
House Sparrow	卌 卌 卌 卌 卌 卌 II
House Finch	卌 卌 卌 卌 卌
Blue Jay	卌 卌 III
Chickadee	卌 卌 卌 I
Nuthatch	IIII
Junco	卌 卌 卌 卌 III

Remember:
I = 1 and 卌 = 5

Which kind of bird visited the feeder most often? least often?

▶ Organizing information in a table from least to greatest or greatest to least makes it easier to find and compare data.

House sparrows visited the feeder most often. Nuthatches visited least often.

Birds at My Feeder

Kind	Number
House Sparrow	32
House Finch	25
Junco	23
Chickadee	16
Blue Jay	13
Nuthatch	4

The table and tally chart below show the number of farm animals Alex and Rachel saw on a trip.

Complete the table and tally chart.

	Animal	Number
1.	Cows	?
2.	Pigs	11
3.	Goats	?
4.	Horses	?
5.	Sheep	26
6.	Chickens	?

Animal	Tally
Cows	卌 卌 卌 卌 卌 卌 II
Pigs	
Goats	卌 卌 卌 III
Horses	卌 卌 卌 卌 I
Sheep	
Chickens	卌 卌 卌 卌 卌 III

Problem Solving Use the table and the tally chart from exercises 1–6.

7. Make another table with the data organized from least to greatest.

8. What kind of animal was seen most often? least often?

Graphing Sense

Video Sales in May	
Cartoon	▮ ▮ ▮
Comedy	▮ ▮ ▮ ▮ ▯
Drama	▮ ▮ ▯
Key: Each ▮ = 100 videos.	
Each ▯ = 50 videos.	

A pictograph uses pictures or symbols to represent data. The Key tells how many each symbol stands for.

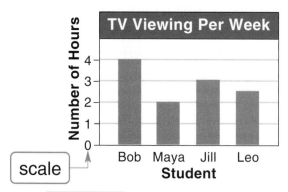

scale

A bar graph uses bars to represent data. The scale tells how much or how many each bar stands for.

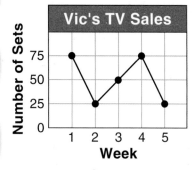

A line graph uses points and lines on a grid to show change over a period of time. A line graph also has a scale.

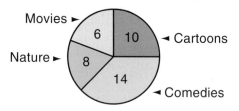

A circle graph uses sections of a circle to compare the parts of a whole.

Choose the graph you would use in each case. Explain why.

1. Compare at a glance the number of books each of your friends reads in a month.

2. Show how the temperature changed during the course of a week.

3. See how the number of classmates who like the beach compares to the total number of classmates.

Probability Experiments

Karim flips a quarter 10 times. Because the quarter has two sides, Karim predicts that it will land heads up half the time and tails up half the time. This is 5 times each.

As he flips the quarter, Karim tallies the results.

Heads	JHT II	7
Tails	III	3

Heads   Tails

Sometimes experiments do not come out as you predict they will. This often happens when you do the experiment a small number of times.

Try these experiments. You may work with a partner.

1. Suppose you flip a coin 10 times. Predict how many times it will land heads up and how many times it will land tails up. Flip it 10 times and tally the results. How close is the result to your prediction?

   Now predict how many times the coin will land heads up and tails up if you flip it 20 times. Flip the coin and tally the results. Compare your tally with a classmate's. Describe how your tallies are alike and how they are different.

2. Put 2 red cubes and 1 yellow cube into a paper bag. If you pick a cube without looking, what color do you think the cube you pick will be? Was your prediction correct?

   Suppose you pick 6 times without looking and put the cube back into the bag after each pick. Predict how many times you would pick a red cube and how many times you would pick a yellow cube. Try the experiment. How close are the results to your predictions?

Dear Student,

Problem solvers are super sleuths. We invite you to become a super sleuth by using these four steps when solving problems.

1 Read **2** Plan **3** Solve **4** Check

Sleuths use clues to find a solution to a problem. When working together to solve a problem, you may choose to use one or more of these strategies as clues:

Strategy File

Use These Strategies
Combine Strategies
Make a Table or List
Interpret the Remainder
Write a Number Sentence
Write an Equation
More Than One Solution

Strategy File

Use These Strategies
Use a Diagram/Graph
Work Backward
Logical Reasoning
Use More Than One Step

Strategy File

Use These Strategies
Choose the Operation
Find a Pattern
Use a Drawing or Model
Guess and Test
More Than One Way
Use Simpler Numbers

Read ▶ **Create a mental picture.**
List the facts and the questions.

As you read a problem, create a picture in your mind.
Make believe you are there in the problem.
This will help you think about:
- what facts you will need;
- what the problem is asking;
- how you will solve the problem.

After reading the problem, it might be helpful
to sketch the picture you imagined so that you
can refer to it.

Name or list all the facts given in the problem.
Be aware of *extra* information not needed.
Look for *hidden* information. Name the
question or questions the problem asks.

Plan ▶ **Choose and outline a plan.**

Plan how to solve the problem by:
- looking at the picture you drew;
- thinking about how you solved similar problems;
- choosing a strategy or strategies for solving the problem.

Solve ▶ **Work the plan.**

Work with the listed facts and the strategy to find the
solution. Sometimes a problem will require you to add,
subtract, multiply, or divide. Multistep problems require
more than one choice of operation or strategy. It is good
to *estimate* the answer before you compute.

Check ▶ **Test that the solution is reasonable.**

Ask yourself:
- "Have you answered the question?"
- "Is the answer reasonable?"

Check the answer by comparing it to the estimate. If
the answer is not reasonable, check your computation.

Algebra
Strategy: Choose the Operation

Number Sentence	Definition
□ + □ = □	Join like groups or quantities.
□ − □ = □	Separate, or take away, from a group. Compare two groups or quantities. Find part of a group. Find how many more are needed.
□ × □ = □	Join only equal groups or quantities.
□ ÷ □ = □	Separate into equal groups. Share a group equally.

Meg collects comic books. She puts 7 comic books into each envelope. How many envelopes does she need for 42 comic books?

Read **Visualize yourself in the problem as you reread it. Focus on the facts and questions.**

Facts: 7 comic books in each envelope
42 comic books

Question: How many envelopes does she need?

Plan You are separating into equal groups.
Divide: 42 ÷ 7 = _?_

Think.......
_?_ × 7 = 42

Solve 42 ÷ 7 = 6
Meg needs 6 envelopes.

Check Multiply to check division:
6 × 7 = 42

Algebra
Strategy: Guess and Test

Pat's bank holds dimes and quarters. There are 4 more dimes than quarters in the bank. The value of all the coins is $2.85. How many quarters are in Pat's bank?

Read Visualize yourself in the problem as you reread it. Focus on the facts and questions.

Facts: bank holds dimes and quarters
4 more dimes than quarters
$2.85 in quarters and dimes

Question: How many quarters are in Pat's bank?

Plan First **guess** a number of quarters. 5 quarters

Add 4 to find the number of dimes. 9 dimes

Then **test** to find whether the value of the coins equals $2.85.

Make a table to record your guesses.

Solve

		Quarter Value	Dime Value	Total Value	Test
	1st	5 quarters = $1.25	9 dimes = $ .90	$1.25 + $ .90 = $2.15	too low
	2nd	6 quarters = $1.50	10 dimes = $1.00	$1.50 + $1.00 = $2.50	too low
	3rd	7 quarters = $1.75	11 dimes = $1.10	$1.75 + $1.10 = $2.85	correct

Check The third guess is correct because:

• 11 dimes is 4 coins more than 7 quarters.

• 7 quarters ($1.75) and 11 dimes ($1.10) equal $2.85.

Algebra
Strategy: Use More Than One Step

Tina, Maya, and Olga need to collect 200 aluminum cans to win a recycling contest. Tina has collected 57 cans, Maya has collected 76 cans, and Olga has collected 64 cans. How many more cans do the girls still need to collect?

Read ▶ **Visualize yourself in the problem as you reread it. Focus on the facts and questions.**

Facts: 200 cans needed.
Tina collected 57 cans.
Maya collected 76 cans.
Olga collected 64 cans.

Question: How many more cans are still needed?

Plan ▶ First find the number of cans collected. Add.

57	+	76	+	64	=	?
Tina's cans		Maya's cans		Olga's cans		number collected

Then find the number of cans the girls still need to collect. Subtract the sum from 200.

200	−	?	=	?
in all		number collected		number still needed

Solve ▶ $57 + 76 + 64 = 197$
The girls collected 197 cans.

$200 - 197 = 3$
The girls need to collect 3 more cans.

Check ▶ Use addition to check your answer.

197	+	3	=	200
cans collected		cans still needed		cans in all

Algebra
Strategy: Write a Number Sentence

A nursery donates 36 trees to a city.
The city plants 4 trees in each of its parks.
At most, how many parks could there be?

Read ▸ **Visualize yourself in the problem as you reread it. Focus on the facts and questions.**

Facts: 36 trees donated
4 trees in each park

Question: How many parks could there be?

Plan ▸ Because the 36 trees are being separated into equal groups of 4 trees each, write a number sentence for division.

$36 \div 4 = \underline{\ ?\ }$
$ \text{parks}$

> **Think**
> Number ÷ Number = Number
> in all   in each   of groups
> group

Solve ▸ Divide to find the quotient.

$$\begin{array}{r} 9 \\ 4\overline{)36} \\ -36 \\ \hline 0 \end{array}$$

> **Think**
> How many 4s
> are in 36? 9

There could be 9 parks.

Check ▸ Multiply the quotient by the divisor.

$$\begin{array}{r} 9 \\ \times\ 4 \\ \hline 36 \end{array}$$

The answer checks!

Applications: Mixed Review

Choose a strategy from the list or use another strategy you know to solve each problem.

1. Olivia works at a zoo gift shop. She sold 6 small, 8 medium, and 4 large T-shirts. How many T-shirts did she sell?

2. Olivia sold 16 posters. Penguins were pictured on 7 of the posters. Pandas were on the rest. How many panda posters did Olivia sell?

3. Stu packed 6 ceramic animals into each small box. How many boxes does he need for 54 ceramic animals?

4. Ryan sent 22 animal buttons to three cousins. Sue received twice as many buttons as Mike and 3 more than Jill. How many buttons did each receive?

5. Lin wants to use 7 animal beads for each of 9 necklaces he is making for the zoo gift shop. How many animal beads will he need?

Use These Strategies
Choose the Operation
Guess and Test
Write a Number Sentence
Use More Than One Step

Use the table for problem 6.

6. Max pays the sale price for 3 key chains, 1 toucan shirt, and 2 fish cards. How much money did he save?

Sale at the Zoo Shop		
Item	Regular Price	Sale Price
Polar Bear Key Chain	$3	$2
Toucan Shirt	$12	$10
Fish Cards	$8	$4

INTRODUCTION TO PROBLEM SOLVING

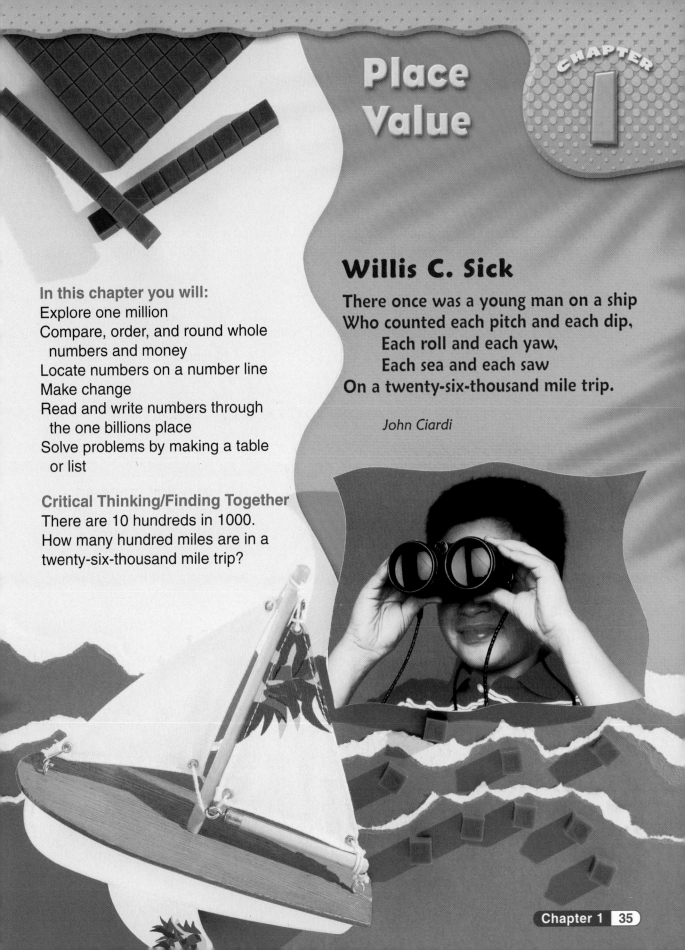

Place Value

CHAPTER 1

In this chapter you will:

Explore one million

Compare, order, and round whole
numbers and money

Locate numbers on a number line

Make change

Read and write numbers through
the one billions place

Solve problems by making a table
or list

Critical Thinking/Finding Together

There are 10 hundreds in 1000.
How many hundred miles are in a
twenty-six-thousand mile trip?

Willis C. Sick

There once was a young man on a ship
Who counted each pitch and each dip,
    Each roll and each yaw,
    Each sea and each saw
On a twenty-six-thousand mile trip.

John Ciardi

1-1

Thousands

A place-value chart makes understanding large numbers easier.

In 206,493 the value of:
2 is 2 hundred thousands or 200,000.
0 is 0 ten thousands or 0.
6 is 6 thousands or 6000.
4 is 4 hundreds or 400.
9 is 9 tens or 90.
3 is 3 ones or 3.

In numbers larger than 9999, use a comma to separate the periods.

Standard Form: 206,493

Word Name: two hundred six thousand,

four hundred ninety-three

Each group of 3 digits is called a period.

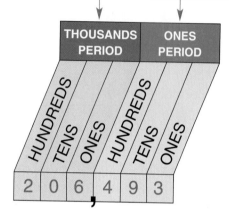

Four-digit numbers may be written with or without a comma.

Practice

Write the place of the red digit. Then write its value.

1. 6,541
2. 7,843
3. 3,962
4. 5,034

5. 27,142
6. 46,359
7. 65,186
8. 92,170

9. 156,143
10. 983,567
11. 495,638
12. 374,826

13. 632,018
14. 275,941
15. 321,235
16. 176,404

17. 205,866
18. 652,048
19. 520,124
20. 804,397

Write the number in standard form.

21. nine hundred four

22. twelve thousand

23. six hundred thousand

24. eight thousand

25. five hundred twenty-one thousand, one hundred twelve

26. sixty-four thousand, seven hundred thirty-five

27. two hundred forty thousand, three hundred ninety-two

28. ninety thousand, four hundred eight

29. one hundred fifteen thousand, five hundred sixty

30. three hundred thousand, two

31. four hundred one thousand, eighteen

32. fifty-four thousand, sixty-eight

Write the word name for each number.

33. 762	**34.** 431	**35.** 605	**36.** 911
37. 4,918	**38.** 1,265	**39.** 7,016	**40.** 3,402
41. 25,461	**42.** 51,824	**43.** 90,160	**44.** 80,007
45. 169,818	**46.** 748,295	**47.** 300,040	**48.** 809,006

CRITICAL THINKING

49. What are the least and the greatest four-digit numbers you can make using all the digits in each set only once?

    a. 1, 2, 3, 4   **b.** 0, 3, 2, 1   **c.** 1, 0, 0, 2

What Is One Million?

The numbers from 1 to 999 are in the ones period. The numbers from 1000 to 999,999 are in the thousands period. Today you will discover the next counting number.

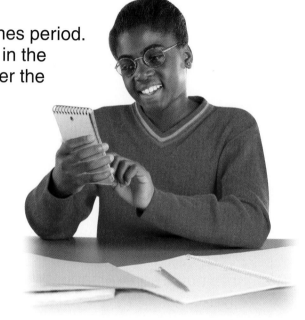

Materials: paper, pencil

Compute the rest of exercise 1. Record each number sentence and the answer.

1. $10 \times 1 = 10$
   $10 \times 10 = 100$
   $10 \times 100 = 1000$
   $10 \times 1000 = \underline{?}$
   $10 \times 10,000 = \underline{?}$
   $10 \times 100,000 = \underline{?}$

2. What patterns do you notice?

The number that is $10 \times 100,000$ is *one million*, or 1,000,000.
One million is the next counting number after 999,999.

3. How is 1,000,000 like 1000; 10,000; and 100,000? How is it different?

$1,000,000 = 10$ hundred thousands
$1,000,000 = 100$ ten thousands

4. How many thousands is one million equal to? how many hundreds?

Suppose you counted one number per second. You would take about

- ? to count to 100.

- $16\frac{1}{2}$ minutes to count to 1000.

- 2 hours and 42 minutes to count to 10,000.

- 1 day to count to 100,000.

- $11\frac{1}{2}$ days to count to 1,000,000!

You may make a table to find the answers to questions 5–7. Explain your answers.

5. If you were 100 days old, would you be older or younger than 1 year old?

6. About how many years old would you be if you were 1000 days old? 10,000 days old? (*Hint:* 1 year = 365 days)

7. About how many years old would you be if you were 100,000 days old? 1,000,000 days old?

Communicate

8. How did you discover how old you would be if you were 100 days old?

9. How did you discover how old you would be if you were 1000; 10,000; 100,000; and 1,000,000 days old?

CHALLENGE

10. If you were to continue the pattern from exercise 1 on page 38, what would the next three entries be?

11. Rewrite the last entry from exercise 10. Which zero do you think is in the millions place? Underline it.

Millions

Recently, the population of Brazil was 184,101,109.

In the millions period of 184,101,109, the value of:
   1 is 1 hundred million, or 100,000,000.
   8 is 8 ten millions, or 80,000,000.
   4 is 4 millions, or 4,000,000.

MILLIONS PERIOD			THOUSANDS PERIOD			ONES PERIOD		
HUNDREDS	TENS	ONES	HUNDREDS	TENS	ONES	HUNDREDS	TENS	ONES
1	8	4	1	0	1	1	0	9

Standard Form: 184,101,109

Word Name: one hundred eighty-four million,

one hundred one thousand,

one hundred nine

Practice

Write the period of the underlined digits.

1. <u>45</u>,678

2. 59,<u>650</u>

3. <u>26</u>,545

4. <u>456</u>,789

5. 567,<u>890</u>

6. <u>148</u>,337

7. <u>9</u>,456,789

8. 567,<u>890</u>,000

9. <u>617</u>,148,337

Write in standard form.

10. thirty-one million

11. three million

12. six hundred million

13. eighty million

14. one hundred twenty million

15. fifty-two million

Write the place of the red digit.
Then write its value.

16. 482,165,016

17. 904,628,153

18. 617,465,089

19. 38,296,145

20. 10,692,534

21. 4,797,123

22. 412,076,531

23. 217,945,310

24. 842,005,301

25. 920,354,876

26. 105,643,129

27. 732,530,481

28. 334,091,685

29. 2,444,656

30. 778,322

Write the word name for each number.

31. 5,460,000

32. 920,015,300

33. 10,300,000

34. 475,000

35. 1,006,005

36. 20,000,012

37. 7,002,502

38. 408,000,201

39. 87,005

Write About It

Brazil is the largest country in South America.

40. The land area of Brazil is three million, two hundred eighty-six thousand, four hundred seventy square miles. How would you write this number in standard form?

41. In Brazil there are two million, one hundred thirty-five thousand, six hundred thirty-seven square miles of forest. Write this number in standard form.

42. The Brazilian city of Rio de Janeiro has an estimated population of 5,974,100. Write this number in words.

Brazil

Place Value

MILLIONS PERIOD			THOUSANDS PERIOD			ONES PERIOD		
HUNDREDS	TENS	ONES	HUNDREDS	TENS	ONES	HUNDREDS	TENS	ONES
8	0	0	5	0	0	0	2	0

▶ Understanding the place of each digit in a number can help you write the number in **expanded form**.

Standard Form	Expanded Form
178	$100 + 70 + 8$
25,613	$20,000 + 5,000 + 600 + 10 + 3$
4,381,256	$4,000,000 + 300,000 + 80,000 + 1000 + 200 + 50 + 6$
60,070,005	$60,000,000 + 70,000 + 5$
800,500,020	$800,000,000 + 500,000 + 20$

▶ Understanding the place of each digit in a number can help you count on and count back by 10, 100, or 1000.

Count on by 10.	Count on by 100.	Count back by 1000.
25,613	25,613	25,613
25,623	25,713	24,613
25,633	25,813	23,613
25,643	25,913	22,613

Practice

Write each number in expanded form.

1. 65　　　**2.** 38　　　**3.** 246　　　**4.** 975

5. 352　　　**6.** 810　　　**7.** 6143　　　**8.** 7924

9. 5491　　　**10.** 4035　　　**11.** 13,827　　　**12.** 62,473

13. 90,303　　　**14.** 184,001　　　**15.** 705,060　　　**16.** 350,900

17. 6,320,079　　　**18.** 19,430,600　　　**19.** 75,260,080

20. 507,104,908　　　**21.** 800,002,100　　　**22.** 300,400,050

Write each number in standard form.

23. 2000 + 400 + 90 + 6

24. 7000 + 100 + 80

25. 30,000 + 5000 + 800 + 20 + 9

26. 800,000 + 90,000 + 4000 + 600 + 50 + 2

27. 7,000,000 + 300,000 + 50,000 + 2000 + 90 + 4

28. 20,000,000 + 70,000 + 5000 + 8

29. 700,000,000 + 300,000 + 4000 + 5

Write the numbers that are 10 more, 100 more, and 1000 more. Then write the numbers that are 10 less, 100 less, and 1000 less.

30. 7825

31. 92,614

32. 365,829

33. 482,565

34. 7,342,675

35. 32,489,267

36. 107,361,072

TEST PREPARATION

37. Which of these is the number 6,090,200?

 A six million, nine thousand, two hundred
 B six million, ninety thousand, two hundred
 C six hundred-ninety thousand, two hundred
 D six million, ninety-two thousand

38. Which of these is four million, fifty-eight thousand, twenty-one?

 F 4,580,021
 G 4,005,821
 H 4,058,021
 J 458,021

39. Which shows the expanded form of 805,034?

 A 800,000 + 5000 + 30 + 4
 B 800,000 + 50,000 + 30 + 4
 C 8,000,000 + 5000 + 30 + 4
 D 800,000 + 5000 + 300 + 4

Estimation

Sometimes it is inconvenient, difficult, or even impossible to report the exact number of items in a group or set.

When you cannot report an exact number, you can use an estimate. An estimate can be a rounded number that tells *about* how much or *about* how many.

Here are some examples of estimates:

- So far, 1,000,000 different species of insects have been discovered.

- One hundred years ago the worldwide population of tigers was 100,000. Today the number of tigers is 7000.

- The age of the oldest bird on record, a cockatoo, was 80 years. It was fully grown when captured in 1902 and died in the London Zoo in 1982.

Discuss these questions with your group:

1. For each example, why is each number reported as an estimate, or rounded number, rather than an exact number?

2. How are all the estimated numbers alike? How are they different?

3. Read the examples again. Do you think estimating is the same as guessing? Why or why not?

Work with your group to estimate the number of fish in the picture below. *Do not try to count all the fish.* You may use a ruler, tracing paper, or any other tools you think might help you.

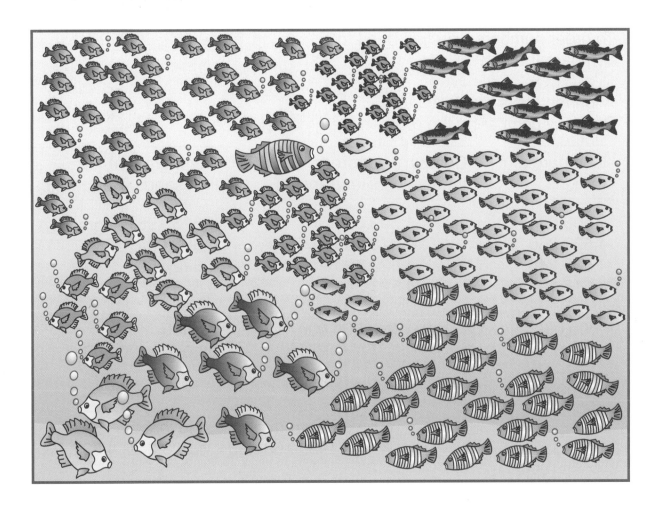

4. What is your estimate of the number of fish in the picture?

5. How did you make your estimate?

6. Compare your method of estimation with your classmates'. What do you notice?

Compare and Order Whole Numbers

Order the numbers from greatest to least.

| 4,603,034; 4,522,260; |
| 4,523,346; 4,613,198 |

To order numbers, you first need to compare them.

Align the digits by place value.
Begin by comparing the digits in the greatest place.

Compare millions.	Compare hundred thousands. Rearrange.	Compare ten thousands. Rearrange.
4,603,034	4,603,034	4,613,198 ← greatest
4,522,260	4,613,198	4,603,034
4,523,346	4,522,260	4,522,260
4,613,198	4,523,346	4,523,346

$4,000,000 =$
$4,000,000$

$600,000 > 500,000$

$10,000 > 0$
$20,000 = 20,000$

Compare thousands.
Rearrange.

4,613,198
4,603,034
4,523,346
4,522,260 ← least

The order from greatest to least:
4,613,198; 4,603,034; 4,523,346; 4,522,260

The order from least to greatest:
4,522,260; 4,523,346; 4,603,034; 4,613,198

$3000 > 2000$

Practice

Compare. Write <, =, or >.

1. 3705 ? 992   Think.............
No thousands.

2. 584,783 ? 584,378

3. 98,050 ? 98,305   **4.** 1,063,582 ? 1,062,975   **5.** 36,758 ? 36,721

Write in order from least to greatest.

6. 671; 680; 707; 679; 702   **7.** 426; 505; 431; 424

8. 4515; 3204; 7661; 1139; 4500   **9.** 843; 839; 87; 841; 836

10. 6714; 6783; 6756; 679; 6744

11. 24,316; 34,316; 24,416; 34,416; 24,404

12. 57,554; 558,641; 5784; 557,590; 579

13. 8,940,505; 840,505; 8,945,405; 894,505

Write in order from greatest to least.

14. 343; 349; 434; 352   **15.** 295; 32; 289; 27; 281

16. 526; 642; 589; 538; 658   **17.** 6028; 628; 686; 6204; 862

18. 8451; 8468; 8450; 8464; 8445

19. 3605; 3679; 369; 3610; 3600

20. 46,824; 46,785; 46,804; 46,815; 46,790

21. 944,747; 9547; 995,754; 959; 94,763

22. 766,094; 7,766,094; 7,766,049; 776,094

CHALLENGE — Algebra

Write a number that can replace the unknown number.

23. $578 < \underline{\ ?\ } < 596$ **24.** $6593 > \underline{\ ?\ } > 6589$

25. $71{,}321 > \underline{\ ?\ } > 71{,}318$ **26.** $165{,}279 > \underline{\ ?\ } > 165{,}267$

27. $8{,}098{,}516 < \underline{\ ?\ } < 8{,}098{,}520$ **28.** $32{,}984{,}021 < \underline{\ ?\ } < 32{,}984{,}028$

Number Sense: Use a Number Line

Halfway points can help you to find numbers
on a number line.

▶ About where on each number line is 75?

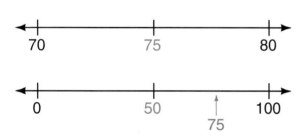

75 is exactly halfway
between 70 and 80.

50 is the halfway point.
75 is exactly halfway
between 50 and 100.

▶ About where on each number line is 142?

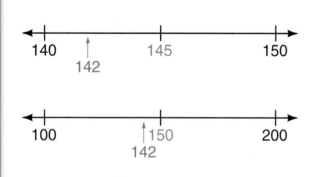

145 is the halfway point.
142 is between 140 and 145.
142 is closer to 140.

150 is the halfway point.
142 is between 100 and 150.
142 is much closer to 150.

Practice

**Write the number that is halfway between
the two numbers.**

1. 20; 30   **2.** 0; 50   **3.** 600; 700   **4.** 0; 200

5. 0; 500   **6.** 0; 80   **7.** 10; 70   **8.** 150; 200

**Draw a number line to show the halfway point
between the two numbers.**

9. 0; 10   **10.** 40; 50   **11.** 0; 60   **12.** 800; 900

13. 0; 1000   **14.** 510; 520   **15.** 1000; 2000   **16.** 0; 2000

About what number is each arrow pointing toward?

17.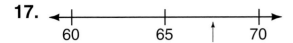
60   65   70

18.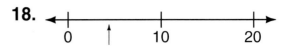
0   10   20

19.
100   150   200

20.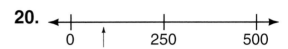
0   250   500

21.
0   10

22.
400   500

23.
150   160

24.
1000   2000

25.
20   30

26.
0   5000

Draw each number line.

27. Draw a number line from 50 to 60. Show the halfway point. Draw an arrow that points toward 53.

28. Draw a number line from 0 to 100. Show the halfway point. Draw an arrow that points toward 40.

29. Draw a number line from 0 to 500. Draw an arrow that points toward 300.

30. Draw a number line from 2000 to 4000. Show the halfway point. Draw an arrow that points toward 3750.

TEST PREPARATION

31. About what number is the arrow pointing toward?

2500   3000

A 2250 **B** 2550 **C** 2625 **D** 225

32. About what number is the arrow pointing toward?

50   60

F 53   **G** 55   **H** 57   **J** 59

1-8

Make Change

Imagine that you are working in a music store. A customer wants to buy a CD that costs $13.88 and gives you a twenty-dollar bill. What coins and bills would you give the customer as change? What would be the value of the change?

twenty-dollar bill

$20.00

To make change:

- Count up from the cost to the amount given.

- Start with the coins that have the least value.

- Use the fewest possible coins and bills.

cost
$13.88 → $13.89 → $13.90 → $14.00 → $15.00 ⟶ **amount given** $20.00

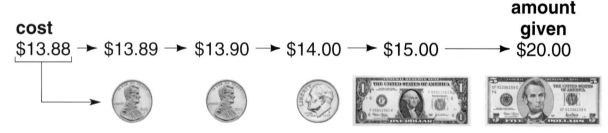

Arrange the money in order.
Count the change: $5.00 + $1.00 + $0.10 + $0.01 + $0.01
                        $5.00 → $6.00 → $6.10 → $6.11 → $6.12

You would give the customer 2 pennies, 1 dime, 1 one-dollar bill, and 1 five-dollar bill as change. The value of the change is $6.12.

Use money. Write the fewest coins and bills you would give as change. Then write the value of the change.

1. Cost: $0.81
Amount given: $1.00

2. Cost: $2.54
Amount given: $3.00

Practice

Use money. Write the fewest coins and bills you would receive as change. Then write the value of the change.

3.
$4.75

Amount given: $10.00

4.
$9.98

Amount given: $20.00

5. Cost: $3.16
   Amount given: $5.00

6. Cost: $4.22
   Amount given: $10.00

7. Cost: $12.99
   Amount given: $15.00

8. Cost: $13.08
   Amount given: $14.00

9. Cost: $13.70
   Amount given: $20.00

10. Cost: $14.10
    Amount given: $20.00

11. Cost: $15.46
    Amount given: $20.00

12. Cost: $19.55
    Amount given: $20.00

13. Cost: $10.60
    Amount given: $20.00

14. Cost: $2.67
    Amount given: $20.00

CHALLENGE · Algebra

Use nickels, dimes, and quarters. List all the ways you can make each amount.

$ .20	
nickels	dimes
4	0
2	1
0	2

15. $0.15

16. $0.30

17. $0.25

18. $0.35

19. $0.50

20. $0.40

21. $0.60

22. $0.75

1-9

Compare and Order Money

Chuck earned $25.35.
Evan earned $24.50.
Who earned more?

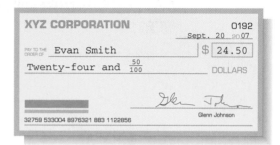

To find who earned more,
compare $25.35 and $24.50.

▶ Compare money as you compare whole numbers.
- Line up the amounts by the pennies.
- Compare digits. Start at the left.

Compare ten dollars.		Compare dollars.

$25.35
$24.50

$25.35
$24.50

$20.00 = $20.00

$5.00 > $4.00

So $25.35 > $24.50. Chuck earned more.

Order $7.49, $7.43, and $6.43 from least to greatest.

▶ Order money as you order whole numbers.

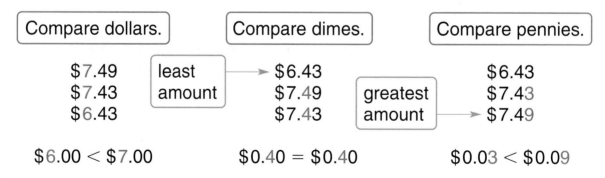

Compare dollars.		Compare dimes.		Compare pennies.

$7.49
$7.43
$6.43

least
amount

→ $6.43
$7.49
$7.43

greatest
amount

$6.43
$7.43
→ $7.49

$6.00 < $7.00

$0.40 = $0.40

$0.03 < $0.09

The order from least to greatest: $6.43, $7.43, $7.49

The order from greatest to least: $7.49, $7.43, $6.43

Compare. Write <, =, or >.

1. $0.07 ? $0.09   **2.** $0.76 ? $0.73   **3.** $0.52 ? $0.52

4. $3.49 ? $4.69   **5.** $8.03 ? $8.50   **6.** $2.81 ? $2.80

7. $5.38 ? $5.36   **8.** $9.75 ? $9.75   **9.** $7.63 ? $7.66

10. $10.30 ? $10.70   **11.** $42.25 ? $25.42   **12.** $87.95 ? $87.75

13. $36.99 ? $36.98   **14.** $77.07 ? $77.70   **15.** $61.18 ? $61.18

16. $1.95 ? $0.19   **17.** $2.67 ? $26.07   **18.** $74.50 ? $7.85

Write in order from least to greatest.

19. $0.76, $0.35, $0.57, $0.83

20. $0.18, $0.15, $0.19, $0.12, $0.17

21. $4.65, $4.62, $4.26, $5.24, $5.42

22. $75.39, $78.36, $7.48, $74.48, $75.93

Write in order from greatest to least.

23. $1.11, $1.10, $1.01, $1.17, $1.71

24. $24.42, $24.48, $24.24, $2.48, $2.84

25. $9.91, $9.19, $91.19, $91.91, $99.11

26. $68.50, $65.80, $68.05, $6.85, $65.08

Problem Solving

27. Jill saved $32.40. Ed saved $34.20. Lynn saved $34.40. Who saved the most money? Who saved the least money?

28. Adam has saved $85.25. Can he buy a jacket that costs $58.82? Explain.

Rounding

Round 26,322 to the nearest ten thousand.

To round a number to a given place, look at the digit to its right.

> If the digit *is less than 5*, round **down**.
> If the digit is *5 or more*, round **up**.

26,322
↓
30,000

| 6 > 5 |
| Round **up** to 30,000. |

Study the following examples.

Round $752.98 to the nearest hundred dollars.

$752.98
↓
$800.00

| 5 = 5 |
| Round **up** to $800.00. |

Round 846,289 to the nearest hundred thousand.

846,289
↓
800,000

| 4 < 5 |
| Round **down** to 800,000. |

Round 23,754,961 to the nearest million.

23,754,961
↓
24,000,000

| 7 > 5 |
| Round **up** to 24,000,000. |

Round each number to its greatest place.

1. 85,990
2. $94.20
3. 549,218
4. $651.99

Round each number to the place of the underlined digit.

5. 56,843
6. $429.28
7. 825,053
8. $10.56

9. 742
10. 36,987,301
11. 12,634,087
12. 221,034

13. $6.42
14. 3198
15. $54.04
16. 10,286

Round each number to the place of the underlined digit.

17. 5̲03   **18.** 85̲7   **19.** 44̲9   **20.** 9̲173   **21.** 342̲6

22. 1̲250   **23.** 7̲314   **24.** 26̲93   **25.** $1.4̲4   **26.** $6̲.70

27. $3̲.95   **28.** $7.5̲6   **29.** $8̲.39   **30.** $55̲.20   **31.** $38̲.98

32. $27̲.49   **33.** $18̲.88   **34.** $71̲.53   **35.** 9̲437   **36.** 1̲878

37. 85̲64   **38.** 29̲46   **39.** 74,8̲06   **40.** 32̲,521   **41.** 60,7̲19

42. 4̲5,133   **43.** $53.6̲8   **44.** $15̲.89   **45.** $94̲.87   **46.** $27̲.95

47. $8̲36.42   **48.** $35̲1.25   **49.** $70̲8.50   **50.** $484̲.62

51. 3̲6,455   **52.** 5̲2,630   **53.** $6̲54.70   **54.** $8̲95.99

55. 7̲43,299   **56.** 2̲50,343   **57.** 5̲71,320

58. 1̲,462,135   **59.** 325̲,523,607   **60.** 62̲,704,810

61. $31,7̲97.60   **62.** 1̲04,279,851   **63.** $97̲,874.69

Problem Solving

64. Springfield Elementary School has seven thousand, three hundred forty-one students. An article in the school newspaper rounded this number to the nearest thousand. What number appeared in the article?

65. Over the past 20 years, 28,514 fifth-grade students have graduated from Springfield Elementary School and moved on to sixth grade at Springfield Middle School. To the nearest ten thousand, how many students have graduated from Springfield Elementary School?

Work with Money

Use the skills and strategies you have learned to solve each problem.

1. Dan buys school supplies for $8.47. He gives the cashier a twenty-dollar bill. The cashier makes change with the fewest possible coins and bills. What coins and bills does Dan receive as change?

2. A sweater is on sale for $18.89. Elena says the sweater costs about $18.00. Rita says it costs about $19.00. Who do you think is right? Why?

3. Juwon receives a total of $75.00 for his birthday. He wants to buy a pair of sneakers that costs $79.95, including tax. Will his birthday money be enough to pay for the sneakers?

4. Neither Mei nor Jaycie has pennies, but they both have $0.45. Mei has 3 coins. Jaycie has 6 coins. Which coins does each girl have?

5. The cost of Ms. Johnson's purchases at the drugstore is $7.82. She gives the clerk a ten-dollar bill and 2 pennies. Since the ten-dollar bill is more than enough to pay for Ms. Johnson's purchases, why might she give the clerk the extra 2 pennies?

6. Would you rather have 5 quarters, 15 dimes, or a one-dollar bill? Why?

7. The table at the right shows how many pennies different classes in Glenn School have collected for charity. Which class collected the fewest pennies? Which class collected the most? How much money did each class collect?

Class	Number of Pennies
4A	1430
4B	1432
4C	1342
3A	1324
3B	1483
3C	1384

Solve each problem. Then explain how you found each answer.

8. Trucker Bob's check at the diner comes to $8.55. He pays with a ten-dollar bill. The cashier has run out of quarters. How can she give Bob change using the fewest possible coins and bills?

9. Dominique has saved $15.00 for a birthday present for her mother. She spends $12.76 for earrings and a pin. Does she have enough money left over to buy a gift bag that costs $2.98?

10. Is $6.53 closer to $6.00 or closer to $7.00? How do you know?

11. Mr. Mackintosh hires students to pick apples in his orchard. The more apples a student picks, the more money he or she earns. Jessie earns $125.75. Zach earns $127.25. Tommy earns $125.27. Sara earns $127.17. Which student earns the most? the least? Does Jessie pick more or fewer apples than Sara?

12. Manny has 9 coins that have a value of $0.88. What coins does Manny have?

13. Alonzo buys a dog collar and a leash at a pet supply store. The dog collar and leash cost $11.56. Alonzo pays with a twenty-dollar bill. If he receives the fewest possible coins and bills as his change, what coins and bills does he receive? What is the value of his change?

14. Tom has 1 quarter, 6 dimes, 3 nickels, and 4 pennies. Rick has 2 quarters, 3 dimes, 2 nickels, and 7 pennies. Harry has 1 half dollar, 1 quarter, and 5 nickels. Whose coins have the greatest value? What is the value of these coins?

Problem-Solving Strategy:
Make a Table or List

Steve has 24 marbles.
Each marble is green or red.
For every green marble, Steve
has 3 red marbles. How many
red marbles does Steve have?

Color	Number of Marbles			
green	1	2	?	?
red	3	?	?	?
total	4	?	?	?

Read **Visualize the facts of the problem as you reread it.**

Facts: Steve has 24 marbles.
For 1 green marble, there are 3 red marbles.

Question: How many red marbles does Steve have?

Plan Make a table.
If Steve has 1 green marble,
he would have 3 red marbles.
Write those numbers in the table.

If Steve has 2 green marbles,
he would have 2 × 3 red marbles.

Solve Complete the table.
Multiply each number of green marbles by 3.
Then add to find a column that shows 24 marbles.

$$\begin{array}{r} \overset{1}{18} \text{ red} \\ + \ 6 \text{ green} \\ \hline 24 \end{array}$$

Color	Number of Marbles					
green	1	2	3	4	5	6
red	3	6	9	12	15	18
total	4	8	12	16	20	24

Steve has 18 red marbles.

Check Check your computation, or act out the problem.

Make a table or list to solve each problem.

1. Mr. Hoody bought 3 shirts and 4 ties. The shirts are blue, gray, and white. The ties are red, brown, green, and yellow. How many ways can he wear the shirts and ties together?

Tie Colors	Blue Shirt	Gray Shirt	White Shirt
red			
brown			
green			
yellow			

Read Visualize the facts of the problem as you reread it.

Facts: 3 shirts: blue, gray, white
4 ties: red, brown, green, yellow

Question: How many ways can the shirts and ties be worn?

Plan Make an organized list.
List each shirt color.
Write the ties that can be worn with each shirt.
Count the total number of combinations.

Solve **Check**

2. Apple juice costs 50¢. The juice machine accepts quarters, dimes, and nickels. Make a list of coin combinations that can be used to buy juice.

3. Adam and Ashlee use three 1–6 number cubes. They look for different ways to roll the sum of 12. How many ways will they find?

4. Calvin has 90 stamps. For every Mexican stamp, Calvin has 8 U.S. stamps. How many Mexican stamps does Calvin have?

5. Write a problem that uses a table or list. Ask a classmate to solve the problem.

Problem-Solving Applications: Mixed Review

Read ▶ **Plan** ▶ **Solve** ▶ **Check**

Solve each problem and explain the method you used.

1. The school book fair wanted to raise $1500. It raised $2500. What is the difference in the amounts?

2. Abigail bought a garden book for $17.89. How much change did she receive from a twenty-dollar bill? What coins and bills could she have received as change?

3. Max sold a science fiction novel that describes life one hundred thousand years from now. What will the date be one hundred thousand years from today?

4. Paperbacks sold for 50¢ each. Hardcover books sold for $1.25 each. Was it more expensive to buy 3 paperbacks or 1 hardcover book?

5. Ray sold handmade bookmarks for 75¢ each. What five coins could be used to pay for 1 bookmark?

6. One book at the sale was printed 100 years ago. In what year was that book printed?

7. The book fair sold 437 books this year. Last year it sold 327 books. In which year were more books sold? how many more?

8. Zena brought 10 dollars to the book fair. She bought 2 books about mountain climbing for $4.20 each. How much change did she get?

Choose a strategy from the list or use another strategy to solve each problem.

9. There were 428 people at the book fair. Three hundred eighteen of them bought books. How many people did not buy a book?

Strategy File

Use These Strategies
Make a Table or List
Choose the Operation
Guess and Test
Write a Number Sentence

10. Stella made a triangular book display. She put 9 books in the first row, 8 books in the second row, 7 books in the third row, and so on. How many books did Stella use in her display?

11. Hank wrote 14 poems. Julio wrote 5 more poems than Hank. How many poems did Julio write?

12. Ray's bookmarks were made of red or blue plastic with purple, white, or yellow fringe. How many different bookmarks could Ray make?

13. Sue reads adventure books. There are 11 books on her desk. She has read 7 books. How many books does Sue have left to read?

14. The book fair charged 30¢ admission. How many different ways could people give the exact amount if no pennies were allowed?

15. In your Math Journal, write the name of the strategy you think is the most fun to use. Explain why you think it is fun. Then write the numbers of the problems you solved by using that strategy.

Write the number in standard form and expanded form. *(See pp. 36–43.)*

1. eight million, forty-three thousand, twelve

2. six hundred thousand, five

Write the place of the red digit. Then write its value.

3. 56,651,020 **4.** 205,640,311 **5.** 67,451

Compare. Write <, =, or >. *(See pp. 46–47, 52–53.)*

6. $77.45 _?_ $74.75 **7.** 1450 _?_ 1450 **8.** 161,905 _?_ 161,950

Write in order from greatest to least.

9. $25.10; $52.10; $51.20 **10.** 6215; 5217; 5451; 5332

11. 31,542; 31,320; 41,310; 51,403 **12.** 446,532; 446,503; 446,330

About what number is each arrow pointing toward? *(See pp. 48–49.)*

13. 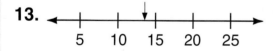 **14.**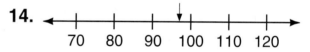

Round each number. *(See pp. 54–55.)*

To the nearest 100,000: **15.** 448,631 **16.** 682,472

To the nearest 1,000,000: **17.** 7,653,447 **18.** 2,153,462

To the nearest 10 dollars: **19.** $12.75 **20.** $57.45

Write the change you would receive.
Then write the value of the change. *(See pp. 50–51, 56–57.)*

21. Cost: $10.72
Amount given: $20.00

22. Cost: $.93
Amount given: $5.00

(See Still More Practice, p. 461.)

Billions

Standard Form:
2,821,700,000

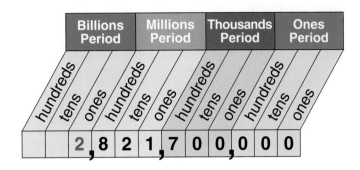

Expanded Form: 2,000,000,000 + 800,000,000 + 20,000,000 + 1,000,000 + 700,000

Word Name:

two billion,

eight hundred twenty-one million,

seven hundred thousand

Write in standard form.

1. one billion, three hundred fifty million, four hundred twenty-nine thousand, sixty-five

2. eight billion, one hundred thirty-one million, six hundred seventy-six thousand, four hundred fifteen

3. four billion, nine hundred three million, seven hundred twelve thousand, five hundred eight

4. 5,000,000,000 + 70,000,000 + 3,000,000 + 500,000 + 8,000

5. 1,000,000,000 + 300,000,000 + 40,000,000 + 30,000 + 900 + 2

Write the word name for each number.

6. 3,480,207,455   7. 8,016,525,719   8. 7,190,402,000

Write in standard form.

1. five hundred eight

2. two hundred four thousand

3. fourteen million, fifteen

4. 700 thousands + 60 tens + 8 ones

Write in expanded form.

5. 420,635,010

6. 56,431

7. 7,532,060

Write in order from least to greatest.

8. $56.20; $50.62; $52.60

9. 72,310; 72,130; 73,303

About what number is each arrow pointing toward?

10.

5   10   15   20   25

11.

70   80   90   100   110   120

Round each number.

To the nearest ten dollars: **12.** $24.31

To the nearest 100,000:   **13.** 732,916

To the nearest 1,000,000: **14.** 6,854,197

Problem Solving

Use a strategy you have learned.

15. Jared has 49 fish. For every carp, Jared has 6 guppies. How many guppies does Jared have?

Tell About It

Explain how you find your answer.

16. Estimate the number of students in your school.

Performance Assessment

17. Robert buys a sandwich and milk. With tax the total is $2.84. He pays with a ten-dollar bill. What bills and coins could he receive in change? What would be the value of the change?

Test Preparation

Choose the best answer.

1. In 576,239 which digit is in the ten thousands place?

  a. 5   **b.** 7
  c. 6   **d.** 3

2. What is the period of the underlined digits?

87,<u>952</u>,310
  a. thousands
  b. millions
  c. ones
  d. not given

3. Which shows the expanded form of 12,082?

  a. 12 + 82
  b. 1000 + 200 + 80 + 2
  c. 12,000 + 80 + 2
  d. 10,000 + 2000 + 80 + 2

4. Compare. Choose <, =, or >.

282,794 _?_ 282,749

  a. <   **b.** =   **c.** >

5. Which number is halfway between the numbers?

1500; 2000

  a. 1800   **b.** 1750
  c. 1700   **d.** 1600

6. Which is ordered greatest to least?

  a. $79.29, $79.92, $79.79
  b. $79.79, $79.92, $79.29
  c. $79.29, $79.79, $79.92
  d. none of these

7. Which shows $37.49 rounded to the nearest dollar?

  a. $37.00   **b.** $40.00
  c. $38.00   **d.** $30.00

8. How much change will you receive?

Cost: $2.18
Amount given: $10.00
  a. $6.82
  b. $7.82
  c. $7.92
  d. $8.82

9. About what number is the arrow pointing toward?

  a. 250   **b.** 235
  c. 225   **d.** 215

10. Compare. Choose <, =, or >.

$31.18 _?_ $31.81

  a. <   **b.** =   **c.** >

11. In 342,961,070 what is the place of the 4?

  a. millions   **b.** ten millions
  c. hundred millions **d.** not given

12. Which is ordered least to greatest?

  a. 618,561; 618,651; 618,516
  b. 618,516; 618,651; 618,561
  c. 618,516; 618,561; 618,651
  d. none of these

13. Choose the fewest coins and bills you would receive as change.

Cost: $9.34
Amount given: $20.00

   a. 1 penny, 1 nickel, 1 dime, 2 quarters, 1 ten-dollar bill
   b. 6 pennies, 6 dimes, 1 ten-dollar bill
   c. 1 penny, 1 nickel, 1 dime, 1 half-dollar, 1 ten-dollar bill
   d. not given

14. Which shows 618,383 rounded to the nearest ten thousand?

   a. 500,000   **b.** 600,000
   c. 620,000   **d.** 618,000

15. Which is ordered greatest to least?

   a. 84,873; 848,732; 8487
   b. 848,732; 84,873; 8487
   c. 8487; 84,873; 848,732
   d. none of these

16. Max has 5 T-shirts: red, blue, green, purple, and yellow. He has 3 pairs of shorts: black, tan, and white. How many ways can Max wear the T-shirts and shorts together?

   a. 15   **b.** 12   **c.** 10   **d.** 8

17. Meg buys art supplies for $13.83. She pays with a twenty-dollar bill. Which shows the fewest coins and bills she can receive as change?

   a. 7 pennies, 1 dime, 1 one-dollar bill, 1 five-dollar bill
   b. 2 pennies, 1 nickel, 1 dime, 1 one-dollar bill, 1 five-dollar bill
   c. 2 pennies, 3 nickels, 1 one-dollar bill, 1 five-dollar bill
   d. not given

18. In 29,706 what is the value of the 9?

   a. 9   **b.** 90
   c. 900   **d.** 9000

19. Choose the standard form of the number.

100,000 + 1000 + 800 + 50 + 3

   a. 101,853   **b.** 110,853
   c. 1,101,853   **d.** 111,853

20. Toni has 24 flowers in a bouquet. Each flower is a daffodil or a tulip. For every daffodil, Toni has 5 tulips. How many tulips does Toni have?

   a. 24   **b.** 15   **c.** 20   **d.** 30

Explain how you solved the problem. Show all your work.

21. Cesar has $11.00 to buy the following items for a project: 1 sea sponge, for $2.97; 1 battery, for $3.39; 1 roll of wire, for $2.98; and 1 bottle of vinegar, for $2.14.

If Cesar rounds the cost of each item to the nearest dollar and adds them together, will he know whether he has enough money for his purchases? Why or why not?

Addition and Subtraction Concepts

MATH MAKES ME FEEL SAFE

Math isn't just adding and subtracting.
Not for me.

Math makes me feel safe
knowing that my brother will always be
three years younger than I am,
and every day of the year will have
twenty-four hours.
That a snowflake landing on my mitten
will have exactly six points,
and that I can make new shapes
from my Tangram pieces
whenever I feel lonely.

Math isn't just adding
and subtracting,
Not for me.

Math makes me feel safe.

Betsy Franco

In this chapter you will:

Use addition properties and strategies
Learn about subtraction concepts
Estimate sums and differences
Check addition and subtraction
Add and subtract whole
  numbers and money
Learn about expressions with variables
Solve problems using logical reasoning

Critical Thinking/Finding Together

Suppose you are the person in the
poem. When your brother is 28 years
old, how old will you be?

Addition Properties

▶ The **properties of addition** can help you
to add quickly and correctly.

Commutative Property of Addition
- Changing the *order* of **addends**
does not change the sum.

$$5 + 6 = 11$$
$$6 + 5 = 11$$

$$\begin{array}{c} 5 \\ +6 \\ \hline 11 \end{array} \quad \begin{array}{c} 6 \\ +5 \\ \hline 11 \end{array}$$

.Think.....
"order"

Identity Property of Addition
- The sum of *zero* and a number
is the same as that number.

$$7 + 0 = 7$$
$$0 + 7 = 7$$

$$\begin{array}{c} 7 \\ +0 \\ \hline 7 \end{array} \quad \begin{array}{c} 0 \\ +7 \\ \hline 7 \end{array}$$

.Think.....
"same number"

Associative Property of Addition
- Changing the *grouping* of the
addends does not change the sum.

$$(4 + 5) + 2 = 4 + (5 + 2)$$

$$9 \quad + 2 = 4 + \quad 7$$
$$11 = 11$$

.Think.....
"grouping"

Always do the computation
in parentheses first.

▶ Use the properties to make adding easier.

Change the order.

Add down.   Add up.

$$\begin{array}{c} 4 \\ 5 \\ 1 \\ +3 \\ \hline 13 \end{array} \begin{array}{c} \\ 9 \\ 10 \\ 13 \end{array} \quad \begin{array}{c} 4 \\ 5 \\ 1 \\ +3 \\ \hline 13 \end{array} \begin{array}{c} 13 \\ 9 \\ 4 \\ \end{array}$$

Change the order
and the grouping.

$$(3 + 7) + 2 + 0 + 5 = 17$$

$$\begin{array}{c} 2 \\ 3 \\ 0 \\ 7 \\ +5 \\ \hline 17 \end{array} \quad 10 \quad + 2 + 0 + 5 = 17$$

10

Add. Name the addition property you used.

1. 3
   +0
   ___
    3

2. 6
   +3
   ___
    9

3. 3
   +6
   ___
    9

4. 8
   +7
   ___
   15

5. 7
   +8
   ___
   14

6. 8
   +0
   ___
    8

7. 0
   +5
   ___
    5

8. 7
    9
    0
   +3
   ___
   15

9. 2
    6
    1
   +4
   ___
    9

10. 5
     4
     2
    +5
    ___

11. 1
     2
     8
    +0
    ___

12. 2
     1
     3
    +9
    ___

13. 1
     9
     7
    +0
    ___

14. 3
     4
     3
    +6
    ___
     9

15. 0 + 6

16. (6 + 4) + 2 + 5

17. 9 + 3 + (4 + 4)

Add the number in the center to each number around it.

18.
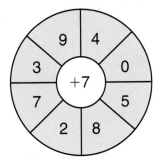

19.
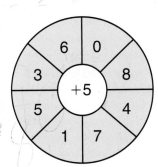

20.
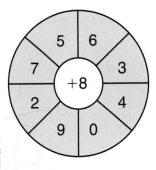

CRITICAL THINKING

Use the scoreboard to answer the questions.

Inning	1	2	3	4	5	6	7	8	9
Bluebirds	5	1	0	0	4	0	1	3	0
Robins	0	2	1	3	0	0	3	3	4

21. Who won the game?

22. What was the final score?

23. After which inning was the score 11 to 9?

24. After which inning was there a tie score?

25. What was the score after 2 innings? 6 innings? 8 innings?

26. How many runs did the Bluebirds and Robins score in the 5th inning?

Update your skills. See page 4.

Addition Strategies

▶ Tyrone and Maria use doubles to find 6 + 7.

| doubles |

Tyrone thinks: 6 + 6 = 12
6 + 7 = 13

Maria thinks: 7 + 7 = 14
6 + 7 = 13

| 1 more than 6 + 6 |

| 1 less than 7 + 7 |

▶ James uses 10 to find 9 + 4.

James thinks: 10 + 4 = 14
So, 9 + 4 = 13.

| 1 less than 10 + 4 |

▶ Tania looks for sums of 10 and doubles when she adds more than two numbers.

```
  2
  5 ⟩10   | 10 + 5 = 15 |
+ 8
 ──
 15
```

```
  6
  3 ⟩12   | 12 + 3 + 2 = 17 |
  6
+ 2
 ──
 17
```

Practice

Find the sum. Use addition strategies.

1. 3 +4	**2.** 5 +6	**3.** 8 +7	**4.** 6 +7	**5.** 5 +4	**6.** 8 +8
7. 9 +5	**8.** 7 +9	**9.** 4 +9	**10.** 9 +9	**11.** 3 +9	**12.** 9 +2

13. 3 + 2

14. 4 + 4

15. 8 + 9

16. 9 + 6

Add mentally. Use addition strategies.

17. 1
     2
   $+9$

18. 3
     3
   $+8$

19. 2
     7
   $+8$

20. 4
     5
   $+4$

21. 3
     7
   $+7$

22. 5
     6
   $+5$

23. 1
     4
     8
   $+2$

24. 4
     2
     3
   $+2$

25. 5
     7
     0
   $+3$

26. 3
     3
     3
   $+3$

27. 6
     2
     4
   $+2$

28. 1
     8
     1
   $+7$

29. $10 + 5$ 30. $9 + 5$ 31. $6 + 5$ 32. $6 + 7$

33. $8 + 10$ 34. $8 + 9$ 35. $9 + 9$ 36. $8 + 8$

37. $3 + 10$ 38. $3 + 4$ 39. $9 + 3$ 40. $4 + 9$

Problem Solving

41. Tara has 6 letters and 5 postcards to mail. Then she loses 3 of the postcards. How many stamps does Tara need?

42. Kim has 4 Canadian stamps, 5 English stamps, and 6 French stamps in his collection. How many stamps does he have altogether?

CHALLENGE

Find the first sum. Predict the second sum and explain your reasoning.

43. $42 + 42$

    $42 + 41$

44. $16 + 16$

    $17 + 16$

45. $35 + 35$

    $45 + 35$

46. $48 + 48$

    $48 + 38$

47. $50 + 50$

    $50 + 65$

48. $20 + 20$

    $20 + 25$

49. $26 + 26$

    $27 + 27$

50. $21 + 21$

    $25 + 25$

Subtraction Concepts

Subtraction has four different meanings.

▶ **Take Away**

Mr. Wu displayed 12 Planet Search videogames. He sold 9 of the games. How many Planet Search games does he have left?

$$12 - 9 = 3$$

He has 3 Planet Search games left.

▶ **Compare**

Jenny had 4 dolls. Inez had 8 dolls. How many more dolls did Inez have than Jenny?

$$8 - 4 = 4$$

Inez had 4 more dolls.

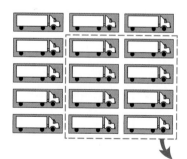

Jenny

Inez

▶ **Part of a Whole Set**

Lisa packed 15 cartons of model trucks. She shipped 8 of the cartons to Ohio. How many cartons were *not* shipped to Ohio?

$$15 - 8 = 7$$

Seven cartons were not shipped to Ohio.

▶ **How Many More Are Needed**

Manny had 6 bull's-eyes in a board game. He needed 10 bull's-eyes to win. How many more bull's-eyes did Manny need?

$$10 - 6 = 4$$

Manny needed 4 more bull's-eyes.

Problem Solving

1. Bobby had 10 action figures. He gave 2 of them away. How many action figures does Bobby have left?

2. Mr. Wu put 5 puppets on a shelf that can hold 14 puppets. How many more puppets can fit on the shelf?

3. Cara had 12 dolls. Three of them were from Russia. How many were from other countries?

4. Mr. Wu sold 8 soft bears and 14 soft rabbits. How many more rabbits did he sell?

Rules for Subtraction

Use these rules to help you subtract quickly and correctly.

When zero is subtracted from a number, the difference is that same number.

$$\begin{array}{r} 4 \\ -0 \\ \hline 4 \end{array} \qquad 4 - 0 = 4$$

When a number is subtracted from itself, the difference is zero.

$$\begin{array}{r} 9 \\ -9 \\ \hline 0 \end{array} \qquad 9 - 9 = 0$$

Subtract.

5.
$$\begin{array}{r} 7 \\ -0 \\ \hline \end{array}$$

6.
$$\begin{array}{r} 5 \\ -5 \\ \hline \end{array}$$

7.
$$\begin{array}{r} 9 \\ -0 \\ \hline \end{array}$$

8.
$$\begin{array}{r} 6 \\ -6 \\ \hline \end{array}$$

9.
$$\begin{array}{r} 4 \\ -4 \\ \hline \end{array}$$

10.
$$\begin{array}{r} 1 \\ -1 \\ \hline \end{array}$$

11.
$$\begin{array}{r} 13¢ \\ -\ 6¢ \\ \hline \end{array}$$

12.
$$\begin{array}{r} 8¢ \\ -8¢ \\ \hline \end{array}$$

13.
$$\begin{array}{r} 3¢ \\ -3¢ \\ \hline \end{array}$$

14.
$$\begin{array}{r} 9¢ \\ -9¢ \\ \hline \end{array}$$

15.
$$\begin{array}{r} 10¢ \\ -\ 5¢ \\ \hline \end{array}$$

16.
$$\begin{array}{r} 12¢ \\ -3¢ \\ \hline \end{array}$$

Write Your Own

17. Use 15 and 8 and use 13 and 5. Make up two different kinds of subtraction problems for your friends to solve.

Expressions and Variables

A **mathematical expression** is a name for a number.
It does not have an equals sign.
It may involve addition or subtraction.

$$10 + 14 \qquad 12 + 12 \leftarrow \boxed{\text{addition expressions}}$$

$$30 - 6 \qquad 28 - 4 \leftarrow \boxed{\text{subtraction expressions}}$$

▶ You can write an expression
based on information in a problem.

Mel has 7 bananas. He eats 3 of them.

What expression shows how many bananas Mel has left?

$$\underline{\text{total number of bananas}} - \underline{\text{number of bananas Mel eats}}$$
$$7 \qquad\qquad - \qquad\qquad 3$$

So, $7 - 3$ shows how many bananas Mel has left.

▶ You can use a letter, or a **variable**, to stand
for an unknown number in an expression.

Sara has 11 apples. She uses some to bake a pie.

What expression shows how many apples Sara has left?

$$\underline{\text{total number of apples}} - \underline{\text{unknown number of apples used}}$$
$$11 \qquad\qquad - \qquad\qquad a$$
$$\uparrow \qquad \boxed{\text{variable}}$$

So, $11 - a$ shows how many apples Sara has left.

▶ You can find the value of an expression with a variable.

- Substitute a number $11 + n$, when $n = 8$
  for the variable:

- Compute: $11 + 8$

Value of the expression: 19

Problem Solving

Choose your own variable to answer each.

1. Alex makes several catches in the first inning of the ball game. He makes two more catches in the last inning. What expression shows how many catches Alex makes in all?

2. Liz correctly answers 93 questions on the quiz. She also correctly answers some extra credit questions. What expression shows how many questions Liz correctly answers altogether?

3. There are 15 booths at the fair. Some of them sell food. What expression shows how many booths at the fair do not sell food?

4. Ann gets some letters in the mail on Monday. She gets 4 more letters on Tuesday. What expression shows how many letters Ann gets in all?

5. Jan swims for several minutes each day. For 8 minutes she does the sidestroke. What expression shows how many minutes Jan does not do the sidestroke?

6. At the zoo, some penguins are in the water. Twelve other penguins are on the rocks. What expression shows how many penguins altogether are at the zoo?

7. Beth has 2 pages of math homework. She also writes some pages for science class. What expression shows how many pages Beth writes in all?

8. Pam's scrapbook has 42 pages. Some of the pages are still blank. What expression shows how many pages in Pam's scrapbook are not blank?

Find the value of each expression.

9. $x + 5$, when $x = 14$

10. $y + 7$, when $y = 15$

11. $15 - c$, when $c = 9$

12. $24 - r$, when $r = 8$

13. $n + 6$, when $n = 11$

14. $s - 9$, when $s = 18$

Addition and Subtraction Sentences

Meg has 5 out of 12 books in a series.
How many books will complete her set?

▶ To find how many books,
write an addition sentence.
Use a variable for the missing addend:

$$5 \quad + \quad n \quad = \quad 12$$

missing addend

To find a missing addend in an addition sentence,
think of a related subtraction fact.

$$12 \quad - \quad 5 \quad = \quad 7$$

minuend − subtrahend = difference

| Addition and subtraction are inverse operations. Subtraction "undoes" addition, and addition "undoes" subtraction. |

$5 + n = 12$
$n = 7$
So, $5 + 7 = 12$.

Meg needs 7 books.

▶ To find a missing minuend or subtrahend
in a subtraction sentence, think of a related
addition or subtraction fact.

Find the missing minuend:

$n - 3 = 8$
$8 + 3 = 11$ ← related facts
$n = 11$
So, $11 - 3 = 8$. ←

Find the missing subtrahend:

$15 - n = 9$
$15 - 9 = 6$ ← related facts
$n = 6$
So, $15 - 6 = 9$. ←

Write the related fact to find the value of the variable.

1. $h + 7 = 10$
2. $y - 8 = 4$
3. $14 - a = 9$
4. $8 + s = 9$
5. $16 - u = 5$
6. $t - 4 = 11$

Find the missing addend, minuend, or subtrahend.

> Remember: You can write $5 + p = 8$ as $8 = 5 + p$.

7. $13 - f = 6$
8. $8 = 5 + p$
9. $c + 4 = 10$
10. $b - 7 = 4$
11. $d + 5 = 13$
12. $r - 8 = 5$
13. $3 = t - 8$
14. $8 + y = 15$
15. $1 = f - 9$
16. $18 - c = 9$
17. $p - 3 = 9$
18. $2 = 9 - x$
19. $b + 3 = 6$
20. $7 = n - 6$
21. $4 + r = 12$
22. $m - 6 = 4$
23. $a + 2 = 6$
24. $7 = c + 5$
25. $13 - v = 5$
26. $8 + s = 16$

Problem Solving

Write an addition or subtraction sentence using a variable. Then find the value of the variable.

27. Nadia is a dog walker. Each week she walks 18 dogs. She walks 10 dogs on the weekend. How many dogs does she walk on weekdays?

28. Mel is a cat sitter. This week he fed 3 fewer cats than last week. This week he fed 9 cats. How many cats did he feed last week?

TEST PREPARATION

29. Find the value of the variable.

    $8 + n = 17$

    A 10   **B** 6   **C** 8   **D** 9

30. Find the value of the variable.

    $p + 9 = 18$

    F 11   **G** 9   **H** 10   **J** 8

Mental Math

Here are some methods to help you add and subtract mentally.

▶ Think of tens or hundreds.

Add: $120 + 30 = n$

.Think...............
$120 = 12$ tens

$$\begin{array}{r} 12 \text{ tens} \\ + \ 3 \text{ tens} \\ \hline 15 \text{ tens} = 150 \end{array}$$

Subtract: $6500 - 400 = x$

.Think...............
$6500 = 65$ hundreds

$$\begin{array}{r} 65 \text{ hundreds} \\ - \ 4 \text{ hundreds} \\ \hline 61 \text{ hundreds} = 6100 \end{array}$$

▶ Look for numbers that are close to a ten or a hundred, and use compensation.

$$\begin{array}{r} 29 \xrightarrow{+1} \quad 30 \\ + 33 \xrightarrow{-1} + 32 \\ \hline 62 \end{array}$$

Add 1 to 29 to make 30.
Subtract 1 from 33 to compensate.

▶ Break apart numbers to find tens and hundreds.

$$\begin{array}{ccc} 38 & + & 14 & = a \\ (30 + 8) & + & (10 + 4) \end{array}$$

.Think...............
Use the associative property of addition.

$$\begin{array}{ccc} (30 + 10) & + & (8 + 4) \\ 40 & + & 12 & = 52 \end{array}$$

$8 + 4 = 10 + 2$

Study these examples.

$$\begin{array}{r} 197 \xrightarrow{+3} \quad 200 \\ + 118 \xrightarrow{-3} + 115 \\ \hline 315 \end{array}$$

$$\begin{array}{ccc} 144 & + & 56 & = n \end{array}$$
Think: $(100 + 44) + (50 + 6)$
$(100 + 50) + (44 + 6)$
$$\begin{array}{ccc} 150 & + & 50 & = 200 \end{array}$$

Add or subtract mentally. Think of tens or hundreds.

1. 40 + 50   **2.** 60 − 10   **3.** 80 − 80   **4.** 50 + 70

5. 690 − 80   **6.** 250 + 20   **7.** 160 + 30   **8.** 5700 − 200

Add mentally. Use compensation.

9.	**10.**	**11.**	**12.**	**13.**	**14.**
98	47	89	38	76	59
+ 62	+ 19	+ 31	+ 23	+ 57	+ 34

15.	**16.**	**17.**	**18.**	**19.**	**20.**
196	288	293	395	349	597
+ 78	+ 99	+ 18	+277	+ 194	+ 224

Add mentally. Break apart numbers.

21.	**22.**	**23.**	**24.**	**25.**	**26.**
64	53	48	72	87	39
+ 27	+ 24	+ 36	+ 25	+ 11	+ 42

27.	**28.**	**29.**	**30.**	**31.**	**32.**
155	136	249	343	411	527
+ 74	+ 83	+ 51	+ 75	+ 88	+ 71

Add mentally.

33.	**34.**	**35.**	**36.**	**37.**	**38.**
50	76	20	70	20	10
87	40	53	30	80	97
+ 50	+ 60	+ 80	+ 62	+ 28	+ 90

DO YOU REMEMBER?

Round each number to the place of the underlined digit.

39. <u>6</u>789   **40.** $6<u>2</u>.43   **41.** $2<u>5</u>.20   **42.** 35,<u>0</u>32   **43.** <u>4</u>1,863

44. 213,<u>6</u>09   **45.** $3<u>3</u>2.09   **46.** <u>5</u>47,028   **47.** $6<u>8</u>0.34

Estimate Sums and Differences

Rounding is one way to estimate sums and differences.

$4360 \rightarrow 4400$

- Round each number to the greatest place of the least number.

- Add or subtract the rounded numbers.

Estimate: 4360 + 654 + 1207

| Round to hundreds. |

$$
\begin{array}{rcr}
4360 & \longrightarrow & 4400 \\
654 & \longrightarrow & 700 \\
+ 1207 & \longrightarrow & + 1200 \\
\hline
& \text{about} & 6300
\end{array}
$$

Estimate: 186,491 − 44,786

| Round to ten thousands. |

$$
\begin{array}{rcr}
186,491 & \longrightarrow & 190,000 \\
- 44,786 & \longrightarrow & - 40,000 \\
\hline
& \text{about} & 150,000
\end{array}
$$

Study these examples.

| Round to dollars. |

$$
\begin{array}{rcr}
\$56.39 & \longrightarrow & \$56.00 \\
- 4.25 & \longrightarrow & - 4.00 \\
\hline
& \text{about} & \$52.00
\end{array}
$$

| Round to hundred thousands. |

$$
\begin{array}{rcr}
208,124 & \longrightarrow & 200,000 \\
+ 632,575 & \longrightarrow & + 600,000 \\
\hline
& \text{about} & 800,000
\end{array}
$$

Practice

Estimate each sum by rounding.

1. $\begin{array}{r} \$.25 \\ + .14 \\ \hline \end{array}$
   about $.40

2. $\begin{array}{r} 53 \\ + 76 \\ \hline \end{array}$

3. $\begin{array}{r} 632 \\ + 149 \\ \hline \end{array}$

4. $\begin{array}{r} \$5.25 \\ + 2.30 \\ \hline \end{array}$

5. $\begin{array}{r} \$37.47 \\ + 42.58 \\ \hline \end{array}$

6. $\begin{array}{r} 1432 \\ 4290 \\ + 3671 \\ \hline \end{array}$

7. $\begin{array}{r} 7859 \\ 523 \\ + 1324 \\ \hline \end{array}$

8. $\begin{array}{r} \$17.89 \\ 4.56 \\ + 10.32 \\ \hline \end{array}$

9. $\begin{array}{r} 22,165 \\ 56,972 \\ + 4,065 \\ \hline \end{array}$

10. $\begin{array}{r} 426,031 \\ 109,764 \\ + 362,801 \\ \hline \end{array}$

11. 314,402 + 23,067

12. 534 + 2414 + 876

13. 642,118 + 153,062

Estimate each difference by rounding.

14. 54 − 23

15. $ .38 − .16

16. 932 − 629

17. $8.57 − 5.08

18. $42.34 − 15.75

19. 6152 − 2830

20. 4819 − 592

21. 43,038 − 3,671

22. 241,701 − 45,089

23. $29.13 − 6.58

Use Estimation to Check

Use estimation to check addition or subtraction to see if your answer is reasonable. Use rounding.

Estimated Sum

3516 ⟶	3500
+ 430 ⟶	+ 400
3946	3900

3946 is close to 3900. The answer is reasonable.

Estimated Difference

67,148 ⟶	70,000
− 45,031 ⟶	− 50,000
22,117	20,000

22,117 is close to 20,000. The answer is reasonable.

Is the answer reasonable? Estimate to check. Use rounding. Then write yes or no.

24. 34 + 15 = 49

25. 61 + 30 = 201

26. 56 − 22 = 34

27. 43 − 21 = 22

28. 121 + 405 = 426

29. $2.61 + $3.28 = $5.89

30. 3021 + 56,078 = 59,099

31. $49.95 − $36.20 = $13.75

32. 75,379 − 15,267 = 60,112

33. 31,714 + 215 = 33,129

34. 546,397 − 42,064 = 504,333

35. 784,412 + 13,561 = 797,973

36. $21.46 + $3.98 + $32.54 = $87.98

2-8

Add and Subtract Money

Suppose you bought a racquet for $54.59 and a pair of tennis shoes for $42.40. How much money would you spend in all? How much more would you pay for the racquet than the shoes?

Round to estimate the sum:

$50.00 + $40.00 = $90.00

To find how much in all,
add: $54.59 + $42.40 = n

$$
\begin{array}{r}
\$54.59 \\
+\ \ 42.40 \\
\hline
\$96.99
\end{array}
$$

You would spend $96.99 in all.

Round to estimate the difference:

$50.00 − $40.00 = $10.00

To find how much more,
subtract: $54.59 − $42.40 = x

$$
\begin{array}{r}
\$54.59 \\
-\ \ 42.40 \\
\hline
\$12.19
\end{array}
$$

You would pay $12.19 more for the racquet.

> Adding and subtracting money is like adding and subtracting whole numbers. Just write the $ and . in the answer.

> $96.99 is close to $90.00. The answer is reasonable.

> $12.19 is close to $10.00. The answer is reasonable.

Study these examples.

$$
\begin{array}{r}
\$304.98 \\
+\ \ 632.01 \\
\hline
\$936.99
\end{array}
\qquad
\begin{array}{r}
\$32.50 \\
+\ \ 6.27 \\
\hline
\$38.77
\end{array}
\qquad
\begin{array}{r}
\$9.98 \\
-\ \ .41 \\
\hline
\$9.57
\end{array}
\qquad
\begin{array}{r}
\$7.24 \\
+\ \ .05 \\
\hline
\$7.29
\end{array}
\qquad
\begin{array}{r}
\$.65 \\
-\ \ .62 \\
\hline
\$.03
\end{array}
$$

> This 0 must be written.

Use rounding to estimate. Then add.

1. $.18
    + .20

2. $.24
    + .34

3. $.50
    + .38

4. $.51
    + .25

5. $7.23
    + 2.55

6. $4.21
    + 1.75

7. $2.22
    + 6.37

8. $17.26
    + 12.73

9. $50.62
    + 24.15

10. $71.40
    + 26.48

11. $324.16
    + 613.41

12. $711.90
    + 130.06

13. $244.87
    + 35.12

14. $516.45
    + 73.23

15. $471.05 + $315.62

16. $523.43 + $56.45

Use rounding to estimate. Then subtract.

17. $.84
    − .62

18. $.66
    − .44

19. $.39
    − .19

20. $8.95
    − 4.51

21. $7.55
    − 2.10

22. $4.67
    − 2.64

23. $3.95
    − 1.85

24. $78.89
    − 74.13

25. $56.39
    − 15.25

26. $678.54
    − 435.32

27. $783.66
    − 572.55

28. $445.78
    − 33.65

29. $976.85
    − 56.44

30. $885.64 − $763.51

31. $594.57 − $63.32

Problem Solving

32. Lauren had $15.95. She bought a pedometer for $4.75. How much money did she have left?

33. Ana bought a bike helmet for $32.25 and elbow pads for $15.60. How much did she spend in all?

Check Addition and Subtraction

▶ To check addition with more than two addends, add up.

```
  → 1899
    1427 ▲
     352
  + 120
  → 1899
```
The answer checks.

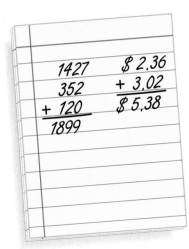

```
 1427      $ 2.36
  352     + 3.02
+ 120      $ 5.38
 1899
```

▶ To check addition with two addends, subtract one addend from the sum. The answer is the other addend.

> Addition and subtraction are inverse operations.

```
  $2.36 ◀        $5.38
+  3.02        −  3.02
  $5.38        → $2.36
```
The answer checks.

▶ To check subtraction, add the difference and the subtrahend. The answer is the minuend.

```
 $8.37
− 2.12
 $6.25
```

```
  $8.37 ◀        $6.25
−  2.12        +  2.12
  $6.25        → $8.37
```
The answer checks.

Add or subtract. Then check the answer.

1. 153 + 516

2. $4.95 − $1.74

3. 762 − 250

4. 2301 + 5090

5. 7799 − 626

6. $24.41 + $11.44

Add or subtract. Then check the answer.

7. $5.06
    + 4.91

8. 2413
    + 5062

9. $8.17
    + .62

10. $6.22
    + 3.56

11. 8251
    + 543

12. $.99
    − .36

13. $7.95
    − 2.62

14. 9388
    − 8072

15. 6975
    − 733

16. $38.46
    − 16.25

17. $11.46
      3.21
    + 24.30

18. 252
    314
    + 321

19. $42.01
    10.25
    + 4.52

20. 6040
    122
    + 36

21. 7411
    + 1505

22. 6359
    − 144

23. $75.59
    − 13.25

24. $8.88
    − 7.37

Problem Solving

25. A scientist discovered 147 fossilized dinosaur eggs in May. From June to December he found 542 more dinosaur eggs. Did he discover at least 600 dinosaur eggs?

26. Trevor bought a fossil shell for $2.30, a fossil field guide for $4.15, and a package of stones for $1.42. He said that he spent $7.75. Was Trevor correct? How do you know?

MENTAL MATH — Algebra

Add or subtract mentally. Look for patterns.

27. 8912
    − 701

    8912
    − 601

    8912
    − 501

    8912
    − 401

    8912
    − 301

28. 1042
    + 111

    1042
    + 212

    1042
    + 313

    1042
    + 414

    1042
    + 515

Problem-Solving Strategy:
Logical Reasoning

Lee, Hoshi, and Yori have their hats and scarves mixed up. Each boy puts on another boy's cap and a different boy's scarf. Hoshi wears Yori's cap. Whose cap and scarf does each boy wear?

Read ▶ **Visualize the facts of the problem as you reread it.**

Facts: Hoshi wears Yori's cap. Each wears another boy's cap and a **different** boy's scarf.

Question: Whose cap and scarf is each boy wearing?

Plan ▶ Draw and label a table.
Fill in the facts you know.
Consider the possible answers.

	Lee	**Hoshi**	**Yori**
cap	Hoshi's	Yori's	Lee's
scarf	Yori's	Lee's	Hoshi's

Solve ▶ Hoshi wears Yori's cap, so he must wear Lee's scarf.

Lee didn't wear his own cap, so he must wear Hoshi's cap and Yori's scarf.

That means that Yori wears Lee's cap and Hoshi's scarf.

Check ▶ Are the answers reasonable?
Is each boy wearing another boy's cap and a different boy's scarf?   Yes.

Use logical reasoning to solve each problem.

1. Mimi, Pedro, and Martin live in three houses in a row on Mountain Lane. Mimi does not live next to Pedro. Pedro lives on a corner. Who lives in the middle house?

Mountain Lane

Read ▷ Visualize the facts of the problem as you reread it.

Facts: Mimi, Pedro, and Martin live on Mountain Lane. Mimi does not live next to Pedro. Pedro lives on a corner.

Question: Who lives in the middle house?

Plan ▷ Pedro cannot live in the middle house.

⋯▷ **Solve** ⋯⋯▷ **Check** ▷

2. What one number could you move from one box to another to make the sums in each box equal?

1	2	3
4	5	6
7	8	9

3. Van has six coins that are worth 57¢ in all. Only one coin is a quarter. What are the other coins?

4. Rudy was born in the month whose name has the most letters. The date is an even 2-digit number. The sum of the digits is 5. What is Rudy's birthday?

5. Mary, Anne, and Rose spent $43.51, $47.46, and $50.44. Rose spent the least and did not buy a blazer. Anne's skirt did not cost the most. How much money did each girl spend? Who bought a sweater?

6. Write a problem modeled on problem 3 above. Have a classmate solve it.

Problem-Solving Applications: Mixed Review

Read ⟩ **Plan** ⟩ **Solve** ⟩ **Check**

Solve each problem and explain the method you used.

1. Deirdre needs 140 yards of white fabric to make costumes for a play. She has 30 yards. How many yards of fabric does she need to buy?

2. Glenn brought home 58 tickets to sell for the school play. He sold 27 tickets. How many does he have left to sell?

3. The theater has 100 seats on the first level and 55 seats in the balcony. How many seats does the theater have?

4. The first act of the play is 69 minutes long. The second act is 54 minutes long. How much longer is the first act?

5. Gini plays the ice queen. She buys a plastic crown for $5.78 and a jar of silver glitter for $1.20. How much does she spend?

6. The director bought 112 boxes of plastic snowflakes and has 37 boxes left. How many boxes has he already used?

7. Bill paints the ice castle door, which is 70 inches tall. The top of the castle is 80 inches higher. How tall is the ice castle?

8. There are 58 penguin puppets in the last scene of the play. Ida has finished making 42 of them. How many does she still have to make?

Choose a strategy from the list or use another strategy you know to solve each problem.

9. The two-act play is 104 pages long. The first act is 53 pages long. How long is the second act?

Strategy File

Use these Strategies
Logical Reasoning
Choose the Operation
Make a Table or List
Guess and Test
Write a Number Sentence

10. The play was performed on Thursday, Friday, and Saturday. Ben, Sue, and Dana went on different nights. Sue went after Dana. Ben missed the first night, so he went the next night. When did Sue and Dana see the play?

11. The cast received 3 curtain calls on Thursday and double that on Friday. On Saturday there were 2 more than on Thursday. What was the total number of curtain calls?

12. There were 142 people in the audience on Thursday night. Forty of them were adults. How many were children?

13. There are 3 bears and 2 penguins in the animal dance line. In how many different ways can the animals be arranged?

14. Jake, Kyle, and Lou play the jester, the king, and the leopard. No one plays a part that begins with the same letter as his name. Kyle decided not to play the jester. Who plays the king?

Use the table for problems 15 and 16.

15. Mr. Mendez bought tickets for 2 adults and 2 children. How much more than ten dollars did he spend?

16. Ms. Shapiro spent $14.40 on tickets. What tickets did she buy?

Tickets	
Adults	**Children**
$3.20	$2.00

Check Your Progress

Find the sum. Name the addition property or strategy you used. *(See pp. 68–71.)*

1. $8 + 0$
2. $9 + 6$
3. $7 + 8$
4. $6 + 5$
5. $6 + 7 + 4$
6. $8 + 0 + 3 + 8$
7. $3 + 7 + 8$

Choose your own variable to write your answer. *(See pp. 74–75.)*

8. Tim called some friends before lunch. After lunch he called 6 more friends. What expression shows how many friends Tim called altogether?

Add or subtract. Then check the answer. *(See pp. 82–85.)*

9.
$$\begin{array}{r} 153 \\ 412 \\ + 323 \\ \hline \end{array}$$

10.
$$\begin{array}{r} 205 \\ 381 \\ + 413 \\ \hline \end{array}$$

11.
$$\begin{array}{r} 3051 \\ + 1738 \\ \hline \end{array}$$

12.
$$\begin{array}{r} \$23.74 \\ 1.12 \\ + \quad .13 \\ \hline \end{array}$$

13.
$$\begin{array}{r} \$42.04 \\ 3.41 \\ + 10.22 \\ \hline \end{array}$$

14.
$$\begin{array}{r} 56 \\ - 16 \\ \hline \end{array}$$

15.
$$\begin{array}{r} 549 \\ - 427 \\ \hline \end{array}$$

16.
$$\begin{array}{r} 798 \\ - 55 \\ \hline \end{array}$$

17.
$$\begin{array}{r} \$94.36 \\ - 40.13 \\ \hline \end{array}$$

18.
$$\begin{array}{r} 6759 \\ - 542 \\ \hline \end{array}$$

Round to estimate. *(See pp. 80–81.)*

19.
$$\begin{array}{r} 42 \\ + 38 \\ \hline \end{array}$$

20.
$$\begin{array}{r} \$54.92 \\ + 23.26 \\ \hline \end{array}$$

21.
$$\begin{array}{r} 568 \\ - 399 \\ \hline \end{array}$$

22.
$$\begin{array}{r} 4327 \\ + 631 \\ \hline \end{array}$$

23.
$$\begin{array}{r} 65,571 \\ - 4,497 \\ \hline \end{array}$$

Find the value of the variable. *(See pp. 74–77.)*

24. $3 + n = 11$
25. $a + 7 = 15$
26. $7 = x + 0$
27. $12 - y = 7$
28. $h - 9 = 8$
29. $9 - c = 0$

Problem Solving
(See pp. 86–89.)

30. The Madison Arts and Crafts Fair had 33 art exhibits and 49 craft exhibits. About how many exhibits were at the Fair?

31. At the City Zoo there are more zebras than lions and more monkeys than zebras. Are there more monkeys or lions?

(See Still More Practice, p. 462.)

The Abacus

The ancient Greeks and Romans used an abacus
to make computations. The abacus is still used
today in Asian cultures.

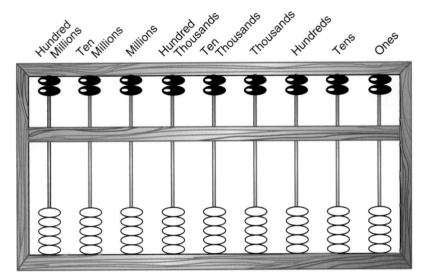

Each black bead
stands for 5 units.

Each white bead
stands for 1 unit.

A number is shown by moving the appropriate beads
to the crossbar.

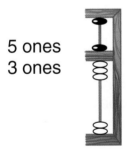

5 ones
3 ones

5 tens
3 tens
4 ones

2 hundreds
5 tens
1 ten
5 ones
2 ones

$5 + 3 = 8$ $50 + 30 + 4 = 84$ $200 + 50 + 10 + 5 + 2 = 267$

Make your own abacus. Use buttons, beads, or counters.

Show each number on your abacus.

1. 39   **2.** 326   **3.** 26   **4.** 681   **5.** 78   **6.** 589

Chapter 2 Test

Add. Name the addition property or strategy you used.

1. $5 + 9$

2. $0 + 7$

3. $9 + 8$

4. $7 + 1 + 7 + 3$

Find the sum or difference. Then check.

5.
$$\begin{array}{r} 172 \\ 205 \\ +\ 22 \\ \hline \end{array}$$

6.
$$\begin{array}{r} 1583 \\ 112 \\ +\ 204 \\ \hline \end{array}$$

7.
$$\begin{array}{r} \$42.63 \\ 5.12 \\ +\ \ \ .14 \\ \hline \end{array}$$

8.
$$\begin{array}{r} \$58.49 \\ -\ 22.41 \\ \hline \end{array}$$

Round to estimate.

9.
$$\begin{array}{r} 846 \\ -\ 230 \\ \hline \end{array}$$

10.
$$\begin{array}{r} 497 \\ +\ 43 \\ \hline \end{array}$$

11.
$$\begin{array}{r} \$24.98 \\ -\ 3.05 \\ \hline \end{array}$$

12.
$$\begin{array}{r} \$32.71 \\ +\ 46.28 \\ \hline \end{array}$$

Find the value of the variable.

13. $5 + x = 13$

14. $n - 9 = 8$

15. $16 = y + 8$

Problem Solving

Use a strategy you have learned.

16. Mike, Bob, and Jeff are 12, 13, and 14 years old. Jeff is the youngest and does not have blond hair. Bob is not the oldest and has brown hair. Mike does not have red hair. How old is each boy? Who has blond hair?

Tell About It

17. Maria went to the grocery store. She bought items that cost $3.09, $1.39, $.20, and $4.15. Did Maria pay more than $10 for the items? Explain how you can use rounding to estimate to find the answer.

Performance Assessment

Write a problem to match the expression.

18. $9 + n$

19. $17 - x$

Test Preparation

Choose the best answer.

1. In 439,587 which digit is in the hundred thousands place?

   a. 4   **b.** 9
   c. 3   **d.** 5

2. Which period is underlined?

   56,631,458   **a.** thousands period
   b. millions period
   c. ones period
   d. not given

3. Which shows the expanded form of 23,401?

   a. 23 + 401
   b. 2000 + 300 + 40 + 1
   c. 23,000 + 400 + 1
   d. 20,000 + 3000 + 400 + 1

4. $18.89
   + 11.26

   a. $20.15   **b.** $30.63
   c. $29.25   **d.** $30.15

5. Which number is halfway between 25 and 75?

   a. 35   **b.** 50
   c. 45   **d.** 55

6. Estimate the sum by rounding.

   $2.51   **a.** $3.00
   .49   **b.** $3.30
   + 1.27   **c.** $3.50
          d. $4.30

7. Find the value of the expression.

   $n - 37$, when $n = 41$

   a. 78   **b.** 41
   c. 14   **d.** 4

8. Which addition property involves the grouping of addends?

   a. commutative
   b. identity
   c. associative
   d. not given

9. Which is **not** a subtraction concept?

   a. take away
   b. zero identity
   c. how many more are needed
   d. compare

10. About what number is the arrow pointing toward?

    a. 1100   **b.** 1400
    c. 1500   **d.** 1600

11. 4 + (3 + 6) + 0 + 2

    a. 9   **b.** 13
    c. 10   **d.** 15

12. In 831,746,053 what is the place of the 1?

    a. millions   **b.** ten millions
    c. hundred millions   **d.** not given

13. Which is ordered greatest to least?

    a. 43,341; 43,413; 43,431
    b. 43,431; 43,413; 43,341
    c. 43,431; 43,341; 43,413
    d. none of these

14. Which shows the best way to check the answer?

    318
    + 194

    a. 194 + 318 = 512
    b. 318 − 194 = 124
    c. 512 − 318 = 194
    d. 512 − 300 = 212

15. Choose the fewest coins and bills you would receive as change.
Cost: $13.27
Amount given: $20.00

  a. 3 pennies, 2 dimes, 2 quarters, 1 one-dollar bill, 1 five-dollar bill
  b. 3 pennies, 2 dimes, 1 half-dollar, 1 one-dollar bill, 1 five-dollar bill
  c. 3 pennies, 7 dimes, 1 one-dollar bill, 1 five-dollar bill
  d. not given

19. Gus buys a fish tank filter for $4.52. He pays with a ten-dollar bill. Which shows the fewest coins and bills he can receive as change?

  a. 8 pennies, 1 nickel, 1 dime, 1 quarter, 1 five-dollar bill
  b. 3 pennies, 2 nickels, 1 dime, 1 quarter, 1 five-dollar bill
  c. 3 pennies, 1 nickel, 4 dimes, 1 five-dollar bill
  d. 3 pennies, 2 dimes, 1 quarter, 1 five-dollar

16. Which shows 1,541,917 rounded to the nearest hundred thousand?

  a. 1,500,000   **b.** 1,540,000
  c. 2,000,000   **d.** 1,600,000

20. In 64,823 what is the value of the 6?

  a. 600   **b.** 6000
  c. 60,000   **d.** 600,000

17. Choose the value of the variable.

$13 = y + 4$

  a. 8   **b.** 9
  c. 13   **d.** 14

21. Choose the standard form of the number.

$300,000 + 70,000 + 400 + 90 + 7$

  a. 307,497   **b.** 3,070,497
  c. 370,497   **d.** 37,497

18. A red car, a blue car, and a green car are parked in a row. The blue car is not next to the green car. The green car is at the beginning of the row. Which car is in the second spot?

  a. red   **b.** blue   **c.** green

22. Sam has 63 model train track pieces. For every curved piece of track, Sam has 8 straight pieces. How many straight pieces of model train track does Sam have?

  a. 7   **b.** 48   **c.** 55   **d.** 56

Explain how you solved the problem. Show all your work.

23. Ms. Applegate tutors three groups containing 2, 3, and 4 students. Mr. Kirsch tutors three groups of 4, 5, and 6 students. Mrs. Levin tutors three groups of 6, 7, and 8 students. If each teacher wants to tutor the same number of students, then which group should be moved from one teacher to another?

Addition and Subtraction

A LOT OF KIDS

There are a lot of kids
Living in my apartment building
And a lot of apartment buildings on my street
And a lot of streets in this city
And cities in this country
And a lot of countries in the world.
So I wonder if somewhere there's a kid I've never met
Living in some building on some street
In some city and country I'll never know—
And I wonder if that kid and I might be best friends
If we ever met.

Jeff Moss

In this chapter you will:

Learn about front-end estimation
Add and subtract larger numbers
 with regrouping
Add three or more addends
Choose the operation to solve
 a problem

Critical Thinking/Finding Together

Mary visited a friend. She drove 126 miles from New York to New Jersey and 140 miles from New Jersey to Pennsylvania. If she traveled a total distance of 425 miles, how far is it from Pennsylvania to New York?

Front-End Estimation

Students in the Hilldale elementary schools held a Read-a-Thon in October. About how many books did they read altogether?

Hilldale Schools	
School	**Books Read**
Central	2534
North	2496
South	3875

▶ To find about how many, use front-end estimation:
2534 + 2496 + 3875

Add the front digits.		Write 0s for the other digits.

$$
\begin{array}{r}
2534 \\
2496 \\
+\ 3875 \\
\hline
7
\end{array}
$$

$$
\begin{array}{r}
2534 \\
2496 \\
+\ 3875 \\
\hline
\text{about } 7000
\end{array}
$$

Rough estimate: 7000

▶ To get a closer estimate, make groups of about 1000 from the other digits.

2<u>534</u> + 2<u>496</u> + 3<u>875</u>

about 1000   about 1000

Think
7000 + 1000 + 1000 = 9000

Adjusted estimate: 9000

Altogether, the students read about 9000 books.

Study these examples.

$$
\begin{array}{r}
\$5.26 \\
1.52 \\
3.78 \\
+\quad 2.45 \\
\hline
\text{about } \$11.00
\end{array}
\quad
\begin{array}{l}
\text{about } \$1 \\
\text{about } \$1
\end{array}
$$

$11 + $1 + $1 = $13
Rough estimate: $11
Adjusted estimate: $13

$$
\begin{array}{r}
738 \\
223 \\
+\quad 569 \\
\hline
\text{about } 1400
\end{array}
\quad
\text{about } 100
$$

1400 + 100 = 1500
Rough estimate: 1400
Adjusted estimate: 1500

Use front-end digits to make a rough estimate. Then adjust.

1. 212
    672
    + 827

2. 358
    143
    + 796

3. 588
    419
    + 622

4. $3.47
    1.30
    + 9.65

5. $6.98
    4.25
    + 6.10

6. 3235
    5871
    + 1886

7. 9139
    2584
    + 4475

8. 5405
    1679
    + 2961

9. $67.99
    73.46
    + 36.49

10. $78.65
    18.98
    + 21.49

11. 635 + 198 + 474 + 360

12. $5.32 + $7.12 + $3.69 + $1.95

13. 283 + 722 + 542 + 156

14. $6.58 + $1.40 + $2.56 + $4.61

Problem Solving Use the table on page 96.

15. Students in Hilldale West School read 4073 books. About how many books did the students in all Hilldale schools read?

Estimate Differences

To estimate differences using front-end estimation:

- Subtract the front digits.
- Write 0s for the other digits.

$73.45	5736	$8.21	963
− 26.50	− 1775	− 7.35	− 315
about $50.00	about 4000	about $1.00	about 600

Estimate the difference. Use front-end estimation.

16. 646
    − 519

17. 441
    − 193

18. 938
    − 256

19. $8.98
    − 3.50

20. $2.56
    − 1.48

21. 7149
    − 3861

22. 5460
    − 1509

23. 8432
    − 5954

24. $49.90
    − 24.95

25. $37.21
    − 18.88

Add with Regrouping

Find the sum of 258 + 177.

First, use rounding to estimate: 258 + 177 → 300 + 200 = 500

Then add: 258 + 177.

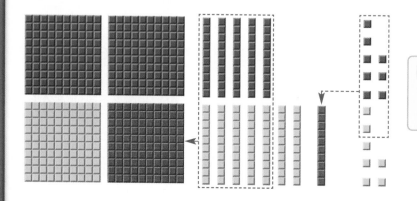

> **Remember:**
> 10 ones = 1 ten
> 10 tens = 1 hundred

Add the ones. Regroup.	Add the tens. Regroup.	Add the hundreds.

h t o
   1
 2 5 8
 + 1 7 7
     5
	h t o
	 1 1
	 2 5 8
	 + 1 7 7
	   3 5
		h t o
		 1 1
		 2 5 8
		 + 1 7 7
		 4 3 5

15 ones = 1 ten 5 ones	13 tens = 1 hundred 3 tens	**Think** 435 is close to 500. The answer is reasonable.

The sum is 435.

Study these examples.

$$
\begin{array}{r}
\overset{1}{} \\
\$.4\ 7 \\
+\ .2\ 9 \\
\hline
\$.7\ 6
\end{array}
\qquad
\begin{array}{r}
\overset{1}{} \\
5\ 2\ 6 \\
+\ 2\ 3\ 7 \\
\hline
7\ 6\ 3
\end{array}
\qquad
\begin{array}{r}
\overset{1}{} \\
\$1.7\ 3 \\
+\ 6.5\ 4 \\
\hline
\$8.2\ 7
\end{array}
\qquad
\begin{array}{r}
\overset{1}{} \\
6\ 5 \\
+\ \ \ 7 \\
\hline
7\ 2
\end{array}
$$

Choose a method to estimate. Then add.

Remember: You can use rounding or front-end estimation.

1. 48
    + 46

2. 37
    + 16

3. 58
    + 22

4. 85
    + 8

5. 73
    + 9

6. 329
    + 543

7. 480
    + 253

8. 675
    + 162

9. 781
    + 47

10. 909
    + 64

11. 168
    + 743

12. 643
    + 259

13. 345
    + 469

14. 877
    + 95

15. 768
    + 99

16. $.78
    + .06

17. $.46
    + .28

18. $1.75
    + 3.61

19. $5.28
    + 2.49

20. $4.65
    + 4.99

21. 75 + 18

22. 389 + 276

23. 581 + 229

24. $.19 + $.66

25. $6.19 + $2.32

26. $3.97 + $4.33

Problem Solving

27. There were 156 Democrats and 137 Republicans in the U.S. House of Representatives in 1878. How many members of the House were there?

28. In 1925 the U.S. Congress was made up of 435 Representatives and 96 Senators. How many members of Congress were there in 1925?

CHALLENGE

29. Find two 3-digit addends with the same digits in each number whose sum is 404.

30. What are the greatest and the least possible addends of two 3-digit numbers whose sum is 555? 999?

Four-Digit Addition

Find the sum of 1279 + 2355.

First, estimate: 1279 + 2355
                  ↓   ↓
              1000 + 2000 = 3000

Then add: 1279 + 2355.

Add the ones. Regroup.	Add the tens. Regroup.	Add the hundreds.	Add the thousands.

th	h	t	o
		1	
1	2	7	9
+ 2	3	5	5
			4

th	h	t	o
	1	1	
1	2	7	9
+ 2	3	5	5
		3	4

th	h	t	o
	1	1	
1	2	7	9
+ 2	3	5	5
	6	3	4

th	h	t	o
	1	1	
1	2	7	9
+ 2	3	5	5
3	6	3	4

| 14 ones = 1 ten 4 ones |

| 13 tens = 1 hundred 3 tens |

The sum is 3634.

> **Think**
> 3634 is close to 3000.
> The answer is reasonable.

Study these examples.

```
  1 1
  4 7 8 0
+ 2 9 5 6
  7 7 3 6
```

```
  1     1
$6 4.3 8
+  1 7.2 5
$8 1.6 3
```

```
    1 1
$5 0.6 7
+    5.4 5
$5 6.1 2
```

Choose a method to estimate. Then add.

1.	3165 + 2917	2.	4227 + 1905	3.	2774 + 6407	4.	5538 + 614

5.	4168 + 3454	6.	6075 + 2845	7.	8264 + 1349	8.	9438 + 395

Practice

Choose a method to estimate. Then find the sum.

9. 3670
+ 3458

10. 5891
+ 2768

11. 6655
+ 1563

12. 8492
+ 945

13. 5329
+ 1398

14. 4921
+ 3486

15. 6482
+ 1843

16. 7560
+ 488

17. $34.27
+ 46.17

18. $65.05
+ 13.98

19. $87.98
+ 10.75

20. $51.75
+ 9.15

Align and add.

21. 6414 + 979

22. 495 + 1272

23. 8067 + 86

24. $28.95 + $56.60

25. $69.75 + $8.94

26. $4.35 + $24.89

27. $6.08 + $44.56

Problem Solving

28. Ms. Davis and Mr. Brown ran for mayor of Newton. Ms. Davis received 2365 votes and Mr. Brown received 4915 votes. How many people voted in the election?

29. A campaign worker spent $23.96 on phone calls and $57.32 for posters. How much did she spend?

30. Three people ran for town manager. Mr. Miller received 4286 votes. Mr. Rush received 3907 votes. Ms. Adams received 7454 votes. Did Mr. Miller and Mr. Rush together receive more or fewer votes than Ms. Adams?

31. Mr. Jones received 2487 votes for sheriff. Mr. Long received double that number. How many votes did Mr. Long receive?

Add Larger Numbers

The Botanical Gardens held a two-day open house. What was the total attendance at the open house?

Attendance	
Saturday	17,465
Sunday	16,592

First, use rounding to estimate: 17,465 + 16,592

$$20,000 + 20,000 = 40,000$$

Then add: 17,465 + 16,592.

Add the ones.

```
  1 7 , 4 6 5
+ 1 6 , 5 9 2
───────────────
            7
```

Add the tens. Regroup.

```
          1
  1 7 , 4 6 5
+ 1 6 , 5 9 2
───────────────
          5 7
```

15 tens = 1 hundred 5 tens

Add the hundreds. Regroup.

```
      1   1
  1 7 , 4 6 5
+ 1 6 , 5 9 2
───────────────
        0 5 7
```

10 hundreds = 1 thousand 0 hundreds

Add the thousands. Regroup.

```
  1 1   1
  1 7 , 4 6 5
+ 1 6 , 5 9 2
───────────────
      4 , 0 5 7
```

14 thousands = 1 ten thousand 4 thousands

Add the ten thousands.

```
  1 1   1
  1 7 , 4 6 5
+ 1 6 , 5 9 2
───────────────
  3 4 , 0 5 7
```

Think
34,057 is close to 40,000. The answer is reasonable.

The total attendance was 34,057.

Add.

1.
```
    1 1
  $ 8.79
+    4.46
  $13.25
```

2.
```
  $6.39
+ 6.21
```

3.
```
  $41.75
+ 54.50
```

4.
```
  $65.49
+ 82.90
```

Choose a method to estimate. Then find the sum.

5.
```
   951
+  735
```

6.
```
   1873
+  2456
```

7.
```
   3298
+  7169
```

8.
```
   24,167
+  31,078
```

9.
```
  $6.75
+  4.37
```

10.
```
  $39.06
+  44.85
```

11.
```
  $57.36
+  28.84
```

12.
```
  $238.91
+  764.07
```

13.
```
   42,615
+  19,218
```

14.
```
   433,099
+  551,908
```

15.
```
   3,612,056
+  8,046,217
```

16.
```
   12,321,566
+   4,878,442
```

17.
```
  $4257.35
+  6152.72
```

18.
```
  $5121.09
+  7028.75
```

19.
```
  $21,564.52
+   5,095.31
```

20.
```
  $34,798.33
+  84,056.82
```

Align and add.

21. 6344 + 5812

22. 14,023 + 91,182

23. 720,279 + 507,090

24. $2.89 + $7.56

25. $28.25 + $66.96

26. $398.99 + $739.62

Problem Solving

27. Visitors to the Botanical Gardens bought 8429 flowering plants and 4872 vegetable plants. How many plants did they buy?

DO YOU REMEMBER?

Add.

28.
```
   4
   6
   7
+  2
```

29.
```
   3
   9
   3
+  4
```

30.
```
   8
   2
   4
+  4
```

31.
```
   9
   0
   1
+  6
```

32.
```
   5
   4
   3
+  4
```

33.
```
   9
   7
   4
+  8
```

Three or More Addends

Ms. Pei drove from Chicago to Kansas City. Then she drove to Indianapolis and Pittsburgh before returning to Chicago. How many miles did she travel?

To find how many miles, add:
499 + 485 + 353 + 452.

First, use front-end digits to estimate and adjust your estimate. Then add.

$$499 + 485 + 353 + 452$$

$$400 + 400 + 300 + 400 + 100 + 100 + 100 = 1800$$

Add the ones. Regroup.	Add the tens. Regroup.	Add the hundreds.
$\begin{array}{r} 1 \\ 4\ 9\ 9 \\ 4\ 8\ 5 \\ 3\ 5\ 3 \\ +\ 4\ 5\ 2 \\ \hline 9 \end{array}$	$\begin{array}{r} 2\ 1 \\ 4\ 9\ 9 \\ 4\ 8\ 5 \\ 3\ 5\ 3 \\ +\ 4\ 5\ 2 \\ \hline 8\ 9 \end{array}$	$\begin{array}{r} 2\ 1 \\ 4\ 9\ 9 \\ 4\ 8\ 5 \\ 3\ 5\ 3 \\ +\ \ 4\ 5\ 2 \\ \hline 1\ 7\ 8\ 9 \end{array}$
19 ones = 1 ten 9 ones	28 tens = 2 hundreds 8 tens	17 hundreds = 1 thousand 7 hundreds

Ms. Pei traveled 1789 miles.

Think
1789 is close to 1800. The answer is reasonable.

Study these examples.

$$\begin{array}{r} 1\ 2 \\ \$1.2\ 7 \\ .3\ 2 \\ .0\ 5 \\ +\ \ .9\ 7 \\ \hline \$2.6\ 1 \end{array}$$

$$\begin{array}{r} 1\ 1\ 1\ 1 \\ 3\ 4,1\ 6\ 1 \\ 3,7\ 2\ 8 \\ +\ \ 7,5\ 6\ 2 \\ \hline 4\ 5,4\ 5\ 1 \end{array}$$

$$\begin{array}{r} 1\ 2 \\ 6\ 5\ 7 \\ 8 \\ 3\ 4 \\ +\ 1\ 2\ 4 \\ \hline 8\ 2\ 3 \end{array}$$

Choose a method to estimate. Then find the sum.

1.
```
   27
   34
   61
 + 58
```

2.
```
   93
    9
   56
 + 82
```

3.
```
 $.33
  .12
  .68
+ .71
```

4.
```
 $.84
  .07
  .55
+ .06
```

5.
```
  247
  191
  322
+ 423
```

6.
```
  316
  875
   26
 +  6
```

7.
```
 $7.32
  5.17
  1.97
+ 3.28
```

8.
```
 $17.05
  21.87
  23.76
+ 31.32
```

9.
```
  1124
  2411
  4312
+ 3442
```

10.
```
  4612
   709
  3327
+ 647
```

11.
```
  13,219
  28,604
+ 26,154
```

12.
```
  29,002
  12,756
+ 14,321
```

13.
```
  35,806
   4,275
+ 71,888
```

14.
```
 $241.55
  897.60
+   43.28
```

Align and add.

15. 163 + 147 + 735 + 28

16. 2905 + 1324 + 655 + 218

17. $17.51 + $32.76 + $14.29

18. $518.87 + $421.08 + $87.99

Problem Solving

19. One month, Mr. Mills made business trips of 163 miles, 429 miles, 59 miles, and 242 miles. How many miles did he travel?

20. Ms. Sims spent $13.48, $19.76, and $9.88 on gasoline last month. How much money did she spend on gasoline?

CRITICAL THINKING

Three of the four addends have a sum of 1000.
Write the addend that does *not* belong.

21. 421, 391, 198, 381

22. 510, 237, 253, 233

23. 173, 125, 225, 602

24. 345, 352, 303, 355

Subtract with Regrouping

How much taller is the Aon Center than the Gas Company Tower?

To find how much taller, subtract: 858 − 749.

First, use rounding to estimate: 900 − 700 = 200. Then subtract.

Height of Tall Buildings in Los Angeles, California	
U.S. Bank Tower	1018 feet
Aon Center	858 feet
Gas Company Tower	749 feet
Arco Center	735 feet
Wells Fargo Tower	723 feet
United California Bank Plaza	717 feet

See if there are enough ones to subtract.

```
  h | t | o
  8 | 5 | 8
- 7 | 4 | 9
```

More ones are needed. Regroup the tens to get more ones.

58 = 5 tens 8 ones
   = 4 tens 18 ones

Subtract the ones.

```
  h |  t  |  o
    |  4  | 18
  8 |  5̶  |  8̶
- 7 |  4  |  9
    |     |  9
```

Subtract the tens.

```
  h |  t  |  o
    |  4  | 18
  8 |  5̶  |  8̶
- 7 |  4  |  9
    |  0  |  9
```

Subtract the hundreds.

```
  h |  t  |  o
    |  4  | 18
  8 |  5̶  |  8̶
- 7 |  4  |  9
  1 |  0  |  9
```

Check by adding.

```
        1
    1 0 9
  + 7 4 9
    8 5 8
```

The Aon Center is 109 feet taller.

.Think..........
109 is close to 200.
The answer is reasonable.

Study these examples.

```
  6  14
  7̶  4̶
- 4  6
  2  8
```

```
  7  13
$ 8̶. 3̶  8
- 7. 9  5
$   . 4  3
```

```
  5  11
  6̶  1̶  2
-     9  1
  5  2  1
```

Estimate mentally. Then find the difference.

1.
$$82 \\ -17$$

2.
$$60 \\ -34$$

3.
$$72 \\ -25$$

4.
$$\$.94 \\ -.58$$

5.
$$\$.43 \\ -.29$$

6.
$$572 \\ -143$$

7.
$$720 \\ -418$$

8.
$$886 \\ -249$$

9.
$$\$3.61 \\ -2.25$$

10.
$$\$6.84 \\ -4.19$$

11.
$$927 \\ -692$$

12.
$$435 \\ -172$$

13.
$$228 \\ -147$$

14.
$$\$5.43 \\ -2.83$$

15.
$$\$9.69 \\ -5.90$$

16.
$$23 \\ -9$$

17.
$$132 \\ -28$$

18.
$$429 \\ -75$$

19.
$$\$.52 \\ -.06$$

20.
$$\$2.75 \\ -.08$$

Align and subtract.

21. $75 - 9$

22. $32 - 8$

23. $480 - 36$

24. $\$6.21 - \$.16$

25. $\$8.19 - \$.54$

26. $\$5.33 - \$.07$

Problem Solving

Use the table on page 106.

27. How much shorter is United California Bank Plaza than the Arco Center?

28. How much taller is Wells Fargo Tower than the United California Bank Plaza?

29. The Aon Center has 62 stories. The Arco Center has 55 stories. How many more stories does the Aon Center have?

30. 777 Tower in Los Angeles is 725 feet tall. Is it taller or shorter than United California Bank Plaza? by how much?

Subtraction: Regroup Twice

How many more home runs did Babe Ruth hit than Frank Robinson?

Subtract: 714 − 586.

Estimate by rounding: 700 − 600 = 100

Then subtract.

Number of Home Runs Hit			
Aaron	755	Killebrew	573
Ruth	714	Jackson	563
Mays	660	Schmidt	548
Robinson	586	Mantle	536
McGwire	583	Foxx	534

More ones are needed. Regroup. Subtract ones.	More tens are needed. Regroup. Subtract tens.	Subtract hundreds.

$$\begin{array}{r} 0\ \ 14 \\ 7\ \cancel{1}\ \cancel{4} \\ -\ 5\ 8\ 6 \\ \hline 8 \end{array}$$

$$\begin{array}{r} 10 \\ 6\ \cancel{0}\ 14 \\ 7\ \cancel{1}\ \cancel{4} \\ -\ 5\ 8\ 6 \\ \hline 2\ 8 \end{array}$$

$$\begin{array}{r} 10 \\ 6\ \cancel{0}\ 14 \\ 7\ \cancel{1}\ \cancel{4} \\ -\ 5\ 8\ 6 \\ \hline 1\ 2\ 8 \end{array}$$

1 ten 4 ones = 0 tens 14 ones	7 hundreds 0 tens = 6 hundreds 10 tens

Check.

$$\begin{array}{r} 1\ \ 1 \\ 1\ 2\ 8 \\ +\ 5\ 8\ 6 \\ \hline 7\ 1\ 4 \end{array}$$

Babe Ruth hit 128 more home runs than Frank Robinson.

Think
128 is close to 100.
The answer is reasonable.

Practice

Choose a method to estimate. Then subtract.

1.
$$\begin{array}{r} 12 \\ 7\ \cancel{2}\ 11 \\ \$8.\cancel{3}\ \cancel{1} \\ -\ 7.8\ 4 \\ \hline \$\ .4\ 7 \end{array}$$

2.
$$\begin{array}{r} \$4.17 \\ -\ 2.38 \\ \hline \end{array}$$

3.
$$\begin{array}{r} \$6.24 \\ -\ 5.75 \\ \hline \end{array}$$

4.
$$\begin{array}{r} \$7.36 \\ -\ 4.88 \\ \hline \end{array}$$

5.
$$\begin{array}{r} 624 \\ -\ 137 \\ \hline \end{array}$$

6.
$$\begin{array}{r} 930 \\ -\ 452 \\ \hline \end{array}$$

7.
$$\begin{array}{r} 846 \\ -\ 669 \\ \hline \end{array}$$

8.
$$\begin{array}{r} 561 \\ -\ 265 \\ \hline \end{array}$$

9.
$$\begin{array}{r} 734 \\ -\ 587 \\ \hline \end{array}$$

Choose a method to estimate.
Then find the difference.

10.
$$
\begin{array}{r}
\overset{11}{} \\
3\cancel{X}16 \\
\cancel{4}\;\cancel{2}\;\cancel{6} \\
-\quad 8\;9 \\
\hline
3\;3\;7
\end{array}
$$

11.
$$
\begin{array}{r}
360 \\
-185 \\
\hline
\end{array}
$$

12.
$$
\begin{array}{r}
922 \\
-734 \\
\hline
\end{array}
$$

13.
$$
\begin{array}{r}
712 \\
-499 \\
\hline
\end{array}
$$

14.
$$
\begin{array}{r}
653 \\
-578 \\
\hline
\end{array}
$$

15.
$$
\begin{array}{r}
835 \\
-\;79 \\
\hline
\end{array}
$$

16.
$$
\begin{array}{r}
561 \\
-\;94 \\
\hline
\end{array}
$$

17.
$$
\begin{array}{r}
454 \\
-\;65 \\
\hline
\end{array}
$$

18.
$$
\begin{array}{r}
946 \\
-\;58 \\
\hline
\end{array}
$$

19.
$$
\begin{array}{r}
137 \\
-\;48 \\
\hline
\end{array}
$$

20.
$$
\begin{array}{r}
\$3.25 \\
-\;1.58 \\
\hline
\end{array}
$$

21.
$$
\begin{array}{r}
\$5.37 \\
-\;2.49 \\
\hline
\end{array}
$$

22.
$$
\begin{array}{r}
\$8.64 \\
-\;4.87 \\
\hline
\end{array}
$$

23.
$$
\begin{array}{r}
\$9.52 \\
-\;.99 \\
\hline
\end{array}
$$

Align and subtract.

24. $456 - 179$

25. $837 - 488$

26. $671 - 95$

27. $\$9.36 - \$7.59$

28. $\$2.91 - \$1.97$

29. $\$5.42 - \$.67$

Problem Solving Use the table on page 108.

30. How many more home runs did Hank Aaron hit than Frank Robinson?

31. How many fewer home runs did Mark McGwire hit than Willie Mays?

32. Did Babe Ruth and Reggie Jackson combined hit more or fewer home runs than Hank Aaron and Mickey Mantle combined? How many more or fewer?

33. Which is the greater difference: between the number of home runs hit by Willie Mays and Mike Schmidt or between the number of home runs hit by Hank Aaron and Willie Mays?

34. What is the combined home run total for Babe Ruth, Mickey Mantle, and Reggie Jackson?

Subtract Larger Numbers

The Mississippi is the second longest river in the United States. How much longer is it than the Colorado River?

U.S. Rivers (Length in Miles)			
Colorado (Texas)	862	Mississippi	2348
Porcupine	569	Missouri	2540
Rio Grande	1900	Tennessee	886

To find how much longer, subtract: 2348 − 862.

Subtract the ones.	More tens are needed. Regroup. Subtract.	More hundreds are needed. Regroup. Subtract.

```
    2 3 4 8
  −   8 6 2
          6
```

```
       2 14
    2 3̶ 4̶ 8
  −   8 6 2
        8 6
```

3 hundreds 4 tens =
2 hundreds 14 tens

```
         12
      1 2̶ 14
    2̶ 3̶ 4̶ 8
  −   8 6 2
      4 8 6
```

2 thousands 2 hundreds =
1 thousand 12 hundreds

Subtract the thousands.	Use addition or estimation to check.

```
         12
      1 2̶ 14
    2̶ 3̶ 4̶ 8
  −   8 6 2
    1 4 8 6
```

1486 + 862 = 2348
or
2300 − 900 = 1400

The Mississippi is 1486 miles longer than the Colorado River.

Study these examples.

```
      13
    5 3̶ 10
    7 6̶ 4̶ 0̶
  − 4 1 9 5
    3 4 4 5
```

```
        12
      0 2̶ 15
    $1̶.3 5̶
  −   .8 9
    $ .4 6
```

```
    5 12 8 13
    $6̶ 2.9̶ 3̶
  −   3 9.0 5
    $2 3.8 8
```

```
             9
        3 1̶0 15
    2 4,0̶ 5̶ 7
  − 1 3,9 6 1
    1 0,0 9 6
```

Estimate mentally. Then find the difference.

1.	2.	3.	4.
521 − 347	825 − 169	6218 − 5354	9743 − 4467

5.	6.	7.	8.
$74.36 − 46.72	$63.35 − 8.16	23,879 − 16,054	167,537 − 48,553

9.	10.	11.	12.
$774.93 − 567.06	$4355.91 − 2687.89	6,211,058 − 4,944,532	9,715,663 − 7,567,774

Align and subtract.

13. $360 - 74$ **14.** $7218 - 533$ **15.** $\$4.21 - \$1.38$

16. $\$672.95 - \$48.77$ **17.** $942{,}118 - 883{,}264$

18. $7{,}721{,}341 - 5{,}044{,}964$ **19.** $\$3127.94 - \$1993.67$

Problem Solving Use the table on page 110.

20. Is the difference in length of the Missouri and Rio Grande rivers greater or less than the length of the Porcupine River?

21. How much shorter is the Tennessee River than the Missouri River?

TEST PREPARATION

22. Find the difference.

77,349
 − 75,682

A 2667   **B** 1347
 C 1667   **D** 2347

23. Find the difference.

$351.09
 −   79.53

F $271.56   **G** $270.96
 H $271.66   **J** $270.56

Zeros in Subtraction

Amy guesses that the number of marbles in a big glass jar at the fair is 1957. The jar has 3000 marbles. How many more marbles are there than Amy's guess?

First, use rounding to estimate: 3000 − 1957

$$3000 - 2000 = 1000$$

Then subtract: 3000 − 1957.

▶ To subtract when the minuend has zeros:

- Align the minuend and the subtrahend by place value.
- Regroup as many times as needed before starting to subtract.
- Subtract.

More hundreds, tens, and ones are needed. Regroup all.	Subtract.	Check.

```
     9  9                    9  9                1  1  1
  2  10 10 10 ◄          2  10 10 10
  3̸  0̸  0̸  0̸            3̸  0̸  0̸  0̸              1  0  4  3
- 1  9  5  7           - 1  9  5  7           +  1  9  5  7
                         1  0  4  3              3  0  0  0
```

3 thousands =
2 thousands 10 hundreds 0 tens 0 ones
2 thousands 9 hundreds 10 tens 0 ones
2 thousands 9 hundreds 9 tens 10 ones

Think
1043 is close to the estimate of 1000.

There are 1043 more marbles than Amy's guess.

Study these examples.

```
        9                      9                       9  9
     7 10 10                4 10 10                 5 10 10 10
  $ 8 . 0̸  0̸            5̸  0̸  0̸             6̸  0̸  0̸  0̸
  -   2 . 4  6          - 4  8  7            -    9  9  4
  $ 5 . 5  4               1  3               5  0  0  6
```

Estimate mentally. Then find the difference.

1.	2.	3.	4.	5.
500 − 374	8070 − 691	400 − 281	700 − 659	900 − 527

6.	7.	8.	9.
6000 − 5783	3050 − 659	7000 − 6291	2000 − 79

10.	11.	12.	13.
300 − 37	4000 − 998	$6.04 − 4.73	$50.00 − 9.64

Align and subtract.

14. $100 - 69$ **15.** $400 - 184$ **16.** $5.00 - $2.38

17. $8000 - 788$ **18.** $6000 - 4893$ **19.** $70.00 - $19.45

20. $806 - 447$ **21.** $9.00 - $5.41   **22.** $1.05 - $.88

23. $9002 - 7865$ **24.** $5000 - 718$ **25.** $40.00 - $16.95

Problem Solving

26. At camp, Mel logged 2005 minutes on the computer. Pam logged 978 minutes the first week and twice as many minutes the second week. Who logged more minutes? How many more?

27. The camp director bought a new laptop for $875.69. She also bought a case of blank CDs for $29.95. She gave the cashier one thousand dollars. How much change did she get?

28. In the first month of camp, 1006 e-mails were sent and received by the campers. In the second month of camp, 677 e-mails were sent and received. About how many fewer e-mails were sent and received the second month of camp?

Write About It

29. Explain in your Math Journal why you gave an estimated or an exact answer for problems 26–28.

Addition and Subtraction Practice

To add or subtract larger numbers:

- Align the addends or align the minuend and subtrahend.
- Start by adding or subtracting at the right.
- Regroup as necessary.

> Remember to estimate the sum or difference first. Then use your estimate to check whether your answer is reasonable.

Add: $567.86 + $341.95.

```
   1     1 1
  $5 6 7.8 6
 + 3 4 1.9 5
  $9 0 9.8 1
```

Subtract: 87,731 − 65,954.

```
            16 12
    6  6  2  11
   8 7,7 3 1
 − 6 5,9 5 4
   2 1,7 7 7
```

Add: 36,428 + 83,985 + 759.

```
   1 2 1 2
   3 6,4 2 8
   8 3,9 8 5
 +       7 5 9
 1 2 1,1 7 2
```

Subtract: $490.00 − $478.81.

```
              9 9
      8 10 10 10
  $4 9 0.0 0
 −  4 7 8.8 1
  $   1 1.1 9
```

Practice

Choose a method to estimate. Then add or subtract.
Watch for + or − .

1. 42,937 + 11,426	**2.** 32,864 + 94,828	**3.** 85,963 + 28,279	**4.** $562.43 + 680.79
5. 94,361 − 22,087	**6.** 75,937 − 12,649	**7.** 82,616 − 51,499	**8.** $262.71 − 140.99
9. 13,584 41,592 + 26,437	**10.** 64,205 39,811 + 52,406	**11.** 82,099 4,157 + 79,862	**12.** $902.67 51.81 + 235.27

Choose a method to estimate. Then find the sum or the difference.

13. $\begin{array}{r} 53,007 \\ - 21,979 \\ \hline \end{array}$ 　14. $\begin{array}{r} 70,064 \\ - 19,155 \\ \hline \end{array}$ 　15. $\begin{array}{r} 80,102 \\ - 9,516 \\ \hline \end{array}$ 　16. $\begin{array}{r} \$600.08 \\ - 59.99 \\ \hline \end{array}$

17. $\begin{array}{r} 98,694 \\ 287 \\ + 5,148 \\ \hline \end{array}$ 　18. $\begin{array}{r} 675 \\ 44,526 \\ + 67 \\ \hline \end{array}$ 　19. $\begin{array}{r} 75,628 \\ 8,073 \\ + 48 \\ \hline \end{array}$ 　20. $\begin{array}{r} \$ 4.97 \\ 826.13 \\ + 65.39 \\ \hline \end{array}$

21. $\begin{array}{r} 81,000 \\ - 19,625 \\ \hline \end{array}$ 　22. $\begin{array}{r} 94,000 \\ - 67,887 \\ \hline \end{array}$ 　23. $\begin{array}{r} 70,000 \\ - 36,678 \\ \hline \end{array}$ 　24. $\begin{array}{r} \$600.00 \\ - 47.89 \\ \hline \end{array}$

Align and add or subtract.

25. $21,863 + 2,684 + 1,326$

26. $82,010 + 395 + 13,692$

27. $65,600 - 1,592$

28. $\$200.00 - \$126.74$

29. $90,506 - 3,729$

30. $\$645.16 + \$8.88 + \$.56$

Problem Solving

31. When it was built, a college stadium had 56,976 seats. Later, 3813 more seats were added. How many people can that stadium seat today?

32. A university stadium has 75,339 seats. A rival university stadium has 69,082 seats. How many more people can be seated in the first stadium than in the rival stadium?

CHALLENGE — Algebra

Find the missing digits.

33. $\begin{array}{r} 923 \\ - 14\square \\ \hline 776 \end{array}$ 　34. $\begin{array}{r} 629 \\ - \square8\square \\ \hline 441 \end{array}$ 　35. $\begin{array}{r} 231 \\ - \square\square\square \\ \hline 85 \end{array}$ 　36. $\begin{array}{r} 856 \\ - 4\square8 \\ \hline \square6\square \end{array}$

Problem-Solving Strategy:
Choose the Operation

The Keep Fit Shop ordered 487 pairs of high-tops. The factory has 1000 pairs in stock. The prices range from $30 to $85. How many pairs of high-tops will the factory have after they fill the order?

Read ▶ **Visualize the facts of the problem as you reread it.**

Facts: 487 pairs ordered
1000 pairs in stock at the factory
Pairs cost $30 to $85.

Question: How many pairs will be left after the order is filled?

Plan ▶ You are separating, or taking away, from a set. Subtract the number of pairs ordered from the number of pairs in stock: 1000 − 487.

You do not need to know the price range to solve the problem.

Solve ▶ Round to estimate the difference.
1000 − 500 = 500
Then subtract.

$$\begin{array}{r} \overset{0\ 9\ 9\ 10}{\cancel{1}\,\cancel{0}\,\cancel{0}\,\cancel{0}} \\ -\ \ 4\ 8\ 7 \\ \hline 5\ 1\ 3 \end{array}$$

The factory will have 513 pairs of high-tops left.

Check ▶ The answer is close to the estimate. It is reasonable.

Add to check subtraction. 513 + 487 = 1000

Choose the operation to solve each problem.

1. Running shoes are on sale for $62.79.
The regular price is $8.55 more.
What is the regular price for the running shoes?

 Read Visualize the facts of the
problem as you reread it.

Facts: $62.79 running shoes on sale
Regular price is $8.55 more.

Question: What is the regular price for
running shoes?

Plan You are joining sets or quantities.
Add the price of running shoes on
sale to the additional cost of
running shoes at regular price.

Solve .... **Check**

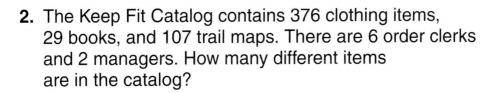

2. The Keep Fit Catalog contains 376 clothing items,
29 books, and 107 trail maps. There are 6 order clerks
and 2 managers. How many different items
are in the catalog?

3. Shipping costs $3 for orders under $10 and $5.50
for orders over $10. What is the total cost of
a $14.98 order?

4. The company received 853 orders in April and
118 more than that in May. How many orders did they
receive in May?

5. The Keep Fit Shop has sponsored a charity bike race
for 15 years. It is 35 miles long. There are rest stops
every 5 miles, including at the finish line.
How many rest stops are there?

Problem-Solving Applications: Mixed Review

Solve each problem and explain the method you used.

1. Jan and Kelly built a giant chain of 1378 plastic dominoes and 2267 wood dominoes. How many dominoes did they use?

2. The chain was 300 feet long. The first 127 feet were plastic dominoes. How many feet of chain were wood dominoes?

3. They set up the chain on the gym floor, which is 10,000 square feet in area. The chain took up 6341 square feet. How much of the gym floor was not covered?

4. Jan and Kelly spent 192 minutes on Friday setting up the dominoes. They worked for 218 minutes on Saturday. How long did it take them to set up the chain?

5. Their project raised $1070. They paid $318 for the dominoes. They gave the rest to charity. How much money did Jan and Kelly donate?

6. Use the graph at the right. How many people were in the audience that saw the domino chain?

7. The plastic dominoes fell in 109 seconds. Then the wood dominoes fell in 189 seconds. How long did it take the entire chain to fall down?

8. Jan and Kelly are planning next year's chain. They will use 2567 plastic dominoes and 3271 wood dominoes. How many dominoes will they use?

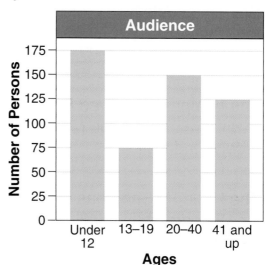

Audience

Number of Persons — Ages: Under 12, 13–19, 20–40, 41 and up

Choose a strategy from the list or use another strategy to solve each problem.

9. A class held a jump rope contest for charity. The winner jumped 9278 times without missing. The second prize went to someone who jumped 8765 times. How many more times did the winner jump?

Strategy File

Use these Strategies
Logical Reasoning
Make a Table or List
Choose the Operation
Guess and Test

10. There were 108 people in the contest. They each paid $2 to enter. The winner won $25. Only 27 jumpers made it to the second round. How many jumpers were eliminated after round one?

11. Paula hopped on her right foot 876 times and then on her left foot 954 times. Then she switched back to her right foot and hopped 212 times before tripping. How many times did she hop in all?

12. Paul, Maria, Gail, and Leroy play Double Dutch. Two people hold ropes and 2 jump. How many different ways could the friends play?

13. Marcia jumped for 47 minutes. How many minutes less than an hour did Marcia jump?

14. Asa, Max, and Jemma came in first, second, and third in the jump rope contest. Max did not win, but he jumped more times than Asa. Who came in first, second, and third?

15. Of the 108 contestants, the number of girls was double the number of boys. How many girls were there? how many boys?

16. Write a problem modeled on problem 12. Have a classmate solve it.

Use front-end digits to make a rough estimate. Then adjust. (See pp. 96–97.)

1. 382
$+216$

2. 4648
$+3175$

3. 7060
-2955

4. $\$63.49$
$-\ \ 19.79$

Add. (See pp. 98–105, 114–115.)

5. $392 + 26$

6. $276 + 477$

7. $4234 + 477$

8. $8312 + 568 + 39$

9. $6178 + 1311 + 452$

10. $\$28.42 + \$63.98$

11. 2527
1198
$+\ \ 456$

12. $\$32.38$
4.43
$+\ \ 20.37$

13. $12{,}476$
$9{,}830$
$+31{,}579$

14. $271{,}042$
$+218{,}924$

Subtract. (See pp. 106–115.)

15. $982 - 54$

16. $2816 - 129$

17. $17{,}150 - 3594$

18. $23{,}881 - 12{,}134$

19. $117{,}923 - 98{,}277$

20. $\$345.04 - \$251.86$

21. 6000
-1406

22. 2603
$-\ \ 186$

23. $\$54.93$
$-\ \ 16.17$

24. $15{,}168$
$-\ \ 7{,}619$

Problem Solving
(See pp. 116–119.)

25. Memorial School has 630 students. If 437 students are girls, how many are boys?

26. There are 127 roses, 416 daisies, and 216 lilies in the flower shop. How many flowers are in the flower shop?

27. The new stadium has 60,000 seats. The old stadium had 45,500 seats. How many more seats than the old stadium does the new stadium have?

28. There were 224 people at the first showing of a new movie. Forty-one people bought popcorn. The second showing had 219 people. How many people went to the new movie today?

(See *Still More Practice*, p. 463.)

Roman Numerals

The ancient Romans used letters to write numbers.

1 = I	4 = IV	7 = VII	10 = X	40 = XL	70 = LXX
2 = II	5 = V	8 = VIII	20 = XX	50 = L	80 = LXXX
3 = III	6 = VI	9 = IX	30 = XXX	60 = LX	90 = XC
					100 = C

Use these rules to read and write Roman numerals:

- When letters that stand for lesser numerals come *after* letters that stand for greater numerals, *add.*
III $\longrightarrow$ 1 + 1 + 1 = 3
VIII $\longrightarrow$ 5 + 3 = 8
LVIII $\longrightarrow$ 50 + 8 = 58

- When a letter that stands for a lesser numeral comes *before* a letter that stands for a greater numeral, *subtract.*
IV $\longrightarrow$ 5 − 1 = 4
IX $\longrightarrow$ 10 − 1 = 9
XL $\longrightarrow$ 50 − 10 = 40

CXLVII = _?_

$$\begin{array}{ccccc} \text{C} & & \text{XL} & & \text{VII} \\ \downarrow & & \downarrow & & \downarrow \\ 100 & + & 40 & + & 7 & = 147 \end{array}$$

Write the Roman numeral in standard form.

1. LXIV   **2.** XXXIX   **3.** LXIX   **4.** CXXVI   **5.** CCVII

Write each as a Roman numeral.

6. 17   **7.** 48   **8.** 300   **9.** 89   **10.** 56   **11.** 234

Chapter 3 Test

Choose a method to estimate. Then add.

1. 509 + 45

2. 283 + 179

3. 8059 + 397

4. 151,209 + 348,964

5. 902,651 + 48,376

6.
```
   176
   205
+ 387
```

7.
```
   374
   162
+  51
```

8.
```
  $78.50
     .99
+   5.38
```

9.
```
  23,154
      96
+  4,129
```

Choose a method to estimate. Then subtract.

10. 750 − 29

11. 5123 − 99

12. 56,150 − 3777

13. 8,731,402 − 5,062,974

14. 9,532,486 − 983,723

15.
```
  5430
−  298
```

16.
```
  3000
− 2951
```

17.
```
  $29.39
−  18.42
```

18.
```
  29,126
−  8,437
```

Problem Solving

Use a strategy you have learned.

19. Mrs. Lee bought 4 items for $29.99, $17.59, $35.79, and $49.99. How much did she pay? If she gave the cashier $135.00, how much change did she receive?

Tell About It

Use front-end digits **and** rounding to estimate the sum. Explain which method of estimation gives an answer closer to the actual sum and why.

20. 659 + 251

Performance Assessment

21. List which three money amounts in the boxes have a sum of about $73. Use estimation to help.

| $63.50 | $1.35 | $3.75 | $8.25 | $58.50 |

Test Preparation

Choose the best answer.

1. Choose the standard form of the number.

ninety-one thousand, four hundred sixty

    a. 9146
    b. 91,046
    c. 91,460
    d. 91,460,000

7. Choose the standard form of the number.

$30,000,000 + 80,000 + 5000 + 6$

    a. 30,085,006
    b. 30,085,060
    c. 30,805,006
    d. 30,850,006

2. Which is ordered greatest to least?

    a. 5718; 57,180; 56,032; 57,099
    b. 57,099; 57,180; 56,032; 5718
    c. 57,180; 57,099; 56,032; 5718
    d. 57,180; 57,099; 5718; 56,032

8. Round 5638 to the nearest thousand.

    a. 5000
    b. 5600
    c. 5700
    d. 6000

3. About what number is the arrow pointing toward?

    a. 225
    b. 250
    c. 255
    d. 270

9. What is the value of the change?

Cost: $14.52
Amount given: $20.00

    a. $5.48
    b. $6.48
    c. $6.52
    d. $6.58

4. Find the missing addend.

$12 = x + 4$

    a. 5
    b. 8
    c. 12
    d. 16

10. Find the missing subtrahend.

$17 - n = 9$

    a. 6
    b. 7
    c. 8
    d. 9

5. $8502 - 647$

    a. 7865
    b. 7855
    c. 9149
    d. not given

11.
```
  $89.60
    .88
+  6.49
```
    a. $95.97
    b. $96.87
    c. $150.48
    d. not given

6. Which is more than 20,000 but less than 28,000?

    a. $15,987 + 13,162$
    b. $29,000 - 900$
    c. $30,255 - 11,065$
    d. $23,154 + 96 + 4129$

12. Which statement is true?

    a. $6 + (3 + 4) = (6 + 3) + 1$
    b. $(6 + 3) + 4 = 6 + (3 + 4)$
    c. $(4 + 3) + 1 = (6 + 3) + 1$
    d. none of these

13. Which is ordered least to greatest?

    a. $43.14, $43.41, $44.13, $43.44
    b. $43.14, $43.41, $43.44, $44.13
    c. $44.13, $43.44, $43.41, $43.14
    d. $43.14, $43.44, $43.41, $44.13

14. What is the period of the underlined digits?

423,578,<u>109</u>

    a. thousands period
    b. millions period
    c. ones period
    d. not given

15. Add.

$$\begin{array}{r} \$62.73 \\ +\ \ \ 6.94 \\ \hline \end{array}$$

    a. $68.57
    b. $68.67
    c. $69.57
    d. $69.67

16. Lynette found 224 clams. She sold 195 clams to a fish store and kept the rest. How many clams did Lynette keep?

    a. 195
    b. 129
    c. 109
    d. 29

17. Subtract.

$$\begin{array}{r} 787,842 \\ -\ 634,367 \\ \hline \end{array}$$

    a. 153,475
    b. 153,485
    c. 153,575
    d. 153,585

18. Find the value of the expression.

$26 + n$, when $n = 17$

    a. 9
    b. 43
    c. 33
    d. 42

19. Which shows the best way to check the answer?

$$\begin{array}{r} 484 \\ -\ 253 \\ \hline \end{array}$$

    a. $484 - 253 = 231$
    b. $484 + 231 = 715$
    c. $231 + 253 = 484$
    d. $242 + 242 = 484$

20. Ty has 45 posters. Some of the posters are of cars and the others are of trains. For each train poster, he has 8 car posters. How many train posters does Ty have?

    a. 40
    b. 32
    c. 8
    d. 5

Tell About It

Explain how you solved the problem. Show all your work.

21. Which statement below is **not** true? Explain why.
- The sum of two odd numbers is always even.
- The difference between an even number and an odd number is always even.

Multiply by One and Two Digits

Is Six Times One a Lot of Fun?

Is six times one a lot of fun?
Or eight times two?
Perhaps for you.
But five times three
Unhinges me,
While six and seven and eight times eight
Put me in an awful state
And four and six and nine times nine
Make me want to cry and whine
So when I get to twelve times ten
I begin to wonder when
I can take a vacation from multiplication
And go out
And start playing again.

Karla Kuskin

In this chapter you will:

Use multiplication properties
Learn about special factors
    and patterns
Explore multiplication models
Estimate and multiply whole
    numbers and money
Solve problems by working
    backward

Critical Thinking/Finding Together

Use base ten blocks to model
and find the product for each
multiplication the girl is thinking of.

Update your skills. See pages 8 and 9.

Multiplication Properties

The **properties of multiplication** can help you to multiply quickly and correctly.

Commutative Property of Multiplication

- Changing the *order* of the factors does not change the product.

.Think....
"order"

$$4 \times 5 = 20$$
$$5 \times 4 = 20$$

$$\begin{array}{r} 5 \\ \times 4 \\ \hline 20 \end{array} \quad \begin{array}{r} 4 \\ \times 5 \\ \hline 20 \end{array}$$

Associative Property of Multiplication

- Changing the *grouping* of the factors does not change the product.

.Think....
"grouping"

$$(1 \times 4) \times 2 = 1 \times (4 \times 2)$$
$$4 \quad \times 2 = 1 \times \quad 8$$
$$8 = 8$$

Identity Property of Multiplication

- The product of *one* and a number is the same as that number.

.Think....
"same number"

$$1 \times 6 = 6$$
$$6 \times 1 = 6$$

$$\begin{array}{r} 6 \\ \times 1 \\ \hline 6 \end{array} \quad \begin{array}{r} 1 \\ \times 6 \\ \hline 6 \end{array}$$

Zero Property of Multiplication

- The product of *zero* and a number is 0.

.Think....
"zero"

$$0 \times 3 = 0$$
$$3 \times 0 = 0$$

$$\begin{array}{r} 3 \\ \times 0 \\ \hline 0 \end{array} \quad \begin{array}{r} 0 \\ \times 3 \\ \hline 0 \end{array}$$

Practice

Find the products. Name the multiplication property you used.

1. $\begin{array}{r} 1 \\ \times 8 \\ \hline \end{array}$ $\begin{array}{r} 8 \\ \times 1 \\ \hline \end{array}$

2. $\begin{array}{r} 9 \\ \times 4 \\ \hline \end{array}$ $\begin{array}{r} 4 \\ \times 9 \\ \hline \end{array}$

3. $\begin{array}{r} 2 \\ \times 6 \\ \hline \end{array}$ $\begin{array}{r} 6 \\ \times 2 \\ \hline \end{array}$

4. $\begin{array}{r} 7 \\ \times 5 \\ \hline \end{array}$ $\begin{array}{r} 5 \\ \times 7 \\ \hline \end{array}$

5. 6×7

6. 8×5

7. 6×0

8. 9×1

Use multiplication properties to complete.

9. $2 \times (3 \times 1) = (2 \times 3) \times 1$
$2 \times \underline{?} = \underline{?} \times 1$
$\underline{?} = \underline{?}$

10. $(3 \times 2) \times 2 = 3 \times (2 \times 2)$
$\underline{?} \times \underline{?} = \underline{?} \times \underline{?}$
$\underline{?} = \underline{?}$

11. $2 \times (5 \times 0) = (2 \times 5) \times \underline{?}$
$\underline{?} \times \underline{?} = \underline{?} \times \underline{?}$
$\underline{?} = \underline{?}$

12. $(1 \times 6) \times 2 = \underline{?} \times (\underline{?} \times \underline{?})$
$\underline{?} \times \underline{?} = \underline{?} \times \underline{?}$
$\underline{?} = \underline{?}$

Use the properties of multiplication to solve.

13. The product is 8. One factor is 8. What is the other factor?

14. If $8 \times 12 = 96$, what is the product of 12×8?

Distributive Property

Distributive Property of Multiplication over Addition
Multiplying a number by a sum is the same as multiplying the number by each addend of the sum and then adding the products.

Think.........................
"same factor across addends"

$5 \times (2 + 1) = (5 \times 2) + (5 \times 1)$
$5 \times \quad 3 \quad = \quad 10 \quad + \quad 5$
$\quad\quad 15 \quad = \quad 15$

Use the distributive property to complete.

15. $4 \times (3 + 2) = (4 \times 3) + (4 \times 2)$
$4 \times \underline{?} = \underline{?} + \underline{?}$
$\underline{?} = \underline{?}$

16. $3 \times (5 + 4) = (3 \times \underline{?}) + (3 \times \underline{?})$
$3 \times \underline{?} = \underline{?} + \underline{?}$
$\underline{?} = \underline{?}$

17. $5 \times (6 + 3) = (\underline{?} \times \underline{?}) + (\underline{?} \times \underline{?})$
$\underline{?} \times \underline{?} = \underline{?} + \underline{?}$
$\underline{?} = \underline{?}$

Multiplication Models

▶ Sharon uses 16 paper clips to make a necklace. How many paper clips will she need to make 2 necklaces?
Multiply: 2 × 16

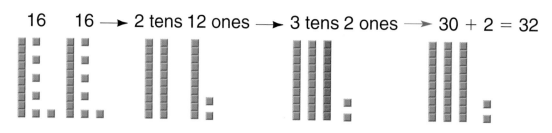

16   16 ⟶ 2 tens 12 ones ⟶ 3 tens 2 ones ⟶ 30 + 2 = 32

2 × 16 = 32   Sharon needs 32 paper clips.

▶ Holly makes a bracelet with 3 rows of beads. Each row has 15 beads. How many beads are in the bracelet?

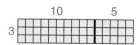

There are 45 beads in the bracelet.

$$
\begin{aligned}
&\quad\ 3 \quad\ \times \quad\ 15 \\
&=\quad 3 \quad\ \times (10 + 5) \\
&= (3 \times 10) + (3 \times 5) \\
&=\quad 30 \quad + \quad 15 \\
&=\qquad\qquad 45
\end{aligned}
$$
3 × 15 = 45

▶ Ito wants to make 4 headbands. Each headband uses 34 elastic bands. How many elastic bands does he need?
Multiply: 4 × 34

> **Think**
> 34 = 3 tens 4 ones

4 × 3 tens = 12 tens = 120   4 × 4 ones = 16 ones = 16

120 + 16 = 136

4 × 34 = 136   Ito needs 136 elastic bands.

Write a multiplication sentence for each model.

1.

2.

3.

4.

5.

6.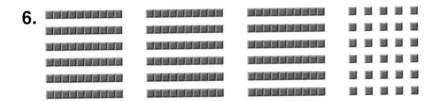

Problem Solving You may use models.

7. Raul has 3 paper-clip chains. Each one is 55 paper clips long. He connects them. How long is the new chain?

8. Monica paints T-shirts. She paints 17 dots on each T-shirt. How many dots does she paint on 9 T-shirts?

9. Marva makes stained-glass designs. One design has 5 rows of squares. There are 10 squares in each row. How many squares does Marva use?

10. Paul and Emma build model boats. Paul uses 25 craft sticks to build a rowboat. Emma uses 20 craft sticks to build a rowboat. How many craft sticks will Paul and Emma each need to build 4 rowboats?

11. Peter uses 52 toothpicks to build a model house. How many toothpicks does he need for 6 model houses?

Special Factors

Look for a pattern when you multiply tens.

  4 × 1 ten = 4 tens
4 × 10 = 40

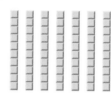 7 × 1 ten = 7 tens
7 × 10 = 70

  2 × 3 tens = 6 tens
2 × 30 = 60

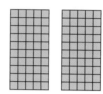 2 × 5 tens = 10 tens
2 × 50 = 100

To multiply tens, hundreds, or thousands:

- Multiply the nonzero digits.
- Count the number of zeros in the factors.
  Then write the same number of zeros in the product.

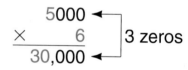

```
  50 ←
×  9    | 1 zero
 450 ←
```

```
 700 ←
×   4    | 2 zeros
2800 ←
```

```
  5000 ←
×    6    | 3 zeros
30,000 ←
```

Write a multiplication sentence for each.

1. 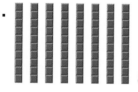 8 × 10 = 80

2.

3.

4.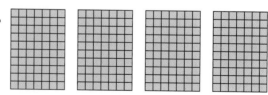

5.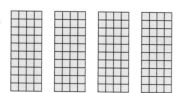

6.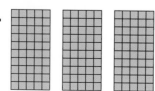

Practice

Copy and complete each multiplication.

7. 6×3 tens $= 6 \times 30 = 180$

8. 5×4 tens $= 5 \times 40 = $?

9. 9×1 hundred $= 9 \times 100 = $?

10. 4×1 thousand $= 4 \times 1000 = $?

11. 7×3 thousands $= $? $\times$? $= $?

Find the product.

12. 4×1 ten

13. 7×3 tens

14. 8×1 hundred

15. 9×6 tens

16. 2×5 hundreds

17. 4×7 hundreds

18. 7×1 thousand

19. 6×3 thousands

20. 5×8 thousands

Use mental math to multiply.
Explain how you got your answer.

21.
$$\begin{array}{r} 90 \\ \times\ 3 \\ \hline \end{array}$$

22.
$$\begin{array}{r} 70 \\ \times\ 2 \\ \hline \end{array}$$

23.
$$\begin{array}{r} 80 \\ \times\ 4 \\ \hline \end{array}$$

24.
$$\begin{array}{r} 50 \\ \times\ 5 \\ \hline \end{array}$$

25.
$$\begin{array}{r} 500 \\ \times\ 3 \\ \hline \end{array}$$

26.
$$\begin{array}{r} 900 \\ \times\ 9 \\ \hline \end{array}$$

27.
$$\begin{array}{r} 400 \\ \times\ 5 \\ \hline \end{array}$$

28.
$$\begin{array}{r} 300 \\ \times\ 8 \\ \hline \end{array}$$

29.
$$\begin{array}{r} 1000 \\ \times\ 6 \\ \hline \end{array}$$

30.
$$\begin{array}{r} 6000 \\ \times\ 4 \\ \hline \end{array}$$

31.
$$\begin{array}{r} 5000 \\ \times\ 7 \\ \hline \end{array}$$

32.
$$\begin{array}{r} 9000 \\ \times\ 6 \\ \hline \end{array}$$

Problem Solving

33. There are 5000 seats at Carver Stadium. Baseball games are played there 4 nights a week. How many tickets can the stadium sell each week?

34. Glen runs the 50-yard dash 8 times. How many yards does he run in all?

35. Ms. Spero swims 8 laps every day. How many laps does she swim in September?

Multiply by One-Digit Numbers

Each of 2 fish tanks holds 24 fish.
How many fish are there?

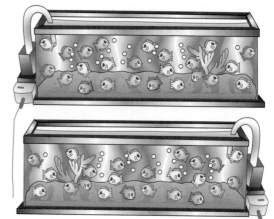

▶ To find how many, join 2 sets of 24.

.Think..........................
24 = 2 tens 4 ones

2 tens 4 ones
+2 tens 4 ones
4 tens 8 ones = 40 + 8 = 48

▶ You can join 2 sets of 24 by using the distributive property.

2 sets of 24 = 2 × 24
= 2 × (20 + 4)
= (2 × 20) + (2 × 4)
= 40 + 8
= 48

▶ You can multiply: 2 × 24

Multiply the ones.

$$\begin{array}{r} 24 \\ \times\ 2 \\ \hline 8 \end{array}$$

2 × 4 ones = 8 ones

Multiply the tens.

$$\begin{array}{r} 24 \\ \times\ 2 \\ \hline 48 \end{array}$$

2 × 2 tens = 4 tens

There are 48 fish.

Multiply.

1. $\begin{array}{r} 12 \\ \times\ 2 \end{array}$ 2. $\begin{array}{r} 22 \\ \times\ 3 \end{array}$ 3. $\begin{array}{r} 13 \\ \times\ 3 \end{array}$ 4. $\begin{array}{r} 11 \\ \times\ 5 \end{array}$ 5. $\begin{array}{r} 14 \\ \times\ 2 \end{array}$ 6. $\begin{array}{r} 12 \\ \times\ 4 \end{array}$

Find the product. Use mental math or paper and pencil.

7. 11
    × 9

8. 34
    × 2

9. 22
    × 4

10. 44
     × 2

11. 12
     × 3

12. 33
     × 3

13. 32
     × 3

14. 13
     × 2

15. 43
     × 2

16. 31
     × 3

17. 26
     × 1

18. 41
     × 2

19. 2 × 23

20. 4 × 22

21. 2 × 33

22. 3 × 31

23. 2 × 42

24. 3 × 21

25. 4 × 21

26. 8 × 11

27. 2 × 14

28. 2 × 31

29. 7 × 11

30. 2 × 32

Problem Solving

31. Fish World received 3 cartons of fish food. There were 12 boxes of food in each carton. How many boxes of fish food did Fish World receive?

32. Niqui displayed 22 fish care booklets on each of 4 shelves. How many fish care booklets did Niqui display on the shelves?

33. Greg filled each of 2 fish tanks with 14 gallons of water. How much water did Greg use to fill the tanks?

34. There were 2 shipments of 42 goldfish each to Fish World. How many goldfish were there in both shipments?

 Write About It

35. Use each of the three methods on page 132 to find the product of 23 × 3. Which method do you find easiest? Why?

36. How is multiplication like addition? How is it different?

4-5

Products: Front-End Estimation

Will 5 games cost more or less than $100?

To find if the games will cost more or less than $100, use front-end estimation.

VIDEO GAME CARTRIDGES
NOW ONLY
$25.95 each

Multiply the front digit of each factor.		Write 0s for the other digits.

$$\begin{array}{r} \$25.95 \\ \times\ \ \ \ \ 5 \\ \hline 10 \end{array}$$

$$\boxed{\begin{array}{r} \$20.00 \\ \times\ \ \ \ \ 5 \\ \hline \$100.00 \end{array}}$$

$$\begin{array}{r} \$25.95 \\ \times\ \ \ \ \ 5 \\ \hline \text{about } \$100.00 \end{array}$$

Write $ and . in the product.

Since $25.95 is greater than $20, the actual cost is close to but greater than $100.

The 5 games will cost more than $100.

Study these examples.

$$\begin{array}{r} 62 \\ \times\ \ 6 \\ \hline \text{about } 360 \end{array}$$

$$\begin{array}{r} \$5.28 \\ \times\ \ \ \ \ 7 \\ \hline \text{about } \$35.00 \end{array}$$

$$\begin{array}{r} 8406 \\ \times\ \ \ \ \ 8 \\ \hline \text{about } 64{,}000 \end{array}$$

$$\begin{array}{r} \$.71 \\ \times\ \ \ \ \ 3 \\ \hline \text{about } \$2.10 \end{array}$$

Practice

Use front-end digits to estimate the product.

1. $\begin{array}{r} 82 \\ \times\ 6 \\ \hline \end{array}$ 2. $\begin{array}{r} 98 \\ \times\ 7 \\ \hline \end{array}$ 3. $\begin{array}{r} 46 \\ \times\ 5 \\ \hline \end{array}$ 4. $\begin{array}{r} \$.73 \\ \times\ \ \ 3 \\ \hline \end{array}$ 5. $\begin{array}{r} \$.57 \\ \times\ \ \ 2 \\ \hline \end{array}$

6. $\begin{array}{r} 473 \\ \times\ \ 8 \\ \hline \end{array}$ 7. $\begin{array}{r} \$9.01 \\ \times\ \ \ \ \ 4 \\ \hline \end{array}$ 8. $\begin{array}{r} 5125 \\ \times\ \ \ \ \ 9 \\ \hline \end{array}$ 9. $\begin{array}{r} 1070 \\ \times\ \ \ \ \ 6 \\ \hline \end{array}$ 10. $\begin{array}{r} \$32.95 \\ \times\ \ \ \ \ \ \ 7 \\ \hline \end{array}$

11. $\begin{array}{r} 849 \\ \times\ \ 4 \\ \hline \end{array}$ 12. $\begin{array}{r} \$6.53 \\ \times\ \ \ \ \ 3 \\ \hline \end{array}$ 13. $\begin{array}{r} 4673 \\ \times\ \ \ \ \ 8 \\ \hline \end{array}$ 14. $\begin{array}{r} 7211 \\ \times\ \ \ \ \ 5 \\ \hline \end{array}$ 15. $\begin{array}{r} \$32.24 \\ \times\ \ \ \ \ \ \ 9 \\ \hline \end{array}$

Use front-end digits to estimate the product.

16.	55 × 2	17.	49 × 9	18.	31 × 7	19.	64 × 6	20.	78 × 3

21.	437 × 9	22.	622 × 5	23.	145 × 4	24.	744 × 7	25.	609 × 8

26.	7832 × 6	27.	8209 × 5	28.	9848 × 4	29.	4633 × 2

30.	$.65 × 9	31.	$8.33 × 7	32.	$34.72 × 5	33.	$21.24 × 6

34. 4 × $7.10   **35.** 2 × $9.67   **36.** 9 × $37.55

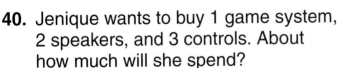 **Problem Solving** **Use front-end estimation.**

37. Will 3 controls cost more or less than $60? Explain why.

38. About how much would a set of 2 speakers cost?

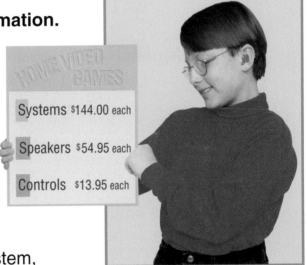

HOME VIDEO GAMES

Systems $144.00 each

Speakers $54.95 each

Controls $13.95 each

39. Will 7 controls cost more than 2 game systems? Explain why.

40. Jenique wants to buy 1 game system, 2 speakers, and 3 controls. About how much will she spend?

TEST PREPARATION

41. Choose the estimated product.

6 × 4863

A 28,800   **B** 24,000   **C** 20,000   **D** 2400

Multiply with Regrouping

Cody needs 102 pushpins. There are 35 pushpins in each packet. Will Cody have enough if he buys 3 packets?

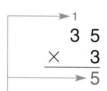

Amarillo

Dallas

Austin

Houston

San Antonio

To find whether Cody will have enough pushpins, find the product: 3×35

First, estimate using front-end digits: 3×35

$$3 \times 30 = 90$$

Then, multiply.

.·Think···
The actual product will be greater than 90.

Multiply the ones. Regroup.

```
      1
    3 5
  ×   3
      5
```

3×5 ones = 15 ones
15 ones = 1 ten 5 ones

Multiply the tens. Add the regrouped tens.

```
      1
    3 5
  ×   3
  1 0 5
```

$105 > 102$

3×3 tens = 9 tens
9 tens + 1 ten = 10 tens

Cody will have enough pushpins.

Practice

Multiply.

1. $\begin{array}{r} 18 \\ \times\ 3 \\ \hline \end{array}$	**2.** $\begin{array}{r} 16 \\ \times\ 5 \\ \hline \end{array}$	**3.** $\begin{array}{r} 38 \\ \times\ 2 \\ \hline \end{array}$	**4.** $\begin{array}{r} 24 \\ \times\ 3 \\ \hline \end{array}$	**5.** $\begin{array}{r} 16 \\ \times\ 4 \\ \hline \end{array}$	**6.** $\begin{array}{r} 25 \\ \times\ 2 \\ \hline \end{array}$
7. $\begin{array}{r} 15 \\ \times\ 7 \\ \hline \end{array}$	**8.** $\begin{array}{r} 29 \\ \times\ 3 \\ \hline \end{array}$	**9.** $\begin{array}{r} 44 \\ \times\ 8 \\ \hline \end{array}$	**10.** $\begin{array}{r} 32 \\ \times\ 6 \\ \hline \end{array}$	**11.** $\begin{array}{r} 22 \\ \times\ 7 \\ \hline \end{array}$	**12.** $\begin{array}{r} 58 \\ \times\ 5 \\ \hline \end{array}$

Use front-end digits to estimate. Then multiply.

13. $\begin{array}{r} 24 \\ \times\ 6 \\ \hline \end{array}$ 14. $\begin{array}{r} 46 \\ \times\ 4 \\ \hline \end{array}$ 15. $\begin{array}{r} 68 \\ \times\ 5 \\ \hline \end{array}$ 16. $\begin{array}{r} 78 \\ \times\ 2 \\ \hline \end{array}$ 17. $\begin{array}{r} 36 \\ \times\ 3 \\ \hline \end{array}$ 18. $\begin{array}{r} 86 \\ \times\ 9 \\ \hline \end{array}$

19. 3×27 20. 4×63 21. 5×84 22. 6×77

23. 9×58 24. 7×45 25. 8×67 26. 9×99

27. 5×59 28. 2×89 29. 3×88 30. 4×96

Problem Solving

31. The school play has 4 acts. Each act is 23 minutes long. How long is the school play?

32. The school cafeteria serves salad 5 times a week. In 22 weeks, how many times is salad served?

33. Hunter Grade School has 6 grades. Each grade has 98 students. How many students go to Hunter?

34. Each row in the school parking lot holds 28 cars. There are 6 rows. How many cars can park in the lot?

35. Ms. Shaw assigns one chapter of a book as homework every week. Each chapter has 87 pages. How many pages will Ms. Shaw's students have read in 7 weeks?

36. Each student in Mr. Klein's class can work at the class computer for 15 minutes at a time. Nine students have worked at the computer today. How many minutes were spent at the computer altogether?

CHALLENGE — Algebra

Find the pattern rule. Complete the pattern.

37. 10, 15, 25, 30, 40, _?_, _?_, _?_   38. 1, 3, 2, 4, 3, 5, _?_, _?_, _?_

39. 24, 30, 28, 34, 32, _?_, _?_, _?_   40. 1, 1, 3, 3, 5, 5, 7, _?_, _?_, _?_

41. 1, 2, 3, 6, 7, 14, _?_, _?_, _?_   42. 2, 4, 6, 12, 14, _?_, _?_, _?_

Multiply Three-Digit Numbers

Each of the 8 families on Pine Road receives a newspaper delivery each day of the year. How many newspapers are delivered on Pine Road each year?

To find how many, multiply: 8 × 365
First, estimate using
front-end digits:

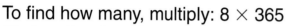

$$8 \times 365$$
$$8 \times 300 = 2400$$

Then multiply.

Multiply the ones. Regroup.

```
      4
    3 6 5
  ×     8
        0
```

8 × 5 ones = 40 ones
40 ones = 4 tens 0 ones

Multiply the tens. Add the regrouped tens. Regroup.

```
    5 4
    3 6 5
  ×     8
      2 0
```

8 × 6 tens = 48 tens
48 tens + 4 tens = 52 tens
52 tens = 5 hundreds 2 tens

Multiply the hundreds. Add the regrouped hundreds.

```
    5 4
    3 6 5
  ×     8
  2 9 2 0
```

8 × 3 hundreds = 24 hundreds
24 hundreds + 5 hundreds = 29 hundreds
29 hundreds = 2 thousands 9 hundreds

Each year, 2920 newspapers are delivered on Pine Road.

....Think....
2920 is close to 2400.
The answer is reasonable.

Use front-end digits to estimate. Then multiply.

1.
$$
\begin{array}{r}
\overset{1}{504} \\
\times\ \ 4 \\
\hline
2016
\end{array}
$$

2.
$$
\begin{array}{r}
101 \\
\times\ \ 3 \\
\hline
\end{array}
$$

3.
$$
\begin{array}{r}
210 \\
\times\ \ 4 \\
\hline
\end{array}
$$

4.
$$
\begin{array}{r}
323 \\
\times\ \ 2 \\
\hline
\end{array}
$$

5.
$$
\begin{array}{r}
223 \\
\times\ \ 3 \\
\hline
\end{array}
$$

6.
$$
\begin{array}{r}
308 \\
\times\ \ 5 \\
\hline
\end{array}
$$

7.
$$
\begin{array}{r}
410 \\
\times\ \ 8 \\
\hline
\end{array}
$$

8.
$$
\begin{array}{r}
271 \\
\times\ \ 7 \\
\hline
\end{array}
$$

9.
$$
\begin{array}{r}
505 \\
\times\ \ 9 \\
\hline
\end{array}
$$

10.
$$
\begin{array}{r}
192 \\
\times\ \ 4 \\
\hline
\end{array}
$$

11.
$$
\begin{array}{r}
634 \\
\times\ \ 6 \\
\hline
\end{array}
$$

12.
$$
\begin{array}{r}
279 \\
\times\ \ 9 \\
\hline
\end{array}
$$

13.
$$
\begin{array}{r}
844 \\
\times\ \ 7 \\
\hline
\end{array}
$$

14.
$$
\begin{array}{r}
575 \\
\times\ \ 8 \\
\hline
\end{array}
$$

15.
$$
\begin{array}{r}
397 \\
\times\ \ 5 \\
\hline
\end{array}
$$

Find the product. Use mental math or paper and pencil.

16. 2×304

17. 3×131

18. 2×642

19. 5×160

20. 6×702

21. 4×261

22. 8×625

23. 7×444

24. 9×368

25. Show how you could use the distributive property to find the product for exercise 16.

Problem Solving

26. The Ecology Club brought 6 bundles of junk mail to the recycling center. Each bundle weighed 275 pounds. How many pounds of junk mail did the Ecology Club recycle?

27. Troop 42 collected 8 bins of cardboard for recycling. Four of the bins held 325 pounds of cardboard each. The other 4 bins held 450 pounds of cardboard each. How many pounds of cardboard did Troop 42 collect?

28. Six of the families on Pine Road each recycled at least 8 aluminum cans each week last year. There are 52 weeks in a year. Altogether, did these families recycle more or less than 2000 aluminum cans last year? Explain.

Multiply Money

Cesar buys 8 notebooks for
the Detective Club. Each
notebook costs $3.39.
What is the total cost?

To find the total cost,
multiply: 8 × $3.39
First, estimate using
front-end digits:

$$\begin{array}{r} \$3.39 \\ \times \qquad 8 \\ \hline \text{about } \$24.00 \end{array}$$

Walkie-Talkies	$8.59 each
Periscopes	$4.58 each
Magnifying Glasses	$7.50 each
Decoder Rings	$ .99 each
Invisible Ink Markers	$1.56 each
Notebooks	$3.39 each

Then multiply.

To multiply money:

- Multiply the same way you multiply whole numbers.

- Write a decimal point in the
product two places from the right.

- Write the dollar sign.

The total cost is $27.12.

$$\begin{array}{r} \text{3 7} \\ \$3.3\,9 \\ \times \qquad 8 \\ \hline \$2\,7.1\,2 \end{array}$$

Think
$27.12 is close to $24.00.
The answer is reasonable.

Study these examples.

$$\begin{array}{r} 1 \\ \$.6\,4 \\ \times \qquad 3 \\ \hline \$1.9\,2 \end{array} \qquad \begin{array}{r} 2 \\ \$2.0\,7 \\ \times \qquad 4 \\ \hline \$8.2\,8 \end{array}$$

Practice

Use front-end digits to estimate. Then multiply.

1. $$\begin{array}{r} \$.46 \\ \times \quad 6 \\ \hline \end{array}$$
2. $$\begin{array}{r} \$.38 \\ \times \quad 8 \\ \hline \end{array}$$
3. $$\begin{array}{r} \$.52 \\ \times \quad 7 \\ \hline \end{array}$$
4. $$\begin{array}{r} \$.74 \\ \times \quad 9 \\ \hline \end{array}$$
5. $$\begin{array}{r} \$.25 \\ \times \quad 3 \\ \hline \end{array}$$

6. $$\begin{array}{r} \$1.05 \\ \times \quad 2 \\ \hline \end{array}$$
7. $$\begin{array}{r} \$5.73 \\ \times \quad 5 \\ \hline \end{array}$$
8. $$\begin{array}{r} \$6.26 \\ \times \quad 4 \\ \hline \end{array}$$
9. $$\begin{array}{r} \$8.30 \\ \times \quad 7 \\ \hline \end{array}$$
10. $$\begin{array}{r} \$4.52 \\ \times \quad 9 \\ \hline \end{array}$$

Use front-end digits to estimate. Then find the product.

11. $\begin{array}{r} \$.42 \\ \times\ \ \ \ 8 \\ \hline \end{array}$

12. $\begin{array}{r} \$.95 \\ \times\ \ \ \ 2 \\ \hline \end{array}$

13. $\begin{array}{r} \$.79 \\ \times\ \ \ \ 3 \\ \hline \end{array}$

14. $\begin{array}{r} \$.12 \\ \times\ \ \ \ 5 \\ \hline \end{array}$

15. $\begin{array}{r} \$8.31 \\ \times\ \ \ \ 4 \\ \hline \end{array}$

16. $\begin{array}{r} \$7.95 \\ \times\ \ \ \ 9 \\ \hline \end{array}$

17. $\begin{array}{r} \$4.36 \\ \times\ \ \ \ 2 \\ \hline \end{array}$

18. $\begin{array}{r} \$8.95 \\ \times\ \ \ \ 6 \\ \hline \end{array}$

19. $\begin{array}{r} \$7.50 \\ \times\ \ \ \ 8 \\ \hline \end{array}$

20. $\begin{array}{r} \$4.31 \\ \times\ \ \ \ 7 \\ \hline \end{array}$

21. $\begin{array}{r} \$6.08 \\ \times\ \ \ \ 5 \\ \hline \end{array}$

22. $\begin{array}{r} \$9.49 \\ \times\ \ \ \ 3 \\ \hline \end{array}$

23. $4 \times \$.53$

24. $6 \times \$.87$

25. $8 \times \$.19$

26. $7 \times \$4.03$

27. $9 \times \$1.71$

28. $3 \times \$7.47$

29. $2 \times \$9.76$

30. $5 \times \$5.98$

31. $4 \times \$6.61$

Problem Solving **Use the sign on page 140.**

32. How much more would 5 periscopes cost than 2 walkie-talkies?

33. How much would 2 periscopes and 3 pairs of walkie-talkies cost?

34. What is the cost of 4 walkie-talkies and 6 invisible ink markers?

DO YOU REMEMBER?

Complete the sentences.
Use the words in the box.

35. Any letter can be used as a _?_ .

36. The _?_ 14 + 7 is another way to write 21.

37. Addition is the _?_ of subtraction.

> difference
> expression
> variable
> inverse operation

Multiply Four-Digit Numbers

Mr. Carter built houses on 6 neighboring plots of land. Each plot is 6,875 square feet. On how many square feet of land did he build the houses?

To find how many square feet, multiply: 6 × 6875

First, estimate using front-end digits:

$$\begin{array}{r} 6875 \\ \times\ \ \ \ \ 6 \\ \hline \text{about } 36{,}000 \end{array}$$

.Think.........................
6875 > 6000, so the answer is greater than 36,000.

Then multiply.

$$\begin{array}{r} {\scriptstyle 5\ \ 4\ \ 3} \\ 6\ 8\ 7\ 5 \\ \times\ \ \ \ \ \ \ \ 6 \\ \hline 4\ 1{,}2\ 5\ 0 \end{array}$$

.Think.........................
41,250 is greater than 36,000. The answer is reasonable.

Mr. Carter built the houses on 41,250 square feet of land.

Study these examples.

$$\begin{array}{r} {\scriptstyle 1\ \ \ \ \ 2} \\ 1\ 4\ 0\ 6 \\ \times\ \ \ \ \ \ \ \ 4 \\ \hline 5\ 6\ 2\ 4 \end{array} \qquad \begin{array}{r} {\scriptstyle 3\ \ \ 1} \\ \$2\ 5.2\ 0 \\ \times\ \ \ \ \ \ \ \ 7 \\ \hline \$1\ 7\ 6.4\ 0 \end{array}$$

Use front-end digits to estimate. Then multiply.
Use mental math when you can.

1. $\begin{array}{r} 2221 \\ \times\ \ \ 3 \\ \hline \end{array}$
2. $\begin{array}{r} 1022 \\ \times\ \ \ 4 \\ \hline \end{array}$
3. $\begin{array}{r} 2432 \\ \times\ \ \ 2 \\ \hline \end{array}$
4. $\begin{array}{r} 3123 \\ \times\ \ \ 3 \\ \hline \end{array}$

5. $\begin{array}{r} 1035 \\ \times\ \ \ 7 \\ \hline \end{array}$
6. $\begin{array}{r} 2164 \\ \times\ \ \ 4 \\ \hline \end{array}$
7. $\begin{array}{r} 1146 \\ \times\ \ \ 6 \\ \hline \end{array}$
8. $\begin{array}{r} 3257 \\ \times\ \ \ 3 \\ \hline \end{array}$

Use front-end digits to estimate. Then find the product.

9.	1415 × 9	10.	6423 × 7	11.	7536 × 5	12.	3341 × 8

13.	4372 × 6	14.	5279 × 4	15.	2523 × 9	16.	8119 × 9

17.	$34.68 × 7	18.	$94.12 × 5	19.	$21.77 × 6	20.	$74.41 × 3

21. 2 × 9455 **22.** 5 × 3408 **23.** 4 × 6472

24. 6 × $36.75 **25.** 8 × $42.56 **26.** 7 × $22.95

Problem Solving

27. Each ranch house in Shady Acres has 1256 square feet of floor space. How many square feet of flooring were used for the 8 ranch houses in Shady Acres?

28. There are 4 miles of roads through Shady Acres. One mile is equal to 5280 feet. How many feet long are all the roads through Shady Acres?

29. In Shady Acres, 2841 houses have 5 people living in them. How many people live in those houses altogether?

Write About It

Predict which product is greater. Multiply to check.

30. 7 × 6321 or 6 × 7321 **31.** 5 × 3451 or 3 × 5451

32. 8 × 9310 or 9 × 8310 **33.** 4 × 9999 or 9 × 4999

34. In your Math Journal, write how you made your predictions.

Patterns in Multiplication

▶ Look for patterns to help you multiply by 10.

$1 \times 35 = 35$	$1 \times 50 = 50$	$1 \times 457 = 457$
$10 \times 35 = 350$	$10 \times 50 = 500$	$10 \times 457 = 4570$
$10 \times 350 = 3500$	$10 \times 500 = 5000$	

▶ Look for patterns or basic facts to help you multiply by tens.

$8 \times 40 = 320$	$9 \times 31 = 279$
$80 \times 40 = 3200$	$90 \times 31 = 2790$
$80 \times 400 = 32,000$	$90 \times 310 = 27,900$

To multiply a number by 10 or by tens:

Hint
The number of zeros in the product should be the same as the number of zeros in **both** the factors.

- Multiply the nonzero digits.
- Count the number of zeros in the factors.
  Then write the same number of zeros in the product.

```
    35                  500  ⌉              457
 ×  10 —1 zero       ×   10 ⌋ 3 zeros    ×   10
  350 —1 zero          5000 ⌉ 3 zeros       4570
```

```
   40 ⌉                 400              31              310
 × 80 ⌋ 2 zeros       ×  80          ×  90          ×   90
 3200 ⌉ 2 zeros       32,000           2790           27,900
```

Multiply mentally.

1. 18 ×10	**2.** 24 ×10	**3.** 57 ×10	**4.** 61 ×10	**5.** 50 ×10

6. 345 ×10	**7.** 638 ×10	**8.** 999 ×10	**9.** 450 ×10	**10.** 690 ×10

Practice

Find the product.

11.	23 $\times 20$	12.	42 $\times 60$	13.	61 $\times 30$	14.	70 $\times 40$	15.	60 $\times 50$
16.	230 $\times\ 20$	17.	420 $\times\ 60$	18.	610 $\times\ 30$	19.	700 $\times\ 40$	20.	600 $\times\ 50$
21.	52 $\times 80$	22.	25 $\times 90$	23.	19 $\times 70$	24.	80 $\times 80$	25.	40 $\times 90$
26.	520 $\times\ 80$	27.	250 $\times\ 90$	28.	190 $\times\ 70$	29.	800 $\times\ 80$	30.	400 $\times\ 90$

Look for a pattern to find each product.

31. 1×78
10×78
10×780

32. 9×60
90×60
90×600

33. 2×78
20×78
20×780

34. 7×60
70×60
70×600

35. 8×50
80×50
80×500

36. 6×35
60×35
60×350

Compute mentally. Explain how you found your answer.

37. How many zeros are in the product when you multiply 10×670?

38. How many zeros are in the product when you multiply 40×500?

MENTAL MATH — Algebra

Find the products mentally.

39. 1×56
10×56
100×56
100×560
100×5600

40. 7×41
70×41
700×41
700×410
700×4100

41. 3×63
30×63
300×63
300×630
300×6300

Products: Rounding to Estimate

A school bought 28 cans of paint for a special school project. The school bought the paint at a discounted price of $5.25 per can. About how much money did the school spend on paint?

To find about how much the school spent, estimate: 28 × $5.25

Rounding is one way to estimate products:

- Round each factor to its greatest place.
- Multiply.

$$\begin{array}{r} \$5.25 \longrightarrow \$5.00 \\ \times \quad 28 \longrightarrow \times \quad 30 \\ \hline \text{about } \$150.00 \end{array}$$

You can write $150.00 as $150.

The school spent about $150 on 28 cans of paint.

Study these examples.

$$\begin{array}{r} 43 \longrightarrow 40 \\ \times 62 \longrightarrow \times 60 \\ \hline \text{about } 2400 \end{array}$$

$$\begin{array}{r} 586 \longrightarrow 600 \\ \times \quad 55 \longrightarrow \times \quad 60 \\ \hline \text{about } 36{,}000 \end{array}$$

$$\begin{array}{r} \$.48 \longrightarrow \$.50 \\ \times \quad 32 \longrightarrow \times \quad 30 \\ \hline \text{about } \$15.00 \end{array}$$

Practice

Estimate each product by rounding.

1. 52
    × 75

2. 68
    × 41

3. 91
    × 22

4. 86
    × 57

5. 47
    × 33

6. 19
    × 62

7. 78
    × 53

8. 29
    × 58

9. 34
    × 92

10. 85
    × 38

11. $.17
    × 27

12. $.36
    × 81

13. $.42
    × 74

14. $.66
    × 65

15. $.26
    × 57

Estimate each product by rounding.

16. 348 × 23	**17.** 551 × 66	**18.** 619 × 72	**19.** 809 × 94	**20.** 748 × 88
21. 315 × 38	**22.** 754 × 24	**23.** 449 × 57	**24.** 938 × 46	**25.** 656 × 53
26. $4.59 × 34	**27.** $6.53 × 76	**28.** $7.24 × 83	**29.** $5.39 × 24	**30.** $8.57 × 79

31. 27 × 426 **32.** 14 × 643 **33.** 36 × 338

34. 27 × $2.04 **35.** 54 × $7.15 **36.** 68 × $7.46

Problem Solving

37. There were 24 gallons of blue paint in each of 17 cartons in the storeroom. About how many gallons of blue paint were in the storeroom?

38. Each sheet of maple wall paneling covers 48 square feet. Mr. Troc sold 22 sheets of the paneling. About how many square feet of paneling did he sell?

39. Each sheet of maple paneling sells for $152. Were the total sales of the 22 sheets of paneling between $2000 and $3000, between $3000 and $4000, or between $4000 and $5000?

DO YOU REMEMBER?

Align and add.

40. 94 + 360 **41.** 78 + 645 **42.** 65 + 940 **43.** 26 + 392

Multiply by Two-Digit Numbers

James baked 24 dozen crescent rolls. How many rolls did James bake?

.Think...............
: 1 dozen = 12 :
....

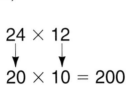

To find how many rolls,
multiply: 24 × 12
First, use rounding
to estimate:

$$24 \times 12$$
$$\downarrow \qquad \downarrow$$
$$20 \times 10 = 200$$

Then multiply.

▶ Here is one way to multiply 24 × 12.

12	.Think.............	12		12		12
×24	: 24 = 20 + 4 :	× 4		×20		×24
	....	48	+	240	=	288

▶ Here is another way to multiply 24 × 12.

Multiply by the ones.	Multiply by the tens.	Add the partial products.

$$\begin{array}{r} 12 \\ \times 24 \\ \hline 48 \end{array}$$

$$\begin{array}{r} 12 \\ \times 24 \\ \hline 48 \\ 240 \end{array}$$

$$\begin{array}{r} 12 \\ \times 24 \\ \hline 48 \\ + 240 \\ \hline 288 \end{array}$$

4 × 12

20 × 12

partial products

.Think ....
: 288 is close to 200.
: The answer is reasonable.
....

James baked 288 crescent rolls.

Use rounding to estimate. Then multiply.

1. 33
× 22

2. 23
× 11

3. 42
× 12

4. 24
× 21

5. 32
× 13

6. 12
× 44

7. 42
× 24

8. 32
× 32

9. 14
× 12

10. 22
× 21

Multiply Money

To multiply money by a 2-digit number:

- Multiply the same way you multiply whole numbers.

- Write a decimal point in the product two places from the right.

- Write the dollar sign in the product.

```
  $ .2 3          $8.00
×   1 3        ×     40
    6 9        $320.00
+ 2 3 0
$ 2 .9 9
```

Multiply.

11. $.52
×   10

12. $6.00
×   50

13. $.23
×   23

14. $.41
×   21

15. $.43
×   20

16. $4.00
×   30

17. $.11
×   85

18. $.12
×   14

19. 40 × $.21

20. 12 × $.43

21. 32 × $3.00

22. $1.00 × 39

23. $.69 × 40

24. $.16 × 17

Problem Solving

25. James makes 12 batches of crescent rolls. Each batch takes 11 minutes to bake. How much baking time in all will he need?

26. James baked crescent rolls for a bake sale. He charged fifty cents per roll and sold 68 rolls. How much money did he earn?

More Multiplying by Two-Digit Numbers

Kara packed 24 pieces of fruit into each of 58 fruit baskets. How many pieces of fruit did Kara pack into the baskets?

To find how many, multiply: 58 × 24

First, use rounding to estimate:

$$
\begin{array}{r}
24 \longrightarrow 20 \\
\times\,58 \longrightarrow \times\,60 \\
\hline
\text{about } 1200
\end{array}
$$

Then multiply.

Multiply by the ones.	Multiply by the tens.	Add the partial products.

$$
\begin{array}{r}
3 \\
2\;4 \\
\times\,5\;8 \\
\hline
1\;9\;2
\end{array}
$$

8 × 24

$$
\begin{array}{r}
2 \\
\cancel{3} \\
2\;4 \\
\times\,5\;8 \\
\hline
1\;9\;2 \\
1\;2\;0\;0
\end{array}
$$

50 × 24

$$
\begin{array}{r}
2 \\
\cancel{3} \\
2\;4 \\
\times\,5\;8 \\
\hline
1\;9\;2 \\
+\,1\;2\;0\;0 \\
\hline
1\;3\;9\;2
\end{array}
$$

.Think.
1392 is close to 1200. The answer is reasonable.

Kara packed 1392 pieces of fruit.

Study these examples.

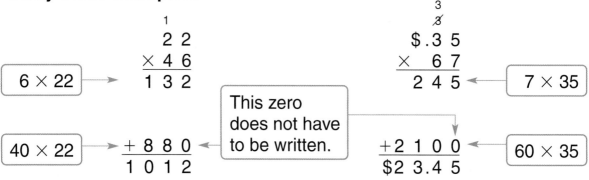

6 × 22

$$
\begin{array}{r}
1 \\
2\;2 \\
\times\,4\;6 \\
\hline
1\;3\;2
\end{array}
$$

40 × 22

$$
\begin{array}{r}
+\,8\;8\;0 \\
\hline
1\;0\;1\;2
\end{array}
$$

This zero does not have to be written.

$$
\begin{array}{r}
3 \\
\cancel{3} \\
\$.3\;5 \\
\times\,6\;7 \\
\hline
2\;4\;5
\end{array}
$$

7 × 35

$$
\begin{array}{r}
+\,2\;1\;0\;0 \\
\hline
\$2\;3.4\;5
\end{array}
$$

60 × 35

Use rounding to estimate. Then multiply.

1. $\begin{array}{r} 21 \\ \times 46 \\ \hline \end{array}$ 2. $\begin{array}{r} 36 \\ \times 18 \\ \hline \end{array}$ 3. $\begin{array}{r} 42 \\ \times 62 \\ \hline \end{array}$ 4. $\begin{array}{r} 57 \\ \times 19 \\ \hline \end{array}$ 5. $\begin{array}{r} 73 \\ \times 31 \\ \hline \end{array}$

6. $\begin{array}{r} 64 \\ \times 39 \\ \hline \end{array}$ 7. $\begin{array}{r} 83 \\ \times 44 \\ \hline \end{array}$ 8. $\begin{array}{r} 56 \\ \times 92 \\ \hline \end{array}$ 9. $\begin{array}{r} 29 \\ \times 75 \\ \hline \end{array}$ 10. $\begin{array}{r} 48 \\ \times 99 \\ \hline \end{array}$

11. $\begin{array}{r} \$.49 \\ \times \quad 32 \\ \hline \end{array}$ 12. $\begin{array}{r} \$.67 \\ \times \quad 58 \\ \hline \end{array}$ 13. $\begin{array}{r} \$.99 \\ \times \quad 64 \\ \hline \end{array}$ 14. $\begin{array}{r} \$.53 \\ \times \quad 28 \\ \hline \end{array}$ 15. $\begin{array}{r} \$.35 \\ \times \quad 76 \\ \hline \end{array}$

16. 95×76 17. 39×55 18. 47×63 19. 25×92

20. 16×52 21. 28×82 22. 34×93 23. 71×37

24. $15 \times \$.94$ 25. $34 \times \$.92$ 26. $85 \times \$.55$ 27. $26 \times \$.78$

Find each product. Describe any pattern you see.

28. $\begin{array}{r} 12 \\ \times 6 \\ \hline \end{array}$ $\begin{array}{r} 12 \\ \times 7 \\ \hline \end{array}$ $\begin{array}{r} 12 \\ \times 8 \\ \hline \end{array}$ $\begin{array}{r} 12 \\ \times 9 \\ \hline \end{array}$ $\begin{array}{r} 12 \\ \times 10 \\ \hline \end{array}$ $\begin{array}{r} 12 \\ \times 11 \\ \hline \end{array}$ $\begin{array}{r} 12 \\ \times 12 \\ \hline \end{array}$

Problem Solving

29. Tyrone put together 62 boxes of canned food. There were 45 cans in each box. How many cans of food were there?

30. Mill Farms donated 85 turkeys to soup kitchens. Each turkey weighed 25 pounds. How many pounds of turkey were donated?

Write About It

31. How does knowing how to multiply by tens help you multiply a 2-digit number by another 2-digit number? Write your answer in your Math Journal.

Multiply with Three-Digit Numbers

Letisha, Marc, Robin, and Tim all made beaded wall hangings. How many beads did Robin use?

	Rows	Beads in Each Row
Tim	35	528
Marc	44	286
Letisha	56	374
Robin	64	225

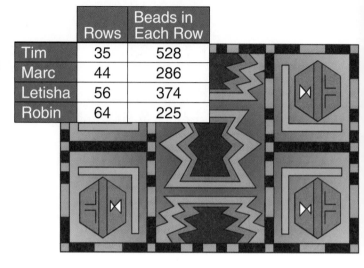

To find how many, multiply: 64 × 225

First, use rounding to estimate: 64 × 225

$$225 \longrightarrow 200$$
$$\underline{\times\ \ 64} \longrightarrow \underline{\times\ \ 60}$$
$$\text{about } 12,000$$

Then multiply.

Multiply by the ones.	Multiply by the tens.	Add the partial products.

$$\begin{array}{r} {\scriptstyle 1\ \ 2} \\ 2\ 2\ 5 \\ \times\ \ \ 6\ 4 \\ \hline 9\ 0\ 0 \end{array}$$

4 × 225

$$\begin{array}{r} {\scriptstyle 1\ \ 3} \\ {\scriptstyle \not{1}\ \ \not{2}} \\ 2\ 2\ 5 \\ \times\ \ \ 6\ 4 \\ \hline 9\ 0\ 0 \\ 1\ 3\ 5\ 0\ 0 \end{array}$$

60 × 225

$$\begin{array}{r} {\scriptstyle 1\ \ 3} \\ {\scriptstyle \not{1}\ \ \not{2}} \\ 2\ 2\ 5 \\ \times\ \ \ 6\ 4 \\ \hline 9\ 0\ 0 \\ +1\ 3\ 5\ 0\ 0 \\ \hline 1\ 4,4\ 0\ 0 \end{array}$$

Think
14,400 is close to 12,000. The answer is reasonable.

Robin used 14,400 beads.

Study these examples.

$$\begin{array}{r} {\scriptstyle 6} \\ {\scriptstyle \not{4}} \\ 3\ 0\ 9 \\ \times\ \ \ 7\ 5 \\ \hline 1\ 5\ 4\ 5 \\ +2\ 1\ 6\ 3\ 0 \\ \hline 2\ 3,1\ 7\ 5 \end{array}$$

$$\begin{array}{r} 1\ 3\ 2 \\ \times\ \ \ 3\ 1 \\ \hline 1\ 3\ 2 \\ +3\ 9\ 6\ 0 \\ \hline 4\ 0\ 9\ 2 \end{array}$$

$$\begin{array}{r} {\scriptstyle 4} \\ {\scriptstyle \not{2}} \\ \$6.5\ 1 \\ \times\ \ \ \ \ 8\ 4 \\ \hline 2\ 6\ 0\ 4 \\ +5\ 2\ 0\ 8\ 0 \\ \hline \$5\ 4\ 6.8\ 4 \end{array}$$

Estimate mentally. Then find the product.

1. 201 × 44	2. 132 × 23	3. 312 × 11	4. 402 × 31	5. 611 × 43

6. 242 × 33 7. 404 × 32 8. 723 × 24 9. 312 × 42 10. 841 × 56

11. 492 × 67 12. 387 × 75 13. 525 × 98 14. 906 × 86 15. 759 × 52

16. $2.37 × 45 17. $4.99 × 68 18. $8.17 × 39 19. $6.30 × 53 20. $7.88 × 47

Multiply.

21. 84 × 634

22. 52 × 928

23. 79 × 837

24. 24 × $5.09

25. 59 × $3.25

26. 46 × $9.72

CRITICAL THINKING

When you do not need an exact answer, you may be able to estimate to solve a problem.

Use the table on page 152 to solve each problem. Estimate or find an exact answer. Then explain how you solved each.

27. How many beads did Tim use?

28. Did Letisha use more or fewer beads than Tim?

29. Did Marc and Robin use about the same number of beads?

30. Who used the most beads? How many beads did that person use?

4-15 Problem-Solving Strategy:
Work Backward

Karl bought some guppies in March.
He had four times as many guppies
by the end of May. He had 46 fish
by the end of June, which was
10 more than at the end of May. How
many guppies did he buy in March?

Read ▸ **Visualize the facts of the problem as you reread it.**

Facts: Karl bought fish in March.
4 times as many in May
10 more than that in June
46 fish in June

Question: How many fish did Karl buy in March?

Plan ▸ Work backward. Use the inverse operation.

- First, find the number of guppies at the end of May:
Subtract 10 from the number of guppies he had in June.

46 − 10 = number in May

- Then find the number of guppies he had in March:
Divide the number of guppies in May by 4.

number in May ÷ 4 = number in March

Solve ▸ 46 − 10 = 36   number in May
36 ÷ 4 = 9   number in March
Karl bought 9 guppies in March.

Check ▸ Start with 9. Use the inverse operation.
9 guppies in March
9 × 4 = 36 in May
36 + 10 = 46 in June   The answer checks.

Work backward to solve each problem.

1. The Torres family came home from the movies at 5:00 P.M. The trip to and from the movie theater was 15 minutes each way.
They spent 1 hour and 45 minutes at the theater. What time did they leave home?

Read ▶ Visualize the facts of the problem as you reread it.

> **Facts:** 5:00 P.M. arrived home
> 15 minutes travel time to the movies
> 15 minutes travel time from the movies
> 1 hour 45 minutes at the movie theater

> **Question:** What time did they leave home?

Plan ▶ Count back each time that was added.
5:00 − 15 minutes − 15 minutes − 1 hour 45 minutes
⎯⎯⎯⎯⎯⎯⎯*time to*⎯⎯⎯*time from*⎯⎯⎯*at the movie theater*

Solve ▶ **Check** ▶

2. Kari had $4.25 left after shopping. She spent $11.80 for party favors and $22.55 for a giant party pizza. How much money did Kari have when she began shopping?

3. Bev, Ruth, and Lisa are sisters. Bev is 8 years older than Ruth. Ruth is 5 years older than Lisa, who is 16 years old. How old is Bev?

4. Don bought two vases for $36 and a lamp for $78. He received $6 change. How much money did he give the cashier?

5. After lunch there were 2 pizzas left over. Grades 1, 2, and 3 each finished 6 pizzas. Grades 4 and 5 each finished 7 pizzas. If the teachers finished 2 pizzas, how many pizzas had been ordered?

Problem-Solving Applications: Mixed Review

Solve each problem and explain the method you used.

1. Oscar's Orchard has 28 McIntosh apple trees. A tree produces about 115 pounds of fruit each year. About how many pounds of apples do the trees produce each year?

2. The orchard has 17 rows of peach trees. There are 16 trees in each row. Does the orchard have more than 300 peach trees?

3. Sonal works for 5 hours every day during harvest. How many hours does she work in thirty days?

4. A fence around the orchard is 894 feet long. Every foot of fencing has three posts. How many posts are in the fence?

5. Customers can pick raspberries for $1.75 per quart. How much would one dozen quarts of berries cost?

6. The pick-your-own price at Oscar's Orchard is $3.25 per bushel of apples. Mr. Ennis picked 8 bushels. How much did he spend?

7. Mr. Ennis uses 3 pounds of apples to make 1 pint of apple butter. How many pounds of apples does he need to make 14 pints of apple butter?

8. Each pot of strawberry plants produces about 8 dozen berries. There are 58 pots of plants. About how many strawberries do 58 pots of plants produce?

Choose a strategy from the list or use another strategy you know to solve each problem.

Strategy File

Use These Strategies
Work Backward
Choose the Operation
Logical Reasoning
Guess and Test

9. Emily picked 34 apples. Half of the apples were Golden Delicious. How many were not Golden Delicious?

10. Mia, Nate, and Rob each picked either apples, pears, or grapes. Mia did not pick pears, and Rob did not pick grapes. Nate shared his apples. Which fruit did each person pick?

11. Tia gave 5 apples to Ms. Lu and half of what she had left to her grandmother. She used the remaining 6 apples in a pie. How many apples had she brought home?

12. Liam picked 124 apples and Cleo picked 152. The pick-your-own apples cost about 4 cents each. Did Cleo spend more than $5?

13. Chad stopped picking fruit at 2:30 P.M. He had picked pears for 1 hour and apples for 45 minutes. When did he start picking?

14. One apple has about 25 seeds. There are about 160 apples in a bushel. About how many seeds are in a bushel of apples?

Use the graph for problems 15 and 16.

15. How many more peach than plum trees were planted in Oscar's Orchard?

16. What kind of trees are double the number of pear trees?

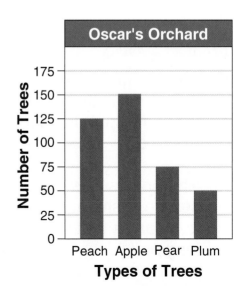

Find the product.   *(See pp. 128–133, 136–145, 148–153.)*

1. 2 × 34   **2.** 6 × 30   **3.** 5 × 68   **4.** 4 × 77

5. 3 × $34.23   **6.** 3 × 450   **7.** 9 × $5.37   **8.** 8 × 6124

9. 10 × 43   **10.** 50 × 30   **11.** 60 × 94   **12.** 10 × 364

13. 53
   × 55

14. 74
   × 38

15. 84
   × 46

16. 30
   × 27

17. 524
   ×   5

18. 608
   × 54

19. 735
   × 46

20. 450
   × 76

21. $6.30
   ×   26

22. $42.50
   ×   6

23. $9.40
   ×   17

24. $5.09
   ×   46

Choose a method to estimate the product.   *(See pp. 134–135, 146–147.)*

25. 8 × 35   **26.** 6 × 736   **27.** 5 × 612   **28.** 9 × $27.50

29. 61 × 54   **30.** 86 × 91   **31.** 32 × $.17   **32.** 16 × 307

Problem Solving   *(See pp. 126–127, 156–157.)*

33. The product is zero. One factor is 8. What is the other factor? What multiplication property does this use?

34. Jamal bicycles 18 kilometers each day. How far does he bicycle in 12 days?

35. Sharon has tiles that are 1 inch square. If she uses them to make a rectangle that is 14 inches long and 5 inches wide, how many tiles will she use?

36. If 9 × 13 = 117, what is the product of 13 × 9? What multiplication property does this use?

(See Still More Practice, p. 464.)

Clustering

Tommy kept a record of his family's daily mileage on a car trip to Mexico. About how many miles long was the trip?

Day	Miles
Sunday	432
Monday	396
Tuesday	394
Wednesday	402

When a number of addends "cluster" around a certain number, an estimate for the sum may be obtained by multiplying that number by the number of addends.

Estimate: 432 + 396 + 394 + 402

400 + 400 + 400 + 400

4 × 400 = 1600 ← estimate sum

The trip was about 1600 miles long.

Estimate the total by clustering.

1. 37 + 41 + 43 + 35

2. 85 + 98 + 87 + 88

3. 105 + 98 + 96

4. 510 + 483 + 503

5. 326 + 289 + 301 + 313

6. 740 + 675 + 690 + 727

7. 2943 + 3201 + 3065

8. 5624 + 4875 + 5133

Problem Solving

9. In Elmsford's schools, East has 489 students, Central has 535 students, and West has 492 students. About how many students are in Elmsford?

10. VideoLand rented out 199 movies on Friday, 248 movies on Saturday, and 218 movies on Sunday. About how many movies was this?

Chapter 4 Test

Find the product.

1. 3×21 **2.** 7×20 **3.** 4×59 **4.** 8×47

5. $6 \times \$10.31$ **6.** 5×360 **7.** $3 \times \$2.29$ **8.** 9×5473

9. 10×77 **10.** 90×80 **11.** 50×26 **12.** 10×133

Choose a method to estimate. Then multiply.

13.
$$\begin{array}{r} 16 \\ \times\, 39 \\ \hline \end{array}$$

14.
$$\begin{array}{r} 54 \\ \times\, 97 \\ \hline \end{array}$$

15.
$$\begin{array}{r} 43 \\ \times\, 21 \\ \hline \end{array}$$

16.
$$\begin{array}{r} 60 \\ \times\, 39 \\ \hline \end{array}$$

17.
$$\begin{array}{r} \$28.58 \\ \times\quad 4 \\ \hline \end{array}$$

18.
$$\begin{array}{r} 307 \\ \times\quad 85 \\ \hline \end{array}$$

19.
$$\begin{array}{r} 442 \\ \times\quad 36 \\ \hline \end{array}$$

20.
$$\begin{array}{r} 590 \\ \times\quad 73 \\ \hline \end{array}$$

21.
$$\begin{array}{r} 3127 \\ \times\quad 5 \\ \hline \end{array}$$

22.
$$\begin{array}{r} \$81.99 \\ \times\quad 2 \\ \hline \end{array}$$

23.
$$\begin{array}{r} 6215 \\ \times\quad 9 \\ \hline \end{array}$$

24.
$$\begin{array}{r} 4356 \\ \times\quad 4 \\ \hline \end{array}$$

25.
$$\begin{array}{r} \$5.50 \\ \times\quad 18 \\ \hline \end{array}$$

26.
$$\begin{array}{r} \$3.25 \\ \times\quad 37 \\ \hline \end{array}$$

27.
$$\begin{array}{r} \$1.52 \\ \times\quad 20 \\ \hline \end{array}$$

28.
$$\begin{array}{r} \$3.07 \\ \times\quad 45 \\ \hline \end{array}$$

Problem Solving

Use a strategy you have learned.

29. Nan had 7 jacks. Then she bought some packs with 6 jacks in each pack. Nan now has 55 jacks. How many packs did she buy?

Tell About It

Solve. Explain how you solved the problem and which multiplication property you used.

30. $4 \times (5 + 6)$

Performance Assessment

Use mental math to find each product. Then draw base ten blocks to check each answer.

31. 8×10 **32.** 3×50 **33.** 2×20

Test Preparation

Choose the best answer.

1. How many ten thousands equal one million?

   a. 10   b. 100
   c. 1000   d. 10,000

2. Which of these numbers is 1000 less than 47,561,389?

   a. 46,561,389
   b. 47,560,389
   c. 47,551,389
   d. 47,561,289

3. Choose the related fact to find the value of the variable.

   $m - 3 = 9$

   a. $12 - 3 = 9$
   b. $9 + 3 = 12$
   c. $12 - 9 = 3$
   d. $m = 12$

4. Subtract.

   $$\begin{array}{r} 23,275,401 \\ - 631,996 \\ \hline \end{array}$$

   a. 24,907,397
   b. 23,643,405
   c. 22,643,405
   d. 22,644,405

5. Which expression matches the problem?

   Paul shoots some baskets. Then he shoots 4 more.

   a. $b + 4$
   b. $b - 4$
   c. $b = 4$
   d. 4

6. Which shows compensation?

   $39 + 42$

   a. $42 + 39$
   b. $(30 + 9) + (40 + 2)$
   c. $40 + 41$
   d. none of these

7. The product is 12. One factor is 1. What is the other factor?

   a. 0   b. 1
   c. 6   d. 12

8. Estimate the difference using front-end estimation.

   $$\begin{array}{r} 8191 \\ - 3766 \\ \hline \end{array}$$

   a. about 8000
   b. about 5000
   c. about 4000
   d. about 11,000

9. Estimate the difference by rounding.

   $$\begin{array}{r} 279,430 \\ - 63,871 \\ \hline \end{array}$$

   a. 340,000
   b. 140,000
   c. 220,000
   d. 210,000

10. Estimate the product by rounding.

    $$\begin{array}{r} \$5.72 \\ \times 24 \\ \hline \end{array}$$

    a. $100.00
    b. $114.00
    c. $120.00
    d. $150.00

11. Add.

    $$\begin{array}{r} \$83,217.41 \\ + 15,328.18 \\ \hline \end{array}$$

    a. $98,545.59
    b. $90,000.00
    c. $98,535.59
    d. $15,328.18

12. Choose the addition property.

    $3 + (6 + 2) + 9 = (3 + 6) + (2 + 9)$

    a. Commutative Property
    b. Identity Property
    c. Associative Property
    d. Zero Property

13. Multiply.

34×6

a. 180
b. 184
c. 204
d. 224

14. Find the product.

$9 \times \$5.09$

a. $5.81
b. $45.09
c. $45.81
d. $46.81

15. Solve the expression when $n = 17$.

$23 - n$

a. 40
b. 6
c. 17
d. 23

16. Which shows the best way to check the answer?

$\$9.57$
$- \ 7.83$

a. $1.74 + $9.57 = $11.31
b. $9.57 + $1.74 = $7.83
c. $11.31 - $7.83 = $9.57
d. $1.74 + $7.83 = $9.57

17. Kim walks 3 miles per hour. By 1:45 P.M. she had walked 9 miles. What time did she start?

a. 10:45 A.M.
b. 11:45 A.M.
c. 12:45 P.M.
d. 1:45 A.M.

18. Emily has 13 packets of seeds. She gives 8 packets to Lisa. How many packets does Emily have now?

a. $8 + 5 = 13$
b. $13 - 8 = 5$
c. $13 + 8 = 21$
d. $13 - 5 = 8$

19. Add.

64,038
21,988
+ 7,945

a. 93,971
b. 92,971
c. 93,871
d. 93,961

20. Find the product.

$43 \times \$9.00$

a. $9.00
b. $27.00
c. $36.00
d. not given

21. Which is more than 40,000 but less than 47,000?

a. $48,000 - 800$
b. $50,650 - 1250$
c. $37,998 + 9001$
d. $30,022 + 765 + 16,525$

22. Dan's Deli sold 134 tuna subs, 246 turkey subs, and 371 ham subs. How many subs did the deli sell?

a. 134
b. 371
c. 600
d. 751

Tell About It

How do multiplication patterns help you solve the problem? Explain. Show all your work.

23. Mr. Kraus received one order for 33 packages of cups. There are 20 cups in each package. He received a second order for 330 packages, and a third order for 3300 packages. How many cups were ordered altogether?

$28 \div 6$

Divide by One Digit

$6 \div 2$

A Remainder of One

The story of Joe might just well explain what happens to numbers when they must remain after division, and they're left behind as lonesome remainders. It seems so unkind!

From *A Remainder of One*
by Elinor J. Pinczes.

$12 \div 9$

In this chapter you will:

Study the meanings and rules
  of division
Investigate patterns, missing
  numbers, and divisibility
Estimate and divide whole
  numbers and money
Explore zeros in division
Learn about the order of
  operations and averages
Solve problems by interpreting
  the remainder

**Critical Thinking/
Finding Together**

Use counters to find the quotient
and the remainder, the number
left over, for each division on
the page.

5-1

Division Rules

▶ You divide when you want to:

- **separate** a set into equal parts.

  Cal has 12 pears. He puts 4 pears into each bag. How many bags does he use?

  $$12 \div 4 = 3$$

  dividend ÷ divisor = quotient

  Cal uses 3 bags.

- **share** a set equally.

  Jo, Meg, and Cara share 12 pears equally. How many pears does each girl get?

  divisor → 3)12 ← dividend

  quotient → 4

  Each girl gets 4 pears.

▶ Here are some rules that can help you to divide correctly.

- When the divisor is one, the quotient is the same as the dividend.

  $$\frac{8}{1)8} \qquad 8 \div 1 = 8$$

- When the divisor and the dividend are the same number, the quotient is always one.

  $$\frac{1}{5)5} \qquad 5 \div 5 = 1$$

- When the dividend is zero, the quotient is zero.

  $$\frac{0}{6)0} \qquad 0 \div 6 = 0$$

- The divisor can never be zero.

  $9 \div 0$ is impossible.

Divide.

1. 6)6
2. 5)0
3. 1)7
4. 3)3
5. 2)0
6. 9)9

7. 4)0
8. 1)5
9. 1)0
10. 4)4
11. 1)2
12. 1)6

Practice

Find the quotient.

13. $2 \div 2$ **14.** $9 \div 1$ **15.** $0 \div 7$ **16.** $8 \div 8$ **17.** $3 \div 1$

18. $0 \div 8$ **19.** $7 \div 7$ **20.** $4 \div 1$ **21.** $0 \div 9$ **22.** $1 \div 1$

23. $5 \div 5$ **24.** $8 \div 1$ **25.** $0 \div 3$ **26.** $0 \div 6$ **27.** $9 \div 9$

Practice

Problem Solving

28. The dividend is 7.
The quotient is 1.
What is the divisor?

29. The divisor is 4.
The quotient is 1.
What is the dividend?

30. The divisor is 5.
The quotient is 5.
What is the dividend?

31. The quotient is 2.
The dividend is 2.
What is the divisor?

32. The dividend is 1.
The quotient is 1.
What is the divisor?

33. The quotient is 0.
What is the dividend?

34. How should 4 friends share 24 apples equally?

35. How should Dale and 4 friends share 15 oranges equally?

36. Sara bakes 8 pies with 64 plums. Emily bakes 5 pies with 45 plums. How many more plums per pie are in Emily's pie than Sara's?

37. Ty packs 8 baskets with 5 peaches to a basket. Jill packs 9 baskets with 3 peaches per basket. How many peaches do Ty and Jill pack together?

MENTAL MATH

Use the rules of division to divide mentally.

38. $0 \div 15$ **39.** $26 \div 26$ **40.** $49 \div 1$ **41.** $0 \div 99$ **42.** $75 \div 1$

43. $429 \div 429$ **44.** $867 \div 1$ **45.** $0 \div 539$ **46.** $938 \div 938$

Update your skills. See page 12.

Relate Multiplication and Division

Division and multiplication are inverse operations.
Division "undoes" multiplication and
multiplication "undoes" division.

Find the related multiplication fact for $36 \div 9 = 4$.

▶ To find the related multiplication fact,
first think about what each number
in the division fact represents.

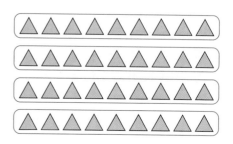

$$36 \quad \div \quad 9 \quad = \quad 4$$

| number in all | number in each group | number of groups |

Then think about the meaning of multiplication.

| number of groups | number in each group | number in all |

$$4 \quad \times \quad 9 \quad = \quad 36$$

.Think...........................
Multiplying 9 "undoes"
dividing by 9.

So, $4 \times 9 = 36$ is the related multiplication fact for $36 \div 9 = 4$.

Study this example.

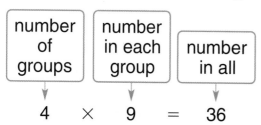

$$6 \quad \times \quad 7 \quad = \quad 42$$

| groups | in each | in all |

$$42 \quad \div \quad 7 \quad = \quad 6 \qquad \text{or}$$

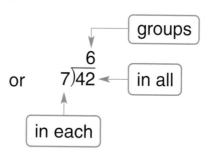

groups

$$6$$
$$7\overline{)42}$$ ← in all

in each

So, $42 \div 7 = 6$ is the related
division fact for $6 \times 7 = 42$.

.Think...........................
Dividing by 7
"undoes"
multiplying 7.

Write a related multiplication fact for each.

1. $27 \div 3 = 9$ **2.** $35 \div 5 = 7$ **3.** $56 \div 7 = 8$ **4.** $24 \div 4 = 6$

5. $18 \div 9 = 2$ **6.** $63 \div 7 = 9$ **7.** $36 \div 6 = 6$ **8.** $14 \div 2 = 7$

9. $1\overline{)9}^{\,9}$ **10.** $9\overline{)36}^{\,4}$ **11.** $6\overline{)48}^{\,8}$ **12.** $8\overline{)40}^{\,5}$

Write a related division fact for each.

13. $8 \times 1 = 8$ **14.** $6 \times 3 = 18$ **15.** $9 \times 5 = 45$ **16.** $8 \times 4 = 32$

17. $9 \times 8 = 72$ **18.** $5 \times 6 = 30$ **19.** $8 \times 2 = 16$ **20.** $6 \times 9 = 54$

21.
$$\begin{array}{r} 8 \\ \times\,3 \\ \hline 24 \end{array}$$

22.
$$\begin{array}{r} 6 \\ \times\,9 \\ \hline 54 \end{array}$$

23.
$$\begin{array}{r} 5 \\ \times\,5 \\ \hline 25 \end{array}$$

24.
$$\begin{array}{r} 7 \\ \times\,4 \\ \hline 28 \end{array}$$

Write four related facts using the given numbers.
Think about fact families.

25. 9, 2, 18
$9 \times 2 = 18$
$2 \times 9 = 18$
$18 \div 2 = 9$
$18 \div 9 = 2$

26. 3, 9, 27

27. 6, 8, 48

28. 7, 6, 42

29. 8, 7, 56

30. 9, 8, 72

31. 3, 7, 21

32. 4, 9, 36

33. 5, 7, 35

34. 9, 7, 63

 Solve the problem. Check using a related fact.

35. A classroom has 9 bulletin boards. Fifty-four thumbtacks are divided equally among the boards. Does each board have more or fewer than 5 tacks?

36. Explain how knowing one fact from a fact family, or set of related facts, helps you know the other facts in that fact family.

Update your skills. See pages 7–8 and 10–12.

Missing Numbers

Jill has 63 nuts. She wants to make 7 equal snack bags for her hiking club. How many nuts will Jill put in each bag?

To find how many nuts, n, divide: $63 \div 7 = n$

> Remember: Division and multiplication are inverse operations, so you can use a related multiplication fact to solve for n.

The related multiplication fact for $63 \div 7 = n$ is $7 \times n = 63$.

$7 \times n = 63$
$n = 9$
So, $63 \div 7 = 9$.

Think
$7 \times n = 63$
$7 \times 9 = 63$

Jill will put 9 nuts in each bag.

Study these examples.

$48 \div n = 8$
$n = 6$
So, $48 \div 6 = 8$.

Think
$n \times 8 = 48$
$6 \times 8 = 48$

$6 \times n = 42$
$n = 7$
So, $6 \times 7 = 42$.

Think
$42 \div 6 = n$
$42 \div 6 = 7$

$n\overline{)36}$ So, $4\overline{)36}$ (both with 9 above)

Think
$n \times 9 = 36$
$4 \times 9 = 36$

$7 \times n = 21$
$n = 3$
So, $7 \times 3 = 21$.

Think
$21 \div 7 = n$
$21 \div 7 = 3$

Find the missing divisor.

1. $6 = 12 \div n$

2. $30 \div a = 5$

3. $8 = 32 \div b$

4. $54 \div c = 6$

5. $49 \div x = 7$

6. $56 \div y = 7$

7. $15 \div z = 3$

8. $2 = 14 \div s$

9. $9 \div t = 1$

Find the value of the variable.

10. $n \times 3 = 6$

11. $15 = a \times 5$

12. $y \times 6 = 36$

13. $56 = a \times 7$

14. $b \times 8 = 72$

15. $c \times 2 = 2$

16. $28 = s \times 4$

17. $t \times 6 = 42$

18. $20 = p \times 4$

19. $9 = 72 \div d$

20. $64 \div r = 8$

21. $v \div 3 = 4$

22. $y \times 6 = 0$

23. $54 = 9 \times p$

24. $a \times 8 = 40$

25. $9\overline{)h}^{\,5}$

26. $2\overline{)m}^{\,0}$

27. $4\overline{)b}^{\,4}$

28. $7\overline{)x}^{\,3}$

29. $9\overline{)c}^{\,2}$

30. $9\overline{)d}^{\,3}$

31. $3\overline{)f}^{\,1}$

32. $6\overline{)x}^{\,8}$

Problem Solving

33. Amy's garden has 9 rows for planting seeds. She has 81 seeds to plant. How many seeds will she plant in each row so each row has the same number of plants?

34. Amy's garden has 8 rows of tomato plants. There is one tomato growing on each plant. There are 72 tomatoes altogether. How many tomato plants are in each row?

DO YOU REMEMBER?

Match each definition with its multiplication property.

35. Changing the grouping of the factors does not change the product.

36. The product of a number and the sum of two addends is the same as multiplying the number by each addend and adding the products.

37. Changing the order of the factors does not change the product.

commutative property

associative property

identity property

zero property

distributive property

Number Patterns

▶ What is the next number in this pattern?

Input	16	8	4	2
Output	8	4	2	?

- First find the rule.

Think: 16, 8, 4, 2
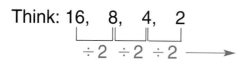
$\div 2 \div 2 \div 2$ ⟶

Rule: Start at 16.
Divide by 2.

- Then complete the pattern.

Input	16	8	4	2
Output	8	4	2	1

Think..........
$2 \div 2 = 1$

The next number in the pattern is 1.

▶ Some patterns result from two different operations and cannot be represented in an input-output table.

What is the next number in the pattern?

2, 7, 6, 11, 10, ?

Think: 2, 7, 6, 11, 10, ?
$+5 \; -1 \; +5 \; -1$ ⟶

Rule: Start at 2. Add 5. Subtract 1.

The next number is 15.

Think ....
$10 + 5 = 15$

Write the rule for each pattern. Then write the next number.

1.

Input	10	12	14	16
Output	12	14	16	?

2.

Input	30	40	50	60
Output	40	50	60	?

Practice

Write the rule. Complete the pattern.

3.

Input	27	18	9	3
Output	9	6	3	?

4.

Input	35	33	31	29
Output	33	31	29	?

5. 42, 38, 34, _?_

6. 4, 8, 16, 32, _?_

7. 16, 20, 18, 22, 20, _?_

8. 54, 51, 52, 49, 50, _?_

9. 4, 12, 10, 30, 28, _?_

10. 5, 10, 13, 26, 29, _?_

11. 1, 4, 4, 7, 7, 10, _?_

12. 10, 12, 6, 8, 4, 6, _?_

Write a pattern of eight numbers for each rule.

13. Rule: Add 6.

14. Rule: Subtract 3.

15. Rule: Multiply by 2.

16. Rule: Add 50.

17. Rule: Add 3. Add 1.

18. Rule: Add 10. Subtract 1.

Problem Solving

19. Mary and Ed play a number game. Mary says several numbers and Ed applies a rule to them. Mary says, "5, 6, 7, 8." Ed says, "15, 18, 21, 24." What is Ed's rule?

20. For every nickel Pat saves her father will give her a quarter. How much will Pat have if she saves 4 nickels?

CHALLENGE

Is the sum or product odd or even? Write _O_ or _E_.

21. Even + Even

22. Even × Even

23. Odd + Odd

24. Odd × Odd

25. Even + Odd

26. Odd × Even

27. In your Math Journal, write two or three examples for each of exercises 21–26 to prove your answers.

Estimate in Division

You can estimate quotients before you divide.

Estimate: 2832 ÷ 8.

- Find where the quotient begins.

    Try dividing thousands.

    8)2832   8 > 2   **Not enough thousands**

    Try dividing hundreds.

    8)2832   8 < 28   **Enough hundreds**

    So the quotient begins in the hundreds place.

    $$\overset{\text{X}}{8)2832}$$

- Find the first digit of the quotient.
  Think of a basic multiplication fact with 8 and a number whose product is close to 28, but not greater than 28.

    hundreds place

    2 × 8 = 16   too small
    3 × 8 = 24 ←
    4 × 8 = 32   too large
    Write 3 in the hundreds place.

    28 is between 16 and 32. Try 3.

    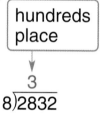

    $$\overset{3}{8)2832}$$

- Since you are estimating, write zeros for the other digits.

    $$\overset{\text{about } 300}{8)2832}$$

Study these examples.

$$\overset{\text{about } 200}{2)523} \qquad \overset{\text{about } 70}{6)425} \qquad \overset{\text{about \$ 6.00}}{5)\$32.75}$$

Write an X in the place where the quotient begins.

1. $\overset{\text{X}}{4)76}$
2. $6)48$
3. $2)451$
4. $7)927$
5. $8)745$

6. $3)127$
7. $5)370$
8. $2)1468$
9. $7)4303$

Estimate the quotient.

10. $9\overline{)95}$ **11.** $6\overline{)43}$ **12.** $2\overline{)87}$ **13.** $5\overline{)38}$ **14.** $4\overline{)92}$

15. $4\overline{)591}$ **16.** $7\overline{)862}$ **17.** $3\overline{)947}$ **18.** $2\overline{)815}$

19. $6\overline{)275}$ **20.** $9\overline{)467}$ **21.** $8\overline{)744}$ **22.** $5\overline{)342}$

23. $7\overline{)2439}$ **24.** $4\overline{)3622}$ **25.** $3\overline{)1729}$ **26.** $9\overline{)5649}$

27. $2\overline{)\$4.94}$ **28.** $3\overline{)\$6.42}$ **29.** $5\overline{)\$17.50}$ **30.** $4\overline{)\$28.58}$

Estimate with Compatible Numbers

Compatible numbers are numbers that are easy to compute mentally.

> Use division facts to find nearby numbers that are compatible.

Estimate: 53 ÷ 6   Estimate: 223 ÷ 7

Divide: 53 ÷ 6   Divide: 223 ÷ 7

Think: 54 ÷ 6 = 9   Think: 210 ÷ 7 = 30
So, 53 ÷ 6 is about 9.   So, 223 ÷ 7 is about 30.

Estimate the quotient. Use compatible numbers.
Write the compatible numbers you used to estimate the quotient.

31. 55 ÷ 8   **32.** 46 ÷ 6   **33.** 362 ÷ 5   **34.** 178 ÷ 3

35. $4\overline{)29}$ **36.** $5\overline{)33}$ **37.** $8\overline{)26}$ **38.** $3\overline{)11}$ **39.** $7\overline{)40}$

40. $3\overline{)61}$ **41.** $4\overline{)84}$ **42.** $2\overline{)63}$ **43.** $5\overline{)56}$ **44.** $3\overline{)91}$

45. $7\overline{)285}$ **46.** $5\overline{)161}$ **47.** $6\overline{)524}$ **48.** $9\overline{)472}$ **49.** $7\overline{)551}$

One Digit-Quotients

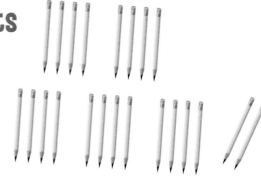

Jaime gave the same number of pencils to each of 5 friends. He had 22 pencils. How many pencils did each friend receive? How many pencils were left over?

To find how many each received, divide: 22 ÷ 5.

Estimate: Think of a basic multiplication fact with 5 and a number whose product is close to 22.

Think

$5\overline{)22}$ 5 > 2   **Not enough tens**

$5\overline{)22}$ 5 < 22   **Enough ones**

The quotient begins in the ones place.

$3 \times 5 = 15$ too small

$5 \times 5 = 25$ too large

22 is between 15 and 25. Try 4.

Divide.	Multiply.	Subtract and compare.	Write the remainder.

$$\begin{array}{r} 4 \\ 5\overline{)22} \end{array}$$

$$\begin{array}{r} \times\ 4 \\ 5\overline{)22} \\ 20 \end{array}$$

$$\begin{array}{r} 4 \\ 5\overline{)22} \\ -20 \\ \hline 2 \end{array}$$

2 < 5

$$\begin{array}{r} 4\ \text{R } 2 \\ 5\overline{)22} \\ -20 \\ \hline 2 \end{array}$$

remainder

Multiply and add to check.

$$\begin{array}{r} 4 \leftarrow \text{quotient} \\ \times\ 5 \leftarrow \text{divisor} \\ \hline 20 \\ +\ 2 \leftarrow \text{remainder} \\ \hline 22 \leftarrow \text{dividend} \end{array}$$

The remainder must always be less than the divisor.

Each friend received 4 pencils. There were 2 pencils left over.

Complete each division.

1. $\begin{array}{r} 6 \\ 4\overline{)24} \\ -24 \\ \hline 0 \end{array}$ ← There is no remainder.

2. $\begin{array}{r} 6 \text{ R } ? \\ 3\overline{)20} \\ -18 \\ \hline 2 \end{array}$

3. $\begin{array}{r} 9 \text{ R } ? \\ 5\overline{)48} \\ -45 \\ \hline ? \end{array}$

4. $\begin{array}{r} ? \text{ R } ? \\ 2\overline{)13} \\ -?? \\ \hline ? \end{array}$

Divide.

5. $2\overline{)15}$ 6. $4\overline{)35}$ 7. $3\overline{)23}$ 8. $5\overline{)17}$ 9. $6\overline{)27}$

10. $6\overline{)14}$ 11. $4\overline{)26}$ 12. $5\overline{)37}$ 13. $7\overline{)50}$ 14. $4\overline{)33}$

15. $6\overline{)55}$ 16. $5\overline{)38}$ 17. $8\overline{)68}$ 18. $2\overline{)19}$ 19. $7\overline{)45}$

20. $8\overline{)23}$ 21. $3\overline{)26}$ 22. $7\overline{)35}$ 23. $7\overline{)29}$ 24. $8\overline{)38}$

25. $9\overline{)64}$ 26. $8\overline{)52}$ 27. $6\overline{)45}$ 28. $9\overline{)71}$ 29. $9\overline{)82}$

Find the quotient and the remainder.

30. $25 \div 3$ 31. $23 \div 7$ 32. $84 \div 9$

33. $50 \div 8$ 34. $38 \div 4$ 35. $57 \div 6$

Problem Solving

36. Caryn put away 36 crayons in boxes. Each box holds 8 crayons. How many boxes could be filled? How many crayons would be left over?

37. Mika put 37 drawings in folders. She put 4 drawings in each folder. How many folders were there? How many extra drawings were there?

38. Bill placed the same number of pencils at each of 6 tables. He began with 44 pencils. At most, how many pencils could he have placed at each table? How many pencils would have been left over?

5-7 Divisibility

A number is divisible by another number when the remainder is zero when the number is divided by the other number.

The chart below shows the divisibility rules for 2, 5, 10, and 3.

Rule A number is divisible	Examples
by 2 if its ones digit is divisible by 2.	10, 32, 154, 3126, 45,398 are divisible by 2.
by 5 if its ones digit is 0 or 5.	40, 75, 820, 6515 are divisible by 5.
by 10 if its ones digit is 0.	30, 170, 4280, 79,360 are divisible by 10.
by 3 if the sum of its digits is divisible by 3.	24 → 2 + 4 = 6 and 6 ÷ 3 = 2. 369 → 3 + 6 + 9 = 18 and 18 ÷ 3 = 6. 24 and 369 are divisible by 3.

All even numbers are divisible by 2.

Practice

Is the number divisible by 2? Write *yes* or *no*.

1. 28 **2.** 75 **3.** 700 **4.** 144 **5.** 807

6. 516 **7.** 343 **8.** 2931 **9.** 1462 **10.** 7749

11. 6847 **12.** 2900 **13.** 75,192 **14.** 27,346 **15.** 92,983

Is the number divisible by 5? Write *yes* or *no*.

16. 64 **17.** 85 **18.** 900 **19.** 245 **20.** 819

21. 703 **22.** 456 **23.** 1820 **24.** 4795 **25.** 9240

26. 8675 **27.** 3299 **28.** 10,000 **29.** 42,685 **30.** 74,007

Is the number divisible by 10? Write *yes* or *no*.

31. 930   **32.** 749   **33.** 6820   **34.** 5000   **35.** 8304

36. 1006   **37.** 4673   **38.** 52,651   **39.** 66,830   **40.** 90,060

41. 230,705   **42.** 562,840   **43.** 1,425,070   **44.** 1,099,801

Is the number divisible by 3? Write *yes* or *no*.

45. 72   **46.** 54   **47.** 253   **48.** 534   **49.** 312

50. 932   **51.** 210   **52.** 842   **53.** 1065   **54.** 4906

55. 12,774   **56.** 20,621   **57.** 37,596   **58.** 64,374

59. Explain in your own words when a number is divisible by 10 and when it is divisible by 3. Write a 2-digit, a 3-digit, and a 4-digit number that support each rule.

Copy and complete the table.

60.

Divisible by	60	88	75	600	494	750	2313	1026	8750
2	yes	?	?	?	?	?	no	?	?
5	yes	?	yes	?	?	?	?	?	?
10	?	?	?	yes	?	?	?	?	?
3	yes	?	?	yes	?	?	?	?	?

CHALLENGE

A number is divisible **by 6** if it is divisible by both 2 and 3.
A number is divisible **by 9** if the sum of its digits is divisible by 9.

Copy and complete the table.

61.

Divisible by	891	1428	6570	9822	12,834	36,459
6	no	?	?	?	?	?
9	?	?	yes	?	?	?

Two-Digit Quotients

Ian cut a 72-inch length of cloth into 2 equal strips.
What was the length of each strip?

To find the length of each strip,
divide: $72 \div 2$.

Estimate: Think of a basic
multiplication fact with 2 and
a number whose product
is close to 7.

Think........
$2\overline{)72}$ $2 < 7$
Enough tens: begin the quotient
in the tens place.

$$3 \times 2 = 6$$
$$4 \times 2 = 8$$
7 is between 6 and 8. Try 3.

Divide the tens.	Multiply.	Subtract and compare.	Bring down the ones.
3 $2\overline{)72}$	$\times 3$ $2\overline{)72}$ 6	3 $2\overline{)72}$ -6 $\overline{1}$ $1 < 2$	3 $2\overline{)72}$ $-6\downarrow$ $\overline{12}$

Repeat the steps to divide the ones.

Estimate: Think of a basic multiplication fact with 2 and
a number whose product is 12.

$$6 \times 2 = 12$$ Try 6.

Divide the ones.	Multiply.	Subtract and compare.	Check.
36 $2\overline{)72}$ $-6\downarrow$ $\overline{12}$	$\times 36$ $2\overline{)72}$ $-6\downarrow$ $\overline{12}$ 12	36 $2\overline{)72}$ $-6\downarrow$ $\overline{12}$ -12 $\overline{0}$	36 $\times\ 2$ $\overline{72}$

Think........
$36 \times 2 = 2 \times 36$

No remainder

The length of each strip was 36 inches.

Complete each division.

$$\begin{array}{r} 1\ 0 \\ 4\overline{)4\ 0} \\ -4\ \downarrow \\ \hline 0\ 0 \\ -\ ? \\ \hline ? \end{array}$$

1.

$$\begin{array}{r} 2\ ? \\ 4\overline{)8\ 4} \\ -8\ \downarrow \\ \hline 0\ 4 \\ -\ \ ? \\ \hline ? \end{array}$$

2.

$$\begin{array}{r} 1\ ? \\ 6\overline{)7\ 8} \\ -?\ \downarrow \\ \hline ?\ ? \\ -?\ ? \\ \hline ? \end{array}$$

3.

$$\begin{array}{r} ?\ ? \\ 2\overline{)3\ 4} \\ -?\ \downarrow \\ \hline ?\ ? \\ -?\ ? \\ \hline ? \end{array}$$

4.

> Remember to use basic facts to help you estimate.

Estimate. Then divide.

5. $5\overline{)60}$ **6.** $6\overline{)84}$ **7.** $4\overline{)64}$ **8.** $7\overline{)91}$ **9.** $3\overline{)69}$

10. $8\overline{)96}$ **11.** $4\overline{)92}$ **12.** $6\overline{)96}$ **13.** $3\overline{)48}$ **14.** $9\overline{)99}$

Find the quotient.

15. $84 \div 3$ **16.** $80 \div 5$ **17.** $56 \div 4$

18. $45 \div 3$ **19.** $90 \div 2$ **20.** $88 \div 2$

CRITICAL THINKING

Read each division problem carefully. Decide whether to use paper and pencil or mental math to solve each problem. Then solve.

Explain which method you used to solve problems 21 and 22.

21. Reg made 80 pom-poms. He sewed 9 pom-poms on each costume. At most, how many costumes were there? How many pom-poms were left over?

22. Kate cut an 80-inch long ribbon into 4 equal parts. How many inches long was each part?

23. If you need to know the remainder, why is it easier to use paper and pencil?

More Two-Digit Quotients

Luz has 80 favors to divide equally into 6 party bags. At most, how many favors can she put in each bag? How many will be left over?

To find how many in each bag, divide: 80 ÷ 6.

Think

6)80   6 < 8   **Enough tens:** begin the quotient in the tens place.

Estimate: Think of a basic multiplication fact with 6 and a number whose product is close to 8.

$1 \times 6 = 6$ ← Try 1.
$2 \times 6 = 12$

Divide the tens.	Multiply.	Subtract and compare.	Bring down the ones.
$\frac{1}{6\overline{)8\ 0}}$	×1 6)8 0 6	1 6)8 0 −6 2 ← 2 < 6	1 6)8 0 −6 2 0

Repeat the steps.

Divide the ones.	Multiply.	Subtract and compare.	Check.
1 3 6)8 0 −6 2 0	× 1 3 6)8 0 −6 2 0 1 8	1 3 R 2 6)8 0 −6 2 0 −1 8 2 ← 2 < 6	1 3 × 6 7 8 + 2 8 0

At most, she could put 13 favors into each bag. There would be 2 favors left over.

Complete each division.

$$
\begin{array}{r}
1 0 \ \ R \ ? \\
\textbf{1. } 5\overline{)5\ 4} \\
-5 \downarrow \\
\hline
4 \\
-\ \ ? \\
\hline
? \\
\end{array}
\qquad
\begin{array}{r}
2\ ? \ \ R \ ? \\
\textbf{2. } 3\overline{)7\ 4} \\
-6 \downarrow \\
\hline
1\ 4 \\
-?\ ? \\
\hline
? \\
\end{array}
\qquad
\begin{array}{r}
1\ ? \ \ R \ ? \\
\textbf{3. } 8\overline{)9\ 8} \\
-\ ? \downarrow \\
\hline
?\ ? \\
-?\ ? \\
\hline
? \\
\end{array}
\qquad
\begin{array}{r}
?\ ? \ \ R\ 3 \\
\textbf{4. } 4\overline{)9\ 9} \\
-8 \downarrow \\
\hline
1\ ? \\
-?\ ? \\
\hline
3 \\
\end{array}
$$

Estimate. Then divide.

5. $4\overline{)49}$ **6.** $2\overline{)81}$ **7.** $5\overline{)92}$ **8.** $6\overline{)83}$ **9.** $3\overline{)92}$

10. $8\overline{)91}$ **11.** $7\overline{)87}$ **12.** $3\overline{)58}$ **13.** $4\overline{)89}$ **14.** $2\overline{)74}$

15. $3\overline{)37}$ **16.** $5\overline{)63}$ **17.** $7\overline{)94}$ **18.** $6\overline{)67}$ **19.** $8\overline{)89}$

20. $5\overline{)86}$ **21.** $2\overline{)93}$ **22.** $4\overline{)51}$ **23.** $2\overline{)47}$ **24.** $7\overline{)79}$

25. $6\overline{)97}$ **26.** $4\overline{)86}$ **27.** $6\overline{)99}$ **28.** $5\overline{)87}$ **29.** $9\overline{)98}$

30. $61 \div 2$ **31.** $47 \div 3$ **32.** $71 \div 4$ **33.** $76 \div 5$

34. $92 \div 9$ **35.** $84 \div 8$ **36.** $96 \div 7$ **37.** $85 \div 6$

Problem Solving

38. There were 65 balloons at Willy's party. He tied 6 balloons to each tree in his yard and the extra balloons to his mailbox. What is the greatest number of trees that could be in Willy's yard? How many balloons did he tie to his mailbox?

39. Val hid 96 eggs in the yard. Each of 7 children found the same number of eggs. What is the greatest number of eggs each child could have found? How many eggs would still have remained hidden?

Three-Digit Quotients

Divide: 745 ÷ 2.

Use the division steps to find three-digit quotients. Remember to use basic facts to help you do the estimate step.

Division Steps

- Estimate.
- Divide.
- Multiply.
- Subtract.
- Compare.
- Bring down.
- Repeat the steps as necessary.
- Check.

- Divide the hundreds.

  Estimate: $\underline{?} \times 2 = 7$
  $3 \times 2 = 6$
  $4 \times 2 = 8$
  Try 3.

  $$\begin{array}{r} 3 \\ 2\overline{)7\,4\,5} \\ -6\downarrow \\ \hline 1\,4 \end{array}$$

- Divide the tens.

  Estimate: $\underline{?} \times 2 = 14$
  $7 \times 2 = 14$
  Try 7.

  $$\begin{array}{r} 3\,7 \\ 2\overline{)7\,4\,5} \\ -6\downarrow \\ \hline 1\,4 \\ -1\,4\downarrow \\ \hline 0\,5 \end{array}$$

- Divide the ones.

  Estimate: $\underline{?} \times 2 = 5$
  $2 \times 2 = 4$
  $3 \times 2 = 6$
  Try 2.

  This 0 need not be written.

  $$\begin{array}{r} 3\,7\,2 \ \ R\,1 \\ 2\overline{)7\,4\,5} \\ -6\downarrow \\ \hline 1\,4 \\ -1\,4\downarrow \\ \hline 0\,5 \\ -\ \ 4 \\ \hline 1 \end{array}$$

  Remember: Write the remainder in the quotient.

- Check.

  $$\begin{array}{r} 3\,7\,2 \\ \times\ \ \ 2 \\ \hline 7\,4\,4 \\ +\ \ \ \ 1 \\ \hline 7\,4\,5 \end{array}$$

Complete each division.

1.
```
      1 2 5  R 3
   5)6 2 8
    -5↓
     1 2
    -? ?↓
       2 8
      -? ?
         3
```
Check.
```
      1 2 5
   ×      5
      6 2 5
   +      ?
      6 2 8
```

2.
```
      2 4 3  R 2
   3)7 3 1
    -6↓
     1 3
    -1 2↓
         1 1
        -  ?
           2
```
Check.
```
      2 4 3
   ×      3
      7 2 9
   +      ?
      7 3 1
```

3.
```
      2 6 ?
   3)8 0 7
    -?↓
     2 0
    -? ?↓
         2 7
        -? ?
           0
```
Check.
```
      2 6 ?
   ×      3
      ? ? ?
```

4.
```
      ? 2 ?  R  ?
   2)6 5 1
    -6↓
     0 5
    - ?↓
        1 1
       -1 0
          ?
```
Check.
```
      ? 2 ?
   ×      2
      ? ? ?
   +      ?
      6 5 1
```

Estimate. Then divide.

5. 2)632 **6.** 4)976 **7.** 3)733 **8.** 4)762 **9.** 7)931

10. 5)568 **11.** 7)868 **12.** 4)907 **13.** 6)918 **14.** 4)872

15. 8)936 **16.** 5)860 **17.** 2)524 **18.** 7)802 **19.** 2)922

20. 3)988 **21.** 3)537 **22.** 6)714 **23.** 5)815 **24.** 3)884

Problem Solving

25. At the supermarket 950 apples were placed in 3 piles. Each pile contained the same number of apples. At most, how many apples were there in each pile? How many apples were left over?

More Quotients

Handcraft Toys had 274 trains to ship to 8 stores. The same number of trains were shipped to each store. At most, how many trains did each store receive? How many trains were left over?

To find how many each received, divide: 274 ÷ 8.

Think
8)274   8 > 2   **Not enough hundreds**
8)274   8 < 27   **Enough tens**

Estimate: 3 × 8 = 24 ← Try 3.
4 × 8 = 32

Think
Which basic fact has a product close to 27, but not greater than 27?

Divide the tens.	Divide the ones.	Check.

Divide the tens.

```
       3
  8)2 7 4
  −2 4 ↓
     3 4
```

Divide the ones.

```
      3 4  R 2
  8)2 7 4
  −2 4 ↓
     3 4
    −3 2
       2
```

Check.

```
      3 4
   ×    8
    2 7 2
  +     2
    2 7 4
```

Each store received at most 34 trains.
There were 2 trains left over.

Practice

Complete each division.

1.
```
      7 ?
  8)6 0 8
  −5 6 ↓
     ? 8
   −? ?
       ?
```

2.
```
      8 ?  R  ?
  5)4 3 3
  −? ? ↓
     3 ?
   −? ?
       3
```

3.
```
      ? ?  R 4
  6)3 5 8
  −3 0 ↓
     ? 8
   −? ?
       4
```

4.
```
      ? ?  R  ?
  9)4 7 2
  −4 ? ↓
     ? 2
   −? ?
       ?
```

Estimate. Then find the quotient.

5. $3\overline{)105}$ 6. $4\overline{)232}$ 7. $6\overline{)258}$ 8. $3\overline{)186}$ 9. $5\overline{)130}$

10. $6\overline{)436}$ 11. $7\overline{)201}$ 12. $5\overline{)359}$ 13. $4\overline{)354}$ 14. $7\overline{)182}$

15. $9\overline{)756}$ 16. $3\overline{)202}$ 17. $9\overline{)337}$ 18. $6\overline{)576}$ 19. $8\overline{)197}$

20. $6\overline{)220}$ 21. $4\overline{)228}$ 22. $7\overline{)195}$ 23. $5\overline{)295}$ 24. $6\overline{)335}$

25. $7\overline{)308}$ 26. $9\overline{)823}$ 27. $8\overline{)692}$ 28. $7\overline{)666}$ 29. $9\overline{)717}$

Divide.

30. $657 \div 9$ 31. $267 \div 8$ 32. $396 \div 4$

33. $462 \div 5$ 34. $498 \div 6$ 35. $591 \div 7$

Problem Solving

36. The dividend is 272. The quotient is 34. What is the divisor?

37. The dividend is 359. The divisor is 7. What is the remainder?

38. Peg packs 594 wooden animals into 6 boxes of the same size. At most, how many wooden animals does she pack into each box?

39. Janice has 12 dozen wooden pegs to put into plastic containers. Each container holds six pegs. How many containers does Janice need to fit all the pegs?

40. There are 147 tops at the factory store. If the same number of tops are sold on each of 5 days, what is the greatest number of tops that could be sold each day? How many tops would not be sold?

41. Brendan carves 193 figurines of people for dollhouses. There are 4 people in each dollhouse family. At most, how many families does he carve? How many figurines are left over?

Zeros in the Quotient

Liz, Darcy, and Emma have to hang 317 fliers.
Can they split the fliers evenly between them?

Divide: 317 ÷ 3

Materials: base ten blocks, paper, pencil

Step 1 Model 317. Then share the hundreds equally into 3 sets.

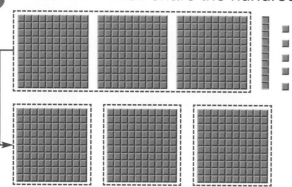

How many hundreds are in each equal set?
Are there any hundreds left over?

$$
\begin{array}{r}
1 \\
3\overline{)3\ 1\ 7} \\
-3 \\
\hline
0\ 1
\end{array}
$$

Step 2 You cannot share 1 ten into the 3 sets.
Regroup the 1 ten as 10 ones.

How many tens are there now? How many ones?

$$
\begin{array}{r}
1\ 0 \\
3\overline{)3\ 1\ 7} \\
-3 \\
\hline
0\ 1 \\
-\ 0 \\
\hline
1\ 7
\end{array}
$$

Step 3 Share the ones equally into the 3 sets.

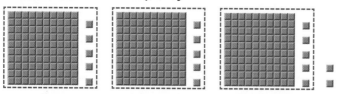

How many ones are in each equal set? How
many ones are left over? What is the quotient
and the remainder when you divide 317 by 3?

$$
\begin{array}{r}
1\ 0\ 5\ \text{R}\ 2 \\
3\overline{)3\ 1\ 7} \\
-3 \\
\hline
0\ 1 \\
-\ 0 \\
\hline
1\ 7 \\
-1\ 5 \\
\hline
2
\end{array}
$$

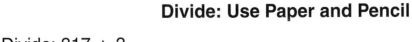

Divide: Use Paper and Pencil

Divide: $317 \div 3$.

..Think...

$3\overline{)317}$ $3 = 3$ **Enough hundreds**

Estimate: $\underline{\ ?\ } \times 3 = 3$
$1 \times 3 = 3$ ← Try 1.

| Divide the hundreds. | Divide the tens. | Divide the ones. | Check. |

Divide the hundreds.

$$
\begin{array}{r}
1 \\
3\overline{)317} \\
-3 \downarrow \\
\hline
0\,1
\end{array}
$$

Divide the tens.

$$
\begin{array}{r}
1\,0 \\
3\overline{)317} \\
-3\downarrow \\
\hline
0\,1 \\
-0\downarrow \\
\hline
1\,7
\end{array}
$$

$3 > 1$ **Not enough tens** Write 0 in the tens place.

Divide the ones.

$$
\begin{array}{r}
1\,0\,5 \ \text{R}\,2 \\
3\overline{)317} \\
-3\downarrow \\
\hline
0\,1 \\
-0\downarrow \\
\hline
1\,7 \\
-1\,5 \\
\hline
2
\end{array}
$$

Check.

$$
\begin{array}{r}
1\,0\,5 \\
\times3 \\
\hline
3\,1\,5 \\
+2 \\
\hline
3\,1\,7
\end{array}
$$

Divide and check. You may use base ten blocks.

1. $4\overline{)800}$ **2.** $2\overline{)600}$ **3.** $3\overline{)390}$ **4.** $4\overline{)840}$ **5.** $5\overline{)550}$

6. $3\overline{)918}$ **7.** $4\overline{)824}$ **8.** $8\overline{)832}$ **9.** $9\overline{)954}$ **10.** $6\overline{)642}$

11. $6\overline{)609}$ **12.** $2\overline{)817}$ **13.** $4\overline{)842}$ **14.** $7\overline{)745}$ **15.** $5\overline{)508}$

16. $5\overline{)841}$ **17.** $9\overline{)985}$ **18.** $2\overline{)615}$ **19.** $3\overline{)902}$ **20.** $8\overline{)847}$

Communicate

21. Examine the divisors and the first two digits of the dividends in exercises 6–20. Explain how you can predict that a zero will probably be in the tens place in the quotient?

Practice

Larger Numbers in Division

Divide: 4925 ÷ 7.

.Think.

$7\overline{)4925}$ 7 > 4 **Not enough thousands**

$7\overline{)4925}$ 7 < 49 **Enough hundreds**

- Divide the hundreds.

  Estimate: $\underline{\ ?\ } \times 7 = 49$

  $7 \times 7 = 49$

  Try 7.

  $$\begin{array}{r} 7 \\ 7\overline{)4\,9\,2\,5} \\ -4\,9\downarrow \\ \hline 0\,2 \end{array}$$

- Divide the tens.

  Estimate: 7 > 2

  Not enough tens

  Write 0 in the
  tens place.

  $$\begin{array}{r} 7\,0 \\ 7\overline{)4\,9\,2\,5} \\ -4\,9\downarrow \\ \hline 2 \\ -\ \ 0\downarrow \\ \hline 2\,5 \end{array}$$

- Divide the ones.

  Estimate: $\underline{\ ?\ } \times 7 = 25$

  $3 \times 7 = 21$

  $4 \times 7 = 28$

  Try 3.

  $$\begin{array}{r} 7\,0\,3 \quad \text{R 4} \\ 7\overline{)4\,9\,2\,5} \\ -4\,9\downarrow \\ \hline 0\,2 \\ -\ \ 0 \\ \hline 2\,5 \\ -2\,1 \\ \hline 4 \end{array}$$

- Check.

  $$\begin{array}{r} 7\,0\,3 \\ \times7 \\ \hline 4\,9\,2\,1 \\ +4 \\ \hline 4\,9\,2\,5 \end{array}$$

Complete each division.

1.
$$\begin{array}{r} 2\,3\,?\,? \\ 4)\overline{9\,5\,6\,0} \\ -\,? \\ \hline ?\,5 \\ -\,?\,? \\ \hline ?\,6 \\ -\,?\,? \\ \hline ?\,0 \end{array}$$

2.
$$\begin{array}{r} 5\,?\,?\ \text{R}\ ? \\ 4)\overline{2\,2\,4\,2} \\ -\,?\,? \\ \hline 2\,4 \\ -\,?\,? \\ \hline 0\,2 \\ -\,? \\ \hline ? \end{array}$$

3.
$$\begin{array}{r} 3\,?\,?\ \text{R}\ ? \\ 7)\overline{2\,5\,0\,1} \\ -\,?\,? \\ \hline 4\,0 \\ -\,3\,5 \\ \hline 5\,1 \\ -\,4\,9 \\ \hline ? \end{array}$$

Estimate. Then divide.

4. $4)\overline{7576}$ 5. $6)\overline{1344}$ 6. $3)\overline{8217}$ 7. $7)\overline{2982}$ 8. $5)\overline{7870}$

9. $8)\overline{4336}$ 10. $2)\overline{5566}$ 11. $9)\overline{1962}$ 12. $3)\overline{4545}$ 13. $7)\overline{4361}$

14. $6)\overline{2418}$ 15. $8)\overline{7249}$ 16. $9)\overline{4567}$ 17. $7)\overline{5320}$ 18. $8)\overline{3600}$

19. $4)\overline{6204}$ 20. $6)\overline{5043}$ 21. $5)\overline{9990}$ 22. $3)\overline{8181}$ 23. $3)\overline{1311}$

24. $9)\overline{28844}$ 25. $7)\overline{32255}$ 26. $9)\overline{27722}$ 27. $8)\overline{28844}$ 28. $9)\overline{36756}$

Find the quotient.

29. $1332 \div 6$

30. $2562 \div 4$

31. $2454 \div 5$

32. $1753 \div 7$

33. $4638 \div 6$

34. $6834 \div 7$

Problem Solving

35. Felipe has 2943 stamps. He keeps an equal number of stamps in each of 3 stamp albums. Does Felipe keep more than 960 stamps in each stamp album?

36. In 9 months Jill collected 941 stamps and Joe collected 931 stamps. The total number of stamps they collected each month was the same. How many stamps did they collect each month?

Divide Money

Meghan bought 4 identical garden spades for $95.92. What did each spade cost?

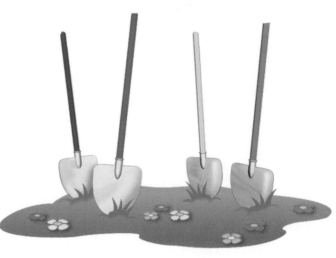

To find the cost of each, divide: $95.92 ÷ 4.

Write the dollar sign and decimal point in the quotient above the dollar sign and decimal point in the dividend.

Divide as usual.

Check.

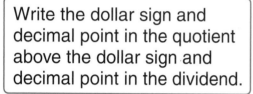

$$\begin{array}{r} \$\qquad. \\ 4\overline{)\$9\,5.9\,2} \end{array}$$

$$\begin{array}{r} \$2\,3.9\,8 \\ 4\overline{)\$9\,5.9\,2} \\ -8 \\ \hline 1\,5 \\ -1\,2 \\ \hline 3\,9 \\ -3\,6 \\ \hline 3\,2 \\ -3\,2 \\ \hline \end{array}$$

$$\begin{array}{r} \$2\,3.9\,8 \\ \times\qquad 4 \\ \hline \$9\,5.9\,2 \end{array}$$

Each spade cost $23.98.

Study these examples.

$$\begin{array}{r} \$.0\,7 \\ 7\overline{)\$.4\,9} \\ -4\,9 \\ \hline \end{array}$$

Check.

$$\begin{array}{r} \$.0\,7 \\ \times\quad 7 \\ \hline \$.4\,9 \end{array}$$

There are no dimes in the quotient. Write a zero.

$$\begin{array}{r} \$\ .9\,0 \\ 5\overline{)\$4.5\,0} \\ -4\,5 \\ \hline 0\,0 \end{array}$$

Check.

$$\begin{array}{r} \$\ .9\,0 \\ \times\quad 5 \\ \hline \$4.5\,0 \end{array}$$

Complete each division.

1.
```
        $2.0 1
    4)$8.0 4
     -8 ↓
        0
      -? ↓
        ?
      -?
```

2.
```
        $  5.? ?
    9)$4 9.9 5
     -? ? ↓
        4 9
      -4 5 ↓
        ? ?
      -? ?
```

3.
```
        $.1 ?
    7)$.8 4
     -? ↓
       1 4
     -? ?
```

4.
```
        $ .0 ?
    8)$0.5 6
      -5 6
```

Estimate. Then find the quotient.

5. 5)$1.35   6. 2)$4.94   7. 4)$2.44   8. 7)$2.31   9. 2)$8.58

10. 4)$20.84   11. 8)$24.16   12. 6)$6.12   13. 3)$24.72   14. 5)$18.10

15. 9)$49.77   16. 6)$14.82   17. 7)$27.93   18. 8)$20.88   19. 5)$26.00

20. 7)$21.63   21. 7)$17.01   22. 4)$63.00   23. 9)$73.53   24. 6)$22.20

Problem Solving

25. Help Meghan copy and complete the order form.

Amount	Description	Cost per Item	Total Cost
2 pairs	Gardening Gloves	?	$23.96
3	Lawn Chairs	?	$50.94
6	Tulip Bulbs	$.95	?
8	Daylily Plants	?	$98.80
5	Flower Pots	?	$14.95
24	Gladiola Bulbs	$1.45	?
4	Trowels	?	$31.96
2	Grass Rakes	$18.09	?
		Total	?

Order of Operations

Tim and Tom were given this problem to solve.

$$6 + 54 \div 2 - 4 \times 5 = n$$

Tim did this:

$$6 + 54 = 60$$
$$60 \div 2 = 30$$
$$30 - 4 = 26$$
$$26 \times 5 = 130$$

Tom did this:

$$54 \div 2 = 27$$
$$4 \times 5 = 20$$
$$6 + 27 = 33$$
$$33 - 20 = 13$$

Whose answer was correct?

Tom's answer was correct.
He used the mathematical rules
called the order of operations.

These are the rules for the
order of operations:

Solve
us first.

- *First* multiply or divide.
  Work in order from left to right.

- *Then* add or subtract.
  Work in order from left to right.

Solve
us next.

$$6 + 54 \div 2 - 4 \times 5 = n \qquad\qquad 6 + 27 - 20 = 13$$

First multiply and divide
from left to right.

Then add and subtract
from left to right.

Study these examples.

$$100 - 6 \times 7 \div 2 = x$$
$$100 - \quad 42 \div 2 = x$$
$$100 - \qquad 21 \quad = 79$$

$$3 \times 4 \times 6 + 5 \div 5 = a$$
$$12 \times 6 + 5 \div 5 = a$$
$$72 \quad + \quad 1 \quad = 73$$

Use the order of operations to solve.

1. $18 - 5 + 6$

2. $9 + 6 - 7$

3. $8 \times 6 \div 4$

4. $54 \div 6 \times 3$

5. $20 + 20 - 16$

6. $85 - 15 \times 2$

7. $10 \div 5 + 5 \times 3$

8. $8 - 4 \div 4 + 4$

9. $24 + 4 \div 4 - 5$

10. $35 - 5 + 10 \div 2$

11. $6 \times 6 + 10 \div 5 - 1$

12. $64 \div 8 \times 10 - 40 - 5$

13. $30 \div 6 \times 9 + 9 - 1$

14. $25 \times 3 - 50 \div 2 + 25$

15. $18 + 6 \div 2 - 11 + 5$

16. $20 \div 4 + 54 \div 6 + 4$

17. $7 \times 30 - 10 + 150 \div 3$

18. $45 \div 5 - 1 + 3 \times 7$

19. $44 \div 2 \times 3 - 12 + 4$

20. $20 \times 5 - 50 \times 2 + 0$

21. $30 + 20 - 25 \div 5 \times 5$

22. $200 \div 4 \times 3 - 50 + 1$

TEST PREPARATION

23. Which part of the expression do you solve first?

$20 \times 10 - 4 \div 2 + 8$

A $2 + 8$ **B** $4 \div 2$ **C** 20×10 **D** $10 - 4$

24. Use the order of operations to solve.

$50 \times 3 - 24 \div 6 + 10$

F 31   **G** 136   **H** 156   **J** 236

25. $46 \times 8 + 10 - 50 \div 2 + 75 \div 3 - 100$

A 728   **B** 278   **C** 89   **D** 94

Find the Mean

Aidan scored 75, 85, 90, 80, and 90 on math tests last term. What was his **mean**, or average, test score?

To find the mean:

| Add the numbers. | | Divide the sum by the number of addends. |

```
   75
   85
   90
   80
 + 90
  420
```

Think..........
5 addends

```
        84 ◄──── mean
   5)420
   − 40↓
      20
    − 20
```

Aidan's mean test score was 84.

Study this example.

Find the mean: $2.44, $3.68, $4.20, $1.64

```
$  2.44
   3.68
   4.20
 + 1.64
 $11.96
```

Think..........
4 addends

```
        $  2.99 ◄──── mean
   4)$11.96
    −  8 ↓
       3 9
     − 3 6↓
        36
      − 36
```

Practice

Find the mean.

1. 36, 42, 72

2. 256, 498

3. 93, 126, 117

4. 500, 250

5. 49, 93, 86

6. 88, 0, 78, 90

Find the mean.

7. 23, 37, 41, 19

8. 56, 18, 42, 64

9. 633, 495, 711

10. 420, 504, 297

11. $4.32, $.88, $4.00, $.76

12. 488, 128, 952, 720

13. 72, 216, 96, 108

14. $1.84, $2.76, $4.08, $2.32

15. 58, 77, 95, 49, 81

16. 93, 102, 115, 83, 42

17. 517, 423, 648, 212, 555

18. $4.25, $6.71, $3.24, $5.06, $4.94

19. $8.44, $.31, $2.97, $3.13, $.80

Problem Solving

Use the information in the grade book.

20. What was Carly's mean test score? Was her mean score greater or less than Dawn's?

21. Did the five students have a higher mean score on Test A or Test B?

Students' Names	Test Scores				
	A	B	C	D	E
Bob	75	63	77	80	90
Carly	82	73	68	72	85
Dawn	75	76	83	87	94
Eric	82	68	85	85	80
Gary	86	85	92	82	70

22. Did the five students have the lowest mean score on Test A, Test B, or Test C?

23. List Bob, Dawn, and Eric in order from the highest mean to the lowest mean.

TEST PREPARATION

24. What is the mean of $3.24, $1.03, $5.69, and $.72?

A $1.99　　**B** $2.49　　**C** $2.67　　**D** $3.56

Problem-Solving Strategy:
Interpret the Remainder

A diner has 98 mugs. The shelves they get stored on can hold only 8 mugs each. How many shelves are needed to store the mugs?

Read **Visualize the facts of the problem as you reread.**

Facts: 98 mugs in all
8 mugs on each shelf

Question: How many shelves are needed?

Plan Divide because a whole is being separated into equal groups of 8. Find the remainder.

The quotient and the remainder will tell how many shelves are needed to hold all the equal groups of 8 mugs, plus any remaining mugs.

$$98 \quad \div \quad 8 \quad = \underline{?} \; R \; \underline{?}$$

number of mugs   mugs on each shelf

Solve

$$\begin{array}{r} 12 \text{ R } 2 \\ 8\overline{)98} \\ -8 \\ \hline 18 \\ -16 \\ \hline 2 \end{array}$$

Think
Since 12 shelves do not hold 98 mugs, increase the quotient by 1.

$12 + 1 = 13$

13 shelves are needed to store the mugs.

Check Multiply and add to check division.
$12 \times 8 = 96$ and $1 \times 2 = 2$
$96 + 2 = 98$ The answer checks.

Interpret the remainder to solve each problem.

1. Jason uses 9-inch strips of plastic. He can buy a 75-inch roll of plastic or a 125-inch roll of plastic. Which roll will have less wasted material?

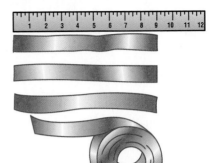

> **Read** ⟩ Visualize the facts of the problem as you reread.
>
> **Facts:** 9-inch strips of plastic
> 75-inch or 125-inch roll of plastic
>
> **Question:** Which roll will have less plastic left over when it is cut into 9-inch strips?
>
> **Plan** ⟩ Divide both 75 inches and 125 inches by 9.
> Compare the remainders.
> Look for the smaller remainder.
>
> ⟩ **Solve** ⟩ ⟩ **Check** ⟩

2. Each CD bin at Sound City holds 8 disks. How many bins are needed to hold 195 disks?

3. Each treasure hunt team will have 5 people. So far 42 people have signed up. How many more people are needed to make every team equal? How many teams will there be?

4. Boxes of juice are sold in packs of 6. The Day Center needs 103 boxes of juice. How many packs should the center buy?

5. A soccer card club has 7 members. Together they have 1305 cards. How many more cards do they need to share the cards equally?

6. Write a problem that uses a remainder. Have a classmate solve it.

Problem-Solving Applications: Mixed Review

Read ▸ **Plan** ▸ **Solve** ▸ **Check**

Solve each problem and explain the method you used.

1. Nora buys a 32-minute cartoon DVD. Each cartoon is 4 minutes long.
   a. How many cartoons are on the DVD?

   b. The DVD costs $6. How much does Nora spend for each cartoon?

2. Alex watches a 1-hour cartoon special. How many 5-minute cartoons can be shown if there are no commercials? What if there are 15 minutes of commercials?

3. A cartoon channel shows 192 cartoons each day. If it shows 8 cartoons each hour, how many hours a day does the channel broadcast?

4. There are 64 characters in a film. Half of them are animals. Of the remaining characters, 8 are puppets. The remaining characters are an even number of boys and girls. How many girls are there?

5. A movie is 84 minutes long. A hopping frog appears every third minute. How many times does the frog appear?

Use the pictograph for problem 7.

6. Fourth-grade students used cartoons to illustrate their stories. How many more students used space creatures than animals?

Fourth-Grade Students	
People	☺ ☺ ☺ ☺ ◖
Animals	☺ ☺ ☺ ◖
Space Creatures	☺ ☺ ☺ ☺ ☺ ☺

Key Each ☺ = 6 students.
Each ◖ = 3 students.

Choose a strategy from the list or use another strategy you know to solve each problem.

Strategy File

Use These Strategies
Interpret the Remainder
Choose the Operation
Logical Reasoning
Write a Number Sentence

7. Mae draws 24 pictures to make 1 second of an animated cartoon. How many pictures does she draw for a 1-minute cartoon?

8. A cartoon, made up of 5760 drawings, uses the same number of drawings for each of the 4 minutes it runs. How many drawings are used per minute?

9. Chris watches a 30-minute cartoon show. If it shows as many 8-minute cartoons as possible, explain if a 7-minute cartoon can also be shown in that time?

10. A DVD includes 4 cartoons. They are 5 minutes, 6 minutes, 8 minutes, and 9 minutes long. What is their average length?

11. Another cartoon DVD is 60 minutes long and costs $8.95. How much will 3 DVDs cost?

12. Three cartoon characters are a chicken, a dog, and an octopus. Flick has more legs than Click, but fewer legs than Glick. Name each animal.

13. A video store orders 60 cartoon DVDs. Each shipping box holds 8 discs. How many boxes will the store receive?

14. Two fourth-grade classes go on a field trip to a cartoon studio. The vans taking the students each hold 7 students. How many vans are needed for 47 students?

15.  Write a problem modeled on problem 13. Have a classmate solve it.

Estimate. Then divide. *(See pp. 172–175, 178–191.)*

1. $4\overline{)32}$ 2. $9\overline{)45}$ 3. $3\overline{)27}$ 4. $5\overline{)65}$ 5. $6\overline{)72}$

6. $2\overline{)53}$ 7. $6\overline{)93}$ 8. $4\overline{)75}$ 9. $6\overline{)86}$ 10. $9\overline{)909}$

11. $3\overline{)723}$ 12. $5\overline{)621}$ 13. $8\overline{)337}$ 14. $7\overline{)256}$ 15. $4\overline{)160}$

16. $6\overline{)\$36.36}$ 17. $8\overline{)\$72.64}$ 18. $5\overline{)\$17.55}$ 19. $7\overline{)2772}$ 20. $8\overline{)4074}$

Write the rule. Complete the pattern. *(See pp. 170–171.)*

21. 4, 7, 10, 13, _?_ , _?_

22. 2, 6, 18, 54, _?_ , _?_

23. 8, 15, 13, 20, 18, _?_ , _?_

24. 69, 64, 66, 61, _?_ , _?_

Answer *yes* or *no*. Then explain why. *(See pp. 176–177.)*

25. Is 45 divisible by 2? by 3? by 5? by 10?

26. Is 300 divisible by 2? by 3? by 5? by 10?

Write the related division or multiplication fact. *(See pp. 166–167.)*

27. $72 \div 9 = 8$ 28. $7 \times 9 = 63$ 29. $27 \div 3 = 9$

Find the value of the variable. *(See pp. 168–169.)*

30. $4 = n \div 9$ 31. $a \times 6 = 54$ 32. $7 \div b = 0$

Find the mean. *(See pp. 194–195.)*

33. 67, 36, 89, 44

34. 436, 219, 116

Problem Solving
(See pp. 178–181, 194–195.)

35. An equal number of crayons were put on each of 8 tables. There were 84 crayons. How many crayons were not put on tables?

36. What was Billy's mean score for basketball if he scored the following points: 24, 30, 18, 15, 28?

(See Still More Practice, p. 465.)

Factor Trees

A composite number has more than two factors.

$$6 = 1 \times 6$$
$$= 2 \times 3$$

A prime number is greater than 1 and has exactly two factors, itself and 1.

$$5 = 1 \times 5$$

The factors of a number that are prime are called prime factors.

You can use a factor tree to help you find all the prime factors, or the prime factorization, of a number.

Look at these factor trees for 12.

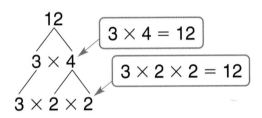

$$3 \times 4 = 12$$

$$3 \times 2 \times 2 = 12$$

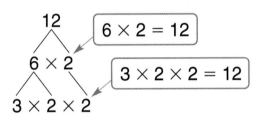

$$6 \times 2 = 12$$

$$3 \times 2 \times 2 = 12$$

3 and 2 are prime numbers.
So the prime factorization of 12 is $3 \times 2 \times 2$.

Copy and complete each factor tree.

1. 30
    6×5
    $? \times 2 \times ?$

2. 40
    4×10
    $? \times 2 \times ? \times ?$

3. 54
    6×9
    $3 \times ? \times ? \times ?$

4. 36
    $9 \times ?$
    $? \times ? \times ? \times ?$

Draw a factor tree for each number.

5. 16

6. 10

7. 20

8. 24

9. 27

10. 32

11. 48

12. 35

13. 56

14. 72

Chapter 5 Test

Estimate. Then divide.

1. $6\overline{)45}$
2. $5\overline{)880}$
3. $8\overline{)268}$
4. $7\overline{)\$8.26}$
5. $6\overline{)660}$

6. $2\overline{)408}$
7. $6\overline{)804}$
8. $5\overline{)610}$
9. $7\overline{)700}$
10. $3\overline{)406}$

11. $4\overline{)\$24.16}$
12. $3\overline{)\$13.23}$
13. $7\overline{)\$7.84}$
14. $8\overline{)\$12.48}$
15. $9\overline{)\$11.70}$

Write the rule. Complete the pattern.

16. 3, 7, 11, 15, __?__, __?__ .

17. 57, 54, 51, 48, __?__, __?__ .

18. 1, 2, 4, 8, __?__, __?__ .

19. 3, 8, 7, 12, 11, __?__, __?__ .

Use the order of operations to solve.

20. $6 \times 5 + 10 \div 5$

21. $32 \div 8 \times 10 - 5 - 10$

Problem Solving

Use a strategy you have learned.

22. Each shelf holds 8 dictionaries. Jean has 37 dictionaries. How many shelves does she need to hold all the dictionaries?

23. On four days Jan read 156 pages, 274 pages, 856 pages, and 306 pages. What was the mean number of pages read by Jan per day?

Tell About It

Explain how you find the value of the variable.

24. $48 \div n = 8$

25. $7 \times a = 35$

Performance Assessment

What might the missing numbers be? Explain why.

26. The divisor is 1. What are the dividend and quotient?
27. The dividend is 0. What are the quotient and divisor?
28. The quotient is 1. What are the divisor and dividend?

Choose the best answer.

1. Choose the standard form of the number.

   $90,000,000 + 500,000 + 10 + 7$

   a. 90,517
   b. 9,500,017
   c. 90,005,017
   d. 90,500,017

8. Round $947.84 to the nearest ten dollars.

   a. $1000.00
   b. $ 950.00
   c. $ 940.00
   d. $ 900.00

2. Which expression matches the problem?

   Liam puts 7 bags in his wagon. Then he puts in some more bags.

   a. $b + 7$
   b. $7 + b$
   c. $7 - b$
   d. $b - 7$

9. $863.69
   $- 651.18$

   a. $1514.87
   b. $212.51
   c. $211.51
   d. $112.51

3. $48,166$
   $+ 57,369$

   a. 90,797
   b. 95,348
   c. 105,535
   d. not given

10. $80,000$
    $- 47,789$

    a. 32,211
    b. 42,211
    c. 47,789
    d. not given

4. What is the period of the underlined digits?

   $\underline{56},722,086$

   a. billions
   b. hundreds
   c. thousands
   d. millions

11. $38.43
    $\times \quad 3$

    a. $115.29
    b. $12.81
    c. $94.29
    d. $38.46

5. 7×88

   a. 81
   b. 95
   c. 556
   d. 616

12. Find the value of the variable.

    $3\overline{)r}^{\,0}$

    a. $r = 0$
    b. $r = 1$
    c. $r = 3$
    d. $r = 30$

6. 60×530

   a. 3180
   b. 12,800
   c. 30,900
   d. not given

13. $5.27
    $\times \quad 46$

    a. $168.28
    b. $224.86
    c. $242.42
    d. not given

7. $6\overline{)97}$

   a. 11 R6
   b. 12 R3
   c. 16 R1
   d. not given

14. $8\overline{)968}$

    a. 101
    b. 121
    c. 131
    d. not given

15. Which is a related multiplication fact

for $21 \div 7 = 3$?
a. $3 \times 7 = 21$
b. $7 \times 4 = 28$
c. $21 \div 3 = 7$
d. $21 = 7 + 14$

16. Divide.

$6\overline{)\$37.38}$
a. $6.23
b. $6.38
c. $36.38
d. not given

17. What is the pattern rule for
55, 48, 41, 34, 27, . . . ?

a. Start at 55, subtract 48
b. Start at 55, subtract 27
c. Start at 27, subtract 7
d. Start at 55, subtract 7

18. Align and add.

$63,138.55 + $45,864.21
a. $109,002.76
b. $109,092.76
c. $108,902.76
d. $17,274.34

19. Which multiplication property
is used?

$9 \times 1 = 9$
a. Commutative
b. Associative
c. Identity
d. Zero

20. Find the mean.

96, 164, 328,
157, 70
a. 328
b. 258
c. 164
d. 163

21. Which shows the best way to check
the answer?

$\begin{array}{r} 1859 \\ -\ 1584 \\ \hline \end{array}$
a. $1859 - 1584 = 275$
b. $1859 + 1584 = 3443$
c. $275 + 1584 = 1859$
d. $275 + 1859 = 2134$

22. The elevation of Mt.
Luna is 737 feet. The
elevation of Mt. Rose is
488 feet. How much
taller is Mt. Luna than
Mt. Rose?
a. 737 ft
b. 488 ft
c. 349 ft
d. 249 ft

23. Choose the related fact to find the
value of f.

$15 - f = 8$
a. $f = 8$
b. $15 - 7 = 8$
c. $15 - 8 = 7$
d. $15 - 5 = 10$

24. Add.

$\begin{array}{r} 7028 \\ +\ 2109 \\ \hline \end{array}$
a. 10,137
b. 9137
c. 9127
d. 4919

Use estimation to solve. Choose the method. Using your method, do you think the estimate is less than or greater than the actual product? How would another method of estimation change your answer? Explain.

25. Jose has 466 rare coins. Nel has about 8 times that
number. About how many rare coins does Nel have?

Measurement

CHAPTER 6

In this chapter you will:

Estimate and compute with customary
and metric units, with renaming
Investigate time and temperature
–both Fahrenheit and Celsius
Solve problems using more than one step

Critical Thinking/Finding Together

Measure the length of various objects
using the nonstandard units below.

- **cubit** (distance from elbow
  to fingertip)
- **span** (distance between
  outstretched thumb and pinky)

from
TAKE A NUMBER

Imagine a world
Without mathematics:

No rulers or scales,
No inches or feet,
No dates or numbers
On house or street,
No prices or weights,
No determining heights,
No hours running through
Days and nights.
No zero, no birthdays,
No way to subtract
All of the guesswork
Surrounding the fact.
No sizes for shoes,
Or suit or hat....
Wouldn't it be awful
To live like that?

Mary O'Neill

6-1

Measure with Inches

You can use a ruler to measure an object to the nearest inch, nearest half inch, and nearest quarter inch.

When you measure length, align the object you are measuring with the beginning of the ruler.

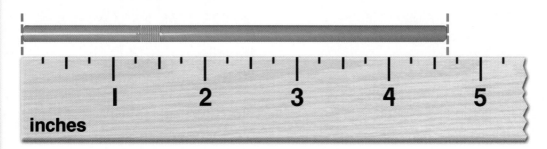

inches

- To the nearest inch, the straw is about 5 in. long.

- To the nearest half inch, the straw is about $4\frac{1}{2}$ in. long.

- To the nearest quarter inch, the straw is about $4\frac{3}{4}$ in. long.

Think
Each inch on the ruler is divided into 2 half inches and 4 quarter inches.

Practice

Measure each to the nearest inch, nearest half inch, and nearest quarter inch.

1.

2. 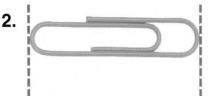   3.

Draw a line segment for each length.

4. 3 in.
5. $2\frac{1}{4}$ in.
6. $1\frac{1}{2}$ in.
7. $4\frac{3}{4}$ in.

8. $5\frac{1}{2}$ in.
9. $3\frac{3}{4}$ in.
10. $6\frac{1}{4}$ in.
11. 4 in.

Practice

Estimate the length of each to the nearest inch.
Then measure each line to check your estimates.

12. |—————————————————————|

13. |———————————————————————————|

14. |————————|

15. |———————————————————|

16. |—————————————————————————————————|

Use an inch ruler to measure objects.

17. Measure the length and width of some of the objects in your classroom. Record each measurement. Discuss your results with your class.

Problem Solving

18. Could you use the ruler at the right to measure the line in exercise 14? How?

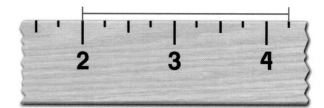

19. What is the length of the red line in the figure at the right?

CHALLENGE

Draw a line segment for each length. Label each line segment.

20. $2\frac{1}{4}$ in., 2 in., $2\frac{3}{4}$ in., $2\frac{1}{2}$ in.

21. Order the labeled line segments from longest to shortest.

Rename Units of Length

Can Don fit a shelf that is 72 in. long in a closet that is 5 ft wide?

Compare: 72 in. __?__ 5 ft

Before you can compare measurements in different units, you need to rename the measurements using the same units.

▶ You can make a table to rename units. Rename 5 ft as inches.

ft	1	2	3	4	5
in.	12	24	36	48	60

This table shows equivalent measures of length.

Think
1 ft = 12 in.

5 ft = 60 in.   72 > 60   So 72 in. > 5 ft.

▶ You can multiply the larger unit to rename units.

5 ft = __?__ in.
5 ft = (5 × 12) in.

5 ft = 60 in.   72 > 60   So 72 in. > 5 ft.

Don cannot fit a shelf that is 72 in. long in a closet that is 5 ft wide.

Rename each unit of measure. Make a table or compute with paper and pencil. Use the Table of Measures on page 500 to help.

1. 2 yd = __?__ in.

2. 8 ft = __?__ in.

3. 18 ft = __?__ yd

4. 7 ft = __?__ in.

5. 4 yd = __?__ ft

6. 4 yd = __?__ in.

Practice

Compare. Write <, =, or >.
You may make a table or compute.

7. 6 yd _?_ 9 ft

8. 8 ft _?_ 84 in.

9. 36 in. _?_ 3 ft

10. 7 ft _?_ 108 in.

11. 20 yd _?_ 45 ft

12. 8 yd _?_ 18 ft

Mile

The mile (mi) is a customary unit of length.

Miles are used to measure long lengths called distances.

5280 feet (ft) = 1 mile (mi)
1760 yards (yd) = 1 mile (mi)

It takes about 25 minutes to walk 1 mile.

Compare. Write <, =, or >.

13. 2 mi _?_ 3520 yd

14. 5280 yd _?_ 3 mi

15. 3 mi _?_ 21,120 ft

16. 10,560 ft _?_ 2 mi

17. 6 mi _?_ 42,240 ft

18. 7040 yd _?_ 4 mi

Problem Solving

19. The width of the teachers' parking lot at Harlington Elementary School is 34 yd. How many feet wide is it?

20. The Public Library is 1810 yd from Luz's house and 5045 ft from Tanya's house. Whose house is closer to the library?

21. Which is the most reasonable distance a person can walk in two hours, 4 miles, 4 yards, 4 inches, or 4 feet?

Compute Customary Units

▶ Last month a sunflower was
4 feet 7 inches tall. Then it grew
1 foot 8 inches taller. How tall
is the sunflower now?

To find how tall it is now,
add: 4 ft 7 in. + 1 ft 8 in.

Add the smaller units first. Rename units as needed.

```
  4 ft   7 in.
+ 1 ft   8 in.
  5 ft  15 in.  = 5 ft + 1 ft + 3 in. = 6 ft 3 in.
```

15 in. = 12 in. + 3 in.
= 1 ft + 3 in.   The sunflower is 6 ft 3 in. tall now.

▶ A lilac stem was 7 feet 7 inches tall.
Sam pruned 2 feet 5 inches off the stem.
How tall was the stem after pruning?

To find how tall, subtract: 7 ft 7 in. − 2 ft 5 in.

Subtract the smaller units first. Rename units as needed.

```
  7 ft 7 in.
− 2 ft 5 in.
  5 ft 2 in.
```
The stem was 5 ft 2 in. tall after pruning.

Study these examples.

```
   8 yd 1 ft       3 ft = 1 yd
+  2 yd 2 ft
  10 yd 3 ft = 10 yd + 1 yd = 11 yd
```

```
  4 ft 11 in.
−      9 in.
  4 ft  2 in.
```

Add.

1. 6 ft 2 in.
    + 3 ft 5 in.

2. 7 yd 1 ft
    + 1 yd 1 ft

3. 3 yd 2 ft
    + 5 yd

4. 8 ft 6 in.
    +   5 in.

5. 10 ft 3 in.
    + 4 ft 10 in.

6. 5 ft 8 in.
    + 7 ft 11 in.

7. 6 ft 9 in. + 9 ft 5 in.

8. 4 yd 2 ft + 3 yd 2 ft

Subtract.

9. 4 ft 8 in.
    − 1 ft 3 in.

10. 9 ft 4 in.
     − 9 ft 2 in.

11. 7 yd 2 ft
     −   2 ft

12. 2 yd 2 ft
     − 2 yd

13. 12 ft 9 in.
     − 2 ft 4 in.

14. 8 ft 10 in.
     − 5 ft 6 in.

15. 9 ft 7 in. − 4 ft 3 in.

16. 4 ft 6 in. − 2 ft 6 in.

Problem Solving

17. Amy's fence is 18 ft 10 in. long. She adds a 3 ft 5 in. section to the fence. How long is the fence then?

18. Joe painted 6 ft of a fence that is 20 ft 6 in. long. How much of the fence is not painted?

CHALLENGE

Subtract. Rename when necessary.

19. ³⁄4 ft ¹⁶⁄4 in.
     − 1 ft 6 in.
     ─────────
     2 ft 10 in.

     | Regroup 1 ft as 12 in. |

20. 8 ft 6 in.
     − 3 ft 11 in.

21. 9 yd 2 ft
     − 8 yd 4 ft

22. 5 ft 1 in.
     − 4 ft 11 in.

23. 12 ft
     − 6 ft 8 in.

Update your skills. See page 15.

Customary Units of Capacity

The customary units for measuring
capacity are cup, pint, quart, and gallon.

Each unit can be measured
in fluid ounces (fl oz).
8 fluid ounces is equal to 1 cup.

Customary Units of Capacity		
8 fluid ounces (fl oz) = 1 cup (c)		
2 cups = 1 pint (pt)		
2 pints = 1 quart (qt)		
4 quarts = 1 gallon (gal)		

▶ How many fluid ounces are
equal to 3 pints?

To find how many fluid ounces,
rename pints as cups. Then rename
cups as fluid ounces.

3 pt = $\underline{\ ?\ }$ fl oz
3 pt = (3 × 2) c
3 pt = 6 c
3 pt = (6 × 8) fl oz
3 pt = 48 fl oz

.Think................
1 pt = 2 c
1 c = 8 fl oz

Remember: Multiply to
rename larger units as
smaller units.

48 fluid ounces are equal to 3 pints.

▶ How many cups are equal to 16 fluid ounces?

To find how many cups, rename fluid ounces as cups.

16 fl oz = $\underline{\ ?\ }$ c
16 fl oz = (16 ÷ 8) c
16 fl oz = 2 c

.Think................
1 c = 8 fl oz

Divide to rename smaller
units as larger units.

2 cups are equal to 16 fluid ounces.

Study this example.

42 fl oz = $\underline{\ ?\ }$ c

$$\begin{array}{r} 5\ \text{R2} \\ 8\overline{)42} \\ -40 \\ \hline 2 \end{array}$$

remaining fluid ounces

42 fl oz = 5 c 2 fl oz

Complete each table to find equivalent measures.

1.

gal	1	2	?	4	?
qt	4	8	?	?	20
pt	8	?	24	?	?

2.

pt	1	2	3	?	5
c	2	?	?	8	?
fl oz	16	32	?	?	?

Rename each unit of capacity.

3. 2 pt = _?_ c

4. 8 c = _?_ fl oz

5. 16 qt = _?_ gal

6. 2 gal = _?_ qt

7. 10 pt = _?_ c

8. 48 pt = _?_ gal

Compare. Use <, =, or >.

9. 6 pt _?_ 12 c

10. 9 qt _?_ 2 gal

11. 3 c _?_ 36 fl oz

12. 2 qt _?_ 10 c

13. 54 fl oz _?_ 6 c

14. 32 fl oz _?_ 1 qt

Problem Solving

15. Would you need 6 c, 6 pt, or 6 gal of paint to paint a room?

16. Would you drink 1 fl oz, 1 c, or 1 qt of milk at lunch?

17. Ted's pail holds 2 qt of water. He filled the pail 6 times to wash his mother's car. How many gallons of water did Ted use?

18. How many 14-fl oz cans of broth are needed for a recipe that calls for 1 qt of broth?

MENTAL MATH

Rename each unit of capacity mentally.

19. 1 qt = _?_ pt

20. 1 c = _?_ fl oz

21. 1 gal = _?_ qt

22. 1 pt = _?_ c

Customary Units of Weight

The ounce (oz), the pound (lb), and the ton (T) are customary units of weight.

| 16 ounces (oz) = 1 pound (lb) |
| 2000 pounds (lb) = 1 ton (T) |

A letter weighs about 1 ounce.

A compact car weighs about 1 ton.

Practice

Write *oz, lb,* or *T* for the unit you would use to measure the weight of each.

1. a carrot

2. an elephant

3. an electric guitar

4. a fire engine

5. a person

6. a toaster

7. a dog

8. a canary

9. a dump truck

Choose the letter of the best estimate.

10. an orange
  a. 6 oz
  b. 1 lb
  c. 2 lb

11. a cat
  a. 30 lb
  b. 12 oz
  c. 12 lb

Complete each table to find equivalent measures.

12.

oz	16	32	?	64	?	?
lb	1	2	3	?	5	6

13.

lb	2000	?	6000	?	?
T	1	2	?	4	?

Compare. Write <, =, or >. You may make a table to help.

14. 5 lb ? 96 oz　　**15.** 6 T ? 12,000 lb　　**16.** 4 lb ? 58 oz

17. 8 lb ? 112 oz　　**18.** 144 oz ? 6 lb　　**19.** 8500 lb ? 5 T

20. 48 oz ? 2 lb　　**21.** 2 T ? 2000 lb　　**22.** 10 lb ? 1600 oz

Match. Write the letter of the tool you would use to measure each.

23. length of a pencil

a. ruler

24. water for a vase

b. scale

25. length of the classroom

c. measuring cup

26. weight of a person

d. yardstick

Problem Solving

27. Akeem has 5 sisters. He gives a 4-oz plum to each sister. In all do the plums weigh more or less than 1 lb?

28. A truck can carry 3000 lb of cargo. Can it carry two tractors that each weigh 1000 lb and a 625-lb plow?

29. Can a truck that weighs 7500 lb safely cross a bridge with a 3 T weight limit?

DO YOU REMEMBER?

Complete the sentences. Use the words in the box.

In the subtraction sentence 67 − 24 = 33:

30. The ? is 67.

31. The ? is 24.

32. The ? is 33.

| difference |
| addend |
| subtrahend |
| minuend |

6-6

Measure with Metric Units

The decimeter (dm) is a metric unit of length.

| 10 centimeters (cm) = 1 decimeter (dm) |

▶ In base ten blocks each ten rod is about 1 decimeter long.

▶ You can use a metric ruler to measure an object to the nearest centimeter or the nearest decimeter.

The length of the piece of yarn is between 8 cm and 9 cm.
It is closer to 8 cm.
To the nearest centimeter, the piece of yarn is 8 cm long.
To the nearest decimeter, the piece of yarn is 1 dm long.

Practice

Measure each to the nearest centimeter.

1. ├──────────────┤

2. ├──────────────────────┤

3. ├────────────────────────────────┤

Draw a line segment for each length.

4. 2 cm   **5.** 8 cm   **6.** 12 cm   **7.** 10 cm   **8.** 2 dm

9. 16 cm   **10.** 1 dm   **11.** 20 cm   **12.** 3 dm   **13.** 3 cm

Estimate each to the nearest centimeter and to the nearest decimeter. Then measure to check your estimates.

14. the length of your shoe

15. the length of a pencil case

16. the width of your hand

17. the length of your desk

18. the length of a dollar bill

19. the length of this book

20. the width of this book

21. For exercises 14–20, was it easier to estimate in centimeters or in decimeters? Why?

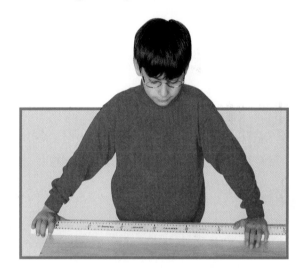

22. Josh and Ray measure the same wall. Josh says it is 360 centimeters long. Ray says it is 36 decimeters long. Can they both be right? Explain your answer.

23. Lila needs 63 cm of balsa wood to make a model plane. The three pieces she has are 3 dm long, 2 dm long, and 8 cm long. How many more cm of balsa wood does Lila need?

24. Find and explain the meanings of these prefixes commonly used in the metric system of measurement.

> centi-
> milli-
> deci-
> kilo-

Update your skills. See page 17.

Work with Metric Units

The millimeter (mm) and the kilometer (km) are other metric units of length.

| 10 millimeters (mm) = 1 centimeter (cm) |
| 100 millimeters (mm) = 1 decimeter (dm) |
| 10 decimeters (dm) = 1 meter (m) |
| 1000 meters (m) = 1 kilometer (km) |

▶ A dime is about 1 millimeter thick.

centimeters

It takes about 15 minutes to walk 1 kilometer.

▶ Make a table or compute to rename units.

Compare: 3000 m __?__ 4 km

.Think.........
1 km = 1000 m

• Make a table:

m	1000	2000	3000
km	1	2	3

3 < 4   So 3000 m < 4 km.

• Multiply:

4 km = (4 × 1000) m
4 km = 4000 m

3000 < 4000
So 3000 m < 4 km.

Compare: 40 cm __?__ 3 dm

.Think.........
1 dm = 10 cm

• Make a table:

cm	10	20	30	40
dm	1	2	3	4

4 > 3   So 40 cm > 3 dm.

• Divide:

40 cm = (40 ÷ 10) dm
40 cm = 4 dm

4 > 3
So 40 cm > 3 dm.

Compare. Write <, =, or >.
You may make a table or compute.

1. 40 km _?_ 400 m

2. 2000 mm _?_ 200 cm

3. 9 dm _?_ 900 cm

4. 6 m _?_ 80 dm

5. 7 dm _?_ 7000 mm

6. 500 cm _?_ 5 dm

7. 2000 m _?_ 5 km

8. 9 dm _?_ 1 m

9. 8000 cm _?_ 80 m

Problem Solving **Use the map below.**

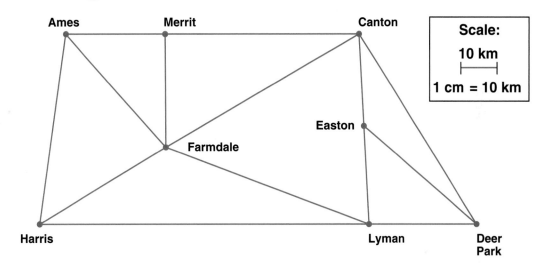

Ames   Merrit   Canton

Scale:
10 km
├──────┤
1 cm = 10 km

Easton

Farmdale

Harris   Lyman   Deer Park

10. What is the shortest route from Ames to Lyman? About how many kilometers long is this route?

11. Mr. Yuan wants to travel from Harris to Deer Park to Canton. About how many kilometers will he travel?

12. Ms. Rau must travel from Lyman to Merrit. Should she go through Farmdale or through Canton? Why?

13. What is the shortest route from Deer Park to Ames? from Easton to Harris? About how long is each route?

14. The distance from City A to City B is 40 miles. What is the distance from City A to City C?

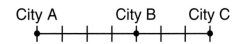

City A   City B   City C

Update your skills. See page 18.

Metric Units of Capacity

The milliliter (mL) is a metric unit of liquid capacity.

1000 milliliters (mL) = 1 liter (L)

There are about 20 drops of water in 1 mL.

Practice

Choose the letter of the best estimate.

1. bottle of liquid soap   **a.** 1 mL   **b.** 10 mL   **c.** 1 L

2. gasoline for a car   **a.** 48 mL   **b.** 48 L   **c.** 480 L

3. bowl of soup   **a.** 5 mL   **b.** 500 mL   **c.** 5 L

4. ladle of soup   **a.** 25 mL   **b.** 250 mL   **c.** 250 L

5. water in an aquarium   **a.** 60 mL   **b.** 600 mL   **c.** 60 L

Write *mL* or *L* for the unit you would use to measure the capacity of each.

6. large jug of apple cider   7. tablespoon of syrup

8. glass of juice   9. bucket

10. washing machine   11. cup

Complete the table to find equivalent measures.

12.

L	1	2	?	?	?	6	?	?
mL	1000	?	3000	?	?	?	7000	?

Compare. Write <, =, or >.
You may make a table or compute.

13. 2 L ? 200 mL   **14.** 5 L ? 6000 mL   **15.** 8 L ? 8000 mL

16. 15 L ? 1500 mL   **17.** 4000 mL ? 3 L   **18.** 9000 mL ? 10 L

Write in order from the least amount to the greatest amount.

19. 4 L, 40 mL, 400 mL, 4 mL   **20.** 200 L, 20 mL, 20 L, 2 mL

21. 38 L, 380 mL, 380 L, 138 L   **22.** 24 L, 2400 mL, 240 mL, 240 L

Problem Solving

23. Mr. Wood's van can travel 5 km on 1 L of gasoline. How much gasoline does the van use to travel 50 kilometers?

24. Mrs. Wood's water jug holds 4 L of water. It has 500 mL of water in it now. How much more water is needed to fill the jug?

25. Ellen and Allen both carry small canteens. Each canteen holds 750 mL of water. How much water, in liters, do they need to fill both canteens?

26. The Woods began their trip with 75 L of gasoline in their gas tank. They used 68 L of gasoline. How much gasoline was left in the tank?

27. Ellen filled her 750-mL canteen four times in one day. How many liters of water did she use?

TEST PREPARATION

28. Which would most likely be measured in milliliters?

    A a full bathtub
    B a teaspoon of honey
    C a carton of milk
    D a bucket of water

29. Ty's thermos holds 2 L. How many milliliters does it hold?

    F 2 mL   **G** 20 mL
    H 200 mL   **J** 2000 mL

Update your skills. See page 19.

Metric Units of Mass

The gram (g) is a metric unit of mass.

| 1000 grams (g) = 1 kilogram (kg) |

A paper clip has a mass of about 1 gram.

1 gram (g)   about 1 gram (g)

Practice

Choose the letter of the best estimate.

1. an egg   **a.** 90 g   **b.** 9 kg   **c.** 90 kg

2. a shark   **a.** 100 g   **b.** 1000 g   **c.** 1000 kg

3. a worm   **a.** 14 g   **b.** 14 000 g **c.** 14 kg

4. a small dog   **a.** 880 g   **b.** 8 kg   **c.** 88 kg

5. a slice of bread   **a.** 2 g   **b.** 28 g   **c.** 28 kg

Write *g* or *kg* for the unit you would use to measure the mass of each.

6. a dinosaur   **7.** a mouse   **8.** a math book

9. a bag of oranges   **10.** a feather   **11.** a crayon

12. a paper clip   **13.** a bag of flour   **14.** a flower

Complete the table to find equivalent measures.

15.

kg	1	?	3	?	?	?	?	8
g	1000	?	?	4000	?	?	?	?

Compare. Write <, =, or >.
You may make a table or compute.

16. 2 kg __?__ 20 g

17. 5 kg __?__ 5000 g

18. 9 kg __?__ 90 000 g

19. 8 kg __?__ 9000 g

20. 80 g __?__ 8 kg

21. 6000 g __?__ 5 kg

Problem Solving

22. A penny has a mass of about 3 g. About what is the mass of a roll of 50 pennies? of 2 rolls of 50 pennies?

23. Pete puts 150 g of turkey into each turkey sandwich. How many kilograms of turkey does he need for 20 sandwiches?

24. Each loaf of bread that Pete uses has a mass of 500 g. He orders 10 loaves of bread. Is this more than or less than 8 kilograms?

25. A carton holds up to 30 kg. Pete has 28 kg of canned goods and 4000 g of side dishes. Can he pack them all into the carton?

26. Pete cooks two turkeys. The first has a mass of 11 000 g. The second has a mass of 17 kg. Which turkey has the greater mass? how much greater?

27. Find objects in your classroom that you think have a mass of about 50 g. Then use a balance to check your guesses. How close were your guesses?

28. The weights of three objects were compared. Which object is the heaviest?

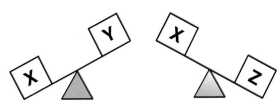

CRITICAL THINKING — Algebra

Choose reasonable numbers so that each picture makes sense.

29.
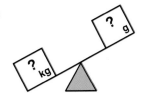

30.
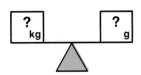

31.
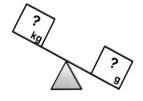

Temperature

A thermometer is used
to measure temperature.

Temperature can be measured
in degrees Fahrenheit (°F)
or in degrees Celsius (°C).

▶ Each line on the Fahrenheit
scale stands for 2°F.
Room temperature in
degrees Fahrenheit is
about 68°F.

Each line on the Celsius
scale stands for 1°C.
Room temperature in
degrees Celsius is
about 20°C.

▶ Use a minus sign to write
temperatures below zero.

Write: ⁻5°F
Read: 5 degrees Fahrenheit
below zero

Write: ⁻10°C
Read: 10 degrees Celsius
below zero

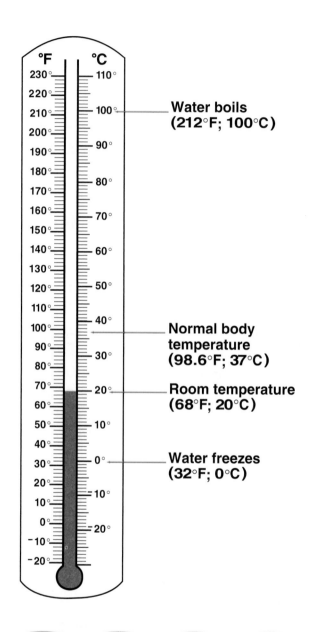

Water boils
(212°F; 100°C)

Normal body
temperature
(98.6°F; 37°C)

Room temperature
(68°F; 20°C)

Water freezes
(32°F; 0°C)

Practice

Write the letter of the better estimate.

1. hot summer day

    a. 90°C   **b.** 90°F

2. ice skating weather

    a. ⁻10°C   **b.** 10°C

Write each temperature.

3.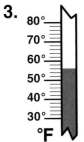

4.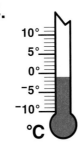

5.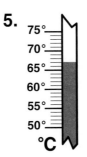

6.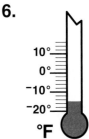

Compare. Write <, =, or >.
You may use the thermometer on page 224.

7. 30°C _?_ 120°F   **8.** 100°C _?_ 212°F   **9.** 50°F _?_ 10°C

10. 140°F _?_ 60°C   **11.** ⁻10°F _?_ ⁻20°C   **12.** 100°F _?_ 50°C

Problem Solving Use the thermometer on page 224.

13. At 6:00 A.M. the temperature was 45°F. It rose 13°F by noon. What was the temperature at noon?

14. The temperature was 22°C at 8:00 P.M. If the temperature dropped 3° every hour, what was the temperature at 11:00 P.M.?

15. The temperature was 36°F at 7:00 P.M. It dropped 10°F by midnight. What was the temperature at midnight?

16. At 5:00 A.M. the temperature was ⁻3°C. By noon it was 6°C. By how many degrees did the temperature rise?

17. The temperature rose 11°F from 5:30 A.M. to 10:00 A.M. It was ⁻17°F at 5:30 A.M. What was the temperature at 10:00 A.M.?

18. The temperature rose from 52°C to the temperature shown on the thermometer in exercise 5. How many degrees did the temperature rise?

Write About It

19. Choose Fahrenheit or Celsius to keep a record of the temperature at the same time each day for 7 days in a row. Share your temperature record with your class.

Time

> You can read time after the half hour as minutes **past** the hour or as minutes **to** the next hour.

Read: 26 minutes past 6

Write: 6:26

Read: 43 minutes past 2;
17 minutes to 3

Write: 2:43

> 24 hours = 1 day

```
|————————+————————+————————+————————|
midnight      6:00 A.M.      noon         6:00 P.M.    midnight
12:00 A.M.              12:00 P.M.                    12:00 A.M.
```

Use A.M. for the hours between 12:00 midnight and 12:00 noon.

Use P.M. for the hours between 12:00 noon and 12:00 midnight.

Write the time in minutes past the hour and in minutes to the hour.

1.

2.

3.

4.

5.

6.

Write _A.M._ or _P.M._ to make each statement reasonable.

7. Bill has breakfast at 7:15 _?_

8. School lets out at 3:00 _?_

9. Ann goes to bed at 9:30 _?_

10. School begins at 8:00 _?_

Write the time. Use _A.M._ or _P.M._

11. 10 minutes past 8 in the morning

12. 22 minutes to 10 at night

13. 36 minutes past 4 in the afternoon

14. 8 minutes to 9 in the morning

15. 18 minutes to noon

16. 45 minutes past midnight

Equivalent Units of Time

How many seconds are in 42 minutes?

Multiply to rename larger units as smaller units.
42 min = _?_ s
42 min = (42 × 60) s

| 60 seconds (s) = 1 minute (min) |
| 60 minutes = 1 hour (h) |
| 24 hours = 1 day (d) |
| 7 days = 1 week (wk) |
| 365 days = 1 year (y) |
| 52 weeks = 1 year |
| 12 months (mo) = 1 year |

1 min = 60 s

42 min = 2520 s   There are 2520 seconds in 42 minutes.

Complete each table to find equivalent measures.

17.

d	1	?	3	?
h	24	?	?	96

18.

min	60	?	?	240
h	?	2	?	?

19.

y	?	2	?	?
wk	52	?	?	208

20.

mo	?	?	36	?
y	1	?	?	4

Elapsed Time

Jody arrived at the airport at
11:10 A.M. to meet Lisa.
Lisa's plane landed at 1:24 P.M.
How long did Jody wait for Lisa?

To find the **elapsed time** or
how much time has passed:

- Count the hours by 1s.
- Count the minutes by 5s and 1s.

| Start at 11:10 A.M.
Count the hours
to 1:10 P.M. | 11:10 ⎫ 1 hour
12:10 ⎬ 1 hour
1:10 ⎭ | **2 hours** |

| Count the minutes
to 1:24 P.M. | 1:10 ⎫ 5 minutes
1:15 ⎬ 5 minutes
1:20 ⎬ 1 minute
1:21 ⎬ 1 minute
1:22 ⎬ 1 minute
1:23 ⎬ 1 minute
1:24 ⎭ | **14 minutes** |

Jody waited 2 hours 14 minutes for Lisa.

Write the elapsed time.

1. from 8:05 A.M. to 8:30 A.M.

2. from 1:25 P.M. to 1:50 P.M.

3. from 6:30 A.M. to 6:51 A.M.

4. from 11:15 P.M. to 11:47 P.M.

5. from 11:45 P.M. to 12:04 A.M.

6. from 11:55 A.M. to 12:16 P.M.

7. from 3:25 P.M. to 4:40 P.M.

8. from 8:30 A.M. to 10:05 A.M.

Practice

Elapsed Time on a Calendar

Lisa arrived on June 26 and left on July 8.
How many days did she visit?

Count from June 26 to July 8. Count June 27 as day 1.

JUNE						
S	M	T	W	TH	F	S
			1	2	3	4
5	6	7	8	9	10	11
12	13	14	15	16	17	18
19	20	21	22	23	24	25
(26)	27	28	29	30		

JULY						
S	M	T	W	TH	F	S
					1	2
3	4	5	6	7	(8)	9
10	11	12	13	14	15	16
17	18	19	20	21	22	23
24/31	25	26	27	28	29	30

AUGUST						
S	M	T	W	TH	F	S
	1	2	3	4	5	6
7	8	9	10	11	12	13
14	15	16	17	18	19	20
21	22	23	24	25	26	27
28	29	30	31			

Lisa visited for 12 days.

Rename each unit of time.

9. 2 wk 4 d = _?_ d

10. 3 y 6 mo = _?_ mo

11. 3 y 5 wk = about _?_ wk

12. 2 y 94 d = _?_ d

Remember:
7 d = 1 wk
365 d = 1 y
52 wk = 1 y
12 mo = 1 y

Problem Solving Use the calendar above for exercises 13 and 14.

13. What date is 10 days after July 22?

14. What date is 21 days before July 2?

15. Jody and Lisa left the airport at 2:05 P.M. They drove for 47 minutes before arriving at Jody's house. What time did they arrive at Jody's house?

16. Jody and Lisa will visit their cousin, who lives 1 hour and 10 minutes away. They want to get there at 11:00 A.M. What time should they leave?

Problem–Solving Strategy:
Use More Than One Step

Maria has 3 packages to send to Hawaii in zone 8. One weighs 3 lb and the others weigh 4 lb each. How much money will she save if she uses 4-day delivery instead of paying $13.40 for using 2-day delivery?

Weight	Zone 8 Rates	
(lb)	2-day Delivery	4-day Delivery
1	$2.90	—
2	$2.90	$2.85
3	$4.10	$4.05
4	$4.65	$4.60
5	$5.45	$5.40

Read ▶ **Visualize the facts of the problem as you reread it.**

Facts: 1—3-lb package
2—4-lb packages

Question: How much money is saved by using 4-day delivery?

Plan ▶ Plan the steps to follow.

Step 1: Use the prices in the chart. Add to find the cost of sending the packages by 4-day delivery.

3-lb cost + 4-lb cost = total cost

Step 2: Subtract to find the difference.

2-day delivery − 4-day delivery = savings

Solve ▶ **Step 1:** 4-day delivery   **Step 2:** savings

```
        1                              3  10
  $   4.0 5                        $1 3.4̶ 0̶
      4.6 0                        − 1 3.2 5
    + 4.6 0                        $    .1 5
  $1 3.2 5
```

Maria will save $.15 by using 4-day delivery.

Check ▶ Remember to check the computation in each step.

Use more than one step to solve each problem.

1. Paul sends his cousin three 28-oz
   fruitcakes and a 27-oz package of
   poppy seed muffins. What is the
   total weight of the package?

> **Read** Visualize the facts of the problem
> as you reread it.
>
> **Facts:** 3—28-oz fruitcakes
> 1—27-oz package of muffins
>
> **Question:** What is the total weight?
>
> **Plan** Plan the steps to follow.
>
> **Step 1:** Multiply to find the weight of
> the 3 fruitcakes:
>
> 3 × 28 oz
>
> **Step 2:** Add to find the total weight.

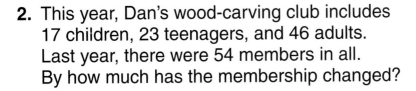

2. This year, Dan's wood-carving club includes
   17 children, 23 teenagers, and 46 adults.
   Last year, there were 54 members in all.
   By how much has the membership changed?

3. Dan works as a wood carver from 8:30 A.M. to
   4:30 P.M. each day. How many hours does
   Dan work in a 5-day work week?

4. Ira sends six 2-lb packages to Hawaii using 4-day
   delivery. How much change will he get from $20?
   (*Hint:* Use the chart on page 230.)

5. Mr. Cheng bought 8 gallons of paint. Each gallon
   cost $12.27. He also bought a paint roller for
   $4.75. What was the total cost?

Solve each problem and explain the method you used.

1. The sun set at 7:52 P.M. It rose the next morning at 5:02 A.M. How much time passed from sunset to sunrise?

2. Ray caught 3 fish that were about 4 lb each. Mary caught 4 fish that were each about the same weight as Ray's. About how many pounds of fish did they catch?

3. Mrs. O'Hara packed 2 pounds of trail mix. Her family ate 7 ounces of the mix. How much was left?

4. Mr. O'Hara brought 3 rolls of fishing line. Each roll holds 525 yards of line. Did he bring more than a mile of line?

5. Mrs. O'Hara caught a 12 kg fish. How much is this in grams?

6. The O'Haras drove to Loon Lake. They left home at 8:25 A.M. Lunch at a rest stop took 45 minutes. They arrived at Loon Lake at 4:00 P.M. How long were they driving?

7. Mary's jug holds 3 L of water. It already has 500 mL in it. How much water should Mary add to fill it?

8. A hiking trail is 4 km long. There are trail markers every 8 m. How many trail markers are there?

Choose a strategy from the list or use another strategy you know to solve each problem.

9. Ray heard a loon's call at 7:48 A.M. and again 13 minutes later. What time did he hear the second call?

10. Mary glues 8 pine needles onto each postcard. She has 130 pine needles. How many postcards can she make?

11. The distance across Loon Lake is 2 miles. Mary rows the boat 2640 yd across. How far away is she from the other side?

12. Six cabins are about evenly spaced along the 3 km perimeter of Moon Lake. About how far apart are the cabins?

13. There were 325 yd of line on Ray's fishing reel. He cuts off 18 feet of line. How much line is left on the reel?

14. The family leaves Loon Lake at 9:00 A.M. and arrives home at 5:30 P.M. Mr. O'Hara drives the first half of the trip and then Mrs. O'Hara drives. About what time does Mrs. O'Hara start driving?

> **Strategy File**
>
> **Use these Strategies**
> Use More Than One Step
> Choose the Operation
> Logical Reasoning
> Interpret the Remainder
> Guess and Test

Use the map for problems 15 and 16.

15. About how long will it take to get from Loon Lake to Moon Lake at a rate of 50 miles per hour?

16. From Moon Lake, Joe wants to visit both Loon and Spoon lakes. What is the distance of the shortest route? the longest route?

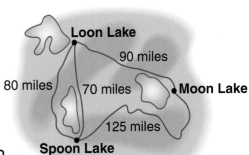

Write *in.*, *ft*, *yd*, or *mi* for the unit you would use to measure each.   *(See pp. 206–209.)*

1. distance across the county
2. width of a creek
3. width of a book
4. length of a pool

Add.   *(See pp. 210–211.)*

5.　3 ft 9 in.
　+ 4 ft 5 in.

6.　4 yd 1 ft
　+ 6 yd 1 ft

7.　9 yd 1 ft
　− 5 yd 1 ft

8.　7 ft 10 in.
　− 6 ft

Rename each unit.   *(See pp. 212–219.)*

9. 4 pt = _?_ c
10. 32 oz = _?_ lb
11. 6000 lb = _?_ T
12. 6 cm = _?_ mm
13. 4000 m = _?_ km
14. 300 mm = _?_ cm

Compare. Write <, =, or >.   *(See pp. 212–223.)*

15. 6 kg _?_ 6000 g
16. 16 fl oz _?_ 2 c
17. 60 mm _?_ 6 m
18. 400 mL _?_ 4 L
19. 16 qt _?_ 1 gal
20. 5000 lb _?_ 1 T
21. 100 cm _?_ 10 m
22. 5 dm _?_ 50 m
23. 50 kg _?_ 1 g

Choose the letter of the better estimate.   *(See pp. 224–225.)*

24. snow skiing weather
　　a. 25°F　　b. 25°C

25. a day for a picnic
　　a. 32°C　　b. 32°F

Write the elapsed time.   *(See pp. 226–229.)*

26. from 11:25 A.M. to 12:15 P.M.
27. from 11:30 P.M. to 7:15 A.M.

Rename each unit of time.   *(See pp. 228–229.)*

28. 2 y 17 w = about _?_ w
29. 42 w 27 d = _?_ d

(See Still More Practice, p. 466.)

Time Zones

The clocks show the time in four different time zones
of the United States when it is 12:00 noon Central time.

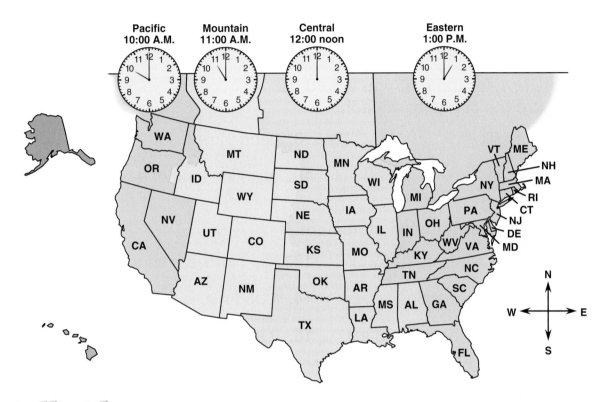

Problem Solving Use the time-zone map.

1. What time is it in California
   when it is 2:00 P.M. in Maine?

2. What time is it in Georgia
   when it is 10:00 A.M. in Iowa?

3. Emily lives in Arizona. She
   will call Nat in Ohio at
   6:30 P.M. Eastern time.
   What is that time in Arizona?

4. Niles will call Chad in Nevada
   at 1:45 P.M. Eastern time
   from New York. What time
   is that in Nevada?

5. It is 2:07 A.M. in Arkansas.
   What time is it in
   a. Texas?   **b.** Oregon?
   c. Vermont?   **d.** Montana?

6. A 6-hour flight to Utah leaves
   Delaware at 1:27 P.M. Eastern
   time. What is the time in
   Utah when the plane arrives?

Compare. Write <, =, or >.

1. 36 in. ___?___ 4 ft   **2.** 900 g ___?___ 9 kg   **3.** 5280 yd ___?___ 2 mi

4. 4 km ___?___ 400 m   **5.** 32 fl oz ___?___ 1 gal   **6.** 14 lb ___?___ 208 oz

Write *mL* or *L* for the unit you would use to measure the capacity of each.

7. glass of milk   **8.** pond

9. cup of soda   **10.** gasoline tank of a car

Write *true* or *false* for each statement.

11. You can ice skate at 30°C.   **12.** You can wear shorts at 90°F.

13. You need a coat at 8°C.   **14.** 11:30 P.M. is school time.

15. Lunch time is about 12:05 P.M.   **16.** It is usually dark at 10:30 A.M.

Problem Solving

Use a strategy you have learned.

17. Joe has saved $24 a week for the last 4 weeks. He wants to buy a ukelele that costs $89.95. Does he have enough money?

Tell About It

Explain how you solved the problem.

18. One basketball player is 2 m tall. Another player is 18 dm tall. Are they both the same height?

Performance Assessment

Find equivalent measures. Complete and extend each table by 3 columns.

19.

pt	1	2
c	2	?
fl oz	?	32

20.

gal	1	?	3
qt	4	?	12
pt	8	16	?

21.

cm	2	4	?
mm	20	?	60

Test Preparation

Choose the best answer.

1. Subtract.

$9.35 - $2.49

    a. $6.86   **b.** $6.96
    c. 686   **d.** 696

2. Which is ordered from the least amount to the greatest amount?

    a. 5800 mL, 58 L, 58 mL, 580 mL
    b. 58 mL, 58 L, 580 mL, 5800 mL
    c. 58 L, 5800 mL, 580 mL, 58 mL
    d. 58 mL, 580 mL, 5800 mL, 58 L

3. Where does the quotient begin?

7)5524

    a. thousands place
    b. hundreds place
    c. tens place
    d. ones place

4. Add.

6 ft 6 in.
+ 3 ft 8 in.

    a. 10 ft 2 in.
    b. 10 ft 14 in.
    c. 9 ft 2 in.
    d. not given

5. Which strategy could best help you find this sum mentally?

6
2
0
+ 4

    a. compensation
    b. make 10
    c. doubles
    d. doubles +1

6. Divide.

4)827

    a. 26 R3
    b. 206 R3
    c. 260 R3
    d. not given

7. Add.

$37.62 + $19.99

    a. $17.23   **b.** $28.73
    c. $47.61   **d.** $57.61

8. Use front-end estimation to estimate the difference.

7884
− 2101

    a. about 5000
    b. 5783
    c. about 9000
    b. 9985

9. Which number is divisible by 3?

    a. 12,955
    b. 19,540
    c. 52,671
    d. 63,959

10. Use the order of operations to solve.

$60 - 4 \times 5 + 30 \div 5$

    a. 46
    b. 62
    c. 286
    d. 392

11. The dividend is 705. The quotient is 141. What is the divisor?

    a. 9
    b. 7
    c. 5
    d. 2

12. Rename the unit of time.

5 weeks = __?__ days

    a. 5
    b. 7
    c. 30
    d. 35

13. Compare. Choose <, =, or >.

32 fl oz __?__ 2 qt

   a. <
   b. =
   c. >

14. Find the value of the variable.

$$7\overline{)m}^{\,6}$$

   a. $m = 6$
   b. $m = 7$
   c. $m = 36$
   d. $m = 42$

15. Which shows the use of compensation to solve?

678 + 97

   a. 97 + 678 = 775
   b. (600 + 78) + (90 + 7) = 775
   c. 675 + 100 = 775
   d. not given

16. Subtract.

652
− 445

   a. 207
   b. 217
   c. 1087
   d. 1097

17. A store manager orders 143 boxes of pens. There are 24 pens in each box. How many pens are there in all?

   a. 2332
   b. 2860
   c. 3322
   d. 3432

18. Compare. Choose <, =, or >.

4 dm __?__ 30 cm

   a. <
   b. =
   c. >

19. Multiply.

8000
×   3

   a. 240,000
   b. 24,000
   c. 2400
   d. 240

20. Which is the correct time?

21 minutes to 8 at night

   a. 7:21 P.M.
   b. 7:39 A.M.
   c. 8:21 P.M.
   d. 7:39 P.M.

21. Find the mean.

517, 524, 628, 424, 727

   a. 727
   b. 564
   c. 424
   d. 303

22. Write the rule. Complete the pattern.

30, 34, 32, 36, 34, 38, __?__

   a. Start at 30; subtract 2; 36
   b. Start at 30; add 4; 42
   c. Start at 30; subtract 4, add 2; 34
   d. Start at 30; add 4, subtract 2; 36

How can you use more than one step to solve the problem? Explain. Show all your work.

23. Scott gets on a scale and sees that he weighs 67 lb. When he gets on the scale holding his puppy, the scale reads 81 lb. When his sister, Sara, gets on the scale holding the puppy, the scale reads 73 lb. How much does Sara weigh?

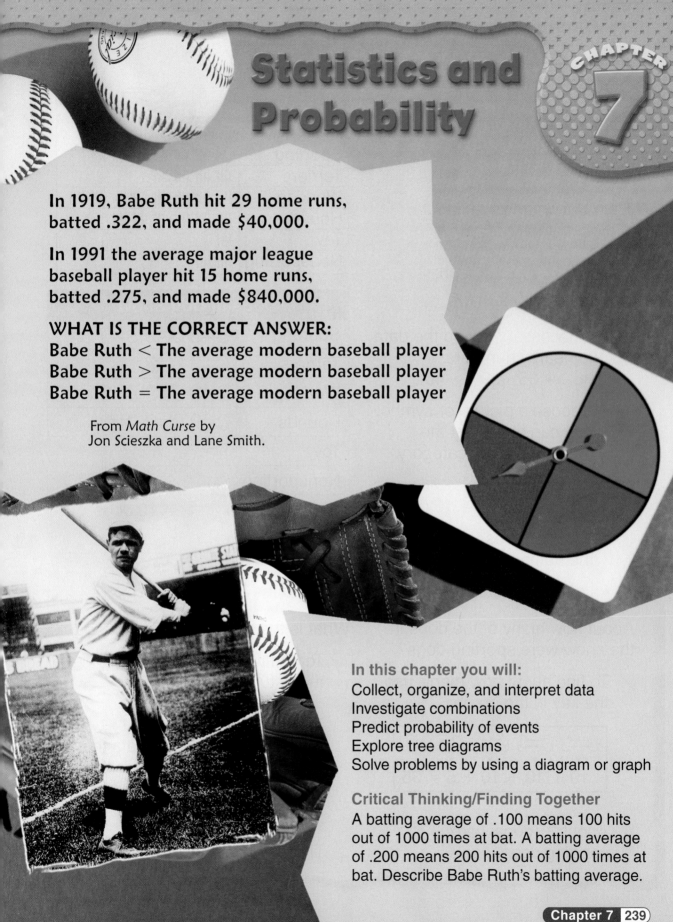

Statistics and Probability

CHAPTER 7

In 1919, Babe Ruth hit 29 home runs, batted .322, and made $40,000.

In 1991 the average major league baseball player hit 15 home runs, batted .275, and made $840,000.

WHAT IS THE CORRECT ANSWER:
Babe Ruth < The average modern baseball player
Babe Ruth > The average modern baseball player
Babe Ruth = The average modern baseball player

From *Math Curse* by
Jon Scieszka and Lane Smith.

In this chapter you will:
Collect, organize, and interpret data
Investigate combinations
Predict probability of events
Explore tree diagrams
Solve problems by using a diagram or graph

Critical Thinking/Finding Together
A batting average of .100 means 100 hits out of 1000 times at bat. A batting average of .200 means 200 hits out of 1000 times at bat. Describe Babe Ruth's batting average.

Update your skills. See pages 25 and 26.

Pictographs

Kai made a tally of the number of dogs in each category in the dog show.

Then Kai organized his data in a pictograph.

▶ To make a pictograph:

- List each category.

- If necessary, round the data to nearby numbers.
  $36 \longrightarrow 35 \quad 39 \longrightarrow 40$

- Choose a picture or symbol that can represent the number in each category.

- Choose a key.
  Let each ⊂⊐ = 10 dogs.

- Draw pictures to represent the number in each category.

- Label the pictograph. Write the title and the key.

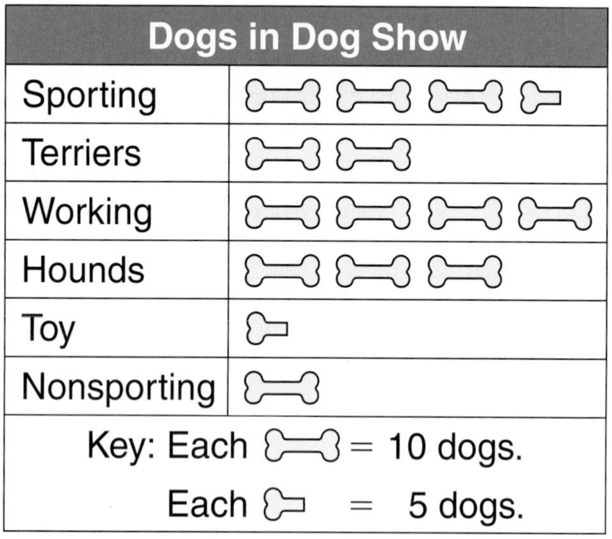

Dogs in Dog Show	
Category	**Tally**
Sporting	⅟⅟⅟ ⅟⅟⅟ ⅟⅟⅟ ⅟⅟⅟ ⅟⅟⅟ ⅟⅟⅟ ⅟⅟⅟ I
Terriers	⅟⅟⅟ ⅟⅟⅟ ⅟⅟⅟ ⅟⅟⅟
Working	⅟⅟⅟ ⅟⅟⅟ ⅟⅟⅟ ⅟⅟⅟ ⅟⅟⅟ ⅟⅟⅟ ⅟⅟⅟ IIII
Hounds	⅟⅟⅟ ⅟⅟⅟ ⅟⅟⅟ ⅟⅟⅟ ⅟⅟⅟ ⅟⅟⅟
Toy	⅟⅟⅟
Nonsporting	⅟⅟⅟ ⅟⅟⅟

Dogs in Dog Show	
Sporting	⊂⊐ ⊂⊐ ⊂⊐ ⊂
Terriers	⊂⊐ ⊂⊐
Working	⊂⊐ ⊂⊐ ⊂⊐ ⊂⊐
Hounds	⊂⊐ ⊂⊐ ⊂⊐
Toy	⊂
Nonsporting	⊂⊐

Key: Each ⊂⊐ = 10 dogs.
Each ⊂ = 5 dogs.

About how many of the dogs in the show were sporting dogs?

▶ To find about how many, use the key in the graph:

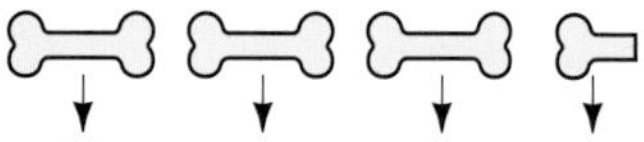

$$10 + 10 + 10 + 5 = 35$$

About 35 dogs were sporting dogs.

What is the median number of dogs?

▶ To find the median, arrange the actual data in order:

5, 10, 20, 30, 36, 39

The median of a set of data that has an even number of items is the average of the two middle numbers:

$20 + 30 = 50 \longrightarrow 50 \div 2 = 25$

The median is 25.

Problem Solving

The pictograph at the right shows the ice cream cones Ida sold at Ida's Ice Cream on a weekend in June.

Ice Cream Cones Sold	
Vanilla	🍦 🍦 🍦 🍦 🍦 🍦
Chocolate	🍦 🍦 🍦 🍦 🍦 🍦 🍦 🍦 🍦
Strawberry	🍦 🍦 🍦 🍦 🍦
Butter Pecan	🍦 🍦 🍦 🍦 🍦 🍦 🍦
Pistachio	🍦 🍦 🍦 🍦
Cherry	🍦 🍦
Key: Each 🍦 = 50 cones. Each 🍦 = 25 cones.	

Use the pictograph.

1. Which flavor was the most popular? How many cones of this flavor did Ida sell?

2. Ida sold 350 cones of one flavor. What flavor was this?

3. What was the median number of ice cream cones sold?

4. How many more cherry cones would Ida need to sell to make a total of 450 cones?

5. How many ice cream cones did Ida sell altogether?

Use each set of data to make a pictograph.

6.

Color of Car	Tally
Black	卌 卌 卌 卌 卌
Gray	卌 卌 卌 卌 卌 卌 卌
Blue	卌 卌
Red	卌 卌 卌
White	卌 卌 卌 卌 卌 卌
Green	卌

7.

Cats in the Cat Show	
Breed	**Number**
American Shorthair	275
Abyssinian	150
Siamese	200
Persian	250
Burmese	125
Manx	50
Rex	50
Himalayan	125

8. Write two questions for each of the pictographs you made.

Practice

DO YOU REMEMBER?

Write the number that is halfway between each pair.

9. 100; 200   **10.** 0; 1000   **11.** 0; 500   **12.** 50; 100   **13.** 1000; 3000

Update your skills. See pages 25 and 26.

Bar Graphs

Heidi found some information about the tallest tree of each species in the United States.

Heidi organized the data she found in a vertical bar graph.

Tallest Trees	
Tree	**Height in Feet**
White Pine	160
Black Cherry	115
White Ash	145
Red Spruce	130
Sugar Maple	135
Red Pine	115

▶ To make a vertical bar graph:

- Use the data from the table to choose an appropriate scale. Start at 0.

- Draw and label the scale on the vertical axis. (*Vertical* means "up and down.")

- Draw and label the horizontal axis. (*Horizontal* means "across.") List the name of each item.

- Draw vertical bars to represent the data.

- Title the graph.

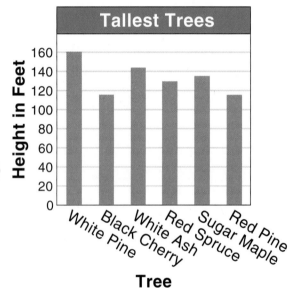

How can you use the bar graph to find how tall the tallest red spruce tree is in the United States?

▶ To find how tall, look at the bar labeled *Red Spruce*.

The top of the bar is *halfway* between 120 and 140.

The number that is *halfway* between 120 and 140 is 130.

So the tallest red spruce tree in the United States is 130 feet tall.

Use the bar graph on page 242.

1. Which tree is 160 feet tall? How much taller is it than the shortest tree?

2. Which two trees are the same height? How tall are they?

Use the table to complete the horizontal bar graph.
Draw bars across to represent the data.

Top Speeds	
Animal	**Miles Per Hour**
Cat	30
Cheetah	70
Elephant	25
Grizzly Bear	30

3.

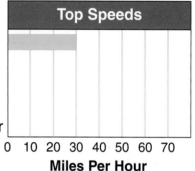
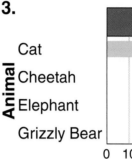

Use the completed horizontal bar graph to interpret the data.

4. Which animal has the shortest bar? Explain why.

5. Which two animals have bars of the same length? What does this mean?

Use the data from the pictograph on page 241 to make a bar graph. Use a scale of 100.

6. For which flavors were fewer than 300 cones sold?

7. Which graph is easier to use to answer exercise 6? Why?

CRITICAL THINKING

The bar graph shows cat food sales.

8. In what way is this graph misleading?

9. How might you fix the graph so it is not misleading?

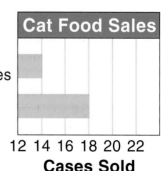

Update your skills. See page 26.

7-3

Line Graphs

A line graph shows how data changes over time.

The Movie Museum keeps track of how many visitors it has each year. About how many visitors did the museum have in 2000?

▶ To find how many:

- Find the year on the horizontal axis.

- Move up to the point.

- Read the number on the **vertical scale** at the left.

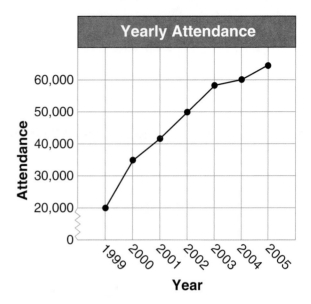

Yearly Attendance

A broken scale is used since the data starts at 20,000.

The point is *about* halfway between 30,000 and 40,000.

The number 35,000 is halfway between 30,000 and 40,000.

So the museum had *about* 35,000 visitors in 2000.

▶ A line graph shows when data increases and when it decreases.

Did attendance at the museum increase or decrease from 1999 to 2005?

The line slants up, so attendance increased.

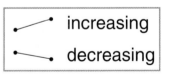

increasing

decreasing

▶ You can often use a line graph to predict how data will continue to change.

Is the museum likely to have fewer than or more than 64,000 visitors in 2006?

The number of visitors has increased since 1999. It is likely that the number of visitors will continue to increase.

Use the line graph on page 244 for exercises 1–6.

1. How many visitors did the museum have in:

   a. 1999   **b.** 2002   **c.** 2003   **d.** 2005

Problem Solving

2. In which years did the museum have more than 50,000 visitors?

3. In which years did the museum have fewer than 40,000 visitors?

4. Between which two years was there a difference of about 2000 visitors?

5. Between which two consecutive years was there a difference of about 15,000 visitors?

6. In 1998, was it likely that the museum had more or fewer than 20,000 visitors? Explain your answer.

Use the line graph at the right.

7. In which years were there the most 4th graders? How many students were there?

8. In which year were there 350 fourth graders?

9. Is the difference in the number of 4th graders from 2000 to 2005 greater or less than that between 1990 and 1995?

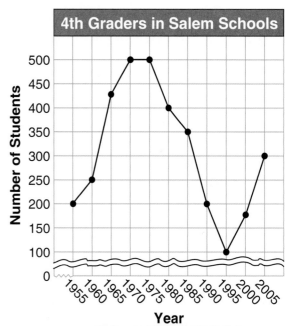

4th Graders in Salem Schools

Use the data in the table to make a line graph and a bar graph.

10. Is the temperature likely to be greater than or less than 27°F on Saturday?

11. Which graph was more helpful when answering exercise 10?

Daily Temperatures	
Sunday	28°F
Monday	33°F
Tuesday	35°F
Wednesday	32°F
Thursday	29°F
Friday	27°F

Surveys and Line Plots

Hours Spent Reading	
Hours	Tally
1	~~IIII~~ I
2	~~IIII~~
3	IIII
4	I
5	
6	
7	I

▶ A survey is a way to collect data by asking a question.

Kay took a survey of her class. She asked her classmates how many hours each day they spend reading.

Kay used the results of her survey to create a line plot.

▶ A line plot shows data by arranging Xs along a number line.

Kay found the range and the mode of the data on her line plot.

To find the range, subtract the least value in the data from the greatest value in the data: $7 - 1 = 6$

So, 6 is the range.

To find the mode, look for the number that has the greatest number of Xs.

1 is the mode.

Hours Spent Reading

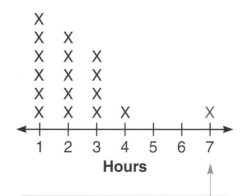

An outlier is a value far from the rest of the data.

Sometimes a set of data has no mode or *more than one* mode.

Use the line plot above to answer each question.

1. How many students spend 2 hours reading each day?

2. How many students read fewer than 2 hours each day?

3. How many more students spent 3 hours reading each day, rather than 4 hours reading each day?

4. How many students were surveyed?

Practice

The tally chart shows the results of Ken's survey about how many of his friends have 2, 3, or 4 cousins.

How Many Cousins?	
Cousins	**Tally**
2	⫴⫴ ‖
3	‖‖
4	⫴⫴ ‖

5. Use the survey results to make a line plot.

6. What is the range of the data?

7. What is the mode of the data?

8. How many friends did Ken survey? How do you know?

9. How many friends have 2 cousins?

10. How many fewer friends have 3 cousins than 4 cousins?

Take a survey.

Ask 6 friends what their favorite even number is from 2 to 10.
Tally the results in a tally chart. Then show the results on a line plot.

11. What is the range of the data?

12. What is the mode of the data?

13. Does your data have an outlier? If yes, what is it?

14. How many friends chose 4 as their favorite even number?

15. Compare your survey results with a friend's results.
Can you draw any conclusions from the data? Explain.

CHALLENGE

This graph is a stem-and-leaf plot. The stems are the tens digits and the leaves are the ones digits.

Dollars Saved	
Stem	**Leaves**
1	0 3 3 4 6 6 8
2	2 3 5 5 7 9
3	0 0 1 3 4 4 6

$2|3 = 23$

16. What is the greatest amount of money saved?

17. What is the least amount of money saved?

18. What is the range?

7-5

Circle Graphs

Community Chorus

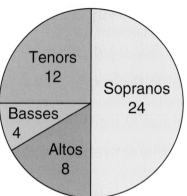

A circle graph shows data as parts of a whole.

This circle graph shows the number of singers who were selected for the Community Chorus.

Which group of singers makes up one half of the chorus?

▶ To find the group of singers that represents one half of the chorus, look for the part of the circle graph that is one half of the circle.

Sopranos is one half of the circle graph. Sopranos make up one half of the chorus.

Which two groups of singers make up one fourth of the chorus?

▶ To find the two groups of singers that represent one fourth of the chorus, find the two parts of the circle graph that together are one fourth of the circle.

Basses and *Altos* together are one fourth of the circle graph. Basses and altos make up one fourth of the chorus.

How many singers make up the Community Chorus?

▶ To find the number that is represented by the whole graph, add the numbers in the sections of the graph:

$$24 + 8 + 4 + 12 = 48$$

Forty-eight singers make up the Community Chorus.

Problem Solving

**Woodvale Students'
Favorite Fruits**

Use the circle graph at the right.

1. Which fruit is the favorite
   of 110 students?

2. How many students named
   melons as their favorite fruit?

3. Which two fruits together
   were the favorites of one
   fourth of the students?

4. Which fruit was chosen most
   by students? How many
   students chose that fruit?

5. Which fruit was chosen as the favorite
   by the fewest students? Which fruit was
   chosen by double that number of students?

6. Were apples more or less popular than bananas
   and pears together? by how many votes?

7. Which three fruits together were the favorites
   of one half of the students? How many
   students was this?

8. How many students are there in Woodvale?

Circle graph labels: Bananas 50, Apples 110, Melons 60, Cherries ▸ 30, Grapes 75, Oranges 125, Pears 50

DO YOU REMEMBER?

Write the heading that matches the information in each column.

9. ?	10. ?	11. ?	
• unit of length	• unit of capacity	• unit of mass	decimeter
			gram
• equivalent to	• about 20 drops	• about the mass	milliliter
10 cm	of water	of a paper clip	millimeter

Combinations

Didi's Diner
※ Early Bird Special ※
$7.95
Choose one from each column.

Main Dish	Side Dish	Vegetable
Roast Chicken	Potato	Broccoli
Grilled Fish	Rice	Spinach
		Carrots

Suppose you went to Didi's Diner. How many different ways could you order the Early Bird Special?

▶ To find how many different ways, draw a tree diagram. Then count the combinations.

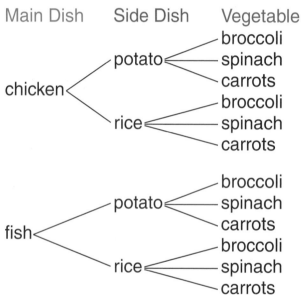

Main Dish	Side Dish	Vegetable	Combination
	potato	broccoli	chicken, potato, broccoli
		spinach	chicken, potato, spinach
chicken		carrots	chicken, potato, carrots
	rice	broccoli	chicken, rice, broccoli
		spinach	chicken, rice, spinach
		carrots	chicken, rice, carrots
	potato	broccoli	fish, potato, broccoli
		spinach	fish, potato, spinach
fish		carrots	fish, potato, carrots
	rice	broccoli	fish, rice, broccoli
		spinach	fish, rice, spinach
		carrots	fish, rice, carrots

You could order the Early Bird Special 12 different ways.

▶ You can also find the number of combinations by multiplying.

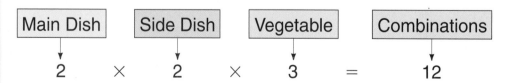

Main Dish	Side Dish	Vegetable	Combinations
2	× 2	× 3	= 12

There are 12 combinations.

Problem Solving **Draw a tree diagram to solve.**

1. One night, the Early Bird Special offered a choice of either ravioli or macaroni and cheese, with either string beans, peas, or cole slaw. How many different ways could you order?

2. Suppose Didi ran out of spinach. How many different ways could you order the Early Bird Special from the menu on page 250?

Draw a tree diagram or multiply to solve.

3. If you order Didi's Breakfast Special, you can choose either scrambled or poached eggs; orange, apple, or grapefruit juice; and whole wheat or white toast. How many combinations of eggs, juice, and toast could you order?

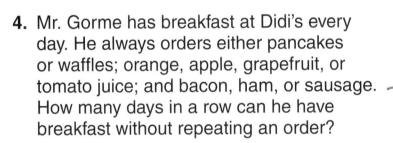

4. Mr. Gorme has breakfast at Didi's every day. He always orders either pancakes or waffles; orange, apple, grapefruit, or tomato juice; and bacon, ham, or sausage. How many days in a row can he have breakfast without repeating an order?

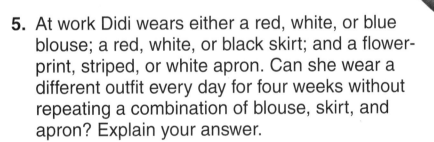

5. At work Didi wears either a red, white, or blue blouse; a red, white, or black skirt; and a flower-print, striped, or white apron. Can she wear a different outfit every day for four weeks without repeating a combination of blouse, skirt, and apron? Explain your answer.

TEST PREPARATION

6. Mr. Gorme drives a delivery van. He must wear a white, blue, or gray shirt with black, blue, or gray pants. Which shows the correct method to find how many combinations of shirt and pants he can wear?

A $3 + 3 = 6$ **B** $2 \times 3 = 6$ **C** $3 \times 3 = 9$ **D** $3 \times 3 \times 3 = 27$

Update your skills. See page 27.

Predict Probability

Probability is the chance that a given event will occur in an experiment.

Random experiments—like tossing a coin, rolling a number cube, spinning a spinner, and selecting an item from a set without looking—mean you do not know what the result, or outcome, of the experiment will be.

What is the probability of the spinner landing on red? on blue? on white?

▶ Two ways to describe probability are in words and as a fraction.

| Probability of an event | = | number of favorable outcomes / number of possible outcomes |

The spinner has 8 *equal* sections. Of the equal sections, 3 are red, 3 are blue, and 2 are white.

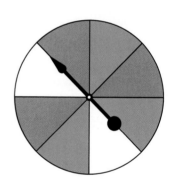

The probability of the spinner landing on

- red is 3 out of 8, or $\frac{3}{8}$.
- blue is 3 out of 8, or $\frac{3}{8}$.
- white is 2 out of 8, or $\frac{2}{8}$.
- not white is 6 out of 8, or $\frac{6}{8}$.

Practice

Use words and a fraction to write the probability of each spinner landing on yellow.

1.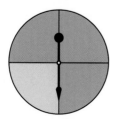

2.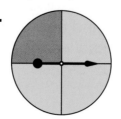

3.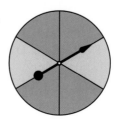

4.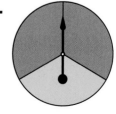

Problem Solving Use the spinner at the right.

5. Use words and fractions to describe the probability of the spinner landing on
   a. blue   **b.** red
   c. green   **d.** yellow

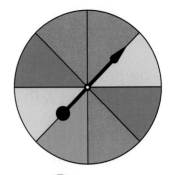

Use the set of marbles.

6. Use words to describe the probability that you would randomly pick a marble that is:
   a. green   **b.** not red
   c. orange   **d.** blue
   e. black   **f.** yellow

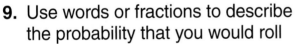

7. Would you be more or less likely to pick yellow than green? black than yellow? red than blue? yellow than orange? Explain why for each.

8. Would you be equally likely to pick black or green? orange or blue? orange or black? black or red? red or blue? Explain why for each.

Use the number cube at the right to find the probability of each event.

9. Use words or fractions to describe the probability that you would roll
   a. 3   **b.** 6
   c. 7   **d.** any number other than 4

CRITICAL THINKING

10. For each spinner, describe in words and fractions the probability of landing on each color.

     a.   **b.**   **c.**

7-8

Events and Outcomes

▶ The probability of an event is affected by whether the experiment is conducted with or without replacement.

Rae put these letters into a bag. She picked a letter at random ten times and **replaced** the letter in the bag each time. Then she graphed her results.

..Think.....................................
The probability of picking B on the 1st pick was 1 out of 3, or $\frac{1}{3}$.
....

What conclusion can Rae draw about the probability of picking B on the 11th pick?

Since Rae puts the card back in the bag after each pick, the contents of the bag do not change. So, the probability of picking B is the same for every pick.

The probability of picking B is always $\frac{1}{3}$.

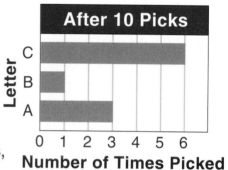

▶ As the number of possible outcomes changes, so does the probability of an event.

Ben put these digits into a bag. He picked a digit at random and **did not replace** it in the bag. He did this for each pick.

What is the probability of Ben picking 0 on the 3rd pick?

Ben's Picks	
Try	Digit
1st	8
2nd	6
3rd	

1st Try: 5 digits in the bag
Probability of picking 0: 1 out of 5; $\frac{1}{5}$

2nd Try: 4 digits in the bag
Probability of picking 0: 1 out of 4; $\frac{1}{4}$

3rd Try: 3 digits in the bag
Probability of picking 0: 1 out of 3; $\frac{1}{3}$

The probability of Ben picking 0 on the 3rd pick is 1 out of 3, or $\frac{1}{3}$.

Problem Solving

Use the information given on page 254.

1. Suppose Ben picks 4 on the 3rd try. What is the probability of his picking 0 on the 4th try?

> Remember: Ben's experiment was without replacement. Rae's experiment was with replacement.

2. If Ben picks 4 on the 3rd try, is it equally likely that he would pick 2 or 0 on the 4th try?

3. Suppose Rae started with A, B, C, D, E, and F. What would be the probability of her picking A on the 1st try? B on the 10th try? E on the 25th try? D on the 100th try?

Conduct a probability experiment.

4. Flip a coin 25 times. Record the outcomes in a tally chart.

5. Display the outcomes of your experiment in a bar graph.

6. What conclusion can you draw about the probability of the 26th flip landing on heads?

Suppose there are 2 red marbles and 2 black marbles in a bag.

7. What is the probability of picking red? black?

8. On the 1st try you pick a red marble and put it in your pocket. On the 2nd try, what is the probability of picking red? of picking black?

Write About It

Make two spinners like the ones at the right. Decide which player is EVEN and which is ODD. Spin both spinners at the same time and find the sum. If the sum is odd, ODD scores 1 point. If the sum is even, EVEN scores 1 point. The winner is the first player to score 10 points. Switch roles and play again.

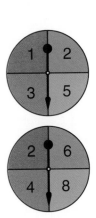

9. List all possible outcomes. Is this game fair or unfair? Explain your answer.

Problem-Solving Strategy:
Use a Diagram/Graph

Jeffrey created the graph at the right. Which of the following could be the title of the graph?

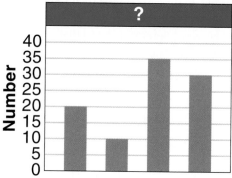

a. Number of students in the 4th grade

b. Number of cars washed at two fairs

c. Number of sides in a rectangle, a triangle, a square, and a pentagon

d. Number of pies sold by four bakeries

Read ▶ **Visualize yourself in the problem as you reread it. Focus on the facts and questions.**

Fact: The graph is a bar graph with four bars.

Question: Which choice is the best title for the graph?

Plan ▶ Study the graph and think about the data it shows.

Solve ▶ Compare each choice to the data in the graph.

- Choice A only refers to one grade. There are four bars in the graph, so Choice A is not correct.

- Choice B refers to two fairs. There are more than two bars in the graph, so Choice B is not correct.

- Choice C is about polygons with no more than 5 sides, which does not match the data in the graph. So Choice C is not correct.

- Choice D refers to four bakeries. There are four bars in the graph, so Choice D is the best choice.

Check ▶ Look again at the data in the graph. Is it reasonable that four bakeries would have sold the number of pies shown in the graph? Yes.

Use a diagram or graph to solve each problem.

1. This tree diagram shows the choices available at a frozen yogurt stand. What questions can you ask using this diagram?

Flavor	Serving	Extras
chocolate	cup	sprinkles / cookie crumbs
	cone	sprinkles / cookie crumbs

Read ▶ Visualize the problem as you reread it.

    Fact: Frozen yogurt can be ordered in different ways.

    Question: What questions can you ask using the diagram?

Plan ▶ Study the diagram and the data it shows. Think about the combinations and the kinds of questions you could ask.

▶ **Solve** ·········▶ **Check** ▶

2. Write a true statement about the data in the line graph.

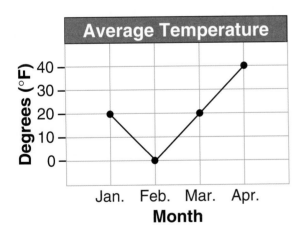

Average Temperature

3. A box of pushpins contains 64 pins in a variety of colors. What questions can you ask using the data in the circle graph?

Pushpin Colors

4. Michael exercised for 12 minutes. He did 20 sit-ups and 10 push-ups. What kind of graph would you use to display the data in the tally chart? Explain why.

Exercise Schedule	
sit-ups	卌 卌 卌 卌
push-ups	卌 卌

Problem-Solving Applications: Mixed Review

Solve each problem and explain the method you used.

1. There were 175 dogs at the Rosedale Pet Show. There were 50 small dogs and 85 medium-size dogs. The rest were large dogs. How many large dogs were in the show? Make a pictograph about the dogs in the pet show.

2. Use words to describe the probability that each type of dog won the Rosedale show.

Use the circle graph for problems 3–5.

3. Were more than half the pets dogs?

4. What fraction of the pets were birds and cats?

5. How many pets were entered in the Rosedale Pet Show?

Rosedale Pet Show

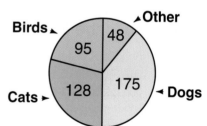

Use the bar graph for problems 6–9.

6. How many turtles were in the pet show?

7. Which type of pet had the fewest entries in the show?

8. How many more gerbils than mice were in the pet show?

9. How many fewer fish than rabbits were in the pet show?

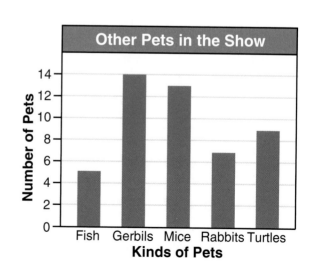

Choose a strategy from the list or use another strategy you know to solve each problem.

Strategy File

Use these Strategies
Use a Diagram/Graph
Use More Than One Step
Choose the Operation
Guess and Test
Logical Reasoning

10. Eight cats were finalists for best cat, and twice as many were semifinalists. There were twice as many quarterfinalists as semifinalists. How many cats were quarterfinalists?

11. Admission to the show was $3.75 for adults and $2.00 for children. Alana spent $13.25 for tickets. What tickets did she buy?

12. A dog-food supplier gave away 560 pounds of dog food. The food was bundled in 4-ounce packages. How many packages were given away?

13. A collie, a turtle, and a canary won the top three prizes. The disappointed collie buried the winner's ribbon. The first- and third-place pets both had four feet. Who won first prize?

Use the line graph for problems 14 and 15.

14. About how many people in all attended the pet show?

15. Between which two days was the increase in attendance the greatest?

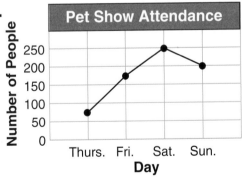

16. Write a problem using one of the graphs from pages 258 or 259. Have a classmate solve it.

Check Your Progress
Lessons 1–10

Use the tally chart to solve problems 1–3. *(See pp. 242–243, 246–247.)*

Meg surveyed her class about the number of pets each student owns.

1. Make a bar graph and a line plot from the data in the tally chart.

2. Find the range and mode of the data in the tally chart.

3. Which number is the outlier? Why?

Family Pets	
Pets	**Tally**
0	IIII
1	IIII III
2	IIII I
3	III
4	
5	
6	I

Use the line graph below to solve problems 4–6. *(See pp. 244–245.)*

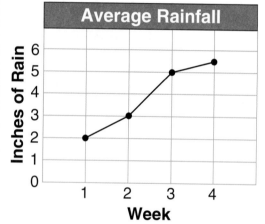

4. In which week was there the most rain?

5. How many inches of rain fell in week 2? week 3?

6. Is week 5 likely to have less than or more than $5\frac{1}{2}$ inches of rain? Explain.

Find the number of combinations. *(See pp. 250–251.)*

7. For lunch, Chad can buy either a tuna fish, chicken, or ham sandwich on either rye, whole-grain, or wheat bread. How many ways can he choose to buy his sandwich?

Use the spinner. *(See pp. 252–253.)*

8. Use words and fractions to write the probability that the spinner will land on

   a. red

   b. blue

   c. yellow

   d. white

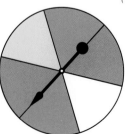

(See Still More Practice, p. 467.)

Double Bar Graphs

A double bar graph is used to compare two similar sets of data. Each set of data is graphed separately, but on the same grid. The *key* identifies the sets of data.

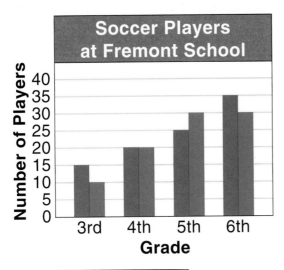

Key: Boys
Girls

The purple bars in the graph stand for the boys. The blue bars stand for the girls.

Problem Solving Use the double bar graph above.

1. How many 5th grade boys play soccer?

2. How many girls play soccer at Fremont School?

3. How many more 6th grade boys play soccer than 6th grade girls?

4. How many fewer 3rd grade boys play soccer than 5th grade girls?

5. In which grade do the same number of boys and girls play soccer?

6. How many soccer players are there at Fremont School?

7. How many more 5th graders play soccer than 3rd graders?

8. Is it likely that more than 35 7th grade boys play soccer?

Number of Students

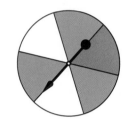

Use the circle graph at the right.

1. What fraction of students drank

   a. milk?   **b.** juice?   **c.** soda and water?

2. Did fewer students drink milk than water and soda? Explain.

Use the spinner.

3. Use words and fractions to describe the probability of the spinner landing on

   a. white   **b.** red   **c.** blue

Problem Solving

Use a strategy you have learned.

4. How much weight did the puppy gain from March to May?

5. What other questions can you ask using the line graph?

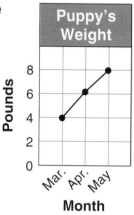

Puppy's Weight

Pounds / Month

Tell About It

Use the line graph from problem 4.

6. Is the puppy's weight likely to be more than 8 pounds in June? Explain why or why not.

Performance Assessment

Draw and color a spinner on which

7. it would be equally likely to land on red or yellow.

8. the probability of landing on red is 1 out of 4, or $\frac{1}{4}$.

Test Preparation

Choose the best answer.

1. What is the value of the underlined digit in <u>6</u>8,325,784?

a. 6 ten millions   b. 6 billions
c. 6 thousands   d. 6 millions

2. Estimate the sum by rounding.

$50.24
3.69
+12.28

a. $54.00
b. $55.00
c. $66.00
d. $70.00

3. 7846 + 685

a. 7531
b. 8521
c. 14,696
d. not given

4. The product is 8. One factor is 1. What is the other factor?

a. 8
b. 6
c. 4
d. 0

5. Find the value of the variable.

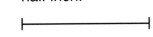

$$n)\overline{56} \quad \frac{8}{}$$

a. 6
b. 7
c. 8
d. 9

6. Find the length to the nearest half inch.

a. $1\frac{1}{2}$ in.   b. $2\frac{1}{2}$ in.

c. 3 in.   d. $3\frac{1}{2}$ in.

7. Round 874,376 to the nearest hundred thousand.

a. 800,000
b. 900,000
c. 880,000
d. 870,000

8. Subtract.

$5.98
− 0.54

a. $5.34
b. $5.42
c. $5.44
d. not given

9. 4000 − 3951

a. 49
b. 149
c. 1049
d. not given

10. Use front-end digits to estimate.

9 × 94

a. 100
b. 700
c. 810
d. 1500

11. What is the next number in the pattern?

27, 9, 3, ?

a. 0
b. 1
c. 3
d. 81

12. Find the length to the nearest centimeter.

a. 7 cm   b. 8 cm   c. 67 cm   d. 80 cm

13. What is the probability of the spinner landing on blue?

a. 1 out of 5; $\frac{1}{5}$ b. 2 out of 5; $\frac{2}{5}$

c. 1 out of 2; $\frac{1}{2}$ d. 3 out of 5; $\frac{3}{5}$

14. How much change will you receive?

Cost: $14.22
Amount given: $20.00

  a. $5.88
  b. $6.78
  c. $6.88
  d. $5.78

19. Estimate the product by rounding.

$$\begin{array}{r} \$7.95 \\ \times \quad 6 \\ \hline \end{array}$$

  a. $42.00
  b. $48.00
  c. $47.00
  d. $43.00

---

15. $23{,}956 - 15{,}987$

  a. 6968   **b.** 7979
  c. 7969   **d.** 39,943

20. $36{,}083 + 24{,}167$

  a. 11,919   **b.** 61,250
  c. 60,250   **d.** 60,240

---

16. Nick puts 42 buns in tins. Each tin holds 8 buns. How many tins can he fill, with how many buns left over?

  a. 5 tins, 2 buns   **b.** 4 tins, 2 buns
  c. 5 tins, 4 buns   **d.** 4 tins, 4 buns

21. Amy has 5 fish. She gives 4 to Meg. Then she buys 6 new fish. How many fish does Amy have now?

  a. 7   **b.** 8
  c. 9   **d.** 10

---

17. 8×3 thousands

  a. 27,000
  b. 24,000
  c. 8,000
  d. 3,000

22. $72 \div 4$

  a. 76
  b. 68
  c. 18
  d. 12

---

18. $3 \, c = \underline{}$ fl oz

  a. 8
  b. 12
  c. 16
  d. 24

23.

$$\begin{array}{r} 9 \text{ ft } 7 \text{ in.} \\ + \, 4 \text{ ft } 6 \text{ in.} \\ \hline \end{array}$$

  a. 12 ft 13 in.
  b. 13 ft 1 in.
  c. 14 ft 1 in.
  d. 13 ft 11 in.

---

24. Which 2 vegetables together were the favorites of one half of the people who voted for their favorite vegetable?

  a. celery and tomato
  b. cucumber and carrot
  c. tomato and cucumber
  d. celery and carrot

Favorite Vegetables

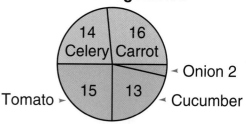

Tell About It — Explain how you solved the problem. Show all your work.

25. The students at Spellman School voted for their favorite color. The results are in the table at the right.

Using the data in the table, what color should the school's new baseball uniforms be?

	6th Grade	7th Grade	8th Grade
Green	25	40	37
Purple	38	35	41
Yellow	32	27	26

Fraction Concepts

CHAPTER 8

Dividing

Here is an apple, ripe and red
    On one side; on the other green.
And I must cut it with a knife
    Across or in between.

And if I cut it in between,
    And give the best (as Mother said)
To you, then I must keep the green,
    And you will have the red.

But Mother says that green is tough
    Unless it comes in applesauce.
You *know* what? I've been sick enough:
    I'll cut it straight across.

David McCord

In this chapter you will:

Explore fractional parts of regions and sets
Learn about equivalent fractions and
    mixed numbers
Identify fractions on a number line
Estimate, compare, and order fractions
Solve problems using logical reasoning

Critical Thinking/ Finding Together

Draw a picture to show what the apple would
look like if it was cut straight across. Why do
you think the boy decided to cut the apple
straight across?

Write Fractions

What fractional part of the whole is yellow? What fractional part of the set is yellow?

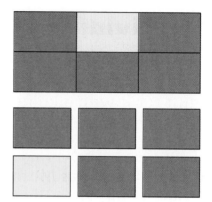

Both the whole and the set have 6 equal parts. One of the equal parts of the whole is yellow. One of the equal parts of the set is yellow.

$\frac{1}{6}$ of the whole is yellow. $\frac{1}{6}$ of the set is yellow.

| The numerator names the number of equal parts. | $\frac{1}{6}$ | The denominator names the total number of equal parts in the whole or the set. |

Write: $\frac{1}{6}$ ← The fraction bar means "divided by."

Read: one sixth
      one divided by six
      one out of six

What fractional part of the whole or of the set is purple?

$\frac{5}{6}$ of the whole is purple. $\frac{5}{6}$ of the set is purple.

numerator ⟶ 5 ← number of equal parts that are purple
denominator ⟶ 6 ← total number of equal parts in the whole or the set

Write: $\frac{5}{6}$

Read: five sixths
      five divided by six
      five out of six

Write each as a fraction. Then circle the denominator.

1. one fourth

2. two tenths

3. one half

4. four fifths

5. three fourths

6. five eighths

7. five sixths

8. three sevenths

9. one twelfth

Write each as a fraction. Then circle the numerator.

10. seven tenths

11. three fifths

12. one eighth

13. one third

14. two sixths

15. nine twelfths

16. seven eighths

17. one ninth

18. four hundredths

Write each fraction in words three different ways. Then draw a picture to show each.

19. $\frac{1}{10}$
20. $\frac{2}{5}$
21. $\frac{1}{6}$
22. $\frac{3}{8}$
23. $\frac{2}{7}$
24. $\frac{5}{12}$

Draw a picture to justify your answer.

25. Michelle designed a banner that was $\frac{7}{8}$ purple. Write this fraction in words.

26. Louis trimmed three tenths of a group of posters in red. Write this as a fraction.

Color fraction strips to show each fraction. Then write about how you decided which strips to use.

27. $\frac{2}{5}$
28. $\frac{1}{2}$
29. $\frac{1}{10}$

30. $\frac{3}{8}$
31. $\frac{5}{6}$
32. $\frac{11}{12}$

8-2

Update your skills. See page 13.

Fractions On a Number Line

A number line can help to show and order whole numbers.

- On a number line the *lesser* of two numbers is to the *left* of the greater number.
- The *greater* of two numbers is to the *right* of the lesser number.

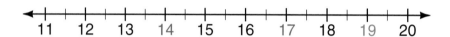

14 is to the *left* of 17.   19 is to the *right* of 17.
So, 14 < 17   So, 19 > 17

Like whole numbers, fractions can be shown on a number line. This number line shows fifths.

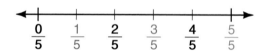

As with whole numbers, the *lesser* of two fractions is to the *left* of the greater fraction. The *greater* of two fractions is to the *right* of the lesser fraction.

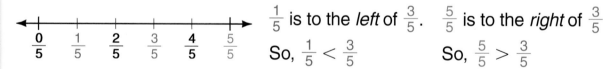

$\frac{1}{5}$ is to the *left* of $\frac{3}{5}$. $\frac{5}{5}$ is to the *right* of $\frac{3}{5}$

So, $\frac{1}{5} < \frac{3}{5}$ So, $\frac{5}{5} > \frac{3}{5}$

Practice

Write the fraction that completes each number line.

1.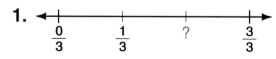

2.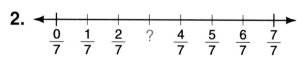

3.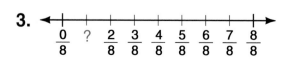

4.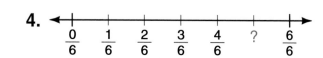

Name the fraction represented by the letter A.

5.

$$\frac{0}{5} \quad \frac{1}{5} \quad \frac{2}{5} \quad \frac{3}{5} \quad A \quad \frac{5}{5}$$

6.

$$\frac{0}{8} \quad \frac{1}{8} \quad \frac{2}{8} \quad \frac{3}{8} \quad \frac{4}{8} \quad A \quad \frac{6}{8} \quad \frac{7}{8} \quad \frac{8}{8}$$

7.

$$\frac{0}{6} \quad A \quad \frac{2}{6} \quad \frac{3}{6} \quad \frac{4}{6} \quad \frac{5}{6} \quad \frac{6}{6}$$

8.

$$\frac{0}{10} \quad \frac{1}{10} \quad \frac{2}{10} \quad \frac{3}{10} \quad \frac{4}{10} \quad \frac{5}{10} \quad \frac{6}{10} \quad A \quad \frac{8}{10} \quad \frac{9}{10} \quad \frac{10}{10}$$

Drawing Number Lines for Fractions

Show $\frac{3}{4}$ on a number line.

- Draw a number line from 0 to 1.

- Divide the number line into 4 equal parts.

- Label the third equal part $\frac{3}{4}$.

Think

$\frac{3}{4}$ is less than 1.

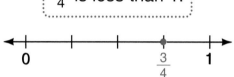

$$0 \qquad\qquad\qquad \frac{3}{4} \qquad 1$$

Show each fraction on a number line.

9. $\frac{1}{3}$ **10.** $\frac{4}{5}$ **11.** $\frac{6}{6}$ **12.** $\frac{5}{8}$ **13.** $\frac{7}{10}$

Name the fraction for letter B.

14.

B

15.

B

16.

B

17.

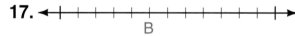

B

CHALLENGE

18. The ant is walking toward the apple. What fraction of the distance has it gone?

19. The ladybug is crawling toward the leaf. What fraction of the distance has it gone?

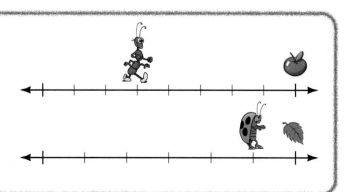

Estimate Fractions

▶ You can use $\frac{1}{2}$ to estimate a fraction of a region.

About what fraction of each region is blue?

about $\frac{1}{2}$ blue

Think
more than $\frac{1}{2}$

about $\frac{3}{4}$ blue

Think
less than $\frac{1}{2}$

about $\frac{1}{3}$ blue

▶ You can use models or a number line to tell whether a fraction is closer to 0, closer to $\frac{1}{2}$, or closer to 1.

Is each of these fractions closer to 0, to $\frac{1}{2}$, or to 1?

$\frac{8}{10}$  $\frac{2}{10}$ $\frac{6}{10}$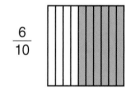

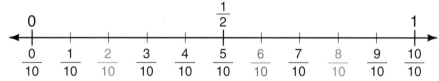

Think
$\frac{1}{2}$ is halfway between 0 and 1.

$\frac{2}{10}$ is between 0 and $\frac{1}{2}$. It is closer to 0.

$\frac{6}{10}$ is between $\frac{1}{2}$ and 1. It is closer to $\frac{1}{2}$.

$\frac{8}{10}$ is between $\frac{1}{2}$ and 1. It is closer to 1.

Write *more than half* or *less than half* to tell about what fraction of each region is shaded.

1.

2.

3.

4.

5.

6.

7.

8.

Use the number lines. Write whether each fraction is *closer to 0, closer to $\frac{1}{2}$, or closer to 1.*

9. $\frac{3}{8}$ 10. $\frac{7}{8}$ 11. $\frac{1}{8}$ 12. $\frac{5}{8}$

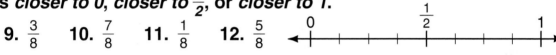

13. $\frac{10}{12}$ 14. $\frac{5}{12}$ 15. $\frac{11}{12}$ 16. $\frac{7}{12}$

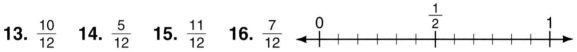

17. $\frac{2}{9}$ 18. $\frac{4}{9}$ 19. $\frac{7}{9}$ 20. $\frac{1}{9}$

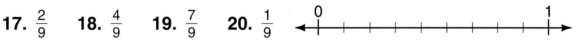

Write whether each fraction is *closer to 0, closer to $\frac{1}{2}$, or closer to 1.* You may use models or number lines.

21. $\frac{3}{10}$ 22. $\frac{1}{8}$ 23. $\frac{4}{5}$ 24. $\frac{3}{7}$ 25. $\frac{1}{12}$ 26. $\frac{2}{3}$

About where on each number line is the arrow pointing?

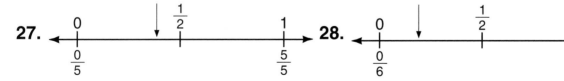

27.   28.

TEST PREPARATION

29. Which fraction is closer to 0?

    A $\frac{5}{6}$ B $\frac{2}{6}$ C $\frac{3}{6}$ D $\frac{4}{6}$

30. Which fraction is closer to 1?

    F $\frac{6}{7}$ G $\frac{1}{7}$ H $\frac{3}{7}$ J $\frac{5}{7}$

8-4

Equivalent Fractions

Equivalent fractions name the *same part* of a region or a set.

Equivalent Fraction Table

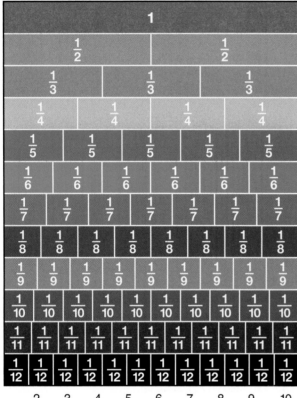

| | | | | | | | | | | | | 1 whole |
| 1 = $\frac{2}{2}$ = $\frac{3}{3}$ = $\frac{4}{4}$ = $\frac{5}{5}$ = $\frac{6}{6}$ = $\frac{7}{7}$ = $\frac{8}{8}$ = $\frac{9}{9}$ = $\frac{10}{10}$ = $\frac{11}{11}$ = $\frac{12}{12}$ | | | | | | | | | | | | |

$$1 = \frac{2}{2} = \frac{3}{3} = \frac{4}{4} = \frac{5}{5} = \frac{6}{6} = \frac{7}{7} = \frac{8}{8} = \frac{9}{9} = \frac{10}{10} = \frac{11}{11} = \frac{12}{12}$$

▶ Use the equivalent fraction table to find the equivalent fraction.

$$\frac{3}{4} = \frac{n}{8}$$

> Remember: A variable stands for an unknown number.

Notice that $\frac{3}{4} = \frac{6}{8}$.

$\frac{3}{4}$ and $\frac{6}{8}$ are equivalent fractions.

They name the same part.

**Write the equivalent fraction. Use the equivalent
fraction table on page 272.**

1. $\frac{1}{2} = \frac{n}{6}$

2. $\frac{1}{4} = \frac{a}{8}$

3. $\frac{2}{5} = \frac{x}{10}$

4. $\frac{4}{8} = \frac{b}{4}$

5. $\frac{2}{3} = \frac{m}{12}$

6. $\frac{5}{10} = \frac{s}{2}$

7. $\frac{3}{12} = \frac{v}{4}$

8. $\frac{2}{3} = \frac{t}{9}$

9. $\frac{1}{3} = \frac{d}{6}$

10. $\frac{2}{4} = \frac{c}{8}$

11. $\frac{2}{3} = \frac{r}{6}$

12. $\frac{1}{5} = \frac{w}{10}$

13. $\frac{1}{3} = \frac{y}{12}$

14. $\frac{2}{6} = \frac{f}{12}$

15. $\frac{3}{4} = \frac{k}{8}$

16. $\frac{3}{5} = \frac{y}{10}$

17. $\frac{1}{2} = \frac{f}{10}$

18. $\frac{3}{4} = \frac{z}{12}$

19. $\frac{2}{2} = \frac{e}{8}$

20. $\frac{1}{3} = \frac{h}{9}$

**Does each pair show equivalent fractions? Explain why or why not.
Then write the equivalent fractions.**

21.

22.

23.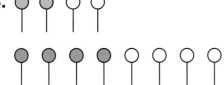

24.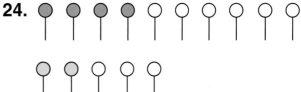

Use fraction strips to show your work.

25. How many fifths are equal
to four tenths?

26. How many twelfths are equal
to five sixths?

CRITICAL THINKING —— *Algebra*

27. Use fraction strips to write all
the fractions from $\frac{1}{2}$ to $\frac{12}{12}$:
a. that are equal to $\frac{1}{2}$.
b. that are equal to 1.

28. Look at fifths and tenths. Then
look at sixths and twelfths.
Name a fraction that is
equivalent to $\frac{2}{7}$.

Write Equivalent Fractions

Suppose you did not have an equivalent fraction table. How would you find equivalent fractions?

$\frac{1}{4}$		$\frac{1}{4}$		$\frac{1}{4}$		$\frac{1}{4}$	
$\frac{1}{8}$	$\frac{1}{8}$	$\frac{1}{8}$	$\frac{1}{8}$	$\frac{1}{8}$	$\frac{1}{8}$	$\frac{1}{8}$	$\frac{1}{8}$

To find equivalent fractions, multiply the numerator and the denominator by the same number.

$$\frac{3}{4} = \frac{n}{8}$$

Think $4 \times 2 = 8$

$$\frac{3 \times 2}{4 \times 2} = \frac{6}{8}$$

So $\frac{3}{4} = \frac{6}{8}$. ← These are equivalent fractions.

Study these examples.

$$\frac{1}{3} = \frac{a}{9}$$

Think $3 \times 3 = 9$

$$\frac{1 \times 3}{3 \times 3} = \frac{3}{9}$$

So $\frac{1}{3} = \frac{3}{9}$.

$$\frac{3}{5} = \frac{12}{n}$$

Think $3 \times 4 = 12$

$$\frac{3 \times 4}{5 \times 4} = \frac{12}{20}$$

So $\frac{3}{5} = \frac{12}{20}$.

Write the equivalent fraction.

1. $\frac{1 \times 2}{3 \times 2} = \frac{?}{?}$

2. $\frac{5 \times 3}{6 \times 3} = \frac{?}{?}$

3. $\frac{2 \times 2}{5 \times 2} = \frac{?}{?}$

4. $\frac{3 \times 4}{4 \times 4} = \frac{?}{?}$

5. $\frac{1 \times 3}{8 \times 3} = \frac{?}{?}$

6. $\frac{3 \times 2}{10 \times 2} = \frac{?}{?}$

7. $\frac{1 \times 3}{7 \times ?} = \frac{3}{?}$

8. $\frac{3 \times ?}{8 \times 2} = \frac{?}{?}$

9. $\frac{2 \times 4}{3 \times ?} = \frac{?}{?}$

10. $\frac{1 \times 5}{4 \times ?} = \frac{?}{?}$

11. $\frac{5 \times ?}{7 \times 2} = \frac{?}{?}$

12. $\frac{2 \times ?}{9 \times 2} = \frac{?}{?}$

Find an equivalent fraction.

13. $\dfrac{3}{4} = \dfrac{n}{12}$

14. $\dfrac{4}{5} = \dfrac{x}{10}$

15. $\dfrac{1}{12} = \dfrac{a}{36}$

16. $\dfrac{1}{2} = \dfrac{b}{10}$

17. $\dfrac{5}{6} = \dfrac{c}{12}$

18. $\dfrac{3}{8} = \dfrac{s}{24}$

19. $\dfrac{5}{9} = \dfrac{t}{27}$

20. $\dfrac{1}{4} = \dfrac{w}{16}$

21. $\dfrac{3}{7} = \dfrac{d}{14}$

22. $\dfrac{2}{5} = \dfrac{r}{25}$

23. $\dfrac{2}{3} = \dfrac{f}{18}$

24. $\dfrac{6}{10} = \dfrac{m}{20}$

25. $\dfrac{1}{6} = \dfrac{z}{30}$

26. $\dfrac{5}{8} = \dfrac{f}{40}$

27. $\dfrac{2}{4} = \dfrac{y}{12}$

Find the missing numerator or denominator.

28. $\dfrac{3}{5} = \dfrac{n}{20}$

29. $\dfrac{a}{7} = \dfrac{12}{21}$

30. $\dfrac{2}{6} = \dfrac{8}{x}$

31. $\dfrac{6}{b} = \dfrac{42}{63}$

32. $\dfrac{d}{11} = \dfrac{4}{22}$

33. $\dfrac{7}{y} = \dfrac{28}{40}$

34. $\dfrac{4}{4} = \dfrac{12}{f}$

35. $\dfrac{s}{9} = \dfrac{12}{36}$

36. $\dfrac{5}{m} = \dfrac{15}{18}$

37. $\dfrac{6}{8} = \dfrac{36}{p}$

38. $\dfrac{r}{9} = \dfrac{21}{27}$

39. $\dfrac{4}{v} = \dfrac{48}{96}$

Write two equivalent fractions for each.

40. $\dfrac{2}{3}$

41. $\dfrac{5}{8}$

42. $\dfrac{1}{11}$

43. $\dfrac{4}{5}$

44. $\dfrac{3}{15}$

45. $\dfrac{5}{6}$

46. $\dfrac{6}{7}$

47. $\dfrac{7}{9}$

48. $\dfrac{6}{12}$

49. $\dfrac{2}{16}$

50. $\dfrac{4}{25}$

51. $\dfrac{2}{18}$

52. $\dfrac{1}{6}$

53. $\dfrac{3}{10}$

54. $\dfrac{3}{4}$

55. $\dfrac{7}{12}$

56. $\dfrac{2}{2}$

57. $\dfrac{8}{9}$

DO YOU REMEMBER? — Algebra

Find the product or the missing factor.

58.
$$\begin{array}{r} n \\ \times\ 1 \\ \hline 48 \end{array}$$

59.
$$\begin{array}{r} 24 \\ \times\ 2 \\ \hline a \end{array}$$

60.
$$\begin{array}{r} 16 \\ \times\ c \\ \hline 48 \end{array}$$

61.
$$\begin{array}{r} r \\ \times\ 4 \\ \hline 48 \end{array}$$

62.
$$\begin{array}{r} 8 \\ \times 6 \\ \hline y \end{array}$$

63. $6 \times n = 24$

64. $b \times 3 = 24$

65. $2 \times a = 24$

Factors

Any whole number can be represented by
one or more rectangles.

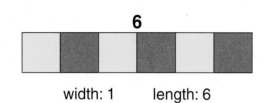

6

width: 1   length: 6

or

6

width: 2   length: 3

Materials: tiles, paper, pencil

Use tiles to find as many different rectangles
as you can for 24. Record each width and length.

	Width	Length
1.	1	24
2.	2	?

1. How many different rectangles did you find?

The widths and lengths stand for the factors of 24.

2. What are all the factors of 24?

Now find as many different rectangles as you can
for 18. Record each width and length.

3. How many different rectangles did you find?

4. What are all the factors of 18?

5. Did 18 and 24 have any rectangles and
factors that were the same? Which ones?

Common factors are numbers that are factors
of two or more products.

6. What are all the common factors
of 24 and 18?

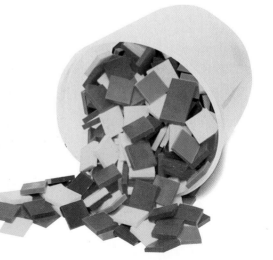

The greatest common factor (GCF) of two or more products is the greatest number that is a factor of those products.

7. What is the greatest common factor (GCF) of 24 and 18?

You can also use multiplication sentences to find all the factors of a number.

$1 \times 24 = 24$
$2 \times 12 = 24$ Factors of 24: 1, 2, 3, 4, 6, 8, 12, and 24
$3 \times 8 = 24$
$4 \times 6 = 24$

8. How would you use multiplication sentences to find all the common factors of two or more numbers?

List all the common factors of each set of numbers. Then circle the GCF.

9. 8 and 12   **10.** 6 and 15   **11.** 9 and 21   **12.** 10 and 30

13. 12 and 16   **14.** 18 and 30   **15.** 25 and 35   **16.** 36 and 42

17. 8, 20, and 40   **18.** 10, 25, and 45   **19.** 18, 48, and 54

Communicate

20. A prime number is greater than 1 and has exactly two factors, itself and 1. Composite numbers have more than two factors. Of the common factors you identified in exercises 17 through 19 above, which are prime numbers and which are composite numbers?

21. Look at the set of numbers at the right. Can the GCF be greater than 12? Explain why or why not. Then find the GCF.

12			42
		30	
	18		48
24			36

Fractions: Lowest Terms

▶ The terms of a fraction are its numerator and its denominator. A fraction is in lowest terms, or simplest form, when its numerator and denominator have no common factor other than 1.

$\frac{2}{5}$ is in lowest terms.

Factors of 2: 1, 2
Factors of 5: 1, 5
Common factor of 2 and 5: 1

$\frac{6}{10}$ is *not* in lowest terms.

Factors of 6: 1, 2, 3, 6
Factors of 10: 1, 2, 5, 10
Common factors of 6 and 10: 1, 2

▶ To rename a fraction as an equivalent fraction in lowest terms or simplest form, divide the numerator and the denominator by their greatest common factor.

Write $\frac{6}{10}$ in lowest terms.

Factors of 6: 1, 2, 3, 6
Factors of 10: 1, 2, 5, 10

$\frac{6 \div 2}{10 \div 2} = \frac{3}{5}$

. Think
The GCF of 6 and 10 is 2.

So $\frac{6}{10}$ in lowest terms is $\frac{3}{5}$.

Factors of 3: 1, 6
Factors of 5: 1, 5

Complete to find the simplest form of each fraction.

1. $\frac{4 \div 4}{8 \div 4} = \frac{?}{?}$

2. $\frac{3 \div 3}{9 \div 3} = \frac{?}{?}$

3. $\frac{6 \div 2}{8 \div 2} = \frac{?}{?}$

4. $\frac{8 \div 2}{10 \div 2} = \frac{?}{?}$

5. $\frac{9 \div ?}{12 \div 3} = \frac{?}{?}$

6. $\frac{14 \div 7}{21 \div ?} = \frac{?}{?}$

7. $\frac{10 \div ?}{25 \div ?} = \frac{?}{5}$

8. $\frac{12 \div ?}{42 \div ?} = \frac{?}{7}$

9. $\frac{16 \div ?}{24 \div ?} = \frac{2}{?}$

Is each fraction in simplest form? Write *yes* or *no*. Explain.

10. $\frac{4}{7}$ 11. $\frac{6}{9}$ 12. $\frac{11}{12}$ 13. $\frac{7}{10}$ 14. $\frac{2}{10}$ 15. $\frac{8}{12}$

Write each fraction in simplest form.

16. $\frac{2}{6}$ 17. $\frac{4}{24}$ 18. $\frac{9}{18}$ 19. $\frac{3}{12}$ 20. $\frac{2}{4}$ 21. $\frac{12}{20}$

22. $\frac{6}{18}$ 23. $\frac{10}{20}$ 24. $\frac{8}{24}$ 25. $\frac{9}{15}$ 26. $\frac{15}{20}$ 27. $\frac{4}{10}$

28. $\frac{6}{24}$ 29. $\frac{8}{14}$ 30. $\frac{6}{15}$ 31. $\frac{10}{12}$ 32. $\frac{7}{21}$ 33. $\frac{5}{15}$

34. $\frac{8}{18}$ 35. $\frac{9}{27}$ 36. $\frac{15}{18}$ 37. $\frac{10}{15}$ 38. $\frac{9}{15}$ 39. $\frac{12}{18}$

Problem Solving Express each answer in simplest form.

40. The chorus sang 12 songs at open house. Four of the songs were folk songs. What fractional part of the songs were folk songs?

41. Of 35 paintings on display in the school lobby, 7 were done in watercolors. What fractional part of the paintings were watercolors?

42. Jamie's parents looked at his notebook. Ten of the 40 pages were filled with math problems. Write this as a fraction in simplest form.

43. Glenda cut out the 26 letters of the alphabet to decorate the classroom. She cut 13 letters from green paper. What fractional part of the letters were green?

44. Writing awards were presented to 30 students. Of the awards, 6 were for poetry and 10 were for essays. What fractional part of the awards were for poetry? for essays?

45. There were 80 fourth graders in Hadley School. Of these, 35 were boys. What fractional part of the fourth graders were girls?

Mixed Numbers

Darryl is baking bread. His recipe calls for
three and two thirds cups of whole-wheat flour.

Think
$1 + 1 + 1 + \frac{2}{3}$, or $3 + \frac{2}{3}$

Write: $3\frac{2}{3}$ Read: three and two thirds

$3\frac{2}{3}$ is a mixed number.

A **mixed number** is made up of a whole number and a fraction.

| whole number | $\rightarrow 3\frac{2}{3} \leftarrow$ | fraction |

Study these examples.

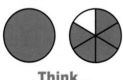

Think
$1 + \frac{5}{6}$

Write: $1\frac{5}{6}$
Read: one and five sixths

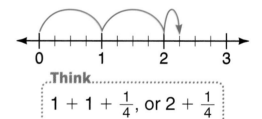

Think
$1 + 1 + \frac{1}{4}$, or $2 + \frac{1}{4}$

Write: $2\frac{1}{4}$
Read: two and one fourth

Write as a mixed number. Then model each.

1. four and three tenths
2. seven and two fifths
3. ten and one ninth
4. eight and five twelfths
5. two and three eighths
6. six and one half

Practice

Write a mixed number for each.

7.

8.

9.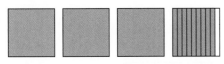

10.

To what mixed number is the arrow pointing?

11.

1   2

12.

4   5

13.

3   4

14.

9   10

Rename as Whole Numbers

Some fractions can be renamed as whole numbers.

Numerator and denominator are the same.

Denominator is 1.

$$\frac{4}{4} = 1$$

$$\frac{4}{1} = 4$$

$$2\frac{4}{4} = 2 + 1 = 3$$

$$\frac{75}{1} = 75$$

$$\frac{1000}{1000} = 1$$

$$\frac{1000}{1} = 1000$$

Rename each as a whole number.

15. $\frac{3}{3}$ 16. $\frac{10}{1}$ 17. $\frac{12}{1}$ 18. $3\frac{12}{12}$ 19. $\frac{9}{1}$

20. $5\frac{11}{11}$ 21. $\frac{15}{1}$ 22. $\frac{19}{1}$ 23. $\frac{14}{14}$ 24. $\frac{36}{1}$

Compare Fractions

▶ Compare: $\frac{5}{8}$ __?__ $\frac{3}{8}$

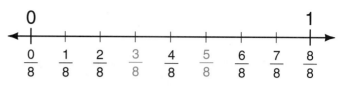

> The denominators are the same.

To compare fractions with the same denominators, compare the numerators.

$\frac{5}{8}$

$\frac{3}{8}$

$5 > 3 \longrightarrow \frac{5}{8} > \frac{3}{8}$

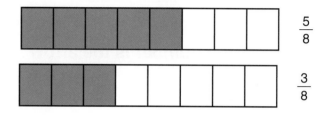

$\frac{5}{8}$

$\frac{3}{8}$

▶ Compare: $\frac{2}{3}$ __?__ $\frac{5}{6}$

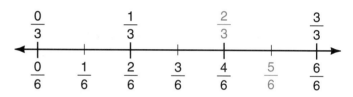

> The denominators are different.

To compare fractions with different denominators, first rename as equivalent fractions with the same denominators. Then compare the numerators.

$\frac{2}{3} = \frac{2 \times 2}{3 \times 2} = \frac{4}{6}$

$\frac{5}{6} = \frac{5}{6}$

$4 < 5 \longrightarrow \frac{4}{6} < \frac{5}{6}$ So $\frac{2}{3} < \frac{5}{6}$.

▶ Compare: $1\frac{2}{5}$ __?__ $1\frac{4}{5}$

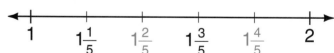

To compare mixed numbers, first compare the whole numbers. Then compare the fractions.

$1\frac{2}{5}$

$1\frac{4}{5}$

$1 = 1$

$2 < 4 \longrightarrow \frac{2}{5} < \frac{4}{5}$ So $1\frac{2}{5} < 1\frac{4}{5}$.

Compare. Write <, =, or >. Use models to help.

1. $\frac{3}{4}$? $\frac{1}{4}$ 2. $\frac{5}{8}$? $\frac{7}{8}$ 3. $\frac{2}{7}$? $\frac{4}{7}$ 4. $\frac{7}{9}$? $\frac{5}{9}$

5. $\frac{1}{6}$? $\frac{5}{6}$ 6. $\frac{4}{5}$? $\frac{4}{5}$ 7. $\frac{7}{10}$? $\frac{3}{10}$ 8. $\frac{11}{12}$? $\frac{5}{12}$

9. $\frac{8}{12}$? $\frac{3}{4}$ 10. $\frac{2}{3}$? $\frac{6}{9}$ 11. $\frac{1}{2}$? $\frac{4}{6}$ 12. $\frac{1}{4}$? $\frac{2}{8}$

13. $\frac{1}{3}$? $\frac{1}{6}$ 14. $\frac{3}{5}$? $\frac{3}{10}$ 15. $\frac{7}{8}$? $\frac{2}{4}$ 16. $\frac{7}{12}$? $\frac{5}{6}$

17. $\frac{6}{10}$? $\frac{3}{5}$ 18. $\frac{1}{2}$? $\frac{4}{8}$ 19. $\frac{3}{4}$? $\frac{10}{12}$ 20. $\frac{3}{10}$? $\frac{1}{2}$

21. $4\frac{3}{4}$? $4\frac{1}{4}$ 22. $1\frac{2}{3}$? $2\frac{1}{3}$ 23. $5\frac{1}{9}$? $2\frac{1}{9}$ 24. $6\frac{2}{5}$? $6\frac{4}{5}$

25. $3\frac{3}{10}$? $3\frac{7}{10}$ 26. $8\frac{5}{8}$? $8\frac{3}{8}$ 27. $2\frac{4}{9}$? $4\frac{2}{9}$ 28. $1\frac{3}{6}$? $1\frac{3}{6}$

Problem Solving

29. Of the evergreen trees in the park, $\frac{3}{10}$ were pines and $\frac{1}{10}$ were spruce. Were there more pines or more spruce in the park?

30. At the feeding station, $\frac{1}{3}$ of the birds were sparrows and $\frac{3}{12}$ were finches. Were there more sparrows or finches at the feeding station?

31. The northern sector of the park had $3\frac{3}{4}$ mi of trails. The eastern sector had $3\frac{1}{4}$ mi of trails. Which sector had more miles of trails?

32. On Monday, $\frac{3}{4}$ of the park's visitors were schoolchildren. On Tuesday $\frac{5}{8}$ of the visitors were schoolchildren. Did more schoolchildren visit the park on Monday or on Tuesday?

CHALLENGE — Algebra

Complete to make each comparison true.

33. $1\frac{2}{3} > 1\frac{?}{?}$ 34. $5\frac{3}{8} < 5\frac{?}{?}$ 35. $2\frac{3}{5} < 2\frac{?}{?}$ 36. $4\frac{3}{4} > 4\frac{?}{?}$

Order Fractions

Order from least to greatest: $\frac{1}{2}, \frac{7}{10}, \frac{3}{10}$

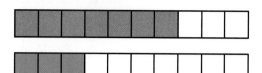

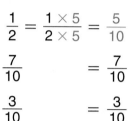

▶ To order fractions with *different denominators:*

- Rename as equivalent fractions with the same denominator.

$$\frac{1}{2} = \frac{1 \times 5}{2 \times 5} = \frac{5}{10}$$

$$\frac{7}{10} \qquad = \frac{7}{10}$$

$$\frac{3}{10} \qquad = \frac{3}{10}$$

- Compare the fractions by comparing the numerators.

$$3 < 5 \longrightarrow \frac{3}{10} < \frac{5}{10}$$

$$5 < 7 \longrightarrow \frac{5}{10} < \frac{7}{10}$$

- Arrange in order from least to greatest.

$$\frac{3}{10}, \frac{5}{10}, \frac{7}{10}$$

The order from least to greatest: $\frac{3}{10}, \frac{1}{2}, \frac{7}{10}$

Order from greatest to least: $\frac{3}{8}, \frac{1}{8}, \frac{7}{8}$

▶ To order fractions with *like denominators:*

- Compare the fractions by comparing the numerators.

$$7 > 3 \longrightarrow \frac{7}{8} > \frac{3}{8}$$

$$3 > 1 \longrightarrow \frac{3}{8} > \frac{1}{8}$$

- Arrange in order from greatest to least.

$$\frac{7}{8}, \frac{3}{8}, \frac{1}{8}$$

The order from greatest to least: $\frac{7}{8}, \frac{3}{8}, \frac{1}{8}$

Write in order from least to greatest. Use models to help.

1. $\frac{4}{6}, \frac{2}{6}, \frac{3}{6}$

2. $\frac{1}{5}, \frac{4}{5}, \frac{2}{5}$

3. $\frac{5}{12}, \frac{9}{12}, \frac{1}{12}$

4. $\frac{1}{8}, \frac{6}{8}, \frac{4}{8}$

5. $\frac{8}{9}, \frac{5}{9}, \frac{7}{9}$

6. $\frac{3}{7}, \frac{5}{7}, \frac{2}{7}$

7. $\frac{8}{10}, \frac{2}{10}, \frac{6}{10}$

8. $\frac{2}{4}, \frac{1}{4}, \frac{3}{4}$

9. $\frac{1}{2}, \frac{1}{4}, \frac{3}{4}$

10. $\frac{5}{6}, \frac{2}{3}, \frac{2}{6}$

11. $\frac{3}{8}, \frac{5}{8}, \frac{1}{4}$

12. $\frac{5}{12}, \frac{1}{6}, \frac{3}{12}$

13. $\frac{3}{10}, \frac{9}{10}, \frac{2}{5}$

14. $\frac{1}{2}, \frac{1}{8}, \frac{6}{8}$

15. $\frac{2}{3}, \frac{5}{12}, \frac{11}{12}$

16. $\frac{7}{9}, \frac{1}{3}, \frac{4}{9}$

Write in order from greatest to least. Use models to help.

17. $\frac{1}{7}, \frac{6}{7}, \frac{4}{7}$

18. $\frac{4}{9}, \frac{8}{9}, \frac{2}{9}$

19. $\frac{1}{10}, \frac{7}{10}, \frac{8}{10}$

20. $\frac{5}{8}, \frac{2}{8}, \frac{7}{8}$

21. $\frac{9}{12}, \frac{3}{12}, \frac{6}{12}$

22. $\frac{3}{6}, \frac{5}{6}, \frac{1}{6}$

23. $\frac{3}{5}, \frac{1}{5}, \frac{4}{5}$

24. $\frac{3}{10}, \frac{9}{10}, \frac{2}{10}$

25. $\frac{1}{6}, \frac{1}{2}, \frac{2}{6}$

26. $\frac{5}{12}, \frac{9}{12}, \frac{1}{2}$

27. $\frac{2}{3}, \frac{2}{9}, \frac{5}{9}$

28. $\frac{3}{12}, \frac{3}{4}, \frac{7}{12}$

Problem Solving

29. Marie cut three lengths of ribbon. They were $\frac{1}{2}$ yd, $\frac{3}{8}$ yd, and $\frac{5}{8}$ yd long. Which was the longest length? Which was the shortest?

30. Brad lives $\frac{3}{4}$ mi from school. Donna lives $\frac{1}{4}$ mi from school, and Chris lives $\frac{1}{2}$ mi from school. Who lives closest to school?

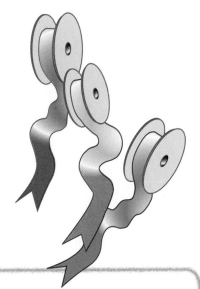

DO YOU REMEMBER?

Choose a word from the box to complete each sentence.

31. To find the __?__ of data, subtract the least number from the greatest number.

32. The __?__ is the number that shows up most frequently in a set of data.

median
mode
range

Algebra

8-11

Problem-Solving Strategy:
Logical Reasoning

Gwen, Maraya, and Sonia each buy a bracelet.
One is $6\frac{5}{8}$ in., one is $6\frac{1}{2}$ in., and the third is $6\frac{4}{8}$ in.
Gwen's bracelet is longer than Sonia's.
How long is Maraya's bracelet?

Read | **Visualize the facts of the problem as you reread it.**

Facts: Bracelets are $6\frac{5}{8}$ in., $6\frac{1}{2}$ in., and $6\frac{4}{8}$ in.
Gwen's bracelet is longer than Sonia's.

Question: How long is Maraya's bracelet?

Plan | To compare mixed numbers:
First, compare the whole number parts. $\quad 6 = 6 = 6$
Then, compare the fraction parts. $\quad \frac{5}{8}\ \underline{?}\ \frac{1}{2}; \quad \frac{1}{2}\ \underline{?}\ \frac{4}{8}$

Solve | Compare: $\frac{5}{8}\ ?\ \frac{1}{2}$

$$\frac{5}{8} \qquad = \frac{5}{8}$$
$$\frac{1}{2} = \frac{1 \times 4}{2 \times 4} = \frac{4}{8}$$

$5 > 4 \longrightarrow \frac{5}{8} > \frac{4}{8} \longrightarrow$ So $\frac{5}{8} > \frac{1}{2}$.

Compare: $\frac{1}{2}\ ?\ \frac{4}{8}$

$$\frac{1}{2} = \frac{1 \times 4}{2 \times 4} = \frac{4}{8}$$
$$\frac{4}{8} \qquad = \frac{4}{8}$$

$4 = 4 \longrightarrow \frac{4}{8} = \frac{4}{8} \longrightarrow \frac{1}{2} = \frac{4}{8}$.

So $6\frac{5}{8} > 6\frac{1}{2}$ and $6\frac{5}{8} > 6\frac{4}{8}$.

Two bracelets are the same length. Gwen's is longer
than Sonia's, so Gwen's bracelet is $6\frac{5}{8}$ in. long.
Sonia's and Maraya's must be equal in length. $6\frac{1}{2}$ in. $= 6\frac{4}{8}$ in.

Check | Draw 3 lines: $6\frac{5}{8}$ in., $6\frac{1}{2}$ in., $6\frac{4}{8}$ in. Then compare.

Use logical reasoning or an analogy to solve each problem.

1. Can you complete the analogy?

   $\frac{1}{2}$ is to $\frac{2}{4}$ as $\frac{3}{6}$ is to _?_

       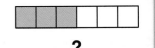
   ?

> **Read** **Facts:** $\frac{1}{2}$ and $\frac{2}{4}$ are related.

Question: What fraction is related to $\frac{3}{6}$ in the same way?

> **Plan** To solve an analogy, first read it aloud. Then draw and label the fractions.
> One half is to two fourths as three sixths is to what?
>
> Think about how $\frac{1}{2}$ and $\frac{2}{4}$ are related.

> **Solve** ....▶ **Check**

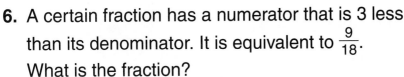

2. $\frac{5}{10}$ is to $\frac{10}{10}$ as $\frac{4}{8}$ is to _?_

3. **ABAB** is to **CDCD** as **ABBA** is to _?_

4. 8 is to $\frac{16}{24}$ as 6 is to _?_

5. One worm is $4\frac{1}{4}$ in. long, another is $4\frac{3}{8}$ in. long, and a third is $4\frac{5}{8}$ in. long. The longest worm is in the garden and the shortest worm is on a leaf. Which worm is on a leaf?

6. A certain fraction has a numerator that is 3 less than its denominator. It is equivalent to $\frac{9}{18}$. What is the fraction?

7. $1\frac{1}{2}$ is to 1 as $3\frac{1}{2}$ is to _?_

8. 6 is to $\frac{12}{18}$ as 4 is to _?_

Problem-Solving Applications: Mixed Review

Solve each problem and explain the method you used.

1. A bouquet of a dozen flowers has 4 roses. The rest are carnations. What fractional part of the bouquet is roses? is carnations?

2. Pete plants $\frac{3}{8}$ of the garden with tomatoes, $\frac{1}{2}$ with peas, and $\frac{1}{8}$ with peppers. Order the sections from largest to smallest.

3. Delia's garden is $\frac{9}{12}$ flowers and $\frac{4}{16}$ herbs. Are there more flowers or herbs in her garden?

4. A garden has $\frac{1}{10}$ red, $\frac{1}{5}$ white, $\frac{2}{10}$ yellow, and $\frac{2}{5}$ pink roses. Of which color are there the most roses? the least? Which colors share an equal number?

5. One plant is $7\frac{10}{16}$ in. tall. Another is $7\frac{3}{4}$ in. tall. The herb is the shorter plant. How tall is it?

> Remember: Express fractions in simplest form.

6. Marci has 12 sections in her flower garden and 16 sections in her herb garden. If both gardens are equal in size, which has smaller sections?

Use the circle graph for problems 7 and 8.

7. About what fractional part of Greta's garden is tulips? is red tulips?

8. What flowers make up equal parts of Greta's garden?

Greta's Garden

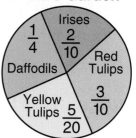

Choose a strategy from the list or use another strategy you know to solve each problem.

Strategy File

Use these Strategies
Logical Reasoning
Guess and Test
Use a Diagram/Graph
Use More Than One Step
Make a Table or List

9. For every sunflower seed Deven plants, he also plants 4 zinnia seeds. Deven plants 45 seeds in all. How many zinnia seeds does he plant?

10. Diego has 10 pots. He puts marigolds in $\frac{2}{5}$ of the pots and daisies in $\frac{1}{2}$ of the pots. Are there more pots with daisies or marigolds?

11. A fraction has a denominator that is 8 greater than its numerator. It is equivalent to $\frac{1}{3}$. What is the fraction?

12. The circle graph at right shows how many rows of each kind of vegetable Kito has planted in his garden. What questions can you ask using the circle graph?

Kito's Garden

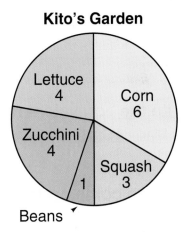

Lettuce 4
Corn 6
Zucchini 4
Squash 3
1
Beans

13. Ms. Tallchief plants 2 red and 2 pink geraniums in a row in her window box. How many different arrangements can she make?

14. Two fractions are equivalent. The denominator of one is the same as the numerator of the other. What are some possibilities for the two fractions?

15. Lila plants tulips, daffodils, and lilies. The flowers take up $\frac{2}{6}$, $\frac{2}{12}$, and $\frac{1}{2}$ of her garden. She plants twice as many tulips as lilies. What fraction of her garden does each flower take up?

Write each as a fraction. *(See pp. 266–267.)*

1. one half

2. three eighths

3. five sevenths

4. four out of nine

5. six-tenths

6. two divided by three

Write the fraction represented by the letter A. *(See pp. 268–269.)*

7.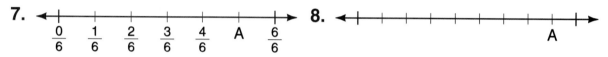

8.

Tell whether the fraction is closer to 0, $\frac{1}{2}$, or 1. *(See pp. 270–271.)*

9. $\frac{6}{7}$

10. $\frac{2}{9}$

11. $\frac{6}{10}$

12. $\frac{9}{11}$

Write the equivalent fraction. *(See pp. 272–275.)*

13. $\frac{1}{9} = \frac{5}{n}$

14. $\frac{7}{10} = \frac{14}{x}$

15. $\frac{6}{9} = \frac{y}{54}$

16. $\frac{3}{4} = \frac{18}{a}$

Find the common factors for each set of numbers. Then circle the greatest common factor. *(See pp. 276–277.)*

17. 8, 12

18. 6, 16

19. 12, 20

Write each fraction in simplest form. *(See pp. 278–279.)*

20. $\frac{10}{15}$

21. $\frac{6}{12}$

22. $\frac{8}{24}$

23. $\frac{4}{20}$

24. $\frac{15}{40}$

Write in order:
least to greatest.   **greatest to least.** *(See pp. 282–285.)*

25. $\frac{4}{10}, \frac{7}{10}, \frac{4}{5}$

26. $\frac{11}{12}, \frac{3}{4}, \frac{2}{12}$

27. $\frac{6}{9}, \frac{1}{3}, \frac{4}{9}$

28. $\frac{4}{5}, \frac{3}{10}, \frac{7}{10}$

Compare. Write <, =, or >. *(See pp. 280–283.)*

29. $2\frac{7}{14}$? $3\frac{4}{14}$

30. $\frac{10}{12}$? $\frac{9}{12}$

31. $1\frac{2}{3}$? $2\frac{1}{3}$

(See Still More Practice, p. 468.)

Ratio and Percent

You can use a ratio to compare the number of violins to the number of trombones.

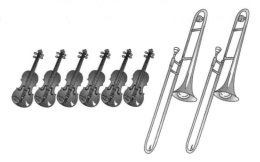

The ratio of violins to trombones is 6 to 2.

▶ You can write a ratio in three ways.

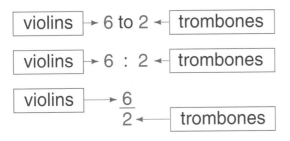

> When you write a ratio, be sure to write the numbers in the correct order.

The ratio of violins to trombones: 6 to 2, 6:2, or $\frac{6}{2}$

The ratio of trombones to violins: 2 to 6, 2:6, or $\frac{2}{6}$

▶ If you write a ratio as a fraction with a denominator of 100, you can express that ratio as a percent (%).

fraction:	$\frac{8}{100}$	$\frac{10}{100}$	$\frac{85}{100}$	$\frac{100}{100}$
	↓	↓	↓	↓
percent:	8%	10%	85%	100%

Write each ratio three ways.

1. 4 clarinets to 7 trumpets
2. 10 oboes to 1 piano
3. 5 cellos to 8 tubas
4. 9 bassoons to 6 saxophones

Write each ratio as a percent.

5. $\frac{50}{100}$
6. $\frac{1}{100}$
7. $\frac{75}{100}$
8. 25:100
9. 99:100

Write each percent as a fraction.

10. 30%
11. 5%
12. 62%
13. 48%
14. 150%

Write each as a fraction.

1. five sixths **2.** seven eighths **3.** two divided by ten **4.** four out of seven

Write the equivalent fraction.

5. $\dfrac{3}{4} = \dfrac{n}{12}$ **6.** $\dfrac{1}{5} = \dfrac{5}{a}$ **7.** $\dfrac{1}{3} = \dfrac{3}{x}$ **8.** $\dfrac{2}{7} = \dfrac{d}{21}$

Find the common factors for each set. Then circle the GCF.

9. 12, 24   **10.** 18, 36, 12

Write each in simplest form.

11. $\dfrac{8}{12}$ **12.** $\dfrac{6}{10}$ **13.** $\dfrac{12}{36}$ **14.** $\dfrac{14}{28}$ **15.** $\dfrac{8}{10}$

Write in order from greatest to least.

16. $\dfrac{14}{21}, \dfrac{3}{7}, \dfrac{3}{21}$ **17.** $\dfrac{1}{3}, \dfrac{8}{9}, \dfrac{4}{9}$

Problem Solving

Use a strategy you have learned.

18. Chet, Juan, and Ty walked around the track. Chet walked farther than Juan. Ty walked the farthest. If they walked $\dfrac{3}{5}$ mi, $\dfrac{2}{5}$ mi, $\dfrac{5}{10}$ mi, how far did each boy walk?

Tell About It

What fractions are shown? Explain why they are equivalent.

19.

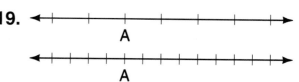

Performance Assessment

20. Extend the number line to show 1.

Draw a number line and locate each point.

21. $\dfrac{0}{4}$ **22.** $\dfrac{3}{4}$ **23.** $\dfrac{1}{2}$

Choose the best answer.

1. $\$.86$
   $- \quad .81$

   a. $\$.15$
   b. $\$.05$
   c. $\$1.67$
   d. $\$.50$

2. Choose the rule for the pattern.

   14, 11, 12, 9, 10

   a. Start at 11; $-3, +1$
   b. Start at 14; -3
   c. Start at 14; $-3, +2, -1$
   d. Start at 14; $-3, +1$

3. Choose the value of the variable.

$$a\overline{)63}^{\,9}$$

   a. $a = 54$
   b. $a = 9$
   c. $a = 8$
   d. $a = 7$

4.   5768
   $\times \quad 6$

   a. 34,608
   b. 34,668
   c. 34,208
   d. 30,608

5. $\$.79 + \$.17$

   a. $\$1.06$
   b. $\$.62$
   c. $\$.86$
   d. $\$.96$

6. Round the number to the place of the underlined digit.

   40<u>2</u>,516,970

   a. 400,000,000
   b. 401,000,000
   c. 402,000,000
   d. 403,000,000

7. $6\overline{)217}$

   a. 35 R7
   b. 36
   c. 36 R1
   d. 36 R2

8. Sam puts 220 g of raisins into each snack bag. How many kilograms of raisins does he need for 15 bags?

   a. 3300 kg   **b.** 15 kg
   c. 4 kg   **d.** 3 kg

9. Choose the value of the variable.

   $19 = n + 8$

   a. $n = 8$
   b. $n = 11$
   c. $n = 19$
   d. $n = 27$

10.   603
   $\times \quad 7$

   a. 4271
   b. 4221
   c. 4201
   d. 596

11. 3 yd = _?_

   a. 9 ft
   b. 36 ft
   c. 8 ft
   d. 96 in.

12. Choose the multiplication property.

   $(3 \times 5) \times 2 = 3 \times (5 \times 2)$

   a. commutative property
   b. associative property
   c. identity property
   d. zero property

13. Compare. Choose $<$, $=$, or $>$.

58 fl oz ___?___ 8 c

    a. $<$
    b. $=$
    c. $>$

14. There are 3 blue cubes and 2 red cubes in a bag. What is the probability of picking a red cube?

    a. $\frac{1}{2}$ **b.** $\frac{2}{3}$ **c.** $\frac{3}{4}$ **d.** $\frac{2}{5}$

15. Choose the equivalent fraction.

$\frac{3}{6}$

    a. $\frac{9}{12}$ **b.** $\frac{6}{18}$ **c.** $\frac{9}{18}$ **d.** $\frac{12}{18}$

16. Choose the fraction for the letter A.

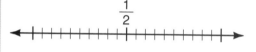

    a. $\frac{2}{5}$ **b.** $\frac{3}{6}$ **c.** $\frac{3}{5}$ **d.** $\frac{4}{5}$

17. Choose the fraction in lowest terms.

    a. $\frac{4}{8}$ **b.** $\frac{6}{7}$ **c.** $\frac{2}{6}$ **d.** $\frac{2}{4}$

18. Compare. Choose $<$, $=$, or $>$.

70 dm ___?___ 6 m

    a. $<$
    b. $=$
    c. $>$

19. At 1:00 A.M. the temperature was 2°C. By 4:00 A.M. it was -5°C. How many degrees did the temperature drop?

    a. 7 degrees   **b.** 5 degrees
    c. 3 degrees   **d.** 2 degrees

20. Choose the missing denominator.

$\frac{3}{7} = \frac{12}{n}$

    a. $n = 7$
    b. $n = 21$
    c. $n = 24$
    d. $n = 28$

21. Which fraction is closer to $\frac{1}{2}$?

    a. $\frac{14}{20}$ **b.** $\frac{12}{20}$ **c.** $\frac{9}{20}$ **d.** $\frac{8}{20}$

22. Which fraction completes the analogy?

5 is to $\frac{15}{20}$ as 7 is to ___?___

    a. $\frac{21}{28}$ **b.** $\frac{20}{25}$ **c.** $\frac{14}{21}$ **d.** $\frac{28}{35}$

Tell About It

Draw a picture to help solve the problem.

23. Amy has a 1-foot plank of wood. She cuts the plank into 8 equal parts. Write the fraction which names, in feet, 2 pieces of Amy's cut plank of wood. Explain how you found the numerator and the denominator.

Fractions: Addition and Subtraction

LITTLE BITS

"Will you have some pie?"
Said Jane. Said I,
"Well, just a little. Just a bit."
But I found when I had eaten it
That just *one* little-bit wouldn't do.
So I told Jane to make it *two*.

Then was I happy with what I got?
Well, little-bits can't make a lot.
For little-bits are small, you see.
So I told Jane to make it *three*.

Three little-bits are not much more
Than *two*. So I said, "Make it *four*."

And I ate them up. Then asked for *five*.
Then *six*. Till Jane said, "Sakes alive,
Here are two more and that makes *eight*.
If you don't stop you'll eat the plate!"
"*Eight* little-bits." I said, "are fine.
But would you care to make it *nine*?"

From "Little Bits" by John Ciardi.

In this chapter you will:

Add and subtract fractions and mixed numbers
Estimate sums and differences of mixed numbers
Explore multiples
Relate fractions and probability
Find fractional parts of numbers
Solve problems by using simpler numbers

Critical Thinking/ Finding Together

Suppose Jane's pie was cut into 10 equal pieces. Name in lowest terms each fractional part of the pie that was eaten. What fractional part of the pie is left?

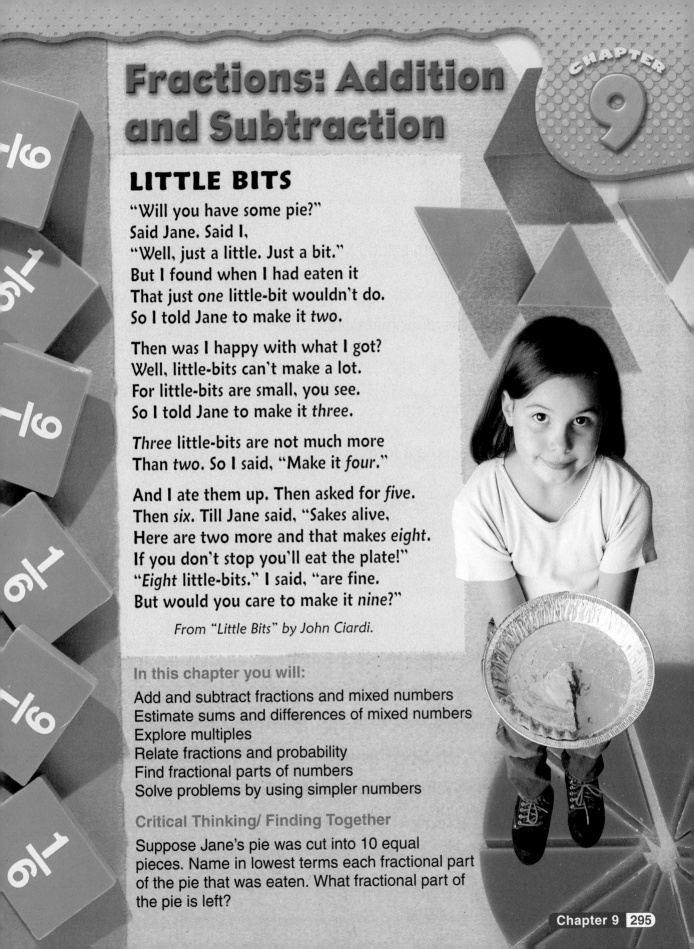

Add Fractions: Like Denominators

Pam walked $\frac{3}{10}$ mile from her house to school. Then she walked $\frac{5}{10}$ mile from school to the bus stop. How far did Pam walk?

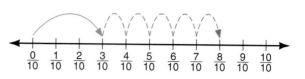

To find how far Pam walked, add: $\frac{3}{10} + \frac{5}{10}$

| The denominators are the same. |

To add fractions with like denominators:

- Add the numerators.

$$\frac{3}{10} + \frac{5}{10} = \frac{8}{}$$

.Think.........
$3 + 5 = 8$

- Write the like denominator.

$$\frac{3}{10} + \frac{5}{10} = \frac{8}{10}$$

- Write the sum in simplest form.

$$\frac{8}{10} = \frac{8 \div 2}{10 \div 2} = \frac{4}{5}$$

| Factors of 8: 1, 2, 4, 8 | → | Factors of 10: 1, 2, 5, 10 | → | GCF: 2 |

Pam walked $\frac{4}{5}$ mile.

Study these examples.

$$\begin{array}{r} \frac{4}{9} \\ + \frac{5}{9} \\ \hline \frac{9}{9} = 1 \end{array}$$ ← simplest form

$$\begin{array}{r} \frac{2}{7} \\ + \frac{3}{7} \\ \hline \frac{5}{7} \end{array}$$

$$\frac{1}{10} + \frac{2}{10} + \frac{4}{10} = \frac{7}{10}$$

Practice

Add. Write the sum in simplest form.
You can use a number line to help.

1. $\frac{1}{4} + \frac{2}{4}$

2. $\frac{5}{8} + \frac{2}{8}$

3. $\frac{1}{3} + \frac{1}{3}$

4. $\frac{2}{7} + \frac{4}{7}$

Find the sum in simplest form.

5. $\frac{2}{9} + \frac{1}{9}$

6. $\frac{1}{6} + \frac{2}{6}$

7. $\frac{2}{10} + \frac{4}{10}$

8. $\frac{2}{5} + \frac{3}{5}$

9. $\frac{1}{8} + \frac{5}{8}$

10. $\frac{3}{7} + \frac{4}{7}$

11. $\frac{4}{12} + \frac{6}{12}$

12. $\frac{2}{6} + \frac{2}{6}$

13. $\frac{3}{4} + \frac{1}{4}$

14. $\frac{2}{9} + \frac{4}{9}$

15. $\frac{4}{10} + \frac{4}{10}$

16. $\frac{2}{8} + \frac{2}{8}$

17. $\begin{array}{r}\frac{1}{9}\\[2pt]+\ \frac{3}{9}\\ \hline\end{array}$

18. $\begin{array}{r}\frac{3}{5}\\[2pt]+\ \frac{1}{5}\\ \hline\end{array}$

19. $\begin{array}{r}\frac{2}{10}\\[2pt]+\ \frac{3}{10}\\ \hline\end{array}$

20. $\begin{array}{r}\frac{3}{8}\\[2pt]+\ \frac{5}{8}\\ \hline\end{array}$

21. $\begin{array}{r}\frac{5}{12}\\[2pt]+\ \frac{3}{12}\\ \hline\end{array}$

22. $\begin{array}{r}\frac{1}{2}\\[2pt]+\ \frac{1}{2}\\ \hline\end{array}$

23. $\begin{array}{r}\frac{5}{7}\\[2pt]+\ \frac{2}{7}\\ \hline\end{array}$

24. $\begin{array}{r}\frac{2}{8}\\[2pt]+\ \frac{4}{8}\\ \hline\end{array}$

25. $\begin{array}{r}\frac{3}{12}\\[2pt]+\ \frac{3}{12}\\ \hline\end{array}$

26. $\begin{array}{r}\frac{1}{12}\\[2pt]+\ \frac{3}{12}\\ \hline\end{array}$

27. $\frac{2}{12} + \frac{1}{12} + \frac{7}{12}$

28. $\frac{3}{10} + \frac{2}{10} + \frac{5}{10}$

29. $\frac{1}{8} + \frac{5}{8} + \frac{2}{8}$

Problem Solving Write each answer in simplest form.

30. Mr. Lom rode his bicycle for $\frac{1}{4}$ hour before breakfast and $\frac{1}{4}$ hour after supper. For how much time did he ride his bicycle?

31. Jake cycled $\frac{3}{8}$ mile from his house to Rick's. Then he cycled $\frac{5}{8}$ mile from Rick's to Hal's. How far did Jake cycle?

TEST PREPARATION

32. For every $\frac{1}{10}$ mile that an adult walks, he or she burns about 10 calories. About how many calories would an adult burn walking $\frac{2}{10}$ mile in the morning and $\frac{7}{10}$ mile in the evening?

A 10 calories

B 20 calories

C 70 calories

D 90 calories

Subtract Fractions: Like Denominators

Kevin had $\frac{7}{8}$ yard of felt. He used $\frac{3}{8}$ yard to make a pirate's hat. How much felt was left?

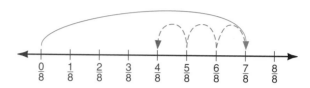

To find how much was left, subtract: $\frac{7}{8} - \frac{3}{8}$

To subtract fractions with like denominators:

- Subtract the numerators.

$$\frac{7}{8} - \frac{3}{8} = \frac{4}{}$$

.....Think.........
$7 - 3 = 4$

- Write the like denominator.

$$\frac{7}{8} - \frac{3}{8} = \frac{4}{8}$$

- Write the difference in simplest form.

$$\frac{4}{8} = \frac{4 \div 4}{8 \div 4} = \frac{1}{2}$$

| Factors of 4: 1, 2, 4 | → | Factors of 8: 1, 2, 4, 8 | → | GCF: 4 |

There was $\frac{1}{2}$ yard of felt left.

Study these examples.

$$\begin{array}{r} \frac{3}{4} \\ -\frac{3}{4} \\ \hline \frac{0}{4} = 0 \end{array}$$ ← simplest form →

$$\begin{array}{r} \frac{7}{9} \\ -\frac{5}{9} \\ \hline \frac{2}{9} \end{array}$$

Find the difference in simplest form.
You can use a number line to help.

1. $\frac{9}{10} - \frac{2}{10}$ **2.** $\frac{3}{5} - \frac{2}{5}$ **3.** $\frac{4}{7} - \frac{2}{7}$ **4.** $\frac{3}{4} - \frac{1}{4}$

Subtract. Write the difference in simplest form.

5. $\dfrac{6}{9} - \dfrac{3}{9}$ **6.** $\dfrac{2}{3} - \dfrac{1}{3}$ **7.** $\dfrac{5}{6} - \dfrac{4}{6}$ **8.** $\dfrac{5}{8} - \dfrac{5}{8}$

9. $\dfrac{11}{12} - \dfrac{5}{12}$ **10.** $\dfrac{8}{10} - \dfrac{2}{10}$ **11.** $\dfrac{4}{5} - \dfrac{4}{5}$ **12.** $\dfrac{6}{8} - \dfrac{2}{8}$

13. $\dfrac{8}{9} - \dfrac{2}{9}$ **14.** $\dfrac{10}{12} - \dfrac{1}{12}$ **15.** $\dfrac{3}{6} - \dfrac{1}{6}$ **16.** $\dfrac{7}{10} - \dfrac{3}{10}$

17. $\begin{array}{r} \frac{3}{4} \\ -\frac{2}{4} \\ \hline \end{array}$ **18.** $\begin{array}{r} \frac{7}{9} \\ -\frac{1}{9} \\ \hline \end{array}$ **19.** $\begin{array}{r} \frac{11}{12} \\ -\frac{8}{12} \\ \hline \end{array}$ **20.** $\begin{array}{r} \frac{9}{10} \\ -\frac{7}{10} \\ \hline \end{array}$ **21.** $\begin{array}{r} \frac{1}{2} \\ -\frac{1}{2} \\ \hline \end{array}$

22. $\begin{array}{r} \frac{2}{7} \\ -\frac{2}{7} \\ \hline \end{array}$ **23.** $\begin{array}{r} \frac{4}{5} \\ -\frac{1}{5} \\ \hline \end{array}$ **24.** $\begin{array}{r} \frac{5}{6} \\ -\frac{1}{6} \\ \hline \end{array}$ **25.** $\begin{array}{r} \frac{10}{12} \\ -\frac{6}{12} \\ \hline \end{array}$ **26.** $\begin{array}{r} \frac{6}{10} \\ -\frac{2}{10} \\ \hline \end{array}$

Problem Solving   Write the answer in simplest form.

27. Nora bought $\dfrac{5}{6}$ yard of calico. Wayne bought $\dfrac{2}{6}$ yard of calico. How much more calico did Nora buy than Wayne?

28. Jo used $\dfrac{5}{8}$ yard of red linen to make a skirt. She used $\dfrac{1}{8}$ yard of blue linen for a scarf. Did she use more red or blue linen? How much more?

29. Ben has $\dfrac{1}{4}$ yard of denim. He needs $\dfrac{3}{4}$ yard for a school project. How much more denim does he need?

DO YOU REMEMBER?

Divide.

30. $6\overline{)8}$ **31.** $4\overline{)13}$ **32.** $8\overline{)43}$ **33.** $5\overline{)27}$ **34.** $2\overline{)11}$ **35.** $3\overline{)20}$

36. $48 \div 7$ **37.** $89 \div 9$ **38.** $65 \div 9$ **39.** $76 \div 8$

Improper Fractions

An improper fraction is a fraction greater than or equal to one. Its numerator is greater than or equal to its denominator.

$\frac{20}{8}$ is an improper fraction since $20 > 8$.

Write $\frac{20}{8}$ as a mixed number in simplest form: $\frac{20}{8} = n$

> **Remember:**
> Read $\frac{20}{8}$ as: twenty eighths
>   twenty divided by eight

▶ To write an improper fraction as a mixed number:

| Divide the numerator by the denominator. | Write the quotient as the whole number. | Write the remainder over the divisor. |

$\frac{20}{8} = 8\overline{)20}^{\,2\ R\ 4}$

2

$\frac{4}{8} = \frac{1}{2}$

> Write the fraction in simplest form.

So $\frac{20}{8} = 2\frac{4}{8} = 2\frac{1}{2}$. [simplest form]

▶ You can also break apart an improper fraction.

$\frac{20}{8} = \frac{8}{8} + \frac{8}{8} + \frac{4}{8} = 2\frac{1}{2}$

$\frac{8}{8} = 1$ $\frac{8}{8} = 1$ $\frac{4}{8} = \frac{1}{2}$

▶ You can use a number line to model an improper fraction.

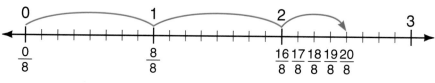

$\frac{0}{8}$ $\frac{8}{8}$ $\frac{16}{8}\,\frac{17}{8}\,\frac{18}{8}\,\frac{19}{8}\,\frac{20}{8}$

$\frac{20}{8} = \frac{8}{8} + \frac{8}{8} + \frac{4}{8} = 2\frac{4}{8} = 2\frac{1}{2}$ ◀ [simplest form]

Write as a whole number or mixed number in simplest form.
Use division, models, or number lines to help.

1. $\frac{12}{3} = 12 \div 3 = 4$ ← $\boxed{\text{simplest form}}$

2. $\frac{9}{4}$

3. $\frac{13}{6}$

4. $\frac{27}{3}$

5. $\frac{30}{10}$

6. $\frac{15}{9}$

7. $\frac{32}{8}$

8. $\frac{20}{6}$

9. $\frac{10}{5}$

10. $\frac{14}{4}$

11. $\frac{70}{12}$

12. $\frac{58}{6}$

13. $\frac{42}{8}$

14. $\frac{33}{6}$

15. $\frac{92}{8}$

16. $\frac{26}{10}$

Add. Write each sum in simplest form.

17. $\frac{3}{5} + \frac{4}{5}$

18. $\frac{2}{3} + \frac{2}{3}$

19. $\frac{4}{6} + \frac{2}{6}$

20. $\frac{2}{4} + \frac{3}{4}$

21. $\frac{4}{6} + \frac{5}{6}$

22. $\frac{7}{8} + \frac{5}{8}$

23. $\frac{4}{7} + \frac{5}{7}$

24. $\frac{7}{9} + \frac{8}{9}$

25. $\frac{10}{12} + \frac{8}{12}$

26. $\frac{3}{10} + \frac{7}{10}$

27. $\frac{1}{2} + \frac{1}{2}$

28. $\frac{7}{8} + \frac{3}{8}$

29. $\frac{14}{5} + \frac{16}{5}$

30. $\frac{20}{8} + \frac{30}{8}$

31. $\frac{25}{3} + \frac{20}{3}$

32. $\frac{23}{9} + \frac{57}{9}$

Problem Solving

33. Max cut $\frac{125}{7}$ feet of wood. Did he cut more or less than 18 feet of wood?

34. Pat put $\frac{94}{6}$ liters of water in her fish tank. Was this more or less than 16 liters?

35. Steve walked $\frac{10}{4}$ miles to the county fair. Did he walk more or less than 2 miles?

36. Kelvin sold $\frac{164}{8}$ gal of cider at the fair. Did he sell more or less than 22 gallons?

37. Sue ate $\frac{5}{2}$ pies in the pie-eating contest. Was this more or less than 3 pies?

38. Mia has $\frac{7}{4}$ yards of fabric. Does she have more or less than 2 yards of fabric?

Estimate with Mixed Numbers

There are $5\frac{1}{8}$ lb of apples, $2\frac{3}{4}$ lb of bananas, and $8\frac{1}{5}$ lb of melons at a picnic. About how many pounds of fruit are at the picnic?

To find about how many pounds, estimate the sum: $5\frac{1}{8} + 2\frac{3}{4} + 8\frac{1}{5}$

▶ To estimate sums of mixed numbers, use front-end estimation.

• Add the whole number parts. $5 + 2 + 8 \rightarrow 15$

• Adjust the estimate with the fraction parts.

$5\frac{1}{8} + 2\frac{3}{4} + 8\frac{1}{5}$

Fractions of $\frac{1}{2}$ or greater are about 1.

Adjusted estimate: $15 + 1 = 16$

There are about 16 lb of fruit at the picnic.

About how many more pounds of melons than bananas are there?

To find about how many more, estimate the difference: $8\frac{1}{5} - 2\frac{3}{4}$

▶ To estimate differences of mixed numbers, use front-end estimation.

• Subtract the whole number parts.

$8 - 2 \rightarrow 6$ ◀ estimated difference

There are about 6 more pounds of melons than bananas.

Practice

Estimate. Use front-end estimation.

1. $6\frac{1}{5} + 9\frac{8}{10}$

2. $8\frac{1}{4} + 8\frac{9}{12}$

3. $3\frac{1}{2} + 7\frac{1}{6}$

4. $1\frac{4}{9} + 4\frac{5}{6}$

5. $5\frac{2}{3} - 2\frac{4}{9}$

6. $9\frac{3}{4} - 4\frac{3}{8}$

7. $7\frac{2}{10} - 5\frac{1}{2}$

8. $6\frac{3}{8} - 4\frac{1}{4}$

Estimate the sum. Use front-end estimation.

9. $3\frac{1}{3}$
    $4\frac{4}{6}$
    $+\ 7\frac{1}{9}$

10. $5\frac{3}{4}$
    $9\frac{1}{8}$
    $+\ 6\frac{1}{4}$

11. $2\frac{1}{6}$
    $8\frac{4}{10}$
    $+\ 6\frac{9}{10}$

12. $9\frac{1}{4}$
    $4\frac{1}{2}$
    $+\ 4\frac{3}{12}$

13. $8\frac{2}{9}$
    $4\frac{5}{6}$
    $+\ 7\frac{1}{3}$

14. $10\frac{4}{10}$
    $8\frac{1}{5}$
    $+\ 10\frac{1}{10}$

15. $7\frac{3}{4}$
    $12\frac{1}{4}$
    $+\ 1\frac{1}{4}$

16. $14\frac{2}{3}$
    $10\frac{1}{6}$
    $+\ 12\frac{2}{9}$

17. $24\frac{2}{10}$
    $16\frac{8}{10}$
    $+\ 10\frac{1}{5}$

18. $15\frac{1}{8}$
    $25\frac{7}{8}$
    $+\ 6\frac{1}{4}$

Estimate the difference. Use front-end estimation.

19. $18\frac{2}{3}$
    $-\ 9\frac{6}{9}$

20. $9\frac{3}{4}$
    $-\ 7\frac{4}{8}$

21. $13\frac{1}{5}$
    $-\ 8\frac{5}{10}$

22. $7\frac{1}{2}$
    $-\ 4\frac{3}{4}$

23. $11\frac{6}{9}$
    $-\ 5\frac{1}{6}$

24. $15\frac{8}{12}$
    $-\ 8\frac{2}{3}$

25. $6\frac{7}{8}$
    $-\ 3\frac{3}{4}$

26. $14\frac{8}{10}$
    $-\ 7\frac{4}{5}$

27. $13\frac{1}{2}$
    $-\ 6\frac{6}{12}$

28. $12\frac{5}{6}$
    $-\ 4\frac{1}{3}$

29. $22\frac{3}{9} - 12\frac{2}{3}$

30. $48\frac{1}{2} - 30\frac{7}{10}$

31. $19\frac{11}{12} - 11\frac{3}{4}$

32. $25\frac{7}{12} - 15\frac{4}{6}$

Problem Solving

33. David brought $5\frac{2}{10}$ lb of potato salad to the picnic. Sue brought $7\frac{1}{2}$ lb of potato salad. About how many pounds of potato salad were there?

34. Jerry traveled $15\frac{3}{4}$ mi to get to the picnic. Emmy traveled $6\frac{1}{2}$ mi less. About how far did Emmy have to travel?

35. Nan brought a watermelon that weighed $20\frac{1}{4}$ lb. The picnickers ate $15\frac{3}{4}$ lb of watermelon. About how many pounds of watermelon were left?

36. Sal needed 37 lb of turkey to feed the picnickers. He bought turkeys that weighed $10\frac{7}{10}$ lb, $16\frac{1}{10}$ lb, and $11\frac{3}{10}$ lb. Did Sal buy enough turkey?

Add and Subtract Mixed Numbers

Akers' Farms displays plants in trays of ten. Lucy buys $2\frac{6}{10}$ trays of plants and her brother buys $1\frac{2}{10}$ trays. How many trays of plants do they buy in all? How many more trays does Lucy buy than her brother?

▶ To find how many they buy in all,

add: $2\frac{6}{10} + 1\frac{2}{10}$

Add the fractions.	Add the whole numbers.	Write in simplest form.
$2\frac{6}{10}$ $+1\frac{2}{10}$ $\overline{\frac{8}{10}}$	$2\frac{6}{10}$ $+1\frac{2}{10}$ $\overline{3\frac{8}{10}}$	$2\frac{6}{10}$ $+1\frac{2}{10}$ $\overline{3\frac{8}{10}} = 3\frac{4}{5}$

They buy $3\frac{4}{5}$ trays in all.

▶ To find how many more trays Lucy buys,

subtract: $2\frac{6}{10} - 1\frac{2}{10}$

Subtract the fractions.	Subtract the whole numbers.	Write in simplest form.
$2\frac{6}{10}$ $-1\frac{2}{10}$ $\overline{\frac{4}{10}}$	$2\frac{6}{10}$ $-1\frac{2}{10}$ $\overline{1\frac{4}{10}}$	$2\frac{6}{10}$ $-1\frac{2}{10}$ $\overline{1\frac{4}{10}} = 1\frac{2}{5}$

Lucy buys $1\frac{2}{5}$ more trays than her brother.

Add. Write the sum in simplest form.

1. $6\frac{2}{6}$
$+ 7\frac{4}{6}$

2. $8\frac{1}{4}$
$+ 5\frac{1}{4}$

3. $4\frac{3}{5}$
$+ 3\frac{1}{5}$

4. $2\frac{3}{8}$
$+ 1\frac{5}{8}$

5. $9\frac{2}{7}$
$+ 6\frac{4}{7}$

6. $5\frac{4}{12}$
$+ 5\frac{6}{12}$

7. $7\frac{2}{9}$
$+ 8\frac{4}{9}$

8. $26\frac{3}{4}$
$+ 17\frac{1}{4}$

9. $36\frac{3}{10}$
$+ 28\frac{5}{10}$

10. $47\frac{3}{8}$
$+ 54\frac{3}{8}$

Subtract. Write the difference in simplest form.

11. $9\frac{10}{12}$
$- 7\frac{7}{12}$

12. $5\frac{2}{3}$
$- 1\frac{1}{3}$

13. $8\frac{3}{4}$
$- 3\frac{1}{4}$

14. $6\frac{4}{5}$
$- 4\frac{2}{5}$

15. $10\frac{7}{8}$
$- 2\frac{5}{8}$

16. $57\frac{5}{6}$
$- 48\frac{2}{6}$

17. $32\frac{6}{7}$
$- 27\frac{1}{7}$

18. $40\frac{8}{9}$
$- 18\frac{5}{9}$

19. $23\frac{9}{10}$
$- 23\frac{3}{10}$

20. $12\frac{1}{2}$
$- 7\frac{1}{2}$

Align and add or subtract. Watch the signs.

21. $18\frac{11}{12} - 9\frac{1}{12}$

22. $14\frac{7}{10} - 8\frac{3}{10}$

23. $21\frac{2}{6} + 5\frac{2}{6}$

24. $31\frac{6}{8} - 9\frac{2}{8}$

25. $1\frac{6}{8} + 19\frac{2}{8}$

26. $6\frac{2}{9} + 17\frac{1}{9}$

27. $30\frac{9}{10} - 2\frac{1}{10}$

28. $42\frac{1}{5} + 8\frac{3}{5}$

Problem Solving

29. The fence around Lucy's garden was $7\frac{4}{12}$ ft high. She put chicken wire at the top so it is now $10\frac{7}{12}$ ft high. How many feet of wire did she add to the height of the fence?

MENTAL MATH

Add or subtract. Watch the signs.

30. $8\frac{7}{8} - 4$

31. $9 + 5\frac{2}{3}$

32. $7\frac{9}{10} + 6$

33. $10\frac{3}{4} - 9$

Multiples

▶ The multiples of a number are all the products that have that number as a factor.

factors ▭→
	0	1	2	3	4	5	6	7	8	9
	×2	×2	×2	×2	×2	×2	×2	×2	×2	×2

Multiples of 2:   0   2   4   6   8   10   12   14   16   18 . . .

factors ▭→
	0	1	2	3	4	5	6	7	8	9
	×3	×3	×3	×3	×3	×3	×3	×3	×3	×3

Multiples of 3:   0   3   6   9   12   15   18   21   24   27 . . .

> You can find the multiples of a number by multiplying or by skip counting.

▶ Common multiples are all the numbers other than 0 that are multiples of two or more numbers.

Multiples of 2: 0, 2, 4, 6, 8, 10, 12, 14, 16, 18, 20, 22, 24, . . .

Multiples of 3: 0, 3, 6, 9, 12, 15, 18, 21, 24, . . .

Common multiples of 2 and 3: 6, 12, 18, 24, . . .

▶ The least common multiple (LCM) of two or more numbers is the least number that is a multiple of those numbers.

Least common multiple (LCM) of 2 and 3: 6

Practice

Is each a multiple of 2? Write *yes* or *no*.

1. 5   2. 40   3. 62   4. 0   5. 29   6. 88

Is each a multiple of 3? Write *yes* or *no*.

7. 33   8. 1   9. 29   10. 60   11. 48   12. 100

Is each a multiple of 4? Write *yes* or *no*.

13. 16   **14.** 7   **15.** 32   **16.** 18   **17.** 42   **18.** 36

Is each a multiple of 5? Write *yes* or *no*.

19. 24   **20.** 15   **21.** 70   **22.** 54   **23.** 30   **24.** 48

List the first eleven multiples of each.

25. 6   **26.** 4   **27.** 9   **28.** 10   **29.** 8   **30.** 5

Write the first four common multiples for each set of numbers. Then write the least common multiple (LCM).

31. 2, 4   **32.** 3, 9   **33.** 4, 8   **34.** 6, 3   **35.** 5, 10

36. 2, 8   **37.** 6, 9   **38.** 8, 12   **39.** 7, 2   **40.** 2, 10

41. 4, 5   **42.** 8, 10   **43.** 4, 6   **44.** 9, 12   **45.** 3, 5

46. 2, 4, and 10   **47.** 3, 9, and 12   **48.** 2, 3, and 9

49. 6, 8, and 12   **50.** 4, 6, and 8   **51.** 5, 6, and 10

CRITICAL THINKING

Write *true* or *false* for each statement. If true, give an example. If false, explain why.

52. All multiples of 3 are divisible by 3.

53. All multiples of 4 are multiples of 8.

54. No multiples of 9 are multiples of 3.

55. Some multiples of 6 are multiples of 12.

56. All multiples of 2 are even numbers.

57. No multiples of 5 are even numbers.

58. Some multiples of 3 are odd numbers.

59. All multiples of 7 are odd numbers.

Add Fractions: Unlike Denominators

Mitchell hiked from camp to Crystal Cave and then to Cedar Lake. How far did Mitchell hike?

To find how far he hiked, add: $\frac{7}{10} + \frac{1}{2}$

$\frac{7}{10}$ mile $\frac{1}{2}$ mile

Camp   Crystal Cave   Cedar Lake

To add fractions with unlike denominators:

- First find the LCM.
- Use the LCM to rename as fractions with like denominators.
- Then add the like fractions.

Multiples of 2: 2, 4, 6, 8, 10, 12 . . .
Multiples of 10: 10, 20, . . .

LCM of 2 and 10: 10

Rename the fractions.

Add the numerators. Write the like denominator.

Write the sum in simplest form.

$$\begin{array}{r}\frac{7}{10} = \frac{7}{10} \\ + \frac{1}{2} = \frac{1 \times 5}{2 \times 5} = \frac{5}{10}\end{array}$$

$$\begin{array}{r}\frac{7}{10} \\ + \frac{5}{10} \\ \hline \frac{12}{10}\end{array}$$

$$\begin{array}{r}\frac{7}{10} \\ + \frac{5}{10} \\ \hline \frac{12}{10} = 1\frac{2}{10} = 1\frac{1}{5}\end{array}$$

Mitchell hiked $1\frac{1}{5}$ miles.

Study these examples.

$$\begin{array}{r}\frac{1}{4} = \frac{1 \times 2}{4 \times 2} = \frac{2}{8} \\ + \frac{3}{8} = \frac{3}{8} \\ \hline \frac{5}{8}\end{array}$$

$$\begin{array}{r}\frac{4}{6} = \frac{4}{6} \\ + \frac{1}{3} = \frac{1 \times 2}{3 \times 2} = \frac{2}{6} \\ \hline \frac{6}{6} = 1\end{array}$$

$$\begin{array}{r}\frac{3}{4} = \frac{3 \times 3}{4 \times 3} = \frac{9}{12} \\ + \frac{1}{12} = \frac{1}{12} \\ \hline \frac{10}{12} = \frac{5}{6}\end{array}$$

Find the sum in simplest form.

1. $\dfrac{6}{8}$
$+\dfrac{1}{4}$

2. $\dfrac{1}{3}$
$+\dfrac{5}{12}$

3. $\dfrac{2}{3}$
$+\dfrac{4}{9}$

4. $\dfrac{1}{2}$
$+\dfrac{5}{8}$

5. $\dfrac{3}{5}$
$+\dfrac{3}{10}$

6. $\dfrac{7}{9}$
$+\dfrac{1}{3}$

7. $\dfrac{8}{10}$
$+\dfrac{1}{5}$

8. $\dfrac{7}{8}$
$+\dfrac{3}{4}$

9. $\dfrac{5}{12}$
$+\dfrac{1}{6}$

10. $\dfrac{2}{3}$
$+\dfrac{5}{6}$

11. $\dfrac{1}{4}$
$+\dfrac{5}{12}$

12. $\dfrac{6}{9}$
$+\dfrac{1}{3}$

13. $\dfrac{11}{12}$
$+\dfrac{3}{4}$

14. $\dfrac{1}{2}$
$+\dfrac{4}{8}$

15. $\dfrac{4}{5}$
$+\dfrac{6}{10}$

16. $\dfrac{2}{3} + \dfrac{1}{6}$

17. $\dfrac{1}{2} + \dfrac{5}{10}$

18. $\dfrac{1}{3} + \dfrac{5}{9}$

19. $\dfrac{3}{4} + \dfrac{2}{12}$

20. $\dfrac{2}{5} + \dfrac{9}{10}$

21. $\dfrac{5}{8} + \dfrac{1}{4}$

22. $\dfrac{3}{4} + \dfrac{7}{12}$

23. $\dfrac{2}{9} + \dfrac{2}{3}$

Problem Solving

24. At camp, campers play water polo, play soccer, swim, and hike. What fraction of the campers play water sports?

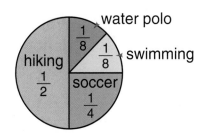

water polo

swimming

hiking $\dfrac{1}{2}$

$\dfrac{1}{8}$

$\dfrac{1}{8}$

soccer $\dfrac{1}{4}$

DO YOU REMEMBER?

Match each definition to the correct term in the box.

25. names the number of equal parts

26. made up of a whole number and a fraction

27. names the total number of parts in the whole or set

> denominator
> numerator
> common factor
> mixed number

Subtract Fractions: Unlike Denominators

Lila had $\frac{11}{12}$ ft of balsa wood. She used $\frac{1}{4}$ ft of the wood to make a miniature chair for her dollhouse. How much wood did Lila have left?

To find how much she had left, subtract: $\frac{11}{12} - \frac{1}{4}$

To subtract fractions with unlike denominators:

- First find the LCM.
- Use the LCM to rename as fractions with like denominators.
- Then subtract the like fractions.

Multiples of 4: 4, 8, 12, 16, 20, . . .
Multiples of 12: 12, 24, 36, . . .

LCM of 4 and 12: 12

| Rename the fractions. | Subtract the numerators. Write the like denominator. | Write the difference in simplest form. |

$$\frac{11}{12} = \frac{11}{12}$$
$$-\frac{1}{4} = \frac{1 \times 3}{4 \times 3} = \frac{3}{12}$$

$$\frac{11}{12}$$
$$-\frac{3}{12}$$
$$\frac{8}{12}$$

$$\frac{11}{12}$$
$$-\frac{3}{12}$$
$$\frac{8}{12} = \frac{2}{3}$$

Lila had $\frac{2}{3}$ ft of wood left.

Study these examples.

$$\frac{3}{4} = \frac{3}{4}$$
$$-\frac{1}{2} = \frac{1 \times 2}{2 \times 2} = \frac{2}{4}$$
$$\frac{1}{4}$$

$$\frac{2}{3} = \frac{2 \times 3}{3 \times 3} = \frac{6}{9}$$
$$-\frac{6}{9} = \frac{6}{9}$$
$$\frac{0}{9} = 0$$

Find the difference in simplest form.

1. $\dfrac{2}{3}$
$-\dfrac{1}{6}$

2. $\dfrac{9}{10}$
$-\dfrac{1}{2}$

3. $\dfrac{7}{9}$
$-\dfrac{2}{3}$

4. $\dfrac{9}{12}$
$-\dfrac{3}{4}$

5. $\dfrac{7}{8}$
$-\dfrac{1}{2}$

6. $\dfrac{7}{10}$
$-\dfrac{1}{5}$

7. $\dfrac{7}{8}$
$-\dfrac{3}{4}$

8. $\dfrac{5}{6}$
$-\dfrac{2}{12}$

9. $\dfrac{2}{3}$
$-\dfrac{2}{9}$

10. $\dfrac{3}{4}$
$-\dfrac{6}{8}$

11. $\dfrac{10}{12}$
$-\dfrac{2}{6}$

12. $\dfrac{6}{8}$
$-\dfrac{1}{2}$

13. $\dfrac{1}{2}$
$-\dfrac{3}{12}$

14. $\dfrac{3}{5}$
$-\dfrac{1}{10}$

15. $\dfrac{8}{9}$
$-\dfrac{2}{3}$

16. $\dfrac{3}{4}$
$-\dfrac{8}{12}$

17. $\dfrac{9}{10}$
$-\dfrac{3}{5}$

18. $\dfrac{8}{9}$
$-\dfrac{1}{3}$

19. $\dfrac{7}{10}$
$-\dfrac{1}{2}$

20. $\dfrac{1}{3}$
$-\dfrac{2}{6}$

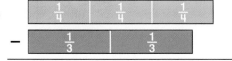 **Write each answer in simplest form.**

21. Kyle worked on his model airplane for $\dfrac{3}{4}$ hour. Lief worked on his model ship for $\dfrac{1}{2}$ hour. How much longer did Kyle work than Lief?

22. Sharon decorated a valentine with pieces of ribbon. She used $\dfrac{2}{6}$ ft of red ribbon and $\dfrac{8}{12}$ ft of white ribbon. How much more white than red ribbon did Sharon use?

23. Clint had a large sheet of paper that was $\dfrac{9}{12}$ yd long. He trimmed $\dfrac{1}{3}$ yd from it. How long was the sheet of paper after trimming?

CHALLENGE

Write the addition or the subtraction shown.

24.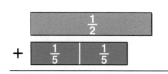

25.

Compute Probability

There are 10 marbles in the jar:
1 is purple, 2 are white, 3 are red, and
4 are yellow. What is the probability that,
without looking, you would pick a marble
of each color?

▶ The probability that you would pick:

- purple is 1 out of 10, or $\frac{1}{10}$.
- white is 2 out of 10, or $\frac{2}{10}$.
- red is 3 out of 10, or $\frac{3}{10}$.
- yellow is 4 out of 10, or $\frac{4}{10}$.

$$\text{Probability of an event} = \frac{\text{number of favorable outcomes}}{\text{number of possible outcomes}}$$

Probability of picking
a red marble: $\frac{3}{10}$

Write: $P(\text{red}) = \frac{3}{10}$ ← 3 red marbles
← 10 total marbles

▶ What is the probability that you would
pick a red *or* a purple marble?

To find the probability of picking red
or purple, add the two probabilities
by adding the fractions.

$$\frac{3}{10} + \frac{1}{10} = \frac{4}{10}$$

$P(\text{red})$ $P(\text{purple})$

Probability of picking red
or purple: $\frac{4}{10}$

Write: $P(\text{red or purple}) = \frac{4}{10}$

Practice

Find the probability of each event. Use the spinner.

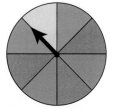

1. $P(\text{green})$
2. $P(\text{yellow})$

3. $P(\text{blue})$
4. $P(\text{green or yellow})$

5. $P(\text{red or blue})$
6. $P(\text{green or yellow or red})$
7. $P(\text{red})$

Find the probability of each event.
Use the cards.

8. P(B)

9. P(E)

10. P(C)

11. P(D)

12. P(A or C)

13. P(B or D)

14. P(A or B or E)

15. P(B or C or D)

16. P(not D)

Find the probability of each event. Use the shapes.

17. P(circle)

18. P(triangle)

19. P(square or triangle)

Certain and Impossible

What is the probability of spinning
red or white or blue?

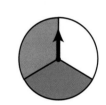

It is **certain** that the spinner will land
on red or white or blue.

$$P(\text{red or white or blue}) = \frac{1}{3} + \frac{1}{3} + \frac{1}{3} = \frac{3}{3} = 1 \longleftarrow \boxed{P(\text{certain}) = 1}$$

What is the probability of spinning green?

It is **impossible** that the spinner will land on green.

$$P(\text{green}) = \frac{0}{3} = 0 \longleftarrow \boxed{P(\text{impossible}) = 0}$$

Find the probability of each event.
Use the marbles on page 312.

20. P(red or yellow or white)

21. P(orange or green)

22. P(red or purple or white or yellow)

Find Part of a Number

There are 12 kittens at the animal shelter. How many kittens are white? How many kittens are gray?

Kittens at the Shelter

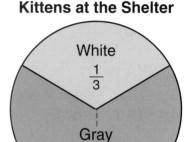

▶ To find how many of each, use the circle graph to find the fractional parts of the whole.

Since the graph shows that $\frac{1}{3}$ of the kittens is white, find $\frac{1}{3}$ of 12.

• Divide 12 into **3** equal parts, or thirds.

$12 \div 3 = 4$
There are 4 in each third.
So $\frac{1}{3}$ of 12 = 4

How many are in two thirds?
$2 \times 4 = 8$
So $\frac{2}{3}$ of 12 = 8

▶ To find a fractional part of a number:

• **Divide** the whole number by the denominator.

• **Multiply** the quotient by the numerator.

$\frac{1}{3}$ of 12: $12 \div 3 = 4 \longrightarrow 1 \times 4 = 4$ So $\frac{1}{3}$ of 12 = 4.

$\frac{2}{3}$ of 12: $12 \div 3 = 4 \longrightarrow 2 \times 4 = 8$ So $\frac{2}{3}$ of 12 = 8.

Of the kittens, 4 are white and 8 are gray.

Practice

Find the part of each number. You may draw a picture.

1. $\frac{1}{5}$ of 15

2. $\frac{1}{3}$ of 9

3. $\frac{1}{2}$ of 14

4. $\frac{1}{8}$ of 40

5. $\frac{1}{4}$ of 24

6. $\frac{1}{9}$ of 36

7. $\frac{1}{7}$ of 42

8. $\frac{1}{5}$ of 50

9. $\frac{1}{6}$ of 30

10. $\frac{1}{6}$ of 24

11. $\frac{1}{8}$ of 16

12. $\frac{1}{2}$ of 8

Find the value of each variable.

13. $\frac{2}{3}$ of 15 = n

14. $\frac{5}{8}$ of 16 = a

15. $\frac{5}{6}$ of 18 = x

16. $\frac{3}{7}$ of 21 = b

17. $\frac{3}{8}$ of 40 = v

18. $\frac{2}{5}$ of 25 = d

19. $\frac{3}{4}$ of 32 = s

20. $\frac{2}{9}$ of 27 = c

21. $\frac{5}{7}$ of 14 = u

22. $\frac{4}{5}$ of 45 = m

23. $\frac{3}{8}$ of 64 = p

24. $\frac{8}{9}$ of 9 = t

Problem Solving

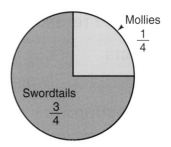

Mollies $\frac{1}{4}$

Swordtails $\frac{3}{4}$

25. There are 16 fish in Fiona's fish tank. How many mollies and swordtails does Fiona have in her tank?

26. Jim raised 28 rabbits. Of these, $\frac{3}{4}$ were black and white. How many were not black and white?

27. Of 30 retrievers at the kennel, $\frac{4}{5}$ were golden retrievers. How many were golden retrievers?

28. Mr. Green has 64 chickens. Of these, $\frac{3}{8}$ are Rhode Island Reds. How many are Rhode Island Reds?

29. Of 150 birds that came to the feeder, $\frac{2}{3}$ were finches. How many were not finches?

CHALLENGE

Find the original number.

$\frac{1}{2}$ of n = 6

Think
Halves mean 2 equal groups.

To find the original number, multiply the whole number by the denominator.

2 × 6 = 12 ⟶ So, $\frac{1}{2}$ of 12 = 6.

↑ Number of groups

↑ Number in each group

Find the original number.

30. $\frac{1}{2}$ of n = 14

31. $\frac{1}{4}$ of n = 24

32. $\frac{1}{5}$ of n = 10

Problem-Solving Strategy: Use Simpler Numbers

A piece of ribbon is $12\frac{7}{8}$ ft long. Kim cuts off two pieces that are $4\frac{3}{8}$ ft each. Does she have enough ribbon left to cut one more piece the same length?

Read

Visualize the facts of the problem as you reread it.

Facts: $12\frac{7}{8}$ ft of ribbon
Two $4\frac{3}{8}$ ft pieces cut from it

Question: Is there $4\frac{3}{8}$ ft left?

Plan

Use simpler numbers to help choose the operation.
Use 12 for the $12\frac{7}{8}$ ft length.

Use 4 for the $4\frac{3}{8}$ ft length.

Add to find the amount of ribbon cut: $4 \text{ ft} + 4 \text{ ft} = 8 \text{ ft}$
Subtract to find the amount of ribbon left: $12 \text{ ft} - 8 \text{ ft} = 4 \text{ ft}$

Solve

Now use the same operations with the numbers in the problem.

$$\begin{array}{r} 4\frac{3}{8} \text{ ft} \\ + 4\frac{3}{8} \text{ ft} \\ \hline 8\frac{6}{8} \text{ ft cut} \end{array} \qquad \begin{array}{r} 12\frac{7}{8} \text{ ft} \\ - 8\frac{6}{8} \text{ ft} \\ \hline 4\frac{1}{8} \text{ ft left} \end{array}$$

Compare: $4\frac{1}{8} < 4\frac{3}{8}$. So Kim does *not* have enough ribbon to cut another piece of the same length.

Check

Add the lengths of the pieces.
Do they equal $12\frac{7}{8}$ ft?

$4\frac{3}{8} + 4\frac{3}{8} + 4\frac{1}{8} = 12\frac{7}{8}$ ✔

Use simpler numbers to solve each problem.

1. Frank checked his kitten's weight on the first day of each month. He kept the information on a chart. How much weight did the kitten gain between April 1 and June 1?

My Kitten's Weight		
April 1	May 1	June 1
$6\frac{4}{8}$ lb	$7\frac{1}{8}$ lb	$7\frac{5}{8}$ lb

Read ▶ Visualize the facts of the problem as you reread it.

Facts: April 1: $6\frac{4}{8}$ lb

June 1: $7\frac{5}{8}$ lb

Question: How much weight did the kitten gain between April 1 and June 1?

Plan ▶ Use 6 for $6\frac{4}{8}$ and 7 for $7\frac{5}{8}$.

Subtract to find the difference. $7 - 6 = \underline{\ ?\ }$
Then use the same operation
with the numbers in the problem.

Solve ⋯⋯▶ **Check**

2. One paper-clip chain is $24\frac{1}{4}$ in. long. Another is $41\frac{1}{4}$ in. long. How long will the chain be if the two chains are connected?

3. Ms. Hanley is running a $26\frac{5}{10}$ mile race. She stops for water after $7\frac{3}{10}$ miles. How much farther does she have to run?

4. A bread recipe calls for $4\frac{3}{8}$ c of white flour, $2\frac{1}{8}$ c of wheat flour, and 1 c of rye flour. How much flour does this recipe use?

Write Your Own

5. Write a problem with fractions or mixed numbers. Use simpler numbers. Then solve it using the original numbers.

Problem-Solving Applications: Mixed Review

Solve each problem and explain the method you used.

1. An oatmeal bar weighs $4\frac{1}{4}$ oz. How much do two oatmeal bars weigh?

2. Bags of granola weigh $6\frac{1}{8}$ oz and $12\frac{3}{8}$ oz. How much heavier is the larger bag?

3. An apple weighs $3\frac{3}{4}$ oz. A pear weighs $4\frac{1}{4}$ oz. About how much do they weigh together?

4. Todd uses 16 tablespoons of jam to make sandwiches. If he spreads each sandwich with $\frac{1}{8}$ of the jam, does he have enough for 10 sandwiches?

5. Of 10 loaves of bread, $\frac{1}{5}$ have sesame seeds. How many loaves have sesame seeds?

6. Carrot bread has 100 calories per slice. Seven tenths of the calories come from carbohydrates. How many calories come from carbohydrates?

7. Nan bought $\frac{1}{8}$ lb of pecans and $\frac{1}{4}$ lb of walnuts. Did she buy more than $\frac{1}{2}$ lb of nuts?

8. A carrot is 9 in. long. Regina cuts it in thirds. How long is each piece?

Choose a strategy from the list or use another strategy you know to solve each problem.

9. Of 24 muffins for sale, $\frac{1}{2}$ are bran, $\frac{1}{4}$ are corn, and the rest are oat. How many oat muffins are for sale?

10. Jan bought half a loaf of rye bread. She gave half of her piece to Ramon. Ramon's piece weighs $\frac{1}{4}$ lb. How much did the original loaf of bread weigh?

11. A carrot has fewer calories than an apple. An oat bar has more calories than an apple. Does a carrot or an oat bar have more calories?

12. Sue's trail mix is $\frac{1}{2}$ toasted oats, $\frac{1}{4}$ raisins, and $\frac{1}{4}$ carob drops. She has 3 oz of raisins. Does she have enough raisins to make 16 oz of mix?

13. Wes ate a snack of 150 calories. The low-fat yogurt he ate had half the calories of the oatmeal cookie. How many calories did the yogurt have?

Strategy File

Use These Strategies
Choose the Operation
Guess and Test
Use Simpler Numbers
Use More Than One Step
Work Backward
Logical Reasoning
Use a Diagram/Graph

Use the pictograph for problems 14–16.

14. What fractional part of the mini-muffins were blueberry muffins?

15. How many more apple muffins than blueberry muffins were there?

16. Liu bought $\frac{1}{2}$ of the cinnamon muffins. How many muffins did she buy?

Mini-Muffin Menu	
apple	⬡ ⬡ ⬡
blueberry	⬡ ⬡
cinnamon	⬡ ⬡ ⬡ ⬡
corn	⬡
Key: Each ⬡ = 5 mini-muffins.	

Add or subtract.
Write the answer in simplest form.

(See pp. 296–301, 304–305, 308–311.)

1. $\dfrac{1}{5}$ $+\dfrac{2}{5}$

2. $\dfrac{5}{8}$ $-\dfrac{3}{8}$

3. $\dfrac{5}{6}$ $+\dfrac{1}{2}$

4. $\dfrac{8}{9}$ $-\dfrac{2}{3}$

5. $\dfrac{7}{10}$ $-\dfrac{2}{20}$

6. $4\dfrac{1}{10}$ $+3\dfrac{1}{10}$

7. $8\dfrac{2}{6}$ $-4\dfrac{1}{6}$

8. $5\dfrac{3}{16}$ $-3\dfrac{3}{16}$

9. $12\dfrac{1}{8}$ $+\ 2\dfrac{1}{8}$

10. $5\dfrac{3}{8}$ $+4\dfrac{1}{8}$

11. $\dfrac{1}{2} + \dfrac{1}{2}$

12. $\dfrac{6}{10} - \dfrac{1}{5}$

13. $\dfrac{1}{4} + \dfrac{7}{8}$

14. $\dfrac{5}{6} - \dfrac{1}{3}$

Write as a whole number or mixed number
in simplest form.

(See pp. 300–301.)

15. $\dfrac{16}{8}$

16. $\dfrac{13}{4}$

17. $\dfrac{15}{6}$

18. $\dfrac{20}{5}$

19. $\dfrac{17}{3}$

Write the least common multiple (LCM) of each set. (See pp. 306–307.)

20. 4, 10

21. 9, 12

22. 9, 6

23. 5, 6

Estimate the sum or difference. (See pp. 302–303.)

24. $11\dfrac{5}{9} - 4\dfrac{2}{3}$

25. $2\dfrac{1}{3} + 3\dfrac{5}{6} + 1\dfrac{1}{9}$

Find the part of each number. (See pp. 314–315.)

26. $\dfrac{1}{3}$ of 18

27. $\dfrac{1}{8}$ of 24

28. $\dfrac{3}{4}$ of 40

29. $\dfrac{5}{8}$ of 24

Problem Solving

(See pp. 312–315.)

30. Of 24 apples, $\dfrac{1}{3}$ are green.

    How many are not green?

31. There are 7 marbles in a bag. Four are red, 2 are blue and 1 is green. What is the probability that the first one picked will be red?

(See *Still More Practice*, p. 469.)

Least Common Denominator

Rafael's cookie recipe called for $\frac{1}{3}$ cup of brown sugar and $\frac{3}{4}$ cup of white sugar. How much sugar did Rafael use?

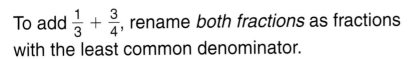

Add: $\frac{1}{3} + \frac{3}{4}$

To add $\frac{1}{3} + \frac{3}{4}$, rename *both fractions* as fractions with the least common denominator.

The least common denominator (LCD) is the least common multiple of the denominators.

Multiples of 3: 0, 3, 6, 9, 12, 15, 18, 21, 24, . . .
Multiples of 4: 0, 4, 8, 12, 16, 20, 24, . . .
So the LCD of $\frac{1}{3}$ and $\frac{3}{4}$ is 12.

Rename the fractions.

$$\frac{1}{3} = \frac{1 \times 4}{3 \times 4} = \frac{4}{12}$$
$$+ \frac{3}{4} = \frac{3 \times 3}{4 \times 3} = \frac{9}{12}$$

Add.

$$\frac{4}{12}$$
$$+ \frac{9}{12}$$
$$\overline{\frac{13}{12}} = 1\frac{1}{12} \leftarrow \boxed{\text{simplest form}}$$

Rafael used $1\frac{1}{12}$ cups of sugar.

Write the LCD for each set of fractions.

1. $\frac{1}{2}, \frac{2}{5}$ **2.** $\frac{3}{4}, \frac{1}{6}$ **3.** $\frac{2}{3}, \frac{3}{8}$ **4.** $\frac{1}{5}, \frac{1}{6}$

5. $\frac{3}{10}, \frac{1}{4}$ **6.** $\frac{4}{5}, \frac{3}{4}$ **7.** $\frac{1}{3}, \frac{1}{5}, \frac{1}{6}$ **8.** $\frac{1}{3}, \frac{1}{4}, \frac{1}{5}$

Add or subtract. Write the answer in simplest form.

9. $\frac{1}{2} + \frac{2}{7}$ **10.** $\frac{1}{4} + \frac{3}{5}$ **11.** $\frac{5}{6} - \frac{1}{9}$ **12.** $\frac{2}{3} - \frac{1}{2}$

13. $\frac{7}{8} - \frac{3}{10}$ **14.** $\frac{9}{10} + \frac{1}{6}$ **15.** $\frac{7}{9} - \frac{3}{8}$ **16.** $\frac{5}{8} + \frac{2}{3}$

Chapter 9 Test

Add or subtract. Write the answer in simplest form.

1. $\frac{3}{10} + \frac{1}{5}$

2. $\frac{1}{6} + \frac{2}{6}$

3. $\frac{7}{8} - \frac{5}{8}$

4. $\frac{2}{3} - \frac{1}{6}$

5. $\frac{4}{5} - \frac{3}{10}$

6. $\frac{7}{8} + \frac{1}{4}$

7. $\frac{8}{10} - \frac{1}{2}$

8. $\frac{2}{3} + \frac{11}{12}$

Write as a whole number or mixed number in simplest form.

9. $\frac{7}{2}$

10. $\frac{16}{5}$

11. $\frac{21}{8}$

12. $\frac{30}{6}$

13. $\frac{38}{7}$

Write the least common multiple (LCM).

14. 2, 6

15. 4, 3

16. 4, 12

17. 5, 7

Find the part of each number.

18. $\frac{1}{2}$ of 26

19. $\frac{2}{3}$ of 21

20. $\frac{3}{5}$ of 25

21. $\frac{5}{8}$ of 64

Problem Solving

Use a strategy you have learned.

22. One necklace is $30\frac{1}{4}$ in. long. Another is $36\frac{1}{2}$ in. long. If the two necklaces are connected, how long will the necklace be?

Tell About It

Explain how you solved the problem.

23. Of 32 apples $\frac{1}{4}$ are red. How many are not red?

Performance Assessment

Use these rule cards. Match the rule card to each pattern, then tell the next number.

Add $\frac{1}{6}$ Add $2\frac{1}{4}$ Subtract $\frac{1}{5}$

24. $\frac{9}{10}, \frac{7}{10}, \frac{5}{10}, \frac{?}{?}$

25. $\frac{5}{12}, \frac{7}{12}, \frac{9}{12}, \frac{?}{?}$

26. $1\frac{3}{4}, 4, 6\frac{1}{4}, \underline{\ ?\ }$

Test Preparation

Choose the best answer.

1. What is the value of the underlined digit in 68,325,784?

  a. 800,000   **b.** 1,000,000
  c. 8,000,000   **d.** 80,000,000

2. What is the cost of 32 CDs at $9.79 each?

  a. $19.58   **b.** $48.95
  c. $312.28   **d.** $313.28

3. How much more than 4000 − 1967 is 1267 + 1967?

  a. 101   **b.** 201
  c. 1091   **d.** none of these

4. 465 is divisible by which number?

  a. 2   **b.** 5
  c. 10   **d.** none of these

5. What fractional part is shaded?

  a. $\frac{1}{3}$ **b.** $\frac{7}{15}$ **c.** $\frac{8}{15}$ **d.** $\frac{3}{4}$

6. $\frac{7}{8}$
$-\frac{3}{8}$

  a. $\frac{1}{3}$ **b.** $\frac{1}{2}$
  c. $\frac{3}{4}$ **d.** not given

7. $3\frac{1}{7} + 2\frac{4}{7}$

  a. $5\frac{5}{14}$ **b.** $5\frac{4}{7}$
  c. $6\frac{5}{7}$ **d.** not given

8. How many minutes have passed from 6:45 P.M. to 7:12 P.M.?

  a. 15 min   **b.** 27 min
  c. 42 min   **d.** 47 min

9. Find the mean of 498, 636, and 714.

  a. 507   **b.** 612
  c. 616   **d.** 1848

10. How many liters of water are there in 8 containers of 750 mL each?

  a. 6 L   **b.** 60 L
  c. 600 L   **d.** 6000 L

11. Add: 4 ft 6 in. + 3 ft 8 in.

  a. 7 ft 2 in.   **b.** 7 ft 4 in.
  c. 8 ft   **d.** 8 ft 2 in.

12. What mixed number is shown?

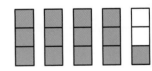

  a. $4\frac{1}{3}$ **b.** $4\frac{1}{2}$ **c.** $5\frac{1}{3}$ **d.** $5\frac{1}{2}$

13. $\frac{1}{3}$
$+\frac{4}{9}$

  a. $\frac{5}{12}$ **b.** $\frac{5}{9}$
  c. $\frac{7}{9}$ **d.** not given

14. $\frac{3}{4}$ of 36 = ?

  a. 9   **b.** 27
  c. 48   **d.** not given

15. Solve: $n - 11$, when $n = 19$

    a. 8   **b.** 10

    c. 19   **d.** 30

16. Beth baby-sits for $4 an hour. She needs $112.00 for a new CD player. How many hours does she need to baby-sit?

    a. 112 hours
    b. 28 hours
    c. 108 hours
    d. 116 hours

17. Rename the unit of capacity.

32 fl oz = __?__ pt

    a. 2   **b.** 4   **c.** 6   **d.** 8

18. Lisa bikes $17\frac{2}{3}$ miles on Saturday. On Sunday, she bikes $4\frac{1}{3}$ miles less than that. How many miles did she ride on the weekend?

    a. $13\frac{1}{3}$ mi   **b.** $30\frac{2}{3}$ mi

    c. 31 mi   **d.** $4\frac{1}{3}$ mi

19. Divide.

$9\overline{)952}$

    a. 105 R7   **b.** 107

    c. 115 R7   **d.** 15 R7

20. Pedro writes 4 pages of a story every hour. By 2:15 P.M. he has written 16 pages. What time did he start writing?

    a. 6:15 P.M.
    b. 10:15 P.M.
    c. 10:15 A.M.
    d. 12:15 P.M.

21. Find the quotient.

$84 \div 6$

    a. 78   **b.** 90   **c.** 16   **d.** 14

22. A certain fraction has a denominator that is 4 more than its numerator. It is equivalent to $\frac{2}{3}$. What is the fraction?

    a. $\frac{10}{14}$ **b.** $\frac{8}{12}$

    c. $\frac{6}{10}$ **d.** $\frac{4}{6}$

23. Which 2 pets make up one half of the students' pets?

    a. hamsters and fish   **b.** cats and birds
    c. fish and cats   **d.** dogs and birds

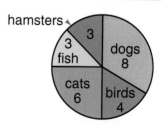

**Explain how you solved the problem.
Show all your work.**

24. Write a question that you are **not** able to ask using the line graph. Explain why the line graph cannot answer the question. Then draw a diagram or graph that can answer your question.

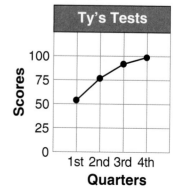

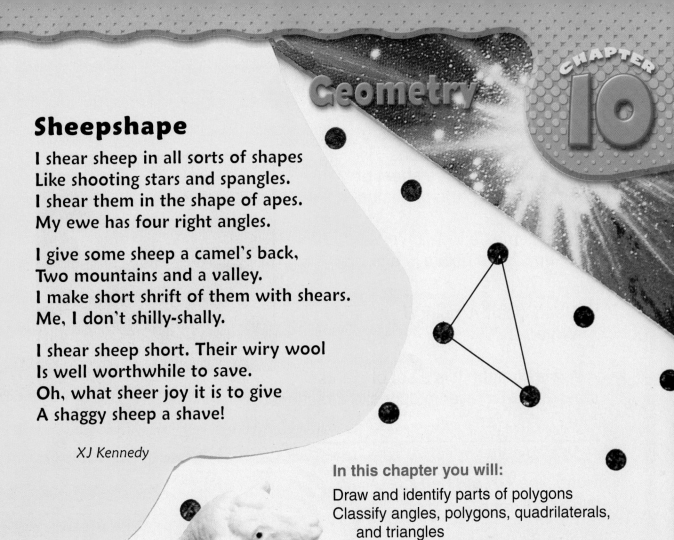

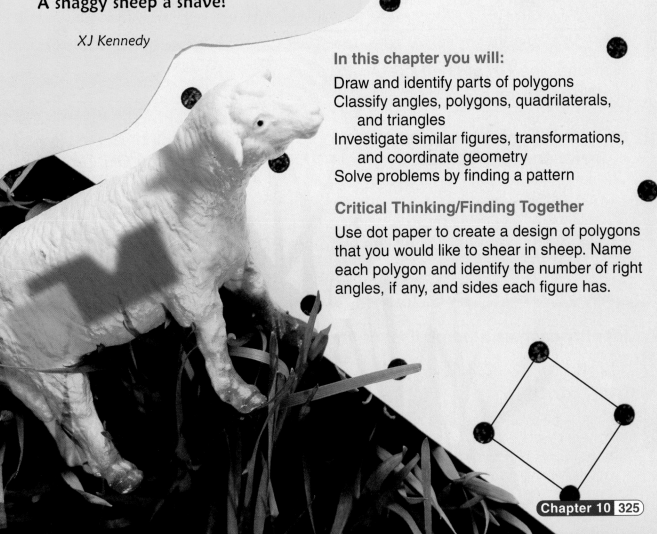

Geometry

CHAPTER 10

Sheepshape

I shear sheep in all sorts of shapes
Like shooting stars and spangles.
I shear them in the shape of apes.
My ewe has four right angles.

I give some sheep a camel's back,
Two mountains and a valley.
I make short shrift of them with shears.
Me, I don't shilly-shally.

I shear sheep short. Their wiry wool
Is well worthwhile to save.
Oh, what sheer joy it is to give
A shaggy sheep a shave!

XJ Kennedy

In this chapter you will:

Draw and identify parts of polygons
Classify angles, polygons, quadrilaterals,
    and triangles
Investigate similar figures, transformations,
    and coordinate geometry
Solve problems by finding a pattern

Critical Thinking/Finding Together

Use dot paper to create a design of polygons
that you would like to shear in sheep. Name
each polygon and identify the number of right
angles, if any, and sides each figure has.

Points, Lines, and Line Segments

▶ A plane is a flat surface that extends indefinitely in all directions. The surface of a table or a sheet of paper are both parts of planes.

▶ A point names a location in space. *A*, *B*, and *X* are points in a plane.

A •   B   • X

Read: point *A*, point *B*, point *X*
Write: *A*, *B*, *X*

▶ A line is straight. It is a set of points that extends forever in opposite directions.

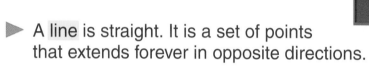

Read: line *GH* **or** line *HG*
Write: $\overleftrightarrow{GH}$ **or** $\overleftrightarrow{HG}$

▶ A line segment is the part of a line between two endpoints.

Line segment *GH* is part of line *GH*.

Read: line segment *DE* **or** line segment *ED*
Write: $\overline{DE}$ **or** $\overline{ED}$

Practice

Identify each as a *point*, *line*, or *line segment*. Use symbols.

1. •R

2.

3.

4.

5.

6. L•

7.

8.

Draw and label each.

9. $\overline{TV}$

10. K

11. $\overleftrightarrow{ST}$

12. $\overline{FG}$

13. D

14. $\overrightarrow{PQ}$

15. $\overline{LM}$

16. Z

Which figures are line segments?

17. **a.** **b.**  **c.** **d.**

18. **a.** **b.**  **c.** **d.**

Name each line two ways.

19.
C   D

20.
K   L

21.
R   S

Name each line segment two ways.

22.
W   X

23.
S   T

24. Q_____R

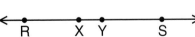

CHALLENGE

You can name a line by naming any two points on the line in any order.

25. Write 6 names for this line: ←———•———————•—•—→
                                        M   O N

26. Write 12 names for this line: ←——•————•—•———•——→
                                         R   X Y   S

Rays and Angles

▶ A ray is the part of a line that starts at an endpoint.
A ray goes on forever in one direction.

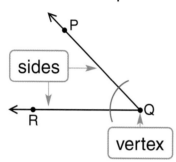

J   K

Read: ray *KJ*
Write: $\overrightarrow{KJ}$

Read the endpoint first.

▶ An angle is formed by two rays with the same endpoint.

sides

P

R   Q

vertex

The rays form the **sides** of the angle.

The common endpoint is the **vertex** of the angle.

Read: angle *Q*, angle *PQR*, or angle *RQP*
Write: ∠*Q* or ∠*PQR* or ∠*RQP*

When you name an angle with three letters, the vertex is always the middle letter.

Practice

Draw and label each figure.

1. ∠*DEF*   **2.** $\overrightarrow{ED}$ **3.** ∠*FED*   **4.** ∠*H*   **5.** ray *EF*

Name each figure.

6.

A
B

7.

C
D
E

8.

G
F
H

Name each angle three ways.

9.

J   I
K

10.

L
M
N

11.

P   Q
O

Measuring Angles

You can measure angles in **degrees** (°) using a **protractor**. Measure an angle by measuring the distance between its sides.

Right Angle	**Acute Angle**	**Obtuse Angle**
	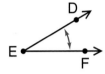	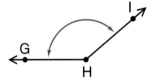
• forms a square corner • measures 90°	• measures less than 90°	• measures more than 90°, but less than 180°

Straight Angle

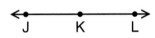

• measures 180°

Use a protractor to tell whether each angle is _right_, _acute_, _obtuse_, or _straight_.

12.

13.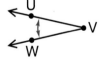

14.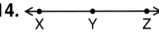

15.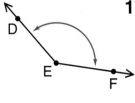

16.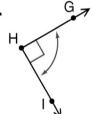

17.

18.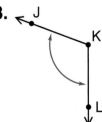

10-3 · Parallel and Perpendicular Lines

▶ **Intersecting lines** are lines that meet or cross at a common point.

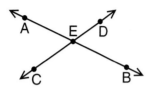

$\overleftrightarrow{AB}$ and $\overleftrightarrow{CD}$ intersect at point E.

▶ **Perpendicular lines** are intersecting lines that form four right angles.

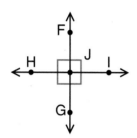

Read: line FG is perpendicular to line HI

Write: $\overleftrightarrow{FG} \perp \overleftrightarrow{HI}$

▶ **Parallel lines** are lines in the same plane that never intersect.

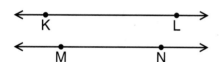

Read: line KL is parallel to line MN

Write: $\overleftrightarrow{KL} \parallel \overleftrightarrow{MN}$

Line segments can also be intersecting, perpendicular, or parallel.

Write *intersecting* or *parallel* to describe each pair of lines.

1.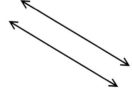

2.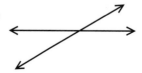

3.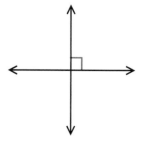

Use the figure at the right.

4. At what point does $\overleftrightarrow{EH}$ intersect $\overleftrightarrow{KL}$?

5. Name the lines that appear to be parallel lines.

6. What kind of angle is $\angle IBA$?

7. Name two pairs of perpendicular lines.

8. Is $\angle FGL$ acute or obtuse?

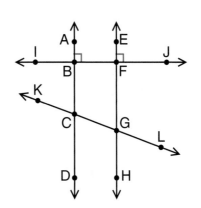

Copy these lines on dot paper.
Use these lines for exercises 9–12.

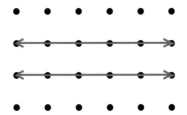

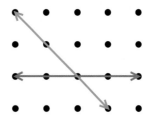

Draw a line segment that:

9. is perpendicular to both red lines.

10. is parallel to the green line and intersects the blue line.

11. intersects one red line but not the other.

12. is perpendicular to the green line.

CRITICAL THINKING

13. Are $\overleftrightarrow{RS}$ and $\overleftrightarrow{XY}$ parallel, intersecting, or neither? Explain your answer in your Math Journal.

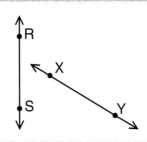

Circles

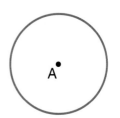

▶ A **circle** is a plane figure. All the points on the circle are the same distance from a given point, called the **center**.

Point *A* is the center of circle *A*.

> A circle is named by its center point.

▶ The parts of a circle have special names.

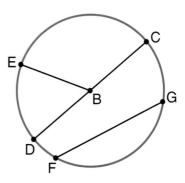

Any line segment with endpoints at the *center* of the circle and *on* the circle is a **radius**.

$\overline{BE}$ is a radius of circle *B*. $\overline{BC}$ and $\overline{BD}$ are also **radii** (plural of radius) of circle *B*.

Any line segment that passes *through* the center of the circle and has *both* endpoints on the circle is a **diameter**.

$\overline{CD}$ is a diameter.

> The length of the diameter is always twice the length of the radius.

Any line segment with *both* endpoints *on* the circle is a **chord**.

$\overline{FG}$ is a chord.

> A diameter is a special chord.

Practice

Use circle *H*.

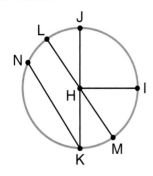

1. Name six points on the circle.

2. Name five line segments that are radii.

3. Name three line segments that are chords. Which one is not a diameter?

Use the circle at the right.

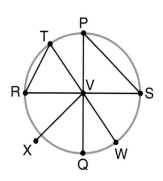

4. Name the circle and its center.

5. How many diameters are shown? Name the diameters.

6. Is $\overline{TR}$ a radius? Explain why or why not.

7. Is $\overline{VX}$ a radius? Explain why or why not.

8. How many radii are shown? Name the radii.

Curves

Simple Closed Curves

A simple closed curve is a path that begins and ends at the same point and does not cross itself.

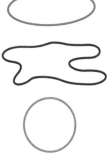

Not Simple   Not Closed

Write *true* or *false*. Use the picture below.

9. Some of the simple closed curves are green.

10. None of the simple closed curves are blue.

11. All circles are simple closed curves.

12. None of the simple closed curves are red.

Polygons

▶ These figures are all polygons:

Remember: Polygons are closed plane figures with straight sides.

The sides of a polygon are line segments that do not cross.

Two sides of a polygon form an angle when they meet at a common endpoint called a vertex (plural: vertices).

These are regular polygons, because they each have sides of equal length and angles of equal measures.

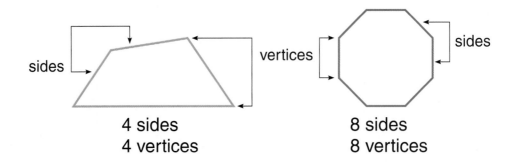

4 sides
4 vertices

8 sides
8 vertices

▶ Most polygons are named for the number of angles they have.

Polygon means "many angles."

Prefix	Number of Angles	Polygon Name
tri-	3	triangle
quadri-	4	quadrilateral
penta-	5	pentagon
hexa-	6	hexagon
octa-	8	octagon

Use dot paper for problems 1–8.

1. Draw a polygon that has 8 sides and 8 vertices. What is its name?

2. Draw a polygon that has 5 sides and 5 vertices. What is its name?

3. Draw a polygon that has 3 sides. How many vertices does it have? What is its name?

4. Draw a polygon that has 6 vertices. How many sides does it have? What is its name?

5. Draw five different quadrilaterals. How many of them have at least one right angle?

6. Draw four different hexagons.

7. Draw an octagon with all right angles. Is this a regular octagon?

8. Do you think the number of sides a polygon has is always equal to the number of its vertices? Use drawings to justify your answer.

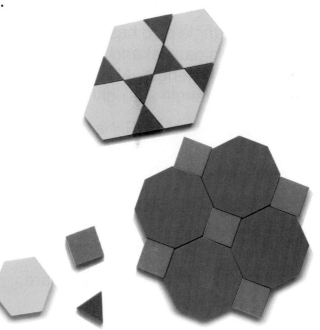

DO YOU REMEMBER?

Match each definition with a term in the box.

9. the numbers other than 0 that are multiples of two or more numbers

10. all the products that have a particular number as a factor

> multiples
> least common multiple
> common multiples

Quadrilaterals

Some quadrilaterals have special names.

> Identical marks indicate congruent sides of the figure.

▶ A **parallelogram** has opposite sides that are parallel *and* that are the same length.

Quadrilateral *ABCD* is a parallelogram.

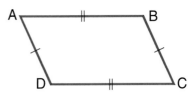

▶ A **rectangle** also has opposite sides that are parallel *and* that are the same length. All the angles of a rectangle are right angles.

Quadrilateral *EFGH* is a rectangle.

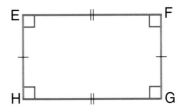

▶ A **square** has opposite sides that are parallel. All its sides are the same length. All the angles of a square are right angles.

Quadrilateral *JKLM* is a square.

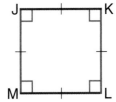

▶ A **rhombus** has opposite sides that are parallel. All four sides are the same length.

Quadrilateral *QRST* is a rhombus.

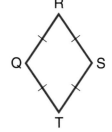

▶ A **trapezoid** has exactly one pair of parallel sides.

Quadrilateral *WXYZ* is a trapezoid.

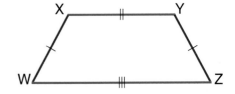

Use the figure at the right.

1. What kind of quadrilateral is figure *DEFL*?

2. What is the special name for figure *BDLK*? figure *JLGI*? figure *ACEM*?

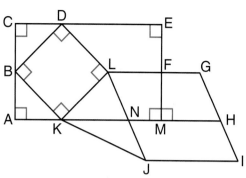

3. Identify 4 quadrilaterals other than those identified in questions **1** and **2**. What are their special names?

Use dot paper to draw a quadrilateral:

4. **a.** with 4 right angles.
   b. with 2 right angles.
   c. with 1 right angle.

5. with 0 right angles and 1 pair of opposite sides that are parallel.

6. whose sides are all equal in length and is *not* a square.

7. with 0 right angles and 0 pairs of opposite sides that are parallel.

8. How are a rectangle and a trapezoid alike? How are they different?

9. Explain why a square is a rectangle, but a rectangle is not a square.

Write About It

Write *true* or *false* for each statement. If a statement is false, explain why.

10. A square is never a rhombus.

11. All trapezoids are parallelograms.

12. All rectangles are parallelograms.

13. A square always has 4 right angles.

14. All quadrilaterals are parallelograms.

15. Some parallelograms are also squares.

10-7 Triangles

These polygons are all triangles. You can classify triangles by their angles and their sides.

▶ These triangles are all right triangles.

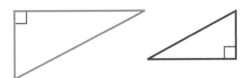

All right triangles have 1 right angle.

▶ These triangles are all isosceles triangles.

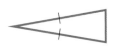

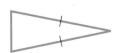

Some isosceles triangles are also right triangles.

All isosceles triangles have at least 2 sides equal in length.

▶ These triangles are all equilateral triangles.

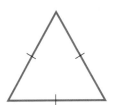

All the sides of an equilateral triangle are equal in length.

▶ These triangles are all scalene triangles.

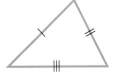

None of the sides of a scalene triangle are equal in length to each other.

Classify each triangle as *right, isosceles, equilateral,*
or *scalene.* Some triangles may be named in more
than one way.

1.

2.

3.

4.

5.

6.

7.

8.

9.

Problem Solving

10. Suppose you wanted to draw an equilateral triangle,
    and you drew one side that measured 5 cm.
    How long would you draw each of the other sides?
    What would be the total length of all the sides?

More Triangles

Here are some
more triangles that
you can classify by
the measure of
their angles.

An obtuse triangle
has one obtuse angle.

An acute triangle has
three acute angles.

Classify each triangle as *obtuse* or *acute.* Use a protractor to help you.

11.

12.

13.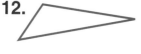

14.

10-8 Similar Figures

Billy used similar figures to make this pattern.

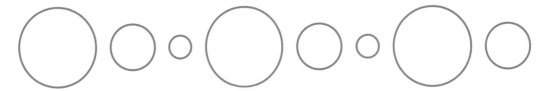

Similar figures have exactly the same shape.
They may or may not be the same size.

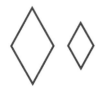  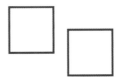

| same shape | same shape | same shape |
| different sizes | different sizes | same size |

All congruent figures are also similar.

Remember: Congruent figures have the same size and the same shape.

Does each set of figures appear to be similar? Write *yes* or *no*.

1.

2.

3.

4.

5.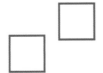

6.

7.

8.

9.

Practice

Choose the letter of the figure that appears to be similar to the first figure.

10. 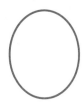　　a. 　　b. 　　c.

11. 　　a. 　　b. 　　c.

12. 　　a. 　　b. 　　c.

13. 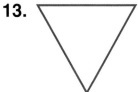　　a. 　　b. 　　c.

Copy each figure onto dot paper. Then draw a figure that is twice as large.

14. 　　　15. 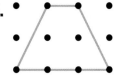　　　16.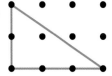

CHALLENGE

Copy and cut out four of these triangles.

17. Fit the triangles together to form a similar triangle.

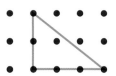HANDS-ON UNDERSTANDING

Transformations: Slides and Flips

Noah and Nicole made these patterns.

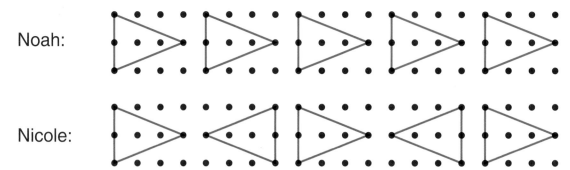

Noah:

Nicole:

Materials: dot paper, pencil, scissors, ruler

Copy the triangle at the right onto dot paper.
Then cut it out.

Place your triangle on another sheet of dot paper. Trace around the triangle to make a pattern in the same way that Noah made his.

1. How did you move the triangle to make the pattern?

Now place the triangle on a third sheet of dot paper. Trace around the triangle to make a pattern in the same way that Nicole made hers.

2. How did you move the triangle to make the pattern?

3. How are your two patterns alike? How are they different?

4. Explain how you know that your patterns are alike and different in the same way as Noah's and Nicole's.

A slide, or translation, is a movement of a figure along a line without flipping or turning.

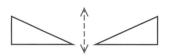

A flip, or reflection, is a movement of a figure over a line so that the figure faces in the opposite direction. The line may be imaginary.

5. Is one of your patterns a translation pattern? Which one?

6. Is one of your patterns a reflection pattern? Which one?

Copy the figures and movements below onto dot paper.

A.   **B.** 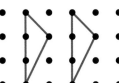   **C.**   **D.**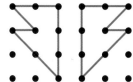

E.   **F.** 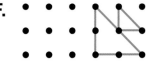   **G.** 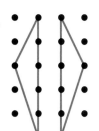   **H.**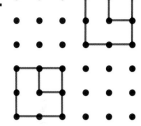

7. Which of the movements are translations? Which are reflections? You may draw lines to help you decide.

Communicate

8. In the figures A and B, what movement would you use to tell whether the figures are congruent?

9. In the figures A–H, are the figures congruent after each transformation? Explain why or why not.

10. Can you slide a figure in any direction? Explain your answer.

11. Can you flip a figure in any direction? Explain your answer.

10-10

Update your skills. See page 22.

Turns

▶ A **turn**, or **rotation**, is the movement
of a figure around a point.

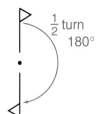 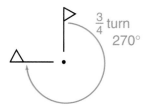 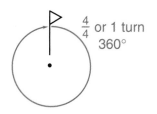

$\frac{1}{4}$ turn 90° $\frac{1}{2}$ turn 180° $\frac{3}{4}$ turn 270° $\frac{4}{4}$ or 1 turn 360°

A full turn measures 360°

▶ You can turn a figure in either direction,
clockwise or counterclockwise.

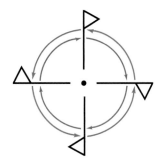

Each new position is a
turn image of the figure.

▶ If you can turn a tracing of a figure
halfway around so that the tracing and
the figure match exactly, the figure has
half-turn symmetry.

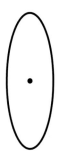 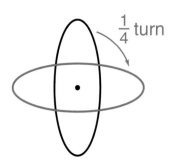 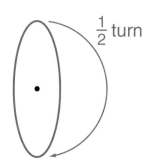

$\frac{1}{4}$ turn $\frac{1}{2}$ turn

This figure has half-turn symmetry.

Which figures are turn images of the first figure?

1.   **a.**   **b.**   **c.**   **d.**

2.   **a.**   **b.**   **c.**   **d.**

3.   **a.**   **b.**   **c.**   **d.**

4.   **a.**   **b.**   **c.**   **d.**

5.   **a.**   **b.**   **c.**   **d.**

Draw the next three figures in the pattern.

6.   ?   ?   ?

Does each figure have half-turn symmetry? Write *yes* or *no*.
You may use tracing paper or dot paper and scissors.

7. 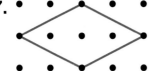   8.    9.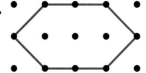

TEST PREPARATION

10. Which of these statements is **not** true?

A If you rotate a figure 360°, the figure ends up in its original position.

B A rotation is the movement of a figure over a line.

C When a figure rotates, it turns.

D Rotating a figure means turning a figure around a point.

Coordinate Geometry

A coordinate grid has two axes:
a horizontal axis called the *x*-axis,
and a vertical axis called the *y*-axis.

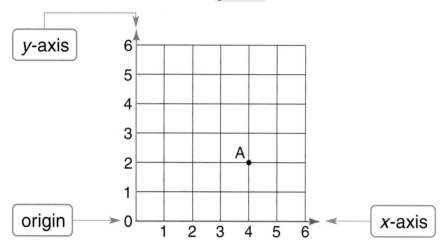

y-axis

origin

x-axis

▶ You can use an ordered pair of numbers (x, y) to
locate points on a coordinate grid.

The *x*-coordinate tells how many spaces
to move horizontally along the *x*-axis.
The *y*-coordinate tells how many spaces
to move vertically along the *y*-axis.

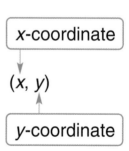

x-coordinate

(x, y)

y-coordinate

The coordinates of point *A* are (4, 2).

▶ The point where the *x*- and *y*-axes intersect
is called the origin. The coordinates of the
origin are (0, 0).

Practice

**Name the *x*- and *y*-coordinates in
each ordered pair.**

1. (4, 2)

2. (5, 1)

3. (3, 0)

4. (1, 1)

5. (2, 3)

6. (0, 4)

Use the graph at the right for exercises 7–18.

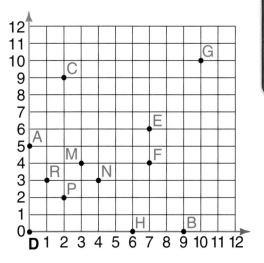

Write the letter of the point for each ordered pair.

7. (0, 0)   **8.** (6, 0)   **9.** (3, 4)

10. (4, 3)   **11.** (2, 2)   **12.** (1, 3)

Write the ordered pair for each point.

13. E   **14.** G   **15.** B

16. C   **17.** F   **18.** A

Graph each ordered pair on a coordinate grid.

19. C (6, 2)   **20.** D (5, 5)   **21.** E (4, 0)   **22.** F (1, 3)   **23.** G (0, 4)

Graph each point on a coordinate grid. Then use line segments to connect the points in order for each pair of figures.

24. A: (1, 2) (4, 2) (1, 7) (1, 2)
     B: (6, 2) (9, 2) (6, 7) (6, 2)

25. A: (1, 6) (8, 6) (8, 9) (1, 6)
     B: (1, 5) (8, 5) (8, 2) (1, 5)

26. A: (1, 1) (5, 1) (1, 4) (1, 1)
     B: (5, 3) (9, 3) (5, 6) (5, 3)

27. A: (4, 4) (4, 8) (1, 8) (4, 4)
     B: (5, 3) (9, 3) (9, 6) (5, 3)

28. Name each movement of the figures in exercises 24–27.

29. Explain how you found the coordinates for point *E* in exercise 13.

30. Explain the difference between locating a point at (3, 4) and locating a point at (4, 3).

31. If the *x*-coordinate is 2 and no further movement is made, then what is the *y*-coordinate? How do you know?

32. If there is no movement for the *x*-coordinate and the *y*-coordinate is 5, then what is the *x*-coordinate? How do you know?

Problem-Solving Strategy:
Find a Pattern

Tyrell draws a spiral on grid paper. He draws 4 line segments. Then he draws 5 more line segments to continue and finish the pattern. How long is the spiral?

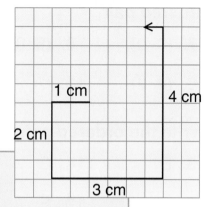

1 cm

2 cm

3 cm

4 cm

Read Visualize the facts of the problem as you reread it.

Facts: The spiral has 4 line segments. The spiral will have 5 more.

Question: How long is the spiral?

Plan Measure the length of each segment. Look for a pattern.

1 cm, 2 cm, 3 cm, 4 cm, . . .

+1 cm +1 cm +1 cm

Solve Add to find the total length. Look for sums of ten.

$$1 + 2 + 3 + 4 + 5 + 6 + 7 + 8 + 9 = 45$$

The spiral is 45 cm long.

Check Cut a 45-cm string and use it to measure the spiral. Check the addition.

Find a pattern to solve each problem. You may use grid paper.

1. Jessie adds one more square to this drawing. It now has 2 lines of symmetry. Where does she add the square? (*Hint:* See page 22.)

Original Drawing

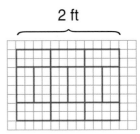

 Read ▶ Visualize the facts of the problem as you reread it.

　　　Facts: Jessie draws this shape. She adds one square. The finished shape has 2 lines of symmetry.

　　　Question: Where does she add the last square?

Plan ▶ Find the line of symmetry in the original drawing. Then think of other ways to fold the shape in half.

▶ **Solve** ▶ ▶ **Check** ▶

2. Jacques paints these shapes in order on a belt: triangle, square, triangle, pentagon, triangle, hexagon. What are the ninth and tenth shapes?

3. Can you cut this shape into 2 congruent hexagons? 2 congruent octagons? (*Hint:* See page 21.)

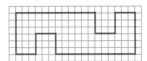

4. Troy makes a gerbil cage. The floor of the cage must have an area of 4 square units. How many different shapes can the floor be?

2 ft

5. A brick border follows this pattern. How many bricks are used in a 10-ft border?

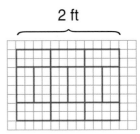

6. Write a problem that uses a pattern. Have a classmate solve it.

Solve each problem and explain the method you used.

1. Sylvia's Sign Shop made an octagonal sign. How many sides does it have? how many angles?

2. Val uses a rope to tie her horse to a post in the middle of a corral. What shape describes the region where the horse can move? Use the shapes at the right to help you.

3. The Dilly Deli ordered a sign in the shape of a pickle outline. Is the sign a simple closed curve?

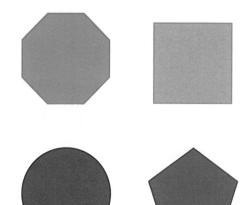

4. Roy orders a square sign from the sign shop. Does his sign have half-turn symmetry?

5. 4 is to square as 8 is to ? .

6. Name the radii shown on circle A at the right.

7. On grid paper draw different figures using 5 squares so that the squares touch along at least one entire side. In how many different ways can the squares be arranged?

Use the table for problems 8–10.

8. How much does a hexagonal sign cost?

9. How much more expensive is a pentagonal sign than a triangular sign?

10. What is the cost of 2 rectangular signs and 1 triangular sign?

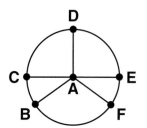

Sign Prices	
Number of Sides (4 ft each)	Price per Side
3	$25
4	$20
5	$45
6	$60

Choose a strategy from the list or use another strategy you know to solve each problem.

Strategy File

Use these Strategies
Find a Pattern
Logical Reasoning
Choose the Operation
Use a Diagram/Graph
Draw a Picture

11. Hank, Don, and Ned are waiting in line. Don is ahead of Ned. Hank has been waiting longer than the others. What is their order in line?

12. A tool measures 16 cm. A plastic tube measures 71 cm. How much longer is the plastic tube?

13. Sylvia cuts a triangle, a square, and a pentagon out of wood. The first shape she cuts has more sides than the second but fewer sides than the third. In what order does she cut the shapes?

14. Marcy cut an equilateral triangle to make 4 congruent signs. Each side of the triangle is 2 ft long. How did Marcy cut the triangle?

15. Sylvia's shop has 8 rows of paint cans. There are 10 cans in the first row, 9 cans in the second row, 8 in the third, and so on. How many cans of paint are there in all?

16. How would you describe the shape of this sign for Farmer Foods? How many angles does it have? What other questions can you answer about this sign?

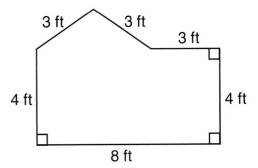

17. Write a problem modeled on problem 12. Have a classmate solve it.

Identify each. *(See pp. 326–339.)*

1. ? ray

2. ? line segment

3. ? perpendicular lines

a.  **b.**  **c.** •B

4. ? vertex

5. ? line

d.  **e.** 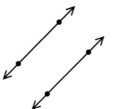 **f.**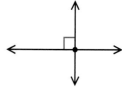

6. ? acute triangle

7. ? circle

8. ? parallel lines

9. ? point

g.  **h.**    **i.**

Draw these.

10. $\overrightarrow{AX}$ **11.** $\angle RST$ **12.** $\overleftrightarrow{XY}$ **13.** right angle *DEF*

Which figure appears to be similar to the first figure? *(See pp. 340–341.)*

14. 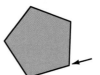   **a.**   **b.**   **c.**

Name the transformation shown. Write *reflection*, *(See pp. 342–343.)*
rotation, or translation.

15.    **16.**   **17.**   **18.**

(See *Still More Practice,* pp. 469–470.)

Coordinate Geometry: Distance

How far is point *A* from point *B*?
How far is point *B* from point *C*?

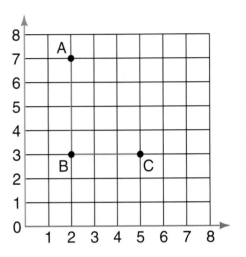

- To find the length of a vertical line segment,
  find the difference between *y*-coordinates.
  A (2,7)
  B (2,3)
  7 − 3 = 4   *A* and *B* are 4 units apart.
  So, line segment $\overline{AB}$ is 4 units long.

- To find the length of a horizontal line
  segment, find the difference between
  x-coordinates.
  B (2,3)
  C (5,3)
  5 − 2 = 3   *B* and *C* are 3 units apart.
  So, line segment $\overline{BC}$ is 3 units long.

**Give the length of the line segment that connects
each set of points. Tell whether the line is vertical
or horizontal.**

1. (3,8) and (3,4)   **2.** (2,8) and (2,4)   **3.** (3,5) and (6,5)

4. (3,6) and (3,5)   **5.** (2,8) and (5,8)   **6.** (1,4) and (9,4)

7. (2,2) and (7,2)   **8.** (3,8) and (3,2)

Problem Solving

9. Name two points that form a 5-unit vertical line
segment when they are connected.

10. Name two points that form a 3-unit horizontal line
segment when they are connected.

Identify each.

1. __?__ perpendicular lines

2. __?__ diameter

3. __?__ radius

4. __?__ reflection

5. __?__ ray

6. __?__ equilateral triangle

a.

b.

c.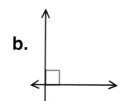

d.

e.

f.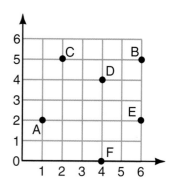

Use the grid to answer each question.

7. What are the *x*- and *y*-coordinates of point *C*?

8. What point is located at (4, 0)?

9. Graph the points *G*(0, 0) and *H*(3, 3) on the grid at the right.

Problem Solving

Use a strategy you have learned.

10. Does each figure have half-turn symmetry?

    a.

    b.

Tell About It

Explain your answer.

11. There are 5 special quadrilaterals. Name, describe, and draw a picture of each kind.

Performance Assessment

Draw each.

12. $\overleftrightarrow{LM}$

13. $\overrightarrow{BA}$

14. point *R*

15. a scalene triangle

16. ∠*DEF*

17. circle *A*

18. $\overline{RS}$

19. an isosceles triangle

Choose the best answer.

1. $90.05
   − 58.93

   a. $32.12   b. $31.12
   c. $41.12   d. $31.02

2. Choose the standard form of two hundred ninety-seven million.

   a. 200,970   b. 2,000,970
   c. 20,970,00   d. 297,000,000

3. Choose the fraction.

   nine elevenths

   a. $\frac{11}{9}$ b. $\frac{9}{10}$ c. $\frac{9}{9}$ d. $\frac{9}{11}$

4. Estimate by rounding.

   $244 + 1749 + 756$

   a. 2700   b. 3000
   c. 2600   d. 2800

5. 11 ft 3 in. + 3 ft 10 in.

   a. 14 ft 1 in.
   b. 15 ft
   c. 15 ft 1 in.
   d. 14 ft 14 in.

6. Which fraction is less than $\frac{5}{9}$?

   a. $\frac{5}{8}$ b. $\frac{6}{9}$ c. $\frac{7}{9}$ d. $\frac{4}{9}$

7. $37.09
   ×   8

   a. $246.72   b. $296.02
   c. $296.72   d. $37.17

8. Choose the compatible numbers to estimate $67 \div 9$.

   a. $70 \div 9$ b. $65 \div 9$
   c. $63 \div 9$ d. $54 \div 9$

9. When the dividend is zero, the quotient is:

   a. never zero.
   b. always zero.
   c. always one.
   d. none of these

10. A week has 7 days. Each day is 24 hours. How many hours is a week?

    a. 31   b. 148
    c. 168   d. 228

11. 2 dm = __?__

    a. 200 cm
    b. 200 mm
    c. 20 m
    d. 20 km

12. Choose the sum in simplest form.

    $$\frac{4}{8} + \frac{2}{8}$$

    a. $\frac{6}{8}$ b. $\frac{2}{4}$ c. $\frac{3}{4}$ d. $\frac{2}{3}$

Use the line plot for exercises 13 and 14.

Favorite Odd Numbers

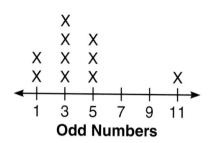

Odd Numbers

13. What is the mode of the data?

    a. 11   **b.** 7   **c.** 3   **d.** 1

14. What is the outlier of the data?

    a. 11   **b.** 7   **c.** 3   **d.** 1

15. Which part of the line graph is labeled *Days*?

  a. vertical axis   **b.** horizontal axis
  c. line of increase **d.** line of decrease

Use the figure for exercises 16–18.

16. Which angle is obtuse?

  a. $\angle ABI$ **b.** $\angle FBA$ **c.** $\angle CDK$ **d.** $\angle FBC$

17. What kind of angle is $\angle ABI$?

    a. acute   **b.** obtuse
    c. right   **d.** straight

18. Which names the parallel lines?

    a. $\overleftrightarrow{FI}$ and $\overleftrightarrow{AE}$

    b. $\overleftrightarrow{AE}$ and $\overleftrightarrow{HK}$

    c. $\overleftrightarrow{GJ}$ and $\overleftrightarrow{HK}$

    d. $\overline{GC}$ and $\overline{HD}$

19. Choose the sum in simplest form.

$$\frac{9}{12} + \frac{3}{4}$$

  a. $1\frac{1}{2}$ **b.** $1\frac{2}{6}$ **c.** $\frac{12}{16}$ **d.** $1\frac{2}{4}$

Tell About It

Show all your work. Explain your answer.

20. Explain how to find the *x*- and *y*-coordinates for the points plotted on the coordinate grid. Name the coordinates of the points.

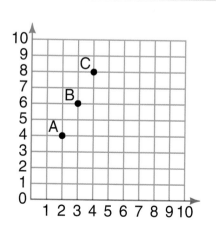

CHAPTER 11

Perimeter, Area, and Volume

POPSICLE STICKS AND GLUE

We're building a village of popsicle sticks,
Just popsicle sticks and glue:

Houses and fences, sidewalks and streets,
A school and a library, too;
Museums, churches, temples, shops,
A playground, a park, and a zoo.

Isn't it wonderful what we can do
With popsicle sticks and a new tube of glue?

Leslie D. Perkins

In this chapter you will:

Use models and formulas
Relate plane and solid figures
Investigate spatial relationships
Solve problems using a drawing or model

Critical Thinking/Finding Together

Use popsicle sticks to build a border around your desk. How many popsicle sticks did you use? Compare your border and the number of sticks used with classmates.

11-1

Update your skills. See page 20.

Use Perimeter Formulas

Perimeter is the distance around a figure.

▶ You can use a formula to find the perimeter of a rectangle.

What is the perimeter of this rectangle?

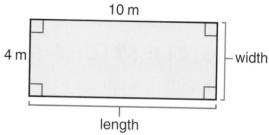

perimeter = length + width + length + width

P = ℓ + w + ℓ + w

P = **2** × ℓ + **2** × w ← formula for perimeter of a rectangle
P = $(2 \times 10) + (2 \times 4)$
P = 20 + 8
P = 28 m

The perimeter of the rectangle is 28 m.

▶ You can also use formulas to find the perimeter of a square and of an equilateral triangle.

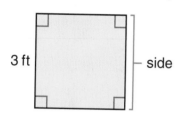

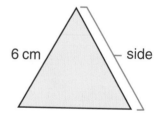

P = side + side + side + side
P = $s + s + s + s$
P = 4 × s ← formula for perimeter of a square
P = 4×3
P = 12 ft

P = side + side + side
P = $s + s + s$
P = 3 × s ← formula for perimeter of an equilateral triangle
P = 3×6
P = 18 cm

Find the perimeter of each. Use a formula.

1.
18 in.

2.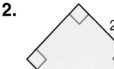
25 mm

3.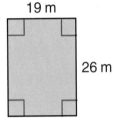
34 ft

4.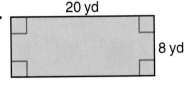
20 yd
8 yd

5.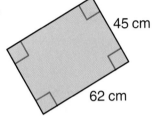
45 cm
62 cm

6.
19 m
26 m

7.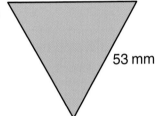
53 mm

8.
37 m

9.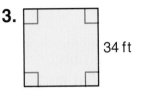
92 in.

Use grid paper to draw a square and a rectangle whose perimeters are:

10. 16 units   **11.** 24 units   **12.** 36 units   **13.** 44 units

Problem Solving **Use a formula.**

14. What is the perimeter of an equilateral triangle with a side that is 17 in. long?

15. What is the perimeter of a square with a side that is 49 m long?

16. What is the perimeter of a rectangle with a length of 72 cm and a width of 14 cm?

17. What is the perimeter of a rectangle with a width of 122 in. and a length of 15 in.?

CHALLENGE

18. Write a formula to find the perimeter of a hexagon whose sides are all the same length.

Practice

11-2

Update your skills. See page 24.

Use Area Formulas

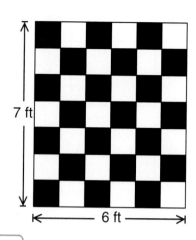

Area is the number of square units needed to cover a flat surface.

What is the area of the rectangle?

▶ To find the area, use the area formula for a rectangle.

area = length × width

$A = \ell \times w$ ← formula for the area of a rectangle

$A = 7 \times 6$

$A = 42$ square feet (sq ft) or 42 ft²

The area of the floor is 42 ft².

Area is always reported in square units.

▶ You can also use a formula to find the area of a square.

area = side × side

$A = s \times s$ ← formula for the area of a square

$A = 9 \times 9$

$A = 81$ square centimeters (sq cm) or 81 cm²

The area of the floor is 81 cm².

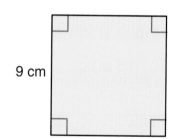

9 cm

Other Square Units for Measuring Area	
Customary Units	**Metric Units**
square inch, sq in., in.²	square millimeter, sq mm, mm²
square yard, sq yd, yd²	square decimeter, sq dm, dm²
square mile, sq mi, mi²	square meter, sq m, m²
	square kilometer, sq km, km²

Find the area. Use the area formula.

1.

9 m
16 m

2.

10 in.

3.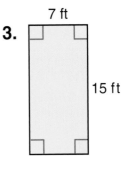

7 ft

15 ft

4.

25 cm

5.

18 m

6.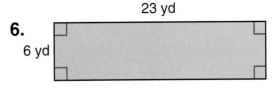

23 yd

6 yd

7.

12 in.

14 in.

8.

15 m

9.

55 cm

40 cm

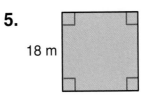
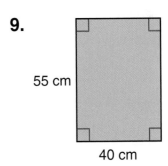
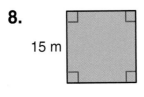

Problem Solving

10. A football field is 120 yd long (including the end zones) and about 55 yd wide. About what is the area of a football field?

11. A baseball infield is a square that is 90 ft along each side, or base line. What is its area?

12. A tennis court is a rectangle that is 78 ft long and 27 ft wide. What is the area of a tennis court?

CHALLENGE

13. Use grid paper and the area formula to draw as many rectangles as you can that each have an area of 24 square units. Are the perimeters of the rectangles equal? Explain.

Update your skills. See pages 20 and 24.

Perimeter and Area

▶ Figures that have the *same* area can have *different* perimeters.

3 in.

4 in.

$A = 12$ in.^{2}
$P = 14$ in.

6 in.

2 in.

$A = 12$ in.^{2}
$P = 16$ in.

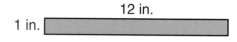

12 in.

1 in.

$A = 12$ in.^{2}
$P = 26$ in.

▶ Figures that have the *same* perimeter can have *different* areas.

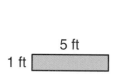

5 ft

1 ft

$P = 12$ ft
$A = 5$ ft^2

2 ft

4 ft

$P = 12$ ft
$A = 8$ ft^2

3 ft

3 ft

$P = 12$ ft
$A = 9$ ft^2

Practice

**For each rectangle, find the area and perimeter.
Then draw another rectangle with the same area
but a different perimeter.**

1. 4 cm

4 cm

2. 8 yd

2 yd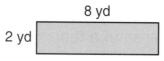

3. 12 m

5 m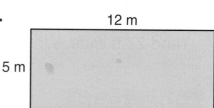

4. 5 km

4 km

5. 6 ft

1 ft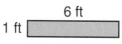

6. 6 in.

4 in.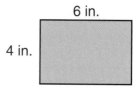

Use grid paper to help to answer each question.

7. Draw two rectangles that have the same area, but different perimeters.

8. Draw two rectangles that have the same perimeter, but different areas.

Complex Figures

▶ To find the area of a complex figure:
  • Separate the figure into known figures.
  • Find the area of each figure.
  • Add the areas.

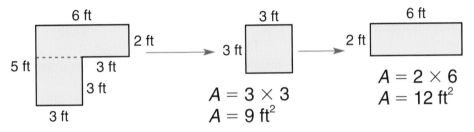

$$A = 9\ \text{ft}^2 + 12\ \text{ft}^2 = 21\ \text{ft}^2$$

▶ To find the perimeter of a complex figure:
  • Add the lengths of its sides.
  5 ft + 6 ft + 2 ft + 3 ft + 3 ft + 3 ft = 22 ft
  $P = 22$ ft

Find the area and perimeter of each complex figure.

9.

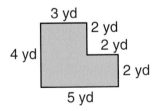

10.

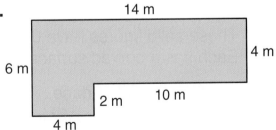

11.

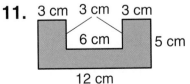

12.

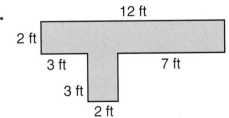

Solid Figures

▶ Polygons, or plane figures are flat. They are two-dimensional.
Solid figures are not flat. They are three-dimensional.

A cube is a solid figure with 6 faces,
12 edges, and 8 vertices.

edge → ← face

← vertex

A face is a flat surface surrounded
by line segments.

Two faces meet at a line segment
called an edge.

Three or more edges meet at a vertex.

▶ These solid figures have faces, edges,
and vertices.

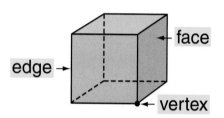 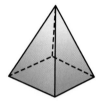

rectangular prism
6 faces
12 edges
8 vertices

triangular prism
5 faces
9 edges
6 vertices

square pyramid
5 faces
8 edges
5 vertices

▶ These solid figures have 0 edges and 0 faces.
Each has a curved surface.

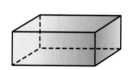 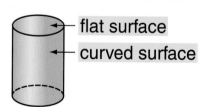  

flat surface

curved surface

cylinder
2 flat surfaces

cone
1 flat surface

sphere
0 flat surfaces

Copy and complete. You need not draw the solid figures.

1.	name	cube	?	?	?	?	?	?
2.	faces	?	?	?	6	?	?	?
3.	edges	12	?	?	?	?	?	?
4.	vertices	?	?	?	?	?	?	6

Problem Solving

5. I have 2 flat surfaces, 0 edges, and 0 vertices. Which solid figure am I?

6. I have 1 flat surface and a curved surface. Which solid figure am I?

7. I have 5 faces and 5 vertices. How many edges do I have? Which solid figure am I?

8. I am shaped like a ball. How many faces, edges, and vertices do I have? Which solid figure am I?

9. I have 6 faces and 12 edges. I am not a rectangular prism. Which solid figure am I?

10. I have 9 edges and 6 vertices. How many faces do I have? Which solid figure am I?

DO YOU REMEMBER?

Write the heading that matches the information in each column.

11. ?

- a line segment
- one endpoint on the circle
- one endpoint at the center

12. ?

- a line segment
- both endpoints on the circle
- passes through the center of the circle

13. ?

- a line segment
- both endpoints on the circle

acute
diameter
chord
point
radius

Solid Figures and Polygons

▶ Each flat surface of a solid figure is a plane figure.

triangular
prism

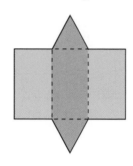

net of a triangular
prism

A net is a flat
pattern that
folds into a
solid figure.

The net shows that a triangular prism is made up
of 5 polygons: 2 triangles and 3 rectangles. The
dashed lines show where to fold the net.

▶ If you could cut a solid figure, the new flat
surfaces you create would be plane figures.

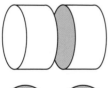

Practice

Name the shape of each shaded flat surface.

1.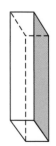

2.

3.

4.

Copy each net on dot paper. Name each polygon.
Then cut, fold, and tape each net to make a solid figure.
Name the solid figure made.

5.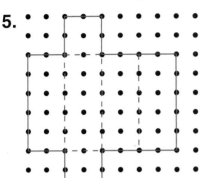

6.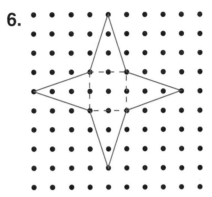

Use dot paper.

7. Draw a net of a cube. Cut out and fold the net.
   Tape the edges together.

Name the shape of the new flat surfaces made by each cut.

8.

9.

10.

11.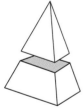

12.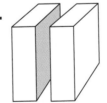

13.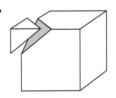

14. Which solid figure can be made
    from the net?

    A sphere   **B** cylinder
    C cone   **D** cube

HANDS-ON UNDERSTANDING

Spatial Relationships

Materials: connecting cubes, paper, pencil

Work in small groups.

Use 36 connecting cubes to build each of these rectangular prisms. Each person in your group should build a different figure.

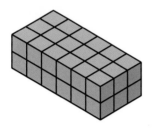 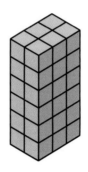 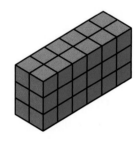

1. Compare the prisms you built. What do you notice?

Take turns. Use 36 cubes to build other rectangular prisms. Ask others in your group to build a prism just like yours. Record the length, width, and height of each prism.

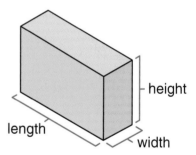

2. How many different rectangular prisms did your group build?

3. How can you be sure that each prism is different from each of the other prisms?

Work together to guess how many connecting cubes you would need to build each of the solid figures in exercises 4, 5, 6, and 7. Record your group's guesses. Then test the guesses by building each figure.

4.

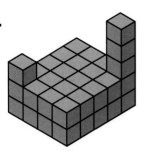

5.

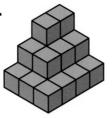

6.

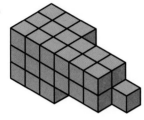

7.

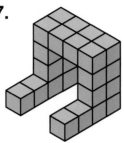

8. How close were your guesses to the actual number of cubes needed to build each figure?

Find the length, width, and height in cubes of each rectangular prism.

9.

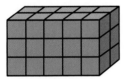

10.

11.

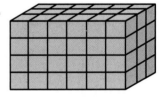

Communicate

12. A rectangular prism has a length of 3 cubes, a width of 2 cubes, and a height of 5 cubes. Does it contain the same number of cubes as the prism in exercise 9? Explain.

Write About It

13. Use connecting cubes to build a solid figure. Draw a picture of the figure on triangle dot paper. Put your drawing in your Math Journal.

Volume

The **volume** of a solid figure is the number of cubic units the figure can contain.

1 cubic unit

▶ You can find the volume of a solid figure by counting the number of cubic units needed to fill it. Or you can build the figure with connecting cubes and then count the cubes.

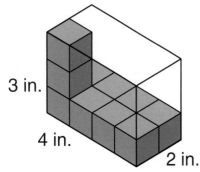

3 in.

4 in.

2 in.

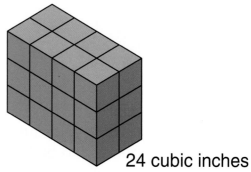

24 cubic inches

The volume of the rectangular prism is 24 cubic inches.

▶ You can also find the volume of a solid figure by multiplying.

Volume = length × width × height

Volume = 6 × 2 × 4 = 48
Volume = 48 cubic meters
Volume is always reported in cubic units.

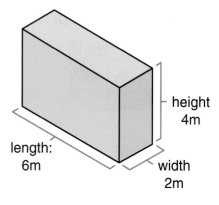

height
4m

length:
6m

width
2m

Find the volume of each.

1.

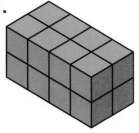

2.

3.

Multiply to find the volume of each.

4.
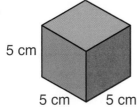
5 cm
5 cm   5 cm

5.
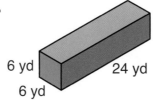
6 yd
6 yd   24 yd

6.
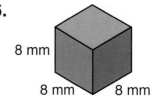
8 mm
8 mm   8 mm

7.
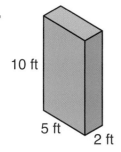
10 ft
5 ft   2 ft

8.
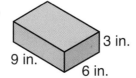
3 in.
9 in.   6 in.

9.
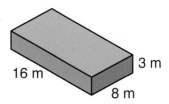
3 m
16 m   8 m

Find the volume to complete the table.

	Length	Width	Height	Volume
10.	7 cm	8 cm	6 cm	? cubic centimeters
11.	9 m	10 m	9 m	? cubic meters
12.	14 mm	4 mm	3 mm	? cubic millimeters
13.	11 yd	5 yd	8 yd	? cubic yards
14.	12 in.	12 in.	4 in.	? cubic inches

Problem Solving

15. Trey has 18 connecting cubes.
How many different rectangular prisms
can he build?

Write About It

16.  Could you compute to find the volume of the figure
in exercise 3? Explain how you would do it.

Problem-Solving Strategy:
Use a Drawing or Model

The Hobby Hut sign is a triangle. The owner wants a light at each vertex and every half foot along each side. Each side is 2 ft long. How many lights will the sign have?

Read ▸ **Visualize the facts of the problem as you reread it.**

Facts: 1 light—at each vertex
1 light—every half foot along each 2-foot-long side

Question: How many lights will the sign have?

Plan ▸ Since each side is 2 ft long, the sign is an equilateral triangle. Draw an equilateral triangle. Use marks for each light. Multiply to find the number of lights:

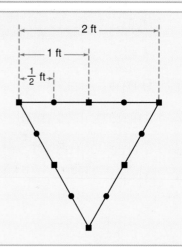

at each vertex ⟶ 3 × 1 = _?_
along each side ⟶ 3 × 3 = _?_

Then add to find the total.

Solve ▸ 1 light at each vertex   3 × 1 = 3
3 lights along each side   3 × 3 = 9
The total number of lights   3 + 9 = 12

The sign will have 12 lights.

Check ▸ Add the number of lights around the figure.
5 + 4 + 3 = 12

Use a drawing or model to solve each problem.

1. A shape made up of tiles that are
1 cm square has an area of
9 sq cm and a perimeter of
12 cm. Describe the shape.

First Try

$A = 9$ sq cm

$P = 18$ cm

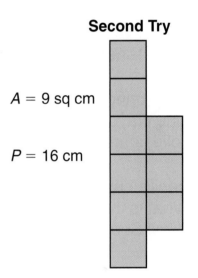

> **Read** Visualize the facts of the problem.

Facts: Area   = 9 sq cm
Perimeter = 12 cm

Question: What is the shape?

Second Try

> **Plan** How should you arrange
1-sq-cm tiles to make a shape
that has an area of 9 sq cm and
a perimeter of 12 cm?

$A = 9$ sq cm

$P = 16$ cm

> **Solve** ·········▶ **Check**

2. How many different rectangles
can you draw that have a perimeter
of 20 units? What is the area of
each rectangle?

3. The volume of a rectangular prism
is 24 cubic centimeters. The flat surface
at the bottom of the prism is 2 cm by 4 cm.
How tall is the prism?

4. How many triangles can you find
in the puzzle on the right?

5. What is the area of the
figure at the right?

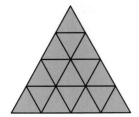

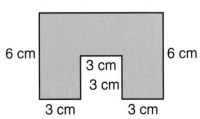

6 cm   6 cm
               3 cm
               3 cm
   3 cm   3 cm

Practice

Problem-Solving Applications: Mixed Review

Read ▸ **Plan** ▸ **Solve** ▸ **Check**

Solve each problem and explain the method you used.

1. Sara babysits for Ollie and shows him how to build a tower with 27 cubes. Each cube has a volume of 1 cubic inch. What is the volume of the tower?

2. Ollie builds a tower with his 1-inch cubes. What shape is the face of each 1-inch cube in Ollie's tower?

3. Trina brings crayons. Both ends of the blue crayon are rubbed flat. What solid figure does the crayon look like?

4. Benji's crib mattress is 34 in. by 30 in. What is the perimeter of the mattress? (*Hint:* See page 20.)

5. Sara draws a hexagon. Each side is 9 cm. What is the perimeter of the hexagon?

6. Trina shows Benji a shape. It has 2 circular flat surfaces. What is the shape?

7. Three children work with blocks to build a rectangular prism. It has a width of 7 in., a length of 8 in., and a height of 10 in. What is the volume of this prism?

8. Trina has a sheet of paper that is $8\frac{1}{4}$ in. by 11 in. What is the perimeter of the paper? (*Hint:* See page 20.)

Choose a strategy from the list or use another strategy you know to solve each problem.

Strategy File

Use These Strategies
Use a Drawing or Model
Use More Than One Step
Logical Reasoning
Write a Number Sentence
Guess and Test
Find a Pattern

9. Ralph has a photo in his wallet. The area of the photo is 6 square inches. How long might each side be?

10. Trina made this bead pattern: 1 sphere, 2 cylinders, 3 cones, 2 spheres, 3 cylinders, 4 cones, and so on. What is the shape of the 20th figure?

11. The shortest side of a quadrilateral is 5 cm. The next side is 10 cm. The length of each succeeding side increases by 5 cm. What is the perimeter of the quadrilateral? (*Hint:* See page 20.)

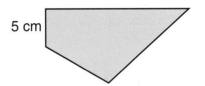
5 cm

12. Ralph's rectangular quilt has an area of 12 sq ft. One side is 3 feet long. What is the perimeter of the quilt?

13. Angie makes giant pillows. The table tells about each pillow. What solid figure does Benji's pillow look like?

14. Which child's pillow is shaped like a cylinder?

	Benji's Pillow	Sara's Pillow	Trina's Pillow
faces	6	0	0
edges	12	0	0
curved surface	0	1	1
flat surface	0	2	1

15. Draw five 1-centimeter squares to make a shape so that any 2 squares touch along at least one entire side. How many different arrangements are possible?

Write Your Own

16. Write a problem that can be solved by using a drawing or model. Have a classmate solve it.

Find the perimeter. Use a perimeter formula.   *(See pp. 358–359.)*

1.
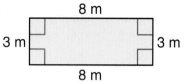

2.
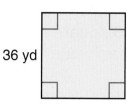

3.
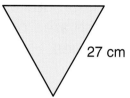

Find the area.   *(See pp. 360–363.)*

4.
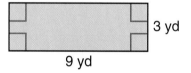

5.

6.
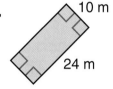

Name each solid figure. Then name the shapes of all flat surfaces on each figure.   *(See pp. 364–367.)*

7.
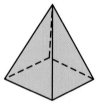

8.
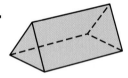

9.

Find the area and perimeter of each figure.   *(See pp. 362–363.)*

10.
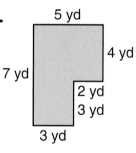

11.
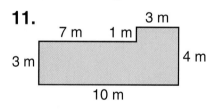

12.
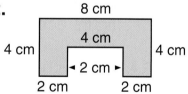

Find the volume.   *(See pp. 370–371.)*

13.
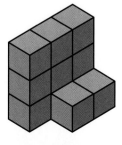

14.
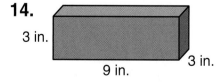

15.
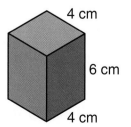

(See Still More Practice, p. 470.)

Missing Cubic Units

Maya used cubes to build this figure.
How many more cubes does she need
to finish making a rectangular prism?

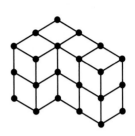

Draw the rectangular prism on triangle dot paper
or use connecting cubes. Then count the
cubes that are missing.

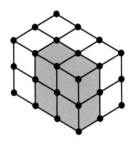

Maya needs 4 more
cubes to finish making
the rectangular prism.

Use triangle dot paper or connecting cubes.

1. How many more cubes are needed
to finish building each cube?

a.
b.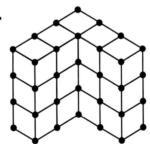
c.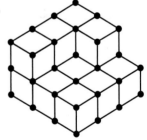

2. How many more cubes are needed to finish
building each rectangular prism?

a.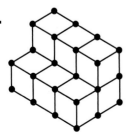
b.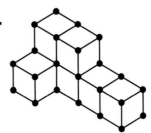
c.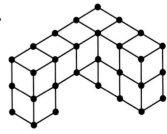

Find the perimeter and area of each figure. Use the formulas.

1.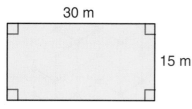
30 m
15 m

2.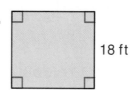
18 ft

3.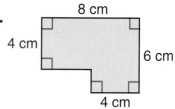
8 cm
4 cm
6 cm
4 cm

Name the shape of the new flat surfaces made by each cut.

4.

5.

6.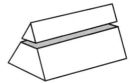

Find the volume.

7.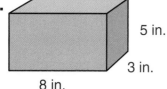
5 in.
3 in.
8 in.

8.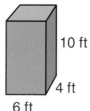
10 ft
4 ft
6 ft

9.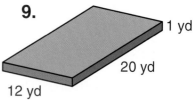
1 yd
20 yd
12 yd

Problem Solving

Use a strategy you have learned.

10. Which solid figure has 5 faces, 9 edges, and 6 vertices? Which solid figure has 2 circular flat surfaces, 0 edges, and 0 vertices?

Tell About It

Explain how you found your answer.

11. The volume of a rectangular prism is 36 cubic cm. A flat surface at the bottom of the prism is 4 cm by 3 cm. How tall is it?

Performance Assessment

12. **a.** Jill Clark wrote her initials on a grid. Estimate the area of her initials.

    b. Write your initials on grid paper and then estimate the area they cover.

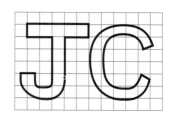

Test Preparation

Choose the best answer.

1. Which is ordered greatest to least?

    a. 4607; 46,070; 45,021; 46,088
    b. 46,088; 46,070; 45,021; 4607
    c. 46,070; 46,088; 45,021; 4607
    d. 46,070; 46,088; 4607; 45,021

2. 65,600 − 1,592

    a. 64,008   **b.** 64,018
    c. 64,192   **d.** not given

3. 8 + 6 ÷ 3 − 2

    a. 2 R2
    b. 8
    c. 14
    d. not given

4. Alana pays $11.96 for 4 identical plants. How much does each plant cost?

    a. $1.56
    b. $1.99
    c. $2.49
    d. $2.99

5. Which is ordered least to greatest?

    a. 4 cm; 300 mm; 40 m; 3 km
    b. 300 mm; 4 cm; 40 m; 3 km
    c. 4 cm; 300 mm; 3 km; 40 m
    d. 3 km; 4 cm; 40 m; 300 mm

6. $5\frac{2}{9} + 8\frac{4}{9}$

a. $13\frac{1}{3}$ **b.** $13\frac{2}{9}$ **c.** $13\frac{2}{3}$ **d.** not given

7. Which is a quadrilateral?

    a. M   **b.** N   **c.** P   **d.** all of these

8. 6907 + 386 + 2999

    a. 9192
    b. 10,292
    c. 13,766
    d. not given

9. 76 × 450

    a. 5850   **b.** 33,900
    c. 34,206   **d.** not given

10. The dividend is 456. The quotient is 76. What is the divisor?

    a. 4
    b. 6
    c. 8
    d. 80

11. Which is normal room temperature?

    a. 20° C
    b. 37° C
    c. 50° C
    d. 68° C

12. Which graph is used to compare the parts of a whole?

    a. circle graph   **b.** bar graph
    c. line graph   **d.** pictograph

13. $\frac{9}{10} - \frac{1}{2}$

    a. $\frac{1}{5}$ **b.** $\frac{4}{5}$ **c.** 1 **d.** not given

14. Find the area.

  6 ft

    a. 12 ft^2
    b. 24 ft^2
    c. 30 ft^2
    d. 36 ft^2

15. Which fraction is closest to $\frac{1}{2}$?

    a. $\frac{9}{11}$ **b.** $\frac{4}{11}$ **c.** $\frac{5}{11}$ **d.** $\frac{8}{11}$

19. $\frac{6}{9} + \frac{1}{3}$

    a. $\frac{8}{9}$ **b.** $\frac{2}{3}$ **c.** 2   **d.** 1

---

16. Choose the GCF
of 18 and 27.

    a. 18
    b. 9
    c. 6
    d. 3

20. How many angles
does a pentagon
have?

    a. 4
    b. 5
    c. 6
    d. 8

---

17. What kind of triangle is shown?

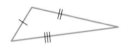

    a. right   **b.** isoceles
    c. equilateral   **d.** scalene

21. Choose the perimeter.

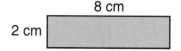

    a. 10 cm   **b.** 16 cm
    c. 20 cm   **d.** 16 cm^2

---

18. Use front-end estimation.

$7\frac{7}{9} + 6\frac{2}{6}$

    a. about 14   **b.** about 12
    c. about 15   **d.** not given

22. Tina draws an octagon. Each side
is 11 mm. What is the perimeter?

    a. $P = 66$ mm   **b.** $P = 19$ mm
    c. $P = 88$ mm   **d.** $P = 55$ mm

---

23. Choose the area and
perimeter of the figure.

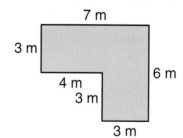

    a. $A = 30$ m^2; $P = 26$ m
    b. $A = 26$ m^2; $P = 30$ m
    c. $A = 21$ m^2; $P = 20$ m
    d. $A = 9$ m^2; $P = 18$ m

Tell About It

**Explain how you solved the problem.
Show all your work.**

23. How many ways can you separate
the figure in exercise 23 in order
to find its area? Describe all the
possible ways.

24. A rectangle has an area of 36 ft^2
and a perimeter of 26 ft. What are
the length and width of the rectangle?

Divide by Two Digits

from
WHO HASN'T PLAYED GAZINTAS?

In your arithmetics
the *problem* is what sticks.
The language isn't bound
by spelling, but by sound.
So 3 gazinta 81.
The answer? 27. Done!
In *long* division, I would hint, a
lot of work gazin gazinta.

Then Tums: the sign of which is X.
Do 8 tums 1-5-6? It checks
at just one thousand two four eight.
Repeat: 1,248.

Computers work at a faster rate.

David McCord

In this chapter you will:

Learn about patterns
Estimate in division
Investigate trial quotients
  and zeros in division
Solve problems with more
  than one step

**Critical Thinking/
Finding Together**
Explain how you can use
base ten blocks to check
that 81 ÷ 3 = 27.

Division Patterns

Use division facts and patterns with zero to divide tens, hundreds, and thousands by multiples of 10.

Remember: Numbers that end in 0 are multiples of 10. They all have 10 as a factor.

Study these division patterns.

Fact: $8 \div 1 = 8$

$80 \div 10 = 8$
$800 \div 10 = 80$
$8000 \div 10 = 800$

Fact: $9 \div 3 = 3$

$90 \div 30 = 3$
$900 \div 30 = 30$
$9000 \div 30 = 300$

Fact: $28 \div 7 = 4$

$280 \div 70 = 4$
$2800 \div 70 = 40$
$28{,}000 \div 70 = 400$

Fact: $10 \div 2 = 5$

$100 \div 20 = 5$
$1000 \div 20 = 50$
$10{,}000 \div 20 = 500$

Look for a pattern to find each quotient.

1. $9 \div 1$
$90 \div 10$
$900 \div 10$
$9000 \div 10$

2. $8 \div 4$
$80 \div 40$
$800 \div 40$
$8000 \div 40$

3. $56 \div 7$
$560 \div 70$
$5600 \div 70$
$56{,}000 \div 70$

4. $6 \div 3$
$60 \div 30$
$600 \div 30$
$6000 \div 30$

5. $32 \div 8$
$320 \div 80$
$3200 \div 80$
$32{,}000 \div 80$

6. $45 \div 9$
$450 \div 90$
$4500 \div 90$
$45{,}000 \div 90$

7. $40 \div 5$
$400 \div 50$
$4000 \div 50$
$40{,}000 \div 50$

8. $30 \div 6$
$300 \div 60$
$3000 \div 60$
$30{,}000 \div 60$

9. $63 \div 7$
$630 \div 70$
$6300 \div 70$
$63{,}000 \div 70$

Divide mentally.

10. $40 \div 20$

11. $20 \div 10$

12. $60 \div 20$

13. $70 \div 10$

14. $360 \div 90$

15. $420 \div 60$

16. $560 \div 80$

17. $250 \div 50$

18. $200 \div 40$

19. $300 \div 50$

20. $400 \div 80$

21. $100 \div 50$

22. $8000 \div 20$

23. $4000 \div 80$

24. $3000 \div 60$

25. $2000 \div 50$

26. $90\overline{)4500}$

27. $80\overline{)6400}$

28. $30\overline{)1200}$

29. $20\overline{)1800}$

30. $30\overline{)21,000}$

31. $40\overline{)20,000}$

32. $70\overline{)35,000}$

33. $90\overline{)81,000}$

34. $50\overline{)40,000}$

35. $60\overline{)54,000}$

36. $30\overline{)24,000}$

37. $40\overline{)36,000}$

Problem Solving

38. How many zeros are in the quotient when you divide 500 by 10?

39. How many zeros are in the quotient when you divide 4800 by 60?

40. How many zeros are in the quotient when you divide 540 by 90?

41. How many zeros are in the quotient when you divide 40,000 by 8?

TEST PREPARATION

Choose the best answer.

42. The quotient is 400. The dividend is 20,000. What is the divisor?

    A 5   **B** 50
    C 500   **D** 5000

43. The divisor is 90. The quotient is 800. What is the dividend?

    F 72   **G** 7200
    H 720   **J** 72,000

Divisors: Multiples of Ten

Forty students share 137 marbles equally. How many marbles does each student get? How many marbles are left over?

To find how many each gets, divide: 137 ÷ 40.

Think

$40\overline{)137}$ 40 > 1   Not enough hundreds

$40\overline{)137}$ 40 > 13   Not enough tens

$40\overline{)137}$ 40 < 137 **Enough ones**

Estimate to place the first digit in the quotient.	137 ÷ 40

Think: 13 ÷ 4 = ? is close to 12 ÷ 4 = 3.
Try 3.

Divide the ones.	Multiply.	Subtract and compare.	Check.

$$\begin{array}{r} 3 \\ 40\overline{)137} \end{array}$$

$$\begin{array}{r} ^\times \quad 3 \\ 40\overline{)137} \\ \rightarrow 120 \end{array}$$

$$\begin{array}{r} 3 \quad R\ 17 \\ 40\overline{)137} \\ -120 \\ \hline 17 \end{array}$$

$$\begin{array}{r} 40 \\ \times \quad 3 \\ \hline 120 \\ +\quad 17 \\ \hline 137 \end{array}$$

Each student gets 3 marbles.
There are 17 marbles left over.

17 < 40

Complete each division.

1. $\begin{array}{r} 4 \ R\ ? \\ 20\overline{)85} \\ -\ ?? \\ \hline ? \end{array}$

2. $\begin{array}{r} 5 \ R\ ? \\ 50\overline{)258} \\ -\ ??? \\ \hline ? \end{array}$

3. $\begin{array}{r} ? \ R\ ? \\ 20\overline{)166} \\ -\ ??? \\ \hline ? \end{array}$

4. $\begin{array}{r} ? \ R\ 35 \\ 80\overline{)675} \\ -\ ??? \\ \hline ?? \end{array}$

Practice

Divide and check.

5. $40\overline{)66}$ **6.** $80\overline{)98}$ **7.** $20\overline{)78}$ **8.** $50\overline{)85}$ **9.** $30\overline{)77}$

10. $70\overline{)356}$ **11.** $90\overline{)548}$ **12.** $80\overline{)567}$ **13.** $40\overline{)283}$ **14.** $50\overline{)454}$

15. $20\overline{)175}$ **16.** $50\overline{)349}$ **17.** $30\overline{)199}$ **18.** $70\overline{)501}$ **19.** $90\overline{)317}$

20. $430 \div 70$ **21.** $312 \div 50$ **22.** $250 \div 40$ **23.** $197 \div 60$

24. $599 \div 80$ **25.** $384 \div 60$ **26.** $672 \div 90$ **27.** $358 \div 40$

Problem Solving

28. Mariah will give an equal number of pencils to each of 60 students. She has 122 pencils. At most, how many pencils can she give to each student? How many pencils will she have left?

29. Brendan is sorting 150 pieces of chalk into boxes. Each box holds 20 pieces of chalk. How many boxes can he fill? How many pieces of chalk will be in the box that is not full?

30. The media center ordered 495 booklets on different health topics. Each of 80 fourth graders will read the same number of booklets. At most, how many booklets will each fourth grader read?

31. Dionne is helping Mr. Rau to stack 256 magazines. They put 30 magazines into each stack. How many stacks of 30 magazines are there? How many magazines are in the last stack?

Write About It

32. In your Math Journal, tell how knowing division patterns helps you to divide by multiples of 10.

> Remember: Numbers that end in 0 are multiples of 10. They all have 10 as a factor.

Estimate Quotients

To estimate quotients with 2-digit divisors, think of nearby numbers that are compatible.

> When one number divides another evenly, the two numbers are compatible.

Estimate using compatible numbers:
664 ÷ 24

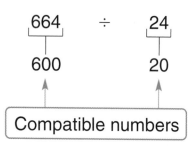

Think: $20\overline{)600}$ with 30 above

So 664 ÷ 24 is about 30.

Study these examples.

Estimate: 96 ÷ 31

.Think...

$$30\overline{)90} \text{ with } 3$$

So 96 ÷ 31 is about 3.

Estimate: $86.43 ÷ 38

.Think...

$$40\overline{)\$80.00} \text{ with } \$2.00$$

So $86.43 ÷ 38 is about $2.00.

Write the compatible numbers you would use to estimate the quotient. Then estimate.

1. 63 ÷ 21   **2.** 89 ÷ 32   **3.** 78 ÷ 19   **4.** 47 ÷ 22

5. 58 ÷ 33   **6.** 67 ÷ 11   **7.** 81 ÷ 44   **8.** 92 ÷ 36

9. 594 ÷ 26   **10.** 905 ÷ 38   **11.** 825 ÷ 18   **12.** 652 ÷ 21

13. 452 ÷ 17   **14.** 395 ÷ 24   **15.** 6475 ÷ 36   **16.** 7959 ÷ 43

Estimate the quotient. Use compatible numbers.

17. 95 ÷ 35   **18.** 87 ÷ 43   **19.** 62 ÷ 12   **20.** 59 ÷ 28

21. 49 ÷ 25   **22.** 81 ÷ 21   **23.** 91 ÷ 29   **24.** 67 ÷ 22

25. 644 ÷ 24   **26.** 841 ÷ 19   **27.** 919 ÷ 29   **28.** 592 ÷ 31

29. 799 ÷ 46   **30.** 652 ÷ 38   **31.** 401 ÷ 22   **32.** 423 ÷ 16

33. 8743 ÷ 36   **34.** 7921 ÷ 45   **35.** 5932 ÷ 24   **36.** 6417 ÷ 38

37. $59.75 ÷ 27   **38.** $4.21 ÷ 19   **39.** $91.39 ÷ 34   **40.** $5.56 ÷ 17

Problem Solving

41. Last week 896 students came to the Folk Art Museum in buses. About the same number of students traveled on each of 28 buses. About how many students were there on each bus?

42. One class spent $75.05 for lunch in the museum cafeteria. There were 19 students in the class, and each student spent about the same amount. About how much money did each student spend for lunch at the museum?

DO YOU REMEMBER?

Divide.

43. $7\overline{)58}$ **44.** $5\overline{)49}$ **45.** $3\overline{)36}$ **46.** $6\overline{)87}$

47. $3\overline{)745}$ **48.** $4\overline{)936}$ **49.** $8\overline{)277}$ **50.** $9\overline{)545}$

51. $2\overline{)\$1.28}$ **52.** $7\overline{)\$7.14}$ **53.** $9\overline{)\$74.43}$ **54.** $6\overline{)\$54.12}$

Two-Digit Dividends

Terry had 92 flower seeds. He planted
22 seeds in each of his flower baskets.
How many flower baskets did Terry
have? How many extra seeds
were there?

To find how many flower baskets,
divide: 92 ÷ 22.

Think

22)92 22 > 9   Not enough tens

22)92 22 < 92 **Enough ones**

| Estimate to place the first digit in the quotient. | 92 ÷ 22
 Think: 9 ÷ 2 = __?__
 Try 4. |

| Divide the ones. | Multiply. | Subtract and compare. | Check. |

$$\begin{array}{r} 4 \\ 22\overline{)92} \end{array}$$

$$\begin{array}{r} \times\ 4 \\ 22\overline{)92} \\ \rightarrow 88 \end{array}$$

$$\begin{array}{r} 4 \ \ R\,4 \\ 22\overline{)92} \\ -88 \\ \hline 4 \end{array}$$

$$\begin{array}{r} 22 \\ \times\ \ 4 \\ \hline 88 \\ +\ \ 4 \\ \hline 92 \end{array}$$

Terry had 4 flower baskets.
There were 4 extra seeds.

4 < 22

Study this example.

40 in. = __?__ yd

| 1 yd = 3 ft
 1 ft = 12 in. |

$$\begin{array}{r} 3\ \ R4 \\ 12\overline{)40} \\ -36 \\ \hline 4 \end{array}$$

40 in. = 3 ft 4 in. or 1 yd 4 in.

| Remember: Divide to rename smaller units as larger units. |

Complete each division.

1. $$24\overline{)48} \quad \begin{array}{r} 2 \\ -48 \\ \hline ? \end{array}$$

2. $$25\overline{)96} \quad \begin{array}{r} 3 \text{ R } \underline{?} \\ -?? \\ \hline 21 \end{array}$$

3. $$44\overline{)89} \quad \begin{array}{r} 2 \text{ R } \underline{?} \\ -88 \\ \hline ? \end{array}$$

4. $$21\overline{)94} \quad \begin{array}{r} ? \text{ R } \underline{?} \\ -84 \\ \hline ?? \end{array}$$

Divide and check.

5. $31\overline{)62}$ 6. $23\overline{)46}$ 7. $42\overline{)84}$ 8. $33\overline{)99}$ 9. $22\overline{)88}$

10. $32\overline{)64}$ 11. $33\overline{)66}$ 12. $41\overline{)82}$ 13. $23\overline{)92}$ 14. $43\overline{)86}$

15. $22\overline{)\$.66}$ 16. $45\overline{)\$.90}$ 17. $31\overline{)\$.93}$ 18. $26\overline{)\$.78}$ 19. $33\overline{)\$.66}$

Divide to rename each measure.

20. 32 fl oz = $\underline{?}$ c

21. 64 oz = $\underline{?}$ lb

22. 66 cm = $\underline{?}$ dm

23. 13 qt = $\underline{?}$ gal

24. 31 dm = $\underline{?}$ m

25. 49 pt = $\underline{?}$ qt

Problem Solving

26. Chris set out 96 tomato plants in a vegetable garden. She placed 24 tomato plants in each row. Did she have more than 5 rows?

27. Mike was putting 95 seed packets in a display. He wanted to put the same number of packets into each of 22 sections. How many packets could he have put into each section? How many packets would he have had left over?

CRITICAL THINKING — **Algebra**

Compare. Write $<$, $=$, or $>$. Estimate or find exact answers.

28. $64 \div 32 \underline{\ ?\ } 72 \div 24$

29. $84 \div 21 \underline{\ ?\ } 96 \div 32$

30. $72 \div 36 \underline{\ ?\ } 96 \div 48$

31. $58 \div 29 \underline{\ ?\ } 90 \div 45$

Three-Digit Dividends

There are 158 people who want to take a boat ride on the lake. How many trips with 45 passengers can the tour boat make? How many passengers will be on the last trip?

To find how many trips, divide: 158 ÷ 45.

Think

$45\overline{)158}$ 45 > 1   Not enough hundreds

$45\overline{)158}$ 45 > 15 Not enough tens

$45\overline{)158}$ 45 < 158 **Enough ones**

Estimate.

158 ÷ 45
Think: 15 ÷ 4 = __?__
Try 3.

Divide the ones.	Multiply.	Subtract and compare.	Check.

$$\begin{array}{r} 3 \\ 45\overline{)158} \end{array}$$

$$\begin{array}{r} \times \quad\quad \\ 3 \\ 45\overline{)158} \\ \rightarrow 135 \end{array}$$

$$\begin{array}{r} 3 \ \text{R}\,23 \\ 45\overline{)158} \\ -135 \\ \hline 23 \leftarrow \boxed{23 < 45} \end{array}$$

$$\begin{array}{r} 45 \\ \times \quad 3 \\ \hline 135 \\ + \quad 23 \\ \hline 158 \end{array}$$

The tour boat can make 3 trips with 45 passengers.
There will be 23 passengers on the last trip.

Study these examples.

$$\begin{array}{r} 6 \\ 63\overline{)378} \\ -378 \\ \hline 0 \end{array}$$

$$\begin{array}{r} 8 \\ 33\overline{)264} \\ -264 \\ \hline 0 \end{array}$$

$$\begin{array}{r} \$ .05 \\ 72\overline{)\$3.60} \\ -360 \\ \hline 0 \end{array}$$

$$\begin{array}{r} \$ .07 \\ 58\overline{)\$4.06} \\ -406 \\ \hline 0 \end{array}$$

Complete each division.

$$\begin{array}{r} 6 \\ 1.\ 51\overline{)306} \\ -??? \\ \hline ? \end{array}$$

$$\begin{array}{r} 9\ R\ \underline{\ ?\ } \\ 2.\ 46\overline{)419} \\ -??? \\ \hline ? \end{array}$$

$$\begin{array}{r} 4\ R\ \underline{\ ?\ } \\ 3.\ 83\overline{)392} \\ -??? \\ \hline ?? \end{array}$$

$$\begin{array}{r} ?\ R\ \underline{\ ?\ } \\ 4.\ 64\overline{)533} \\ -512 \\ \hline ?? \end{array}$$

Divide and check.

5. $22\overline{)176}$ 6. $32\overline{)160}$ 7. $43\overline{)258}$ 8. $57\overline{)285}$ 9. $74\overline{)222}$

10. $61\overline{)122}$ 11. $95\overline{)380}$ 12. $34\overline{)238}$ 13. $62\overline{)248}$ 14. $81\overline{)648}$

15. $42\overline{)146}$ 16. $72\overline{)236}$ 17. $51\overline{)489}$ 18. $21\overline{)109}$ 19. $91\overline{)476}$

20. $63\overline{)456}$ 21. $54\overline{)237}$ 22. $83\overline{)229}$ 23. $75\overline{)474}$ 24. $32\overline{)266}$

25. $67\overline{)\$1.34}$ 26. $92\overline{)\$4.60}$ 27. $71\overline{)\$6.39}$ 28. $83\overline{)\$3.32}$ 29. $44\overline{)\$3.08}$

Problem Solving

30. Each ticket seller sold 82 tickets to a total of 574 passengers. How many ticket sellers were there?

31. The tickets came in rolls of 150. The ticket sellers sold 35 rolls of tickets. How many tickets did they sell?

32. Each tour bus can carry 64 passengers. What is the least number of buses needed for 595 passengers?

MENTAL MATH

Estimate mentally.

Estimate: $168 \div 79$

Think: $80\overline{)160}$ with quotient 2

So $168 \div 79$ is about 2.

33. $164 \div 42$ 34. $218 \div 43$

35. $119 \div 23$ 36. $213 \div 52$

37. $358 \div 62$ 38. $326 \div 51$

Trial Quotients

Sometimes the quotient you try is too large. When this happens, you need to change the estimate.

Divide: 172 ÷ 27.

.Think..
27)172 27 > 1; 27 > 17
27)172 27 < 172 **Enough ones**
....

Estimate.	172 ÷ 27
	Think: 17 ÷ 2 = __?__ Try 8.

Divide the ones. Multiply.	trial quotient	Subtract and compare.	Check.

```
        8                    7                   6  R 10          27
 27)1 7 2            27)1 7 2            27)1 7 2             ×    6
   ► 2 1 6             ► 1 8 9            −1 6 2               1 6 2
                                           1 0 ◄             +  1 0
                                                               1 7 2
```

Too large. Try 7.	Too large. Try 6.	10 < 27

Study this example.

.Think..
35)281 35 > 2; 35 > 28
35)281 35 < 281 **Enough ones**
....

Divide: 281 ÷ 35.

Estimate: 281 ÷ 35.
   Think: 28 ÷ 3 = __?__
      Try 9.

```
        9              8  R 1      Check.
 35)2 8 1       35)2 8 1
   ► 3 1 5        −2 8 0              3 5
                     1             ×   8
                                     2 8 0
                                   +    1
                                     2 8 1
```

Too large.
Try 8.

Complete each division.

1.
$$27\overline{)82} \quad \begin{array}{r} 4 \\ 108 \end{array}$$

$$\longrightarrow \quad 27\overline{)82} \quad \begin{array}{r} 3 \ R\ \underline{\ ?\ } \\ -81 \\ \hline ? \end{array}$$

Try 3.

2.
$$48\overline{)\$2.88} \quad \begin{array}{r} \$\ .07 \\ 3\ 36 \end{array}$$

$$\longrightarrow \quad 48\overline{)\$2.88} \quad \begin{array}{r} \$\ .06 \\ -?\ ?? \\ \hline ? \end{array}$$

Try $ .06.

3.
$$64\overline{)310} \quad \begin{array}{r} 5 \\ ??? \end{array}$$

$$\longrightarrow \quad 64\overline{)310} \quad \begin{array}{r} ?\ R\ \underline{\ ?\ } \\ -??? \\ \hline 54 \end{array}$$

Try 4.

4.
$$86\overline{)657} \quad \begin{array}{r} 8 \\ 688 \end{array}$$

$$\longrightarrow \quad 86\overline{)657} \quad \begin{array}{r} ?\ R\ \underline{\ ?\ } \\ -??? \\ \hline ?? \end{array}$$

Try $\underline{\ ?\ }$.

Divide.

5. $27\overline{)52}$ **6.** $36\overline{)91}$ **7.** $45\overline{)82}$ **8.** $18\overline{)97}$

9. $35\overline{)124}$ **10.** $48\overline{)165}$ **11.** $54\overline{)260}$ **12.** $79\overline{)221}$

13. $66\overline{)542}$ **14.** $94\overline{)638}$ **15.** $87\overline{)569}$ **16.** $49\overline{)202}$

17. $27\overline{)124}$ **18.** $39\overline{)277}$ **19.** $76\overline{)571}$ **20.** $99\overline{)828}$

21. $28\overline{)\$.84}$ **22.** $59\overline{)\$3.54}$ **23.** $78\overline{)\$6.24}$ **24.** $69\overline{)\$5.52}$

Problem Solving

25. Mr. Dean has signed up 180 students for a field trip to the zoo. Each bus can carry 36 students and 4 teachers. How many buses are needed for the field trip?

26. There are 115 chimpanzees at the zoo. No more than 25 chimpanzees can be in each environment. What is the least number of environments there could be at the zoo?

27. The chimpanzees eat 325 bananas each week. The bananas are shipped in crates of 48. How many crates of bananas are needed to feed the chimpanzees?

Greater Quotients

Divide: 995 ÷ 22.

Think

22)995 22 > 9   Not enough hundreds

22)995 22 < 99 **Enough tens**

Estimate.
995 ÷ 22
Think: 9 ÷ 2 = __?__
Try 4.

Divide the tens.	Multiply.	Subtract and compare.	Bring down the ones.

```
    4
22)995
```

```
     ×  4
22)995
    →88
```

```
      4
22)995
  −88
   11
```
11 < 22

```
      4
22)995
  −88↓
  115←
```
partial dividend

Repeat the steps.

Estimate.
115 ÷ 22
Think: 11 ÷ 2 = __?__
Try 5.

Divide the ones.	Multiply.	Subtract and compare.	Check.

```
    45
22)995
  −88↓
  115
```

```
×      45
22)995
  −88↓
  115
  →110
```

```
      45  R 5
22)995
  −88↓
  115
 −110
    5
```
5 < 22

```
    45
  × 22
    90
 +900
  990
 +   5
  995
```

Complete each division.

$$
\begin{array}{r}
26 \\
\textbf{1.}\ 34\overline{)884} \\
-\ ?? \\
\hline
204 \\
-\ ??? \\
\hline
?
\end{array}
\qquad
\begin{array}{r}
2?\ \ \text{R}\ ? \\
\textbf{2.}\ 42\overline{)890} \\
-\ ?? \\
\hline
50 \\
-\ ?? \\
\hline
?
\end{array}
\qquad
\begin{array}{r}
2? \\
\textbf{3.}\ 17\overline{)357} \\
-\ ?? \\
\hline
?? \\
-\ ?? \\
\hline
?
\end{array}
\qquad
\begin{array}{r}
?8\ \ \text{R}\ ? \\
\textbf{4.}\ 19\overline{)536} \\
-\ ?? \\
\hline
??? \\
-\ ??? \\
\hline
?
\end{array}
$$

Divide and check.

5. $15\overline{)95}$ **6.** $12\overline{)92}$ **7.** $18\overline{)79}$ **8.** $16\overline{)68}$ **9.** $11\overline{)74}$

10. $42\overline{)882}$ **11.** $23\overline{)552}$ **12.** $31\overline{)899}$ **13.** $45\overline{)630}$ **14.** $35\overline{)721}$

15. $45\overline{)678}$ **16.** $59\overline{)620}$ **17.** $51\overline{)801}$ **18.** $61\overline{)827}$ **19.** $82\overline{)963}$

20. $11\overline{)316}$ **21.** $18\overline{)723}$ **22.** $16\overline{)522}$ **23.** $15\overline{)187}$ **24.** $19\overline{)799}$

25. $21\overline{)1938}$ **26.** $33\overline{)875}$ **27.** $41\overline{)882}$ **28.** $64\overline{)900}$ **29.** $16\overline{)344}$

30. $32\overline{)\$7.04}$ **31.** $15\overline{)\$1.80}$ **32.** $19\overline{)\$3.99}$ **33.** $24\overline{)\$5.52}$ **34.** $12\overline{)\$5.04}$

Problem Solving

35. Carey picked 865 pears. He put 42 pears into each box. How many boxes did Carey fill? How many pears were left over?

36. Wendell sold two peaches to each of 33 customers for a total of $16.50. What was the cost of each peach?

37. The divisor is 13.
The quotient is 64.
The remainder is 10.
What is the dividend?

38. The quotient is 55.
The divisor is 17.
The remainder is 7.
What is the dividend?

Four-Digit Dividends

Divide: 5481 ÷ 64.

Think

64)5481 64 > 5   Not enough thousands

64)5481 64 > 54 Not enough hundreds

64)5481 64 < 548 **Enough tens**

| Estimate. |

5481 ÷ 64
Think: 54 ÷ 6 = ?
Try 9.

| Divide the tens. Multiply. |

$$\begin{array}{r} 9 \\ 64\overline{)5481} \\ 576 \end{array}$$

| Too large. Try 8. |

$$\begin{array}{r} 8 \\ 64\overline{)5481} \\ 512 \end{array}$$

| Subtract and compare. |

$$\begin{array}{r} 8 \\ 64\overline{)5481} \\ -512 \\ \hline 36 \end{array}$$

| 36 < 64 |

| Bring down the ones. |

$$\begin{array}{r} 8 \\ 64\overline{)5481} \\ -512 \downarrow \\ \hline 361 \end{array}$$

Repeat the steps.

| Divide the ones. Multiply. |

$$\begin{array}{r} 86 \\ 64\overline{)5481} \\ -512 \downarrow \\ \hline 361 \\ 384 \end{array}$$

| Too large. Try 5. |

$$\begin{array}{r} 85 \\ 64\overline{)5481} \\ -512 \downarrow \\ \hline 361 \\ 320 \end{array}$$

| Subtract and compare. |

$$\begin{array}{r} 85 \ \text{R}\,41 \\ 64\overline{)5481} \\ -512 \\ \hline 361 \\ -320 \\ \hline 41 \end{array}$$

| 41 < 64 |

| Check. |

$$\begin{array}{r} 85 \\ \times \quad 64 \\ \hline 340 \\ +5100 \\ \hline 5440 \\ + \quad 41 \\ \hline 5481 \end{array}$$

Complete each division.

$$
\begin{array}{r}
24 \ \text{R} \ \underline{?} \\
1. \ 51\overline{)1273} \\
-102 \\
\hline
253 \\
-??? \\
\hline
? \\
\end{array}
\qquad
\begin{array}{r}
46 \ \text{R} \ \underline{?} \\
2. \ 24\overline{)1107} \\
-96 \\
\hline
147 \\
-??? \\
\hline
? \\
\end{array}
\qquad
\begin{array}{r}
?? \ \text{R} \ \underline{?} \\
3. \ 33\overline{)2179} \\
-198 \\
\hline
199 \\
-??? \\
\hline
? \\
\end{array}
$$

Divide and check.

4. $40\overline{)2459}$　　5. $80\overline{)5346}$　　6. $70\overline{)6842}$　　7. $50\overline{)4779}$

8. $34\overline{)1180}$　　9. $52\overline{)3115}$　　10. $44\overline{)2106}$　　11. $63\overline{)4914}$

12. $72\overline{)4594}$　　13. $96\overline{)7128}$　　14. $22\overline{)1550}$　　15. $84\overline{)5285}$

16. $64\overline{)5084}$　　17. $48\overline{)4128}$　　18. $38\overline{)2242}$　　19. $55\overline{)3226}$

20. $22\overline{)1810}$　　21. $73\overline{)5808}$　　22. $14\overline{)1248}$　　23. $18\overline{)1200}$

24. $92\overline{)\$21.16}$　　25. $51\overline{)\$16.83}$　　26. $88\overline{)\$22.00}$　　27. $67\overline{)\$56.95}$

Problem Solving

28. Each of 45 students bought a copy of *The Great Dinosaurs.* They paid a total of $42.75. How much did one copy of *The Great Dinosaurs* cost?

29. There are 1565 books at the Elmford book fair. If each table can hold 55 books, what is the least number of tables needed for the fair?

30. Each homeroom in Elmford School can seat 36 students. There are 1256 students in the school. What is the least number of homerooms needed for all the students?

31. Students bought 32 copies of *Amazing Science* for a total cost of $95.36 and 32 copies of *SciFi* for a total cost of $110.40. If each student bought 1 copy of each magazine, how much did each student spend?

Zero in the Quotient

Divide: 2865 ÷ 14.

Think
$14\overline{)2865}$ 14 > 2 Not enough thousands
$14\overline{)2865}$ 14 < 28 **Enough hundreds**

| Estimate. | 2865 ÷ 14
Think: 2 ÷ 1 = __?__
Try 2. |

| Divide the hundreds. | Divide the tens. | | Divide the ones. |

$$
\begin{array}{r}
2 \\
14\overline{)2865} \\
-28\downarrow \\
\hline
06
\end{array}
$$

$$
\begin{array}{r}
20 \\
14\overline{)2865} \\
-28\downarrow \\
\hline
6 \\
-0\downarrow \\
\hline
65
\end{array}
$$

14 > 6 **Not enough tens** Write 0 in the tens place. Bring down the ones.

$$
\begin{array}{r}
204\text{ R 9} \\
14\overline{)2865} \\
-28\downarrow \\
\hline
6 \\
-0\downarrow \\
\hline
65 \\
-56 \\
\hline
9
\end{array}
$$

| Check. | 14 × 204 = 2856 ⟶ 2856 + 9 = 2865 |

Study these examples.

$$
\begin{array}{r}
300\text{ R 5} \\
21\overline{)6305} \\
-63\downarrow \\
\hline
0 \\
-0\downarrow \\
\hline
5 \\
-0 \\
\hline
5
\end{array}
$$

| Check. |
$$
\begin{array}{r}
300 \\
\times21 \\
\hline
300 \\
+600 \\
\hline
6300 \\
+5 \\
\hline
6305
\end{array}
$$

$$
\begin{array}{r}
\$3.06 \\
26\overline{)\$79.56} \\
-78\downarrow \\
\hline
15 \\
-0\downarrow \\
\hline
156 \\
-156 \\
\hline
0
\end{array}
$$

| Check. |
$$
\begin{array}{r}
\$3.06 \\
\times26 \\
\hline
1836 \\
+6120 \\
\hline
\$79.56
\end{array}
$$

Complete each division.

$$
\begin{array}{r}
60 \\
\textbf{1.}\ 35\overline{)2100} \\
-210 \\
\hline
? \\
\end{array}
$$

$$
\begin{array}{r}
102 \\
\textbf{2.}\ 57\overline{)5814} \\
-57 \\
\hline
11 \\
-\ ? \\
\hline
1?4 \\
-??? \\
\hline
\end{array}
$$

$$
\begin{array}{r}
\$\ 2.0? \\
\textbf{3.}\ 18\overline{)\$36.90} \\
-36 \\
\hline
9 \\
-? \\
\hline
?0 \\
-?? \\
\hline
\end{array}
$$

$$
\begin{array}{r}
3??\ \ R\ \underline{?} \\
\textbf{4.}\ 24\overline{)7231} \\
-72 \\
\hline
3 \\
-? \\
\hline
?1 \\
-?? \\
\hline
? \\
\end{array}
$$

Divide and check.

5. $45\overline{)3600}$ **6.** $32\overline{)1600}$ **7.** $24\overline{)2166}$ **8.** $56\overline{)3930}$

9. $17\overline{)6800}$ **10.** $25\overline{)5000}$ **11.** $41\overline{)8214}$ **12.** $33\overline{)9927}$

13. $21\overline{)2247}$ **14.** $19\overline{)5852}$ **15.** $32\overline{)9856}$ **16.** $46\overline{)9246}$

17. $15\overline{)9097}$ **18.** $51\overline{)5576}$ **19.** $28\overline{)8538}$ **20.** $34\overline{)7068}$

21. $43\overline{)8735}$ **22.** $13\overline{)9175}$ **23.** $62\overline{)6736}$ **24.** $74\overline{)7904}$

25. $18\overline{)\$37.44}$ **26.** $23\overline{)\$70.61}$ **27.** $85\overline{)\$92.65}$ **28.** $56\overline{)\$60.48}$

Problem Solving

29. Damon bought a 12-yard length of cloth for $48.72. What was the cost per yard?

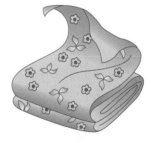

CHALLENGE

Find the quotient and any remainder.

30. $22\overline{)22,154}$ **31.** $32\overline{)64,128}$ **32.** $17\overline{)61,085}$

33. $42\overline{)84,378}$ **34.** $51\overline{)51,408}$ **35.** $24\overline{)96,088}$

Greater Dividends

Repeat the division steps as necessary when you divide greater dividends.

Divide: 26,794 ÷ 52.

Think

$52\overline{)26{,}794}$ 52 > 2; 52 > 26

$52\overline{)26{,}794}$ 52 < 267

Enough hundreds.

Division Steps

- Estimate.
- Divide.
- Multiply.
- Subtract.
- Compare.
- Bring down.
- Repeat the steps as necessary.
- Check.

Estimate.

26,794 ÷ 52
Think: 26 ÷ 5 = __?__
Try: 5.

Divide the hundreds.

```
        5
5 2)2 6,7 9 4
  -2 6 0
      7 9
```

Divide the tens.

```
        5 1
5 2)2 6,7 9 4
  -2 6 0
      7 9
    - 5 2
    2 7 4
```

Divide the ones.

```
        5 1 5  R 14
5 2)2 6,7 9 4
  -2 6 0
      7 9
    - 5 2
    2 7 4
  - 2 6 0
      1 4
```

14 < 52

Check.

```
      5 1 5
   ×    5 2
     1 0 3 0
  +2 5 7 5
   2 6 7 8 0
```

```
   2 6,7 8 0
 +      1 4
   2 6,7 9 4
```

Complete each division.

1.
$$81?\text{ R }3$$
$$43)\overline{35{,}177}$$
$$-34\ 4$$
$$77$$
$$-43$$
$$347$$
$$-???$$
$$3$$

2.
$$5??\text{ R }\underline{\ ?\ }$$
$$85)\overline{42{,}949}$$
$$-42\ 5$$
$$44$$
$$-\ ?$$
$$???$$
$$-???$$
$$24$$

3.
$$???\text{ R }\underline{\ ?\ }$$
$$66)\overline{29{,}786}$$
$$-26\ 4$$
$$3\ 3?$$
$$-?\ ??$$
$$?6$$
$$-??$$
$$??$$

Find the quotient.

4. $91)\overline{56{,}708}$

5. $48)\overline{17{,}751}$

6. $51)\overline{35{,}138}$

7. $75)\overline{62{,}844}$

8. $29)\overline{13{,}479}$

9. $37)\overline{24{,}795}$

10. $63)\overline{42{,}726}$

11. $86)\overline{59{,}843}$

12. $97)\overline{72{,}471}$

13. $43)\overline{\$313.04}$

14. $58)\overline{\$349.74}$

15. $72)\overline{\$214.56}$

16. $21)\overline{137{,}662}$

17. $32)\overline{258{,}412}$

18. $77)\overline{445{,}083}$

Problem Solving

19. During Clean Up the River week, volunteers picked up 23,436 pounds of trash from the banks of the river. Each volunteer picked up an average of 28 pounds of trash. How many volunteers worked to pick up trash?

20. 28,694 pounds of canned goods were collected for the homeless. If each family receives 35 pounds of canned goods, what is the greatest number of families that can be helped?

Problem-Solving Strategy:
Use More Than One Step

Andre needs 14 ft of rope to string between two trees to hang his art show. He buys a spool that has 175 in. of rope. Does Andre have enough rope?

Read ▸ **Visualize the facts of the problem as you reread it.**

Facts: Andre needs 14 ft of rope.
The spool has 175 in.

Question: Does he have enough rope?

Plan ▸ Interpret the hidden information.
Then find whether he has enough rope:
First divide. 175 in. ÷ 12 in. = ___?___ ft
Then compare. 14 ft ___?___ ___?___ ft

Remember:
12 in. = 1 ft

Solve ▸

```
       1 4  R 7
  1 2)1 7 5
   - 1 2
      5 5
    - 4 8
       7
```

Think........
14 R 7 means
14 ft 7 in.

Compare. 14 ft < 14 ft 7 in.
Yes, Andre has enough rope.

Check ▸ Multiply and add to check division.

```
     14          168
   × 12        +  7
     28          175
  + 14
    168
```

The answer checks.

Use more than one step to help you solve each problem.

1. Winnie must make 136 pint-sized yogurt sundaes. She has 66 quarts of yogurt. Does Winnie have enough yogurt?

Read ▶ Visualize the facts of the problem as you reread it.

Facts: 136 pint-sized sundaes
66 quarts of yogurt

Question: Does Winnie have enough yogurt?

Plan ▶ Is there hidden information to interpret? Yes

Remember: 2 pints = 1 quart

Since there must be 136 sundaes, 136 pints of yogurt are needed.
To find out whether she has enough yogurt:
First divide: 136 ÷ 2. Then compare.

Solve ⋯⋯▶ **Check**

2. A nature DVD is 148 minutes long. Can Saundra watch the DVD in $2\frac{1}{2}$ hours?

3. Paulo earns $1196 a year for delivering newspapers. Mia earns $24 a week for mowing lawns. Who earns more money per year?

4. In one full day a satellite transmits 9600 messages. How many fewer messages does it transmit in 1 hour than a satellite that transmits 420 messages in 1 hour?

5. Arcade games cost 1 quarter to play. Byron has $15 in quarters. Explain if he has enough coins to play 50 arcade games.

Problem-Solving Applications: Mixed Review

Solve each problem and explain the method you used.

1. A store displays 252 different wrapping papers equally on 14 racks. How many papers are on each rack?

2. There are 180 toys to be wrapped for a toy drive. 20 people volunteer to wrap. How many toys will each person wrap?

3. A shop sells 10 ft of ribbon for $1.60. How much does 1 ft of ribbon cost?

4. Joe made 24 party invitations at a cost of $1.98. About how much did he spend on each invitation?

5. Joe cuts as many 18-in. strips as he can from a 100-in. roll of ribbon. How much ribbon is left on the roll?

6. Crepe paper streamers are sold in 28-ft rolls. To decorate a gym for a party, 150 ft of crepe paper is needed. How many rolls should be bought?

7. The store sells ready-made bows in packs of 15. Each pack costs $4.20. How much does each bow cost?

8. There were 2880 balloons delivered to 12 area stores. About how many balloons did each store order if each store received the same number of balloons?

9. A complete party package costs $75.90. If 22 friends share the cost, how much will each friend spend?

**Choose a strategy from the list or
use another strategy you know
to solve each problem.**

Strategy File

Use these Strategies
Make a Table
Choose the Operation
Use More Than One Step
Find a Pattern
Use a Diagram/Graph
Interpret the Remainder

10. Birthday candles are sold in packs of 12. How many packs should you buy if you need to put 35 candles on a cake?

11. Jeff makes his own wrapping paper with cat and dog stickers in 8 rows, following this pattern: 2 cats, 4 dogs, 3 cats, 5 dogs, 4 cats. What is the pattern for the last 3 rows?

12. Joan needs 48 party favors. They come in packs of 12. How many packs will she need to buy?

13. A store's display window is filled with 350 balloons. They came in packs of 24. How many packs were used?

14. Kim has $.95. Helium balloons are $11.28 a dozen. Does Kim have enough to buy one balloon?

15. On Mondays a shop gives a discount of 10¢ for every dollar spent. Ted spent $14 on Friday. How much would he have saved if he had shopped on Monday?

16. Al spent $16.28. Julia spent 4 times as much. How much money did she spend?

Use the graph for problems 17 and 18.

17. Of which patterns did the store sell more than 20 but fewer than 40 packs?

18. Of which pattern did the store sell about 15 fewer packs than it did for teddy bears?

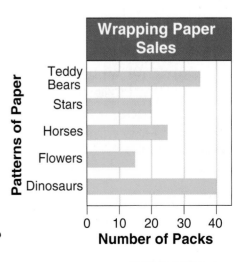

Wrapping Paper Sales

Patterns of Paper: Teddy Bears, Stars, Horses, Flowers, Dinosaurs

Number of Packs: 0 10 20 30 40

Check Your Progress
Lessons 1–12

Divide and check. (See pp. 382–385.)

1. $20\overline{)66}$ 2. $30\overline{)75}$ 3. $70\overline{)351}$ 4. $50\overline{)299}$ 5. $90\overline{)319}$

6. $395 \div 70$ 7. $312 \div 70$ 8. $139 \div 20$ 9. $256 \div 20$

Estimate the quotient. (See pp. 386–387.)

10. $48 \div 20$ 11. $82 \div 39$ 12. $99 \div 47$ 13. $597 \div 19$

14. $4011 \div 38$ 15. $\$69.03 \div 9$ 16. $7482 \div 47$ 17. $\$5.79 \div 19$

Divide and check. (See pp. 388–399.)

18. $22\overline{)66}$ 19. $45\overline{)90}$ 20. $31\overline{)\$.93}$ 21. $13\overline{)\$.65}$ 22. $17\overline{)85}$

23. $56\overline{)280}$ 24. $37\overline{)222}$ 25. $76\overline{)342}$ 26. $42\overline{)\$3.36}$ 27. $75\overline{)\$97.50}$

28. $17\overline{)435}$ 29. $14\overline{)456}$ 30. $13\overline{)286}$ 31. $15\overline{)\$1.80}$ 32. $12\overline{)\$5.04}$

33. $34\overline{)1180}$ 34. $96\overline{)7128}$ 35. $14\overline{)1248}$ 36. $67\overline{)5690}$ 37. $73\overline{)5808}$

38. $17\overline{)6800}$ 39. $19\overline{)5852}$ 40. $13\overline{)9175}$ 41. $28\overline{)8536}$ 42. $74\overline{)7904}$

Problem Solving
(See pp. 404–405.)

43. There are 257 sheets of lined paper for 24 students to share equally. How many sheets of paper does each student get? How many sheets are left over?

44. The rental of a school bus for a field trip is $56.00. Thirty-two students are going on the trip, and will split the cost equally. What is the cost for each student?

45. The dividend is 80. The quotient is 4. What is the divisor?

46. The quotient is 8. The divisor is 31. What is the dividend?

  (See *Still More Practice*, p. 471.)

Logic

You have to read carefully to be sure you do not draw a false conclusion from true statements.

Read these statements and conclusions. All the statements are true.

statements: All dogs have ears.
Sparky is a dog.

conclusion: Sparky has ears.   TRUE

statements: All dogs have ears.
My cat has ears.

conclusion: My cat is a dog.   FALSE

Read the true statements carefully. Then write *true* or *false* for each conclusion.

1. All ducks have feathers.
A chicken has feathers.
A chicken is a duck.

2. All fish can swim.
A salmon is a fish.
A salmon can swim.

3. Ralph is a 4th-grade boy.
All the 4th-grade boys
wore sneakers on Monday.
Ralph wore sneakers
on Monday.

4. All the 4th-grade boys wore
sneakers on Monday.
Maria wore sneakers
on Monday.
Maria is a 4th-grade boy.

5. All triangles are polygons.
A pentagon is a polygon.
A pentagon is a triangle.

6. All squares are parallelograms.
All rectangles are parallelograms.
All rectangles are squares.

7. Triangle *A* has one right
angle. All triangles with
one right angle are right
triangles.
Triangle *A* is a right triangle.

Estimate the quotient.

1. 58 ÷ 33
2. 825 ÷ 18
3. 395 ÷ 24
4. 7959 ÷ 43

5. 29)‾919‾
6. 45)‾7921‾
7. 27)‾5975‾
8. 19)‾841‾
9. 38)‾6417‾

Divide and check.

10. 33)‾66‾
11. 31)‾96‾
12. 24)‾89‾
13. 41)‾$.82‾
14. 23)‾$.92‾

15. 42)‾146‾
16. 34)‾$2.38‾
17. 83)‾$2.49‾
18. 24)‾109‾
19. 54)‾237‾

20. 66)‾542‾
21. 76)‾$5.32‾
22. 49)‾202‾
23. 31)‾$1.24‾
24. 99)‾828‾

25. 45)‾678‾
26. 35)‾745‾
27. 42)‾770‾
28. 25)‾$9.00‾
29. 41)‾8565‾

30. 18)‾5546‾
31. 15)‾$1.80‾
32. 15)‾187‾
33. 88)‾9504‾
34. 73)‾$79.57‾

Problem Solving

Use a strategy you have learned.

35. A bus seats 52 passengers. How many buses are needed to carry 795 passengers from the hotel to the state fair?

Tell About It

Explain how to use compatible numbers to solve this problem.

36. In one week, a hospital's cafeteria serves 5325 meals. About how many meals are served a day?

Performance Assessment

Use these dividends and divisors to make division exercises for the following:

Dividends		Divisors	
1440	2820	40	20

37. A quotient between 60 and 100 with no remainder.

38. A quotient less than 100 with a remainder of 20.

39. A quotient greater than 100.

Choose the best answer.

1. 8 yd 2 ft
  − 3 yd 1 ft

   a. 5 yd 1 ft **b.** 12 yd
   c. 12 yd 1 ft **d.** 13 yd

2. Choose the standard form.

   $800,000,000 + 400,000 + 50,000 + 1$

   a. 84,501 **b.** 804,050,001
   c. 804,501 **d.** 800,450,001

3. Use front-end estimation.

   4387
   × 9

   a. 36,000
   b. 3600
   c. 4000
   d. 39,483

4. How many inches of rain are most likely to fall in August?

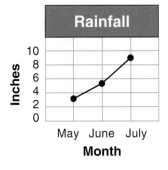

   a. 6 in. **b.** 7 in.
   c. 8 in. **d.** 10 in.

5. Choose the equivalent fraction.

   $\frac{4}{7}$

   a. $\frac{21}{12}$ **b.** $\frac{7}{10}$ **c.** $\frac{12}{21}$ **d.** $\frac{1}{4}$

6. 3 yd = ___?___ in.

   a. 9 **b.** 36
   c. 108 **d.** not given

7. Choose the adjusted estimate.

   $638 + 207 + 669$

   a. about 1200 **b.** about 1300
   c. about 1500 **d.** about 1600

8. Which expression matches the problem?
Liv picks some berries. She eats 9 of them.

   a. $9 - b$
   b. $b - 9$
   c. $9 + b$
   d. $b + 9$

9. How many students went on the roller coaster more than twice?

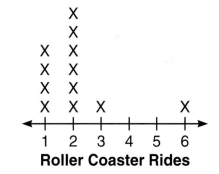

   a. 6 **b.** 2
   c. 9 **d.** 8

10. Choose the difference in simplest form.

   $\frac{5}{6} - \frac{2}{6}$

   a. $\frac{1}{2}$ **b.** $\frac{3}{6}$ **c.** $\frac{7}{12}$ **d.** $\frac{1}{3}$

Use the circle below for exercises 11 and 12.

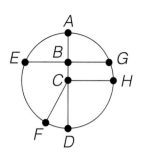

11. Which names a chord?

   a. $\overline{AB}$ **b.** $\overline{EG}$ **c.** $\overline{CH}$ **d.** $\overline{FC}$

12. Which does **not** name a radius?

   a. $\overline{AD}$ **b.** $\overline{CD}$ **c.** $\overline{CH}$ **d.** $\overline{FC}$

13. Choose the angle defined.

measures more than 90°, but less than 180°

   a. right   **b.** acute
   c. obtuse   **d.** straight

14.

$30\overline{)349}$

   a. 12
   b. 110 R19
   c. 11 R19
   d. 11 R11

15. Choose the fraction in simplest form.

$$\frac{9}{27}$$

   a. $\frac{3}{9}$ **b.** $\frac{2}{4}$ **c.** $\frac{1}{2}$ **d.** $\frac{1}{3}$

16. Choose the volume.

   Length: 8 cm
   Width: 7 cm
   Height: 9 cm

   a. 504 cubic cm
   b. 56 cubic cm
   c. 63 cubic cm
   d. 24 cubic cm

17. Find part of the number.

$$\frac{3}{8} \text{ of } 64 = n$$

   a. 8   **b.** 16   **c.** 24   **d.** 11

18. Choose the best compatible numbers to estimate.

$$88 \div 29$$

   a. $90 \div 30$ **b.** $85 \div 30$
   c. $90 \div 20$ **d.** $80 \div 30$

19.

$17\overline{)397}$

   a. 22 R 23
   b. 23
   c. 23 R6
   d. 24

20.

$43\overline{)6904}$

   a. 16 R 24
   b. 160 R 24
   c. 161
   d. 160 R 42

Explain each step you use to solve the problem.

21. Nick the Baker uses 96 fl oz of milk to bake a dozen cakes.
Rick the Baker uses $1\frac{1}{2}$ cups of milk to bake 1 cake.
Who uses more milk in each cake?

Math Class

She talks about the decimal point,
The reasons why—
But on the window, buzzing free,
A fly

With two red eyes
Moves slowly up the pane.
She moves the decimal one place left
And then again

The fly moves up
And up, practiced and slow.
What I have learned of decimal points
Flies know.

Myra Cohn Livingston

Decimals

CHAPTER 13

20.5

In this chapter you will:

Learn about tenths and hundredths
Compare, order, and round decimals
Estimate, add, and subtract decimals
Divide money
Use more than one step to solve
   problems

Critical Thinking/Finding Together

Name the decimal written on the
board. Then name and model the
new decimal when the decimal point
is moved one place to the left.

Tenths and Hundredths

▶ You can write tenths as a fraction or as a decimal.

Fraction: $\frac{3}{10}$

Decimal: 0.3

Read: three tenths

> The *decimal point* separates the whole number part from the decimal part.

> This 0 means *no ones*.

▶ You can write hundredths as a fraction or as a decimal.

Fraction: $\frac{45}{100}$

Decimal: 0.45

Read: forty-five hundredths

Fraction: $\frac{5}{100}$

Decimal: 0.05

Read: five hundredths

> This 0 means *no tenths*.

▶ You can write **equivalent decimals** to name the same part.

$\frac{5}{10}$ or 0.5   = $\frac{50}{100}$ or 0.50

Think
$\frac{5}{10} = \frac{5 \times 10}{10 \times 10} = \frac{50}{100}$

0.5 and 0.50 name the same part.
They are equivalent decimals.

Write as a fraction. Then write as a decimal.

1.

2.

3.

Rename as a fraction in simplest form.

4. 0.5   **5.** 0.25   **6.** 0.6   **7.** 0.4   **8.** 0.75   **9.** 0.8

Use grid paper to model each.
Then write each as a decimal or a fraction.

10. 0.1   **11.** $\frac{37}{100}$ **12.** 0.7   **13.** $\frac{60}{100}$ **14.** 0.09

Are the decimals equivalent? Write *yes* or *no*.

15. 0.6; 0.60   **16.** 0.10; 0.1   **17.** 0.7; 0.07   **18.** 0.02; 0.2

Decimals and Fractions on a Number Line

You can model decimals and fractions on a number line.

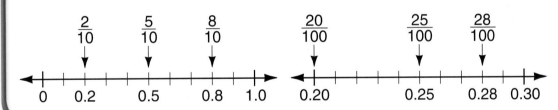

To what decimal and fraction is each arrow pointing?

19.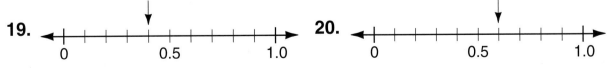

20.

21.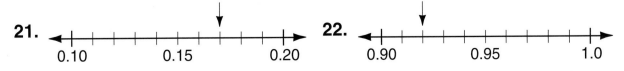

22.

Decimals Greater Than One

You can write a mixed number or a whole number as a decimal.

   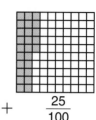

$$1 \quad + \quad 1 \quad + \quad 1 \quad + \quad \frac{25}{100} \quad = 3\frac{25}{100}$$

Mixed Number: $3\frac{25}{100}$

This 3 means *3 ones*.

Decimal: 3.25

decimal point

Read: three **and** twenty-five hundredths

Study these examples.

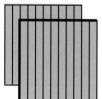 

$2\frac{1}{10} = 2.1$ $1\frac{3}{100} = 1.03$ $3 = 3.0$

two and one tenth   one and three hundredths   three

Practice

Write as a mixed number. Then write as a decimal.

1.

2.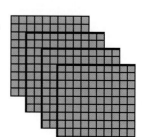

Write each as a decimal.
Then model exercises 3–10 using decimal squares.

3. $5\frac{3}{10}$ **4.** $8\frac{7}{10}$ **5.** $4\frac{2}{10}$ **6.** $7\frac{5}{10}$

7. $9\frac{21}{100}$ **8.** 10 **9.** $3\frac{6}{100}$ **10.** $2\frac{1}{100}$

11. $24\frac{6}{10}$ **12.** $97\frac{17}{100}$ **13.** 50 **14.** $100\frac{9}{100}$

15. three and eight tenths

16. nine and nineteen hundredths

17. twelve and one hundredth

18. one hundred fifty-seven

Write each as a mixed number.

19. 6.4   **20.** 4.30   **21.** 8.08   **22.** 5.01   **23.** 60.02

To what decimal is each arrow pointing?

24.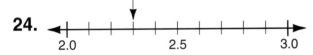

25.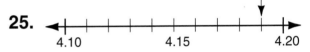

26.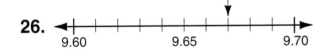

27.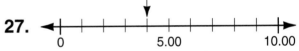

Write a decimal or a mixed number for each situation.

28. Keisha hiked five and two tenths miles.

29. Manny ran in a benefit race that was three and eighty hundredths miles.

30. Seo scored nine and nine hundredths on the horizontal bars competition.

31. Ivan jogged twelve and three tenths miles in two days.

Problem Solving

32. Write a decimal that is:
  a. between 3 and 4.
  b. less than 9 and greater than 8.
  c. between 11 and 12.
  d. greater than 1 and less than 2.

Decimal Place Value

▶ The value of a digit in a decimal depends on its place in the decimal.

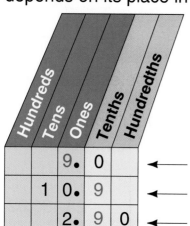

Look at the decimals in the place-value chart.

The value of the digit 9 in each decimal is:

9 ones, or 9.

9 tenths, or 0.9

9 tenths, or 0.9

9 hundredths, or 0.09

9 hundredths, or 0.09

▶ You can write decimals in standard form or in expanded form.

Standard Form	Expanded Form
24.5	20 + 4 + 0.5
3.60	3 + 0.6
961.04	900 + 60 + 1 + 0.04
87.37	80 + 7 + 0.3 + 0.07

Practice

Write the place of the red digit. Then write its value.

1. 2.31　　**2.** 0.49　　**3.** 62.75　　**4.** 11.38　　**5.** 129.04

6. 21.59　　**7.** 5.04　　**8.** 30.03　　**9.** 25.15　　**10.** 53.96

11. 4.10　　**12.** 8.56　　**13.** 509.88　　**14.** 9.14　　**15.** 18.03

Write each decimal in expanded form.

16. 0.23 **17.** 4.07 **18.** 9.94 **19.** 1.8 **20.** 205.6

21. 91.05 **22.** 30.8 **23.** 84.73 **24.** 670.01 **25.** 700.60

Write each in standard form. Then write each word name.

26. 40 + 2 + 0.9 + 0.07

27. 500 + 70 + 5 + 0.2 + 0.06

28. 6 + 0.9 + 0.01

29. 8 + 0.2

30. 0.4 + 0.06

31. 0.1 + 0.01

32. 800 + 5 + 0.03

33. 300 + 20 + 0.8

34. 100 + 0.5 + 0.07

35. 50 + 0.3 + 0.04

Write the word name for the number shown in expanded form.

36. 200 + 30 + 0.6

37. 50 + 7 + 0.01

38. 90 + 0.1 + 0.02

39. 400 + 9 + 0.09

CHALLENGE

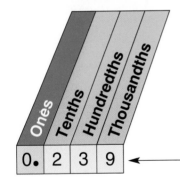

Look at the decimal in the place-value chart.

The value of the digit 9 is:

9 thousandths, 0.009 or $\frac{9}{1000}$

Write each as a decimal.

40. $\frac{657}{1000}$ **41.** $\frac{171}{1000}$ **42.** $\frac{6}{1000}$ **43.** $\frac{83}{1000}$

Write each as a fraction.

44. 0.107 **45.** 0.001 **46.** 0.034 **47.** 0.004

Compare Decimals

Who rode the greater distance?

To find who rode the greater distance,
compare: 2.5 _?_ 2.58

Weekend Bike Rides	
Name	**Distance**
Sheena	2.5 km
Naomi	2.58 km

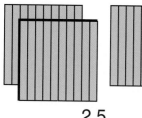

2.5

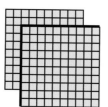

2.58

To compare decimals:

- Align the digits
  by their place value.

  2.5
  2.58

- Start at the left. Compare
  the digits in the greatest place.

  2.5 $2 = 2$
  2.58

- Keep comparing digits until
  you find two digits that
  are *not* the same.

  2.5 $5 = 5$
  2.58

  Think
  $0.5 = 0.50$

  2.50 $0 < 8$
  2.58

So 2.5 < 2.58.

Naomi rode the greater distance, 2.58 km.

Study these examples.

$0.96 _?_ $0.92

$0.96 $9 = 9$
$0.92 $6 > 2$

So $0.96 > $0.92.

42.7 _?_ 4.7

42.7
 4.7

Think
There are no tens
in 4.7.

$4 > 0$

So 42.7 > 4.7.

Compare. Write <, =, or >.
Use grid paper to model exercises 1–8.

1. 0.4 _?_ 0.9

2. 0.22 _?_ 0.18

3. 0.35 _?_ 0.38

4. 0.65 _?_ 0.6

5. 0.7 _?_ 0.70

6. 0.84 _?_ 0.8

7. 2.7 _?_ 1.8

8. 3.5 _?_ 3.9

9. 5.6 _?_ 5.9

10. 5.47 _?_ 5.77

11. 8.03 _?_ 8.30

12. 2.35 _?_ 1.99

13. 23.05 _?_ 8.79

14. 2.17 _?_ 62.1

15. 14.9 _?_ 1.49

16. 100.1 _?_ 100.10

17. 235.0 _?_ 23.5

18. 604.04 _?_ 604.40

19. 839.00 _?_ 839.10

20. 147.5 _?_ 145.7

21. 252.01 _?_ 225.1

22. $5.65 _?_ $3.65

23. $0.76 _?_ $0.76

24. $20.19 _?_ $2.09

25. $1.04 _?_ $1.40

26. $10.00 _?_ $10.25

27. $3.09 _?_ $3.90

Problem Solving

28. Ken's top speed in the bike-a-thon was 32.6 kilometers per hour. Vince's top speed was 32.65 kilometers per hour. Which boy had the greater top speed?

29. Each week before the bike-a-thon, Misha rode his bike 112.5 km and Luke rode his bike 121.5 km. Who rode his bike the lesser distance each week?

30. Elise had a total of $42.75 in pledges for the bike-a-thon and Andres had a total of $42.05. Who had the greater total pledges?

31. This year the bike-a-thon raised $726.50 for charity. The bike-a-thon last year raised $725.75. Was the greater amount raised this year or last year?

Order Decimals

Order the finishing times from fastest to slowest.

Championship Times	
Speed Skating, 500 Meters	
Sarah Hill	40.1 seconds
Patty Carter	40.3 seconds
Mei Wong	38.03 seconds
Tanya Odetta	36.33 seconds

▶ You can use place value to order decimals from least to greatest.

Align by place value.	Compare tens. Rearrange.	Compare ones. Rearrange.	Compare tenths. Rearrange if necessary.
40.1	38.03	36.33 ◄ least	36.33
40.3	36.33	38.03	38.03
38.03	40.1	40.1	40.1
36.33	40.3	40.3	40.3 ◄ greatest
	$30 < 40$	$6 < 8$ $0 = 0$	$0.1 < 0.3$

The order from fastest to slowest: 36.33; 38.03; 40.1; 40.3

or

The order from slowest to fastest: 40.3; 40.1; 38.03; 36.33

▶ You can use a number line to order decimals.

Order from least to greatest: 0.6; 0.4; 0.78; 0.65

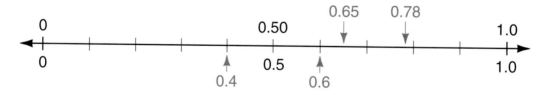

The order from least to greatest: 0.4; 0.6; 0.65; 0.78

or

The order from greatest to least: 0.78; 0.65; 0.6; 0.4

Write in order from least to greatest. You may use a number line.

1. 0.2; 0.9; 0.5

2. 3.5; 3.3; 3.35

3. 1.12; 1.02; 1.2

4. 5; 0.5; 0.05

5. 6.7; 6.77; 6.07; 7.67

6. 2.4; 4.2; 2.44; 4.02

7. 10.03; 1.30; 10.3; 1.33

8. 52.6; 62.5; 6.52; 56.2

9. 83.7; 87.37; 87.3; 83.07

10. 13.3; 33.31; 13.33; 130

Write in order from greatest to least. You may use a number line.

11. 0.1; 0.01; 0.11

12. 2.6; 2.06; 6.26

13. 4.04; 4.40; 4.0

14. 9.99; 9.19; 9.9

15. 1.18; 1.8; 1.81; 1.08

16. 17.6; 16.7; 61.7; 17.76

17. 59.03; 59; 53.9; 53.09

18. 44; 4.04; 40.4; 44.04

19. 90.3; 30.93; 30.09; 39.3

20. 75.01; 75.1; 75.11; 7.51

Problem Solving

21. Erhard Keller won the 500-meter speed skating Olympic gold medal twice with times of 39.44 and 40.3 seconds. Uwe-Jens Mey also won the gold medal twice with times of 36.45 and 37.14 seconds. Order these winning times from slowest to fastest.

Round Decimals

▶ A number line can help you to round decimals.

Round to the nearest tenth: 0.42, 0.45, and 0.48.

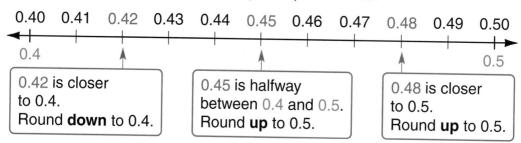

| 0.42 is closer to 0.4. Round **down** to 0.4. | 0.45 is halfway between 0.4 and 0.5. Round **up** to 0.5. | 0.48 is closer to 0.5. Round **up** to 0.5. |

You can round decimals the same way you round whole numbers:

- Find the place you are rounding to.

- Look at the digit to its right.

> Remember: If the digit *is less than 5*, round **down**. If the digit is *5 or more*, round **up**.

Round to the nearest tenth: 1.35, 5.62, and 2.48.

1.35
1.4

> 5 = 5
> Round **up** to 1.4.

5.62
5.6

> 2 < 5
> Round **down** to 5.6.

2.48
2.5

> 8 > 5
> Round **up** to 2.5.

Round to the nearest one: 4.09, 6.7, and 8.54.

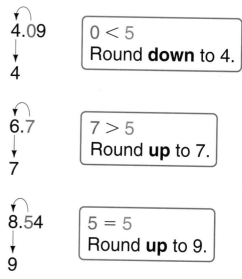

4.09
4

> 0 < 5
> Round **down** to 4.

6.7
7

> 7 > 5
> Round **up** to 7.

8.54
9

> 5 = 5
> Round **up** to 9.

> Do not write zeros to the right of the place you are rounding to.

Round to the nearest one.

1. 7.3   **2.** 9.2   **3.** 3.9   **4.** 1.5   **5.** 12.8

6. 16.2   **7.** 28.5   **8.** 62.4   **9.** 30.8   **10.** 19.7

11. 4.64   **12.** 15.35   **13.** 25.78   **14.** 41.23   **15.** 20.91

16. 17.52   **17.** 71.18   **18.** 49.62   **19.** 24.03   **20.** 3.95

Round to the nearest tenth.

21. 6.27   **22.** 4.64   **23.** 9.75   **24.** 2.20   **25.** 1.11

26. 31.37   **27.** 25.65   **28.** 85.06   **29.** 24.75   **30.** 38.33

31. 9.47   **32.** 13.53   **33.** 27.13   **34.** 82.75   **35.** 63.08

36. 52.71   **37.** 30.59   **38.** 81.11   **39.** 55.05   **40.** 44.89

Problem Solving

41. What is ten and three tenths rounded to the nearest one?

42. What is six and five tenths rounded to the nearest one?

43. What is seventeen hundredths rounded to the nearest tenth?

44. What is nine and five hundredths rounded to the nearest tenth?

45. Is two and fifteen hundredths rounded to the nearest one 2, 2.2, or 3?

46. Is one and fifty hundredths rounded to the nearest tenth 20, 2.0, or 1.5?

TEST PREPARATION

47. Choose the decimal that was rounded to get 6.7.

    A 6.07   **B** 6.59
    C 6.79   **D** 6.68

48. Choose the decimal that was rounded to get 0.8.

    F 0.09   **G** 0.75
    H 0.74   **J** 0.87

Estimate with Decimals

Rounding is one way to estimate
decimal sums and differences.

To estimate sums or differences with decimals:
- Round the decimals to the greatest *nonzero*
  place of the lesser number.
- Then add or subtract.

Estimate: 123.6 + 8.43

$$
\begin{array}{r}
123.6 \longrightarrow 124 \\
+\quad 8.43 \longrightarrow +\quad 8 \\
\hline
\text{about} \quad 132
\end{array}
$$

Estimate: 78.61 − 0.45

$$
\begin{array}{r}
78.61 \longrightarrow 78.6 \\
-\quad 0.45 \longrightarrow -\quad 0.5 \\
\hline
\text{about} \quad 78.1
\end{array}
$$

Study these examples.

$$
\begin{array}{r}
0.92 \longrightarrow 0.9 \\
+0.37 \longrightarrow +0.4 \\
\hline
\text{about} \quad 1.3
\end{array}
$$

$$
\begin{array}{r}
4.7 \longrightarrow 4.7 \\
-0.18 \longrightarrow -0.2 \\
\hline
\text{about} \quad 4.5
\end{array}
$$

$$
\begin{array}{r}
8.8 \longrightarrow 9 \\
+5.1 \longrightarrow +5 \\
\hline
\text{about} \quad 14
\end{array}
$$

Round to estimate the sum or the difference. Watch the signs.

1. 5.9
  + 3.2

2. 9.7
  − 4.6

3. 8.75
  − 1.17

4. 9.38
  + 6.04

5. 4.91
  + 6.73

6. 42.3
  − 6.7

7. 38.5
  + 5.8

8. 56.2
  − 4.84

9. 27.8
  + 6.65

10. 85.43
  − 1.7

11. 0.85
  + 0.63

12. 10.3
  − 0.81

13. 62.77
  + 9.84

14. 48.5
  − 0.69

15. 26.21
  + 0.59

16. 74.36
  + 18

17. 62
  − 7.8

18. 49.95
  − 5.2

19. 405.5
  − 5.76

20. 380.4
  + 2.35

21. 4.5 + 39.03

22. 17.03 − 1.5

23. 47 − 6.62

Practice

Use Front-End Estimation

Front-end estimation is another way to estimate decimal sums and differences.

To make a front-end estimate with decimals:
- Add or subtract the nonzero front digits.

- Write zeros for the other digits.

$$\begin{array}{r} 83.41 \\ +\ 71.3 \\ \hline \text{about} \quad 150.00 \end{array} \qquad \begin{array}{r} 9.3 \\ -4.76 \\ \hline \text{about} \quad 5.00 \end{array} \qquad \begin{array}{r} 0.65 \\ +0.5 \\ \hline \text{about} \quad 1.10 \end{array}$$

Estimate the sum or the difference. Use front-end estimation.

24. $\begin{array}{r} 30.98 \\ +56.44 \end{array}$	**25.** $\begin{array}{r} 8.6 \\ +9.2 \end{array}$	**26.** $\begin{array}{r} 43.21 \\ -12.04 \end{array}$	**27.** $\begin{array}{r} 7.4 \\ -2.9 \end{array}$	**28.** $\begin{array}{r} 58.4 \\ -21.62 \end{array}$
29. $\begin{array}{r} 0.94 \\ -0.55 \end{array}$	**30.** $\begin{array}{r} 0.26 \\ +0.77 \end{array}$	**31.** $\begin{array}{r} 23.2 \\ +96.09 \end{array}$	**32.** $\begin{array}{r} 48.4 \\ -18.36 \end{array}$	**33.** $\begin{array}{r} 74.6 \\ -21.09 \end{array}$
34. $\begin{array}{r} 8.09 \\ +8.9 \end{array}$	**35.** $\begin{array}{r} 6.74 \\ -1.53 \end{array}$	**36.** $\begin{array}{r} 81.2 \\ -27.35 \end{array}$	**37.** $\begin{array}{r} 50.09 \\ +97.79 \end{array}$	**38.** $\begin{array}{r} 59.5 \\ -24.07 \end{array}$

Problem Solving Use front-end estimation.

39. Maria jogged 97.5 miles. Audrey jogged 79.37 miles. About how many more miles did Maria jog than Audrey?

DO YOU REMEMBER?

Find the quotient.

40. $2)\overline{\$37.32}$ **41.** $4)\overline{\$10.40}$ **42.** $9)\overline{\$2.79}$ **43.** $8)\overline{\$64.16}$

44. $24)\overline{\$87.60}$ **45.** $53)\overline{\$57.24}$ **46.** $39)\overline{\$82.29}$ **47.** $42)\overline{\$41.16}$

Add Decimals

Shawn walked 2.1 km in the morning and 1.95 km in the afternoon. How far did he walk altogether?

2.1

1.95

To find how far altogether, add:
2.1 + 1.95

First, round to estimate the sum:
2.1 + 1.95 ⟶ 2 + 2 = 4

Then add.

Line up the decimal points.	Add the hundredths.	Add the tenths. Regroup.	Add the ones.

```
    2.1 0
  + 1.9 5
```
Remember:
2.1 = 2.10

```
    2.1 0
  + 1.9 5
        5
```

```
      1
    2.1 0
  + 1.9 5
      0 5
```

```
      1
    2.1 0
  + 1.9 5
    4.0 5
```

Think
4.05 is close to 4.
The answer is reasonable.

Shawn walked 4.05 km altogether.

Study these examples.

```
    1
    0.8
  + 0.6
    1.4
```

```
  1   1
    5.7 5
    0.9 0
  + 2 8.3 2
    3 4.9 7
```

```
        1
    7 5.0 0
  +   6.4 2
    8 1.4 2
```

Write the decimal point in the sum.

Practice

Round to estimate the sum. Then add.

1. 0.3
  + 0.6

2. 1.4
  + 6.2

3. 0.9
  + 0.7

4. 5.6
  + 9.8

5. 8.5
  + 10.5

6. 0.12
  + 0.43

7. 3.01
  + 0.57

8. 0.84
  + 0.77

9. $2.9
  + 7.83

10. 4.5
  + 2.86

Find the sum.

11. 5.03
+ 8.9

12. 83.8
+ 47.65

13. 90.41
+ 62.7

14. 17.54
+ 5.9

15. 45
+ 9.24

16. 16.75
4.32
+ 10.08

17. 0.7
1.2
+ 8.9

18. 92.3
48.05
+ 18.39

19. 74.32
10.1
+ 0.8

20. 59.11
0.98
+ 100.2

Align and add.

21. 0.3 + 8.44

22. 12.87 + 34

23. 0.95 + 22.6

24. 62 + 0.8

25. 32.5 + 575 + 0.49

26. 367.92 + 0.09 + 5.1

Problem Solving

27. Val ran the first 100 meters of a 200-meter dash in 15.34 seconds. She ran the next 100 meters in 16.9 seconds. What was Val's time in the 200-meter dash?

28. Xavier swam the 100-meter freestyle in 58.95 seconds. If he could keep up that pace for another 100 meters, what would be his time in the 200-meter freestyle?

29. The times for the 4 legs of a relay race were 10.9 seconds, 12.74 seconds, 11.08 seconds, and 10.06 seconds. How long did it take to run the race?

 Write About It

Add. Use mental math or paper and pencil.
Explain in your Math Journal why you chose your methods.

30. 15
+ 5.83

31. 6.75
+ 4.99

32. 13.7
+ 0.05

33. 71.74
+ 86.9

34. 94.7
+ 68.5

35. 8.39
+ 9.92

36. 10.9
+ 10

37. 4.66
+ 0.7

38. 133.04 + 0.8 + 3.47

Subtract Decimals

How much farther is it from the Village to Black Rock than from Old Farm to Sam's Beach?

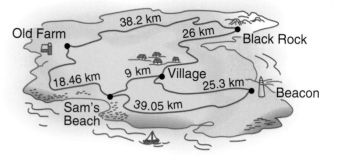

To find how much farther, subtract: 26 − 18.46

First, round to estimate the difference: 26 − 18.46

$$30 - 20 = 10$$

Then subtract.

Line up the decimal points. Regroup.	Subtract the hundredths.	Subtract the tenths.	Regroup. Subtract the ones.

```
        9
    5  10  10
   2  6 . 0  0
 - 1  8 . 4  6
```

Remember: 26 = 26.00

It is 7.54 km farther.

```
        9
    5  10  10
   2  6 . 0  0
 - 1  8 . 4  6
         4
```

```
        9
    5  10  10
   2  6 . 0  0
 - 1  8 . 4  6
       5  4
```

```
      15   9
   1  5  10  10
   2  6 . 0  0
 - 1  8 . 4  6
   7 . 5  4
```

Write the decimal point in the difference.

.Think.........................
7.54 is close to 10.
The answer is reasonable.

Study these examples.

1.2 = 12 tenths

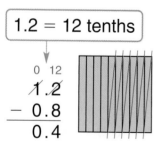

```
   0  12
   1 . 2
 - 0 . 8
   0 . 4
```

```
        9
   0  10  10
   1  0 . 0  5
 -    8 . 2  0
      1 . 8  5
```

```
      7  10
   9 . 8  0
 - 3 . 4  2
   6 . 3  8
```

Round to estimate the difference. Then subtract.

1. 18.7
    − 13.9

2. 24.2
    − 16.7

3. 3.43
    − 2.84

4. 62.19
    − 48.75

5. 75.11
    − 27.25

6. 23.16
    − 15.9

7. 82.6
    − 56.75

8. 64.5
    − 56.48

9. 10
    − 9.07

10. 16
    − 15.5

11. 17
    − 7.4

12. 92.1
    − 0.77

13. 76
    − 8.32

14. 58
    − 9.09

15. 31.2
    − 0.99

Align and subtract.

16. 90.17 − 9.07

17. 40.6 − 2.04

18. 8.34 − 0.5

19. 100 − 55.5

20. 99 − 0.09

21. 76.1 − 75.06

Problem Solving **Use the map on page 428.**

22. How much closer to the Village is the Beacon than Black Rock?

23. How much farther from Old Farm is Black Rock than Sam's Beach?

24. Is the route from Sam's Beach to the Beacon longer or shorter than the distance from Black Rock to Old Farm? How much longer or shorter?

25. How many kilometers would you travel if you went from Old Farm to the Beacon by way of Sam's Beach and the Village?

CHALLENGE

Subtract. Then check by adding.

26. 506.2
    − 175.35

27. 239.07
    − 86.6

28. 400.02
    − 0.8

29. 604
    − 64.91

Divide with Money

Martin designs greeting cards. They cost $0.50 each if you buy them separately, or you can buy a box of 25 cards for $12. Which is the better buy?

To find which is the better buy, find the cost of one boxed card. Then compare the cost to $0.50.

To find the cost of one boxed card, divide: $12 ÷ 25

Before dividing, write a decimal point and two zeros in the dividend.	Divide as usual. Write the dollar sign and decimal point in the quotient.	Check.

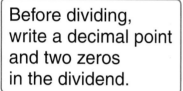

$$25\overline{)\$12.00}$$

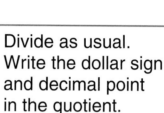

```
     $  .48
25)$12.00
  -10 0↓
    2 00
   -2 00
```

```
  $0.48
×    25
  2 40
+  9 6
$12.00
```

$0.48 < $0.50
So the better buy is a box of 25 cards for $12.

Study this example.

```
             $ 2.25
8)$18.00 ──→ 8)$18.00
             -16 ↓
               2 0↓
              -1 6↓
                 40
                -40
```

Find the quotient.

1. $27 ÷ 6

2. $41 ÷ 5

3. $54 ÷ 8

4. $38 ÷ 4

5. $19 ÷ 2

6. $90 ÷ 8

7. $45 ÷ 6

8. $78 ÷ 8

9. $6 ÷ 24

10. $48 ÷ 32

11. $60 ÷ 16

12. $8 ÷ 10

13. $21 ÷ 14

14. $32 ÷ 20

Divide. Then check.

15. 4)$17

16. 5)$2

17. 8)$60

18. 2)$9

19. 8)$10

20. 4)$5

21. 52)$65

22. 25)$8

23. 48)$12

24. 66)$33

25. 72)$54

26. 84)$21

Tell which is the better buy.

27. 8 erasers for $2.80
    or
    10 erasers for $3

28. 5 notebooks for $10
    or
    9 notebooks for $18.45

29. 6 bottles of shampoo for $21
    or
    8 bottles of shampoo for $22

30. 12 pencils for $3
    or
    10 pencils for $2

31. 20 plums for $14
    or
    16 plums for $12

32. 10 melons for $12
    or
    4 melons for $6

33. 8 juice cartons for $18
    or
    12 juice cartons for $33

34. 6 boxes of detergent for $27
    or
    4 boxes of detergent for $17

Problem-Solving Strategy:
Use More Than One Step

Hector bought 3 jumbo magnets and
1 magnifying glass at the science sale.
How much change did he get from $10?

Science Sale	
mini-magnet	$ .45 each
jumbo magnet	$1.19 each
magnifying glass	$5.78 for 2

Read ▶ **Visualize the facts of the problem.**

Facts: 3 jumbo magnets—$1.19 each
1 magnifying glass—2 for $5.78
paid $10

Question: How much change did Hector get?

Plan ▶ **Step 1:** *Multiply* to find the cost of
3 jumbo magnets.——▶ 3 × $1.19

Step 2: *Divide* to find the cost of
1 magnifying glass.——▶ $5.78 ÷ 2

Step 3: *Add* to find the total cost.

Step 4: *Subtract* to find Hector's change from $10.

Solve ▶

Step 1	Step 2	Step 3	Step 4

```
                                                  9 9
   2                                  1 1      0 10 10 10
 $1.1 9   1 magnifying→ $2.8 9      $3.5 7     $1 0.0 0
 ×    3   glass        2)$5.7 8     +2.8 9     −  6.4 6
 $3.5 7                 −4          $6.4 6     $  3.5 4
                         ─
 3 magnets              1 7                     
                        −1 6        total      Hector's
                         ─          cost       change
                         1 8
                        −1 8
```

Check ▶ Estimate to check: cost of magnets 3 × $1 = $3
cost of magnifying glass $6 ÷ 2 = $3
$10 − $6 = $4 change
The answer $3.54 is close to the estimate of $4.

Use more than one step to solve each problem.

1. Mary wants 4 tubes of oil paint at $4.59 each and 3 brushes at $4.19 each. If she has saved $30.75, how much more money does she need?

Read ▶ Create a mental picture of the problem.

> **Facts:** 4 paint tubes at $4.59 a tube
> 3 brushes at $4.19 a brush
> Mary has saved $30.75.
>
> **Question:** How much more money does Mary need to buy the items?

Plan ▶ Plan the steps to follow.

> Step 1: Multiply to find the cost of 4 paint tubes.
>
> Step 2: Multiply to find the cost of 3 brushes.
>
> Step 3: Add to find the total cost.
>
> Step 4: Subtract $30.75 from the total cost to find how much more money Mary needs.

▶ **Solve** ⋯⋯▶ **Check**

2. Mr. Ortiz collects 7.5 lb of honey in one bucket and 5.5 lb in another. He gives 1.2 lb of honey to a neighbor and 2.1 lb each to two workers. How much honey is left?

3. A shelf is 104.5 cm long. A set of encyclopedias uses 64.6 cm of space, and two books use 2.5 cm each. Is there more than 30 cm of space left? how much more or less?

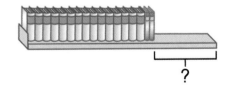

4. It takes Lyn 58.34 s to swim a lap doing the backstroke and 42.15 s to swim a lap doing the crawl. She does 2 laps using the backstroke and 1 using the crawl. How much less than 3 minutes does she swim?

Read Plan Solve Check

Solve each problem and explain the method you used.

1. On Monday, 2.4 cm of rain fell in the morning and another 1.8 cm fell in the afternoon. How much rain fell on Monday?

2. The time between a bolt of lightning and the sound of thunder was 4.72 s. What is this time rounded to the nearest second?

3. A rainstorm lasted 78.2 minutes. How much longer than an hour was the storm?

4. A meteorologist found that the diameter of a hail pellet measured 2.28 cm. What is this measurement to the nearest tenth?

5. The meteorologist found hail pellets with these diameters: 2.28 mm, 1.09 mm, 1.9 mm, 0.98 mm, and 1.42 mm. Order the pellets from smallest to largest.

6. The temperature during a hailstorm started at 11.4°C and then dropped by 0.5 degree. What was the temperature then?

7. Ms. Dell's car received 5 dents during the storm. She paid $85.50 to repair the damage. Each dent cost the same amount to fix. How much did it cost to repair each dent?

8. During a snowstorm, 12.3 dm of snow fell. There were already 45.9 dm of snow on the ground. How much snow was on the ground after the storm?

Choose a strategy from the list or use another strategy you know to solve each problem.

9. At 6:00 A.M. the snow was 1.4 cm deep. It snowed 1.4 cm more every half hour. What time was it when the snow was 11.2 cm deep?

10. A gopher dug a tunnel in the snow. The tunnel began at ground level, rose 2.2 ft, fell 0.7 ft, and then rose another 2.8 ft. How high above ground level did the tunnel end?

11. A winter storm warning lasted 4.5 h. It began at 2:30 P.M. The storm brought 4.3 in. of snow. When did the warning end?

12. Lina broke off 1.2 dm from a long icicle. It melted and lost another 0.8 dm. It was 3.5 dm long at the end of the day. How long was the original icicle?

13. Hugh built a snow sculpture with three large snowballs. They weighed 45.2 lb, 32.7 lb, and 20.1 lb. Luke's snow sculpture used three 28.5 lb snowballs. Whose snow sculpture was heavier? by how much?

Use the line graph for problems 14 and 15.

14. Between which two months did the amount of snowfall change the most on Mt. Sloper?

15. Joan did not ski in March. She did ski during a month that received less than 7 in. of snow. During which month did Joan ski?

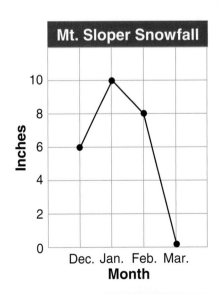

Mt. Sloper Snowfall

Write the place of the underlined digit. (See pp. 416–417.)
Then write its value.

1. 3.<u>1</u>
2. 2.4<u>2</u>
3. 0.<u>9</u>6
4. <u>1</u>.92

5. 59.<u>6</u>
6. <u>8</u>.5
7. 2.2<u>3</u>
8. <u>1</u>5.49

Write as a decimal. (See pp. 412–415.)

9. five tenths
10. thirty-two hundredths

11. three and four tenths
12. eight hundredths

Compare. Write <, =, or >. (See pp. 418–419.)

13. 0.03 _?_ 0.7
14. 9.45 _?_ 12.8
15. 0.64 _?_ 0.05

16. 12.8 _?_ 12.80
17. 7.02 _?_ 7
18. 5.06 _?_ 5.6

Estimate the sum or difference. Then add or subtract. (See pp. 426–429.)

19. $\begin{array}{r} 0.6 \\ +\,0.2 \\ \hline \end{array}$
20. $\begin{array}{r} 4.9 \\ -\,2.73 \\ \hline \end{array}$
21. $\begin{array}{r} 23.5 \\ +\,13.95 \\ \hline \end{array}$
22. $\begin{array}{r} 44 \\ -\,6.8 \\ \hline \end{array}$

Round each to the nearest one. (See pp. 422–423.)
Then round each to the nearest tenth.

23. 12.17
24. 32.74
25. 0.88

Compute. (See pp. 430–431.)

26. $36 ÷ 15
27. 8)$2
28. $5 ÷ 25

Problem Solving
(See pp. 424–429, 434–435.)

29. The weight of one bag of onions is 2.47 lb.
    The weight of another is 0.73 lb.
    Estimate the weight of the two bags of onions.

 (See *Still More Practice*, p. 472.)

Magic Squares

In a magic square each row, column, and diagonal has the same sum, called the magic sum.

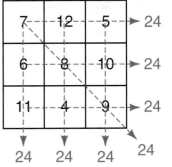

Row Sums	Column Sums
7 + 12 + 5 = 24	7 + 6 + 11 = 24
6 + 8 + 10 = 24	12 + 8 + 4 = 24
11 + 4 + 9 = 24	5 + 10 + 9 = 24

Diagonal Sums

7 + 8 + 9 = 24   5 + 8 + 11 = 24

Copy and complete each magic square.

1.

6	7	?
?	5	9
?	3	?

2.

9	?	7
4	6	?
5	?	?

3.

?	3	?
7	10	?
?	17	5

4.

2.7	3.8	?
5.2	3.6	?
?	3.4	4.5

5.

3.5	7.5	8.5
11.5	?	?
4.5	5.5	?

6.

8.6	7	6.6
5.4	?	?
8.2	7.8	?

7.

?	63	68
?	67	?
?	71	64

8.

2.42	8	5.96
9	5.46	?
4.96	?	?

9.

?	?	24
?	15	?
6	?	12

Hint ....
Use multiples of 3.

Chapter 13 Test

Write the place of the underlined digit. Then write its value.

1. 4.6$\underline{9}$
2. $\underline{4}$7.33
3. $\underline{2}$.26
4. 0.1$\underline{3}$
5. 55.7$\underline{4}$

Write as a decimal.

6. $\frac{25}{100}$

7. $\frac{50}{100}$

8. four and six tenths

9. seven and seven hundredths

Compare. Write <, =, or >.

10. 0.8 _?_ 0.4

11. 0.7 _?_ 0.70

12. 2.43 _?_ 2.39

Write in order from least to greatest.

13. 13.4, 6.5, 13.3, 6.05

14. 2.15, 2.51, 2.05, 2.5

Round to the nearest tenth.

15. 3.94

16. 17.25

17. 12.53

Estimate the sum or difference. Then add or subtract.

18.
$$15 - 3.21$$

19.
$$0.46 + 0.34$$

20.
$$8.79 + 9.7$$

21.
$$2.6 - 0.85$$

Problem Solving

Use a strategy you have learned.

22. Last year Kim measured 153.8 cm. Then she grew 6.8 cm. How tall is she now?

23. Which is the better buy: 25 stickers for $3 or 20 stickers for $2?

Tell About It

Are the decimals equivalent? Explain your answer.

24. 0.6; 0.60

25. 0.10; 0.1

26. 0.7; 0.07

Performance Assessment

27. Draw a number line to show the numbers in the box.

| 9.08 | 9.6 | $9\frac{6}{10}$ | 9.04 | 9.89 |

Test Preparation

Choose the best answer.

1. Round 674,029 to the nearest ten thousand.
   - **a.** 700,000
   - **b.** 680,000
   - **c.** 674,000
   - **d.** 670,000

2. 8000 − 592
   - **a.** 7408
   - **b.** 7518
   - **c.** 7592
   - **d.** not given

3. Estimate.

   $42\overline{)7846}$
   - **a.** 200
   - **b.** 300
   - **c.** 2000
   - **d.** 3000

4. Which type of graph would you use to show changes in data over time?
   - **a.** bar graph
   - **b.** pictograph
   - **c.** circle graph
   - **d.** line graph

5. Is the fraction three sevenths closer to 0, closer to $\frac{1}{2}$, or closer to 1?
   - **a.** 0
   - **b.** $\frac{1}{2}$
   - **c.** 1
   - **d.** cannot tell

6. Which figure has half-turn symmetry?

   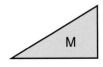 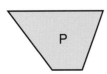
   - **a.** M
   - **b.** N
   - **c.** P
   - **d.** none of these

7. Round to estimate.

   3236 + 5873 + 1884
   - **a.** 8000
   - **b.** 9000
   - **c.** 11,000
   - **d.** 15,000

8. 85 × 409
   - **a.** 5317
   - **b.** 34,725
   - **c.** 34,765
   - **d.** not given

9.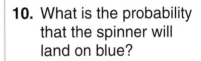
   $$\begin{aligned}8 \text{ ft} \quad 4 \text{ in.}\\ +\ 7 \text{ ft} \ 10 \text{ in.}\end{aligned}$$
   - **a.** 15 ft 4 in.
   - **b.** 15 ft 6 in.
   - **c.** 16 ft 2 in.
   - **d.** 16 ft 6 in.

10. What is the probability that the spinner will land on blue?

    - **a.** $\frac{2}{4}$
    - **b.** $\frac{2}{5}$
    - **c.** $\frac{1}{2}$
    - **d.** $\frac{1}{5}$

11. What is the least common multiple (LCM) of 4 and 6?
    - **a.** 2
    - **b.** 24
    - **c.** 36
    - **d.** none of these

12. What is the volume of a rectangular prism that is 12 m long, 9 m wide, and 7 m high?
    - **a.** 28 cubic meters
    - **b.** 126 cubic meters
    - **c.** 189 cubic meters
    - **d.** 756 cubic meters

13. Choose the equivalent mixed number in simplest form.

$\dfrac{34}{8}$

   a. $3\dfrac{10}{8}$ **b.** $3\dfrac{5}{4}$ **c.** $4\dfrac{1}{4}$ **d.** $4\dfrac{2}{8}$

14. $4 \times (5 + 7) =$?   **a.** $(4 \times 5) + 7$
                         b. $(4 \times 5) + (4 \times 7)$
                         c. $(4 + 5) \times (4 + 7)$
                         d. not given

15. Compare.

  90 g ? 9 kg   **a.** $<$
                        b. $=$
                        c. $>$

16. Choose the value of the underlined digit.

  692.7̲1   **a.** 7
               b. 0.7
               c. 0.07
               d. 70

17. $96\overline{)7128}$ **a.** 740 R24
                 b. 7 R24
                 c. 704 R24
                 d. 74 R24

18. Brendan bought 8 cupcakes at $1.59 each and 5 pies at $5.99 each. How much more did he spend on pies than on cupcakes?

      a. $12.72   **b.** $17.23
      c. $29.95   **d.** $42.67

19. Choose the correct decimal.

  $17\dfrac{9}{100}$

      a. 17.90   **b.** 17.009
      c. 17.09   **d.** 17.99

20.

  $45\overline{)901}$ **a.** 20 R1
               b. 2 R1
               c. 200 R1
               d. not given

21. Choose the rounded sum.

  $\begin{array}{r} 63.6 \\ +\ 9.27 \\ \hline \end{array}$

      a. about 72.8
      b. about 72
      c. about 72.87
      d. about 73

22. Divide.

  $\$36 \div 40$ **a.** $.09
                  b. $.90
                  c. $.99
                  d. $9.00

23. Find the value of the expression.

  $34 - n$,
  when $n = 9$

      a. 9
      b. 43
      c. 25
      d. $34 - 9$

24. The times in seconds for the 4 legs of a relay race were 9.97, 10.15, 10.08, and 9.99. How long did it take to run the race?

      a. 28.99 s   **b.** 39.09 s
      c. 40.19 s   **d.** 44.19 s

Explain how you solved the problem. Show all your work.

25. Round 49.92 to the nearest one.

26. Round 87.99 to the nearest tenth.

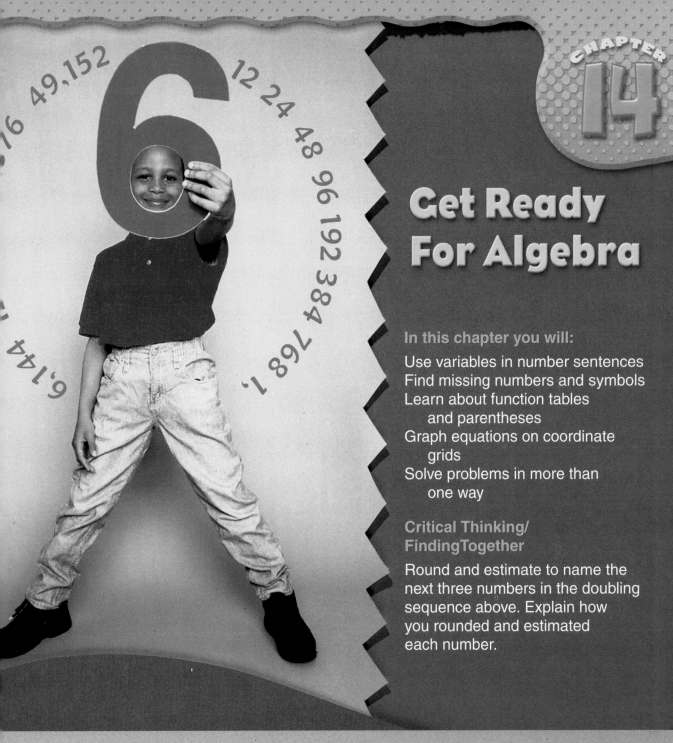

Get Ready For Algebra

In this chapter you will:

Use variables in number sentences

Find missing numbers and symbols

Learn about function tables and parentheses

Graph equations on coordinate grids

Solve problems in more than one way

Critical Thinking/ FindingTogether

Round and estimate to name the next three numbers in the doubling sequence above. Explain how you rounded and estimated each number.

Arithmetic

If you take a number and double it and double it again and then double it a few more times, the number gets bigger and bigger and goes higher and higher and only arithmetic can tell you what the number is when you decide to quit doubling.

From "Arithmetic" by Carl Sandburg.

Algebra
14-1
Equations

A scout troop is planning a trip to a cave. They rent a minibus for $17 per hour. The trip will take 5 hours. How much will the bus cost?

Write an **equation**, or a number sentence, to help you solve the problem.

What do you know?	What do you need to know?	Which operation will you use?
• bus costs $17 per hour • trip takes 5 hours	• how much the bus will cost for 5 hours	• multiplication

Use a variable to stand for the unknown.

- Let n stand for how much the bus will cost.
- Write the equation.　　　　　　　　$5 \times \$17 = n$
- Solve for n.　　　　　　　　　　$\$85 = n$

The bus will cost $85.

Choose the correct equation for each problem. Then solve each problem.

1. The first cave chamber was 18 feet high. The second chamber was only 4 feet high. How much higher was the first chamber?

   a. $4 + 18 = n$
   b. $4 \times 18 = n$
   c. $18 - 4 = n$

2. The scouts discovered 225 bats in the first chamber and 172 in the second. How many bats did they discover in the two chambers?

   a. $225 + 172 = n$
   b. $225 - 172 = n$
   c. $172 \times 225 = n$

Practice

Problem Solving

Write an equation to solve each problem.

3. One chamber was 195 ft below sea level. Another chamber was 119 ft deeper. How many feet below sea level was the second chamber?

4. Each of 24 scouts brought 15 ft of rope. If they laid their ropes end to end to form a long strand, how many feet long would it be?

5. Zack found an arrowhead that was about 1500 years old. Chang found one that was twice as old. About how old was Chang's arrowhead?

6. Lucy's Lunches prepared 24 box lunches for the scouts. The total cost of the lunches was $94.80. What was the cost of each box lunch?

7. Each guide was to lead a team of 5 scouts. There were 24 scouts in all. How many teams of 5 were there? How many guides were needed for all the scouts?

8. The lengths of five passages in a cave are 17.2 mi, 24.5 mi, 18.3 mi, 16.4 mi, and 23.6 mi. What is the total length of the five passages in the cave?

9. Carlsbad Caverns covers 46,755 acres. The Wind Cave covers 28,295 acres. How many more acres does Carlsbad Caverns cover?

10. A cave has 144 miles of underground passages. Exploring 3 miles each day, how many days would it take to explore all the passages?

DO YOU REMEMBER? — Algebra

Find the value of the variable.

11. $7 + n = 15$

12. $n - 5 = 8$

13. $6 \times n = 36$

14. $40 \div n = 8$

15. $12 - n = 5$

16. $n \div 7 = 9$

17. $n \times 4 = 28$

18. $n \div 8 = 1$

19. $n + 5 = 5$

Find Missing Numbers

▶ What number does a stand for?
$$4a = 6 + 6$$

Hint
$4a = 4 \times a$

To solve:

- Compute where possible.

$$4a = 6 + 6$$
$$4a = \quad 12$$

Think
The missing factor is a.

- Solve for the missing factor.

$$a = 12 \div 4$$
$$a = 3$$

- Check.

$$4 \times 3 = 6 + 6$$
$$12 \quad = \quad 12$$

▶ What number does x stand for?
$$3 \times 5 = x \div 2$$

- Compute.

$$3 \times 5 = x \div 2$$
$$15 \quad = x \div 2$$

Think
The missing dividend is x.

- Solve.

$$15 \times 2 = x$$
$$30 = x$$

- Check.

$$3 \times 5 = 30 \div 2$$
$$15 \quad = \quad 15$$

Practice

Find the number that n stands for in each equation.

1. $12 - 5 = n - 7$

2. $4 \times n = 8 \times 3$

3. $40 \div 8 = 30 \div n$

4. $n + 14 = 3 \times 6$

5. $n \div 8 = 22 - 17$

6. $2 \times 4 = 56 \div n$

Find the number that _y_ stands for in each equation.

7. $y \div 3 = 63 \div 7$

8. $9 + 7 = y + 8$

9. $2 \times 10 = 5y$

10. $9 + y = 3 \times 6$

11. $42 \div 7 = 16 - y$

12. $10 + 7 = y - 3$

13. $3y = 18 \div 3$

14. $y - 10 = 7 \times 2$

15. $25 - 15 = y \div 4$

16. $8y = 26 - 26$

17. $9 \times 8 = y \times 72$

18. $100 + y = 9 \times 12$

19. $50 \times 3 = 200 - y$

20. $y \div 2 = 10 \times 25$

21. $12 \times 12 = 130 + y$

22. $y + 99 = 59 + 40$

23. $43 \times y = 0 \div 34$

24. $125 \times 2 = 400 - y$

25. $64 + y + 22 = 100 + 20 + 8$

26. $8 \times 8 \times y = 2 \times 250 + 12$

27. $500 \div 50 \times 95 = y + 2 \times 450$

Find the number that _n_ stands for in each equation.

28. $n + n = 6$

> **Think**
> What number added to itself equals 6?

29. $7 - n = 7$

30. $n \times n = 25$

31. $4n = n$

32. $n \div 5 = n$

33. $n + n = 30$

34. $64 \div n = n$

CHALLENGE

Find the numbers that _m_ and _n_ stand for in each pair of equations.

35. $m + n = 9$
    $m + m = 8$

36. $m \times n = 24$
    $n \times n = 9$

37. $m \times n = 8$
    $n - m = 7$

Functions

▶ The table at the right is called a function table.

For each input number, or numbers that you put into the table, there is only one output. You can find the output number by following the rule.

The input is 12. What is the output?

Input	Rule	Output

$$12 \times 3 = 36$$

The output is 36.

Rule: × 3	
Input	Output
2	6
4	12
5	15
8	24
12	?

▶ What is the rule, or function, for this function table?

Think how each input is related to its output.

$$40 \div 4 = 10 \qquad 32 \div 4 = 8$$
$$28 \div 4 = 7 \qquad 20 \div 4 = 5$$

The rule is ÷ 4.

Rule: ?	
Input	Output
40	10
32	8
28	7
20	5

Practice

Complete each function table.

1.

Rule: + 7	
Input	Output
4	11
8	?
25	?
42	?

2.

Rule: − 11	
Input	Output
12	?
20	?
45	?
63	?

3.

Rule: ÷ 2	
Input	Output
250	?
210	?
180	?
100	?

Complete each function table.

4.

Rule: × 9	
Input	**Output**
5	?
8	?
10	?
25	?
51	?

5.

Rule: ÷ 20	
Input	**Output**
500	?
240	?
180	?
120	?
80	?

6.

Rule: × 43	
Input	**Output**
8	?
15	?
37	?
105	?
232	?

7.

Rule: ?	
Input	**Output**
5	40
8	64
12	96
20	160

8.

Rule: ?	
Input	**Output**
70	55
65	50
58	43
42	27

9.

Rule: ?	
Input	**Output**
15	40
22	47
36	61
44	69

10.

Rule: × 7	
Input	**Output**
?	63
?	77
?	98
?	112

11.

Rule: ÷ 9	
Input	**Output**
?	25
?	22
?	18
?	15

12.

Rule: × 15	
Input	**Output**
?	75
?	120
?	165
?	225

CHALLENGE

13. Which rule describes the pattern shown in the table?

$\bigcirc$	3	4	5
$\diamond$	8	15	24

a. $\bigcirc + 5 = \diamond$

b. $\diamond - 11 = \bigcirc$

c. $\bigcirc \times \bigcirc + 1 = \diamond$

d. $\bigcirc \times \bigcirc - 1 = \diamond$

Update your skills. See page 23.

Graph Equations

The function, or rule, of a function table can be an equation.

Rule: $y = 2x$	
Input (*x*)	Output (*y*)
0	0
1	2
2	4
3	6

$y = 2x$	
When $x = 0$, $y = 0$. $y = 2(0)$ $y = 0$ Write: (0,0)	When $x = 1$, $y = 2$. $y = 2(1)$ $y = 2$ Write: (1,2)
When $x = 2$, $y = 4$. $y = 2(2)$ $y = 4$ Write: (2,4)	When $x = 3$, $y = 6$. $y = 2(3)$ $y = 6$ Write: (3,6)

You can graph an equation on a coordinate grid.

To graph an equation:

- Write the values of *x* and *y* as ordered pairs (*x*,*y*).

- Graph the ordered pairs on a coordinate grid.

- Connect the points with a line.

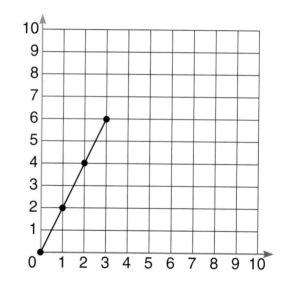

Use the equation $y = x \div 3$ for exercises 1–3.

1. Complete the function table.

2. Write the values of *x* and *y* as ordered pairs.

3. Graph the ordered pairs on a coordinate grid. Connect the points with a line.

Rule: $y = x \div 3$					
Input	*x*	3	6	9	12	15
Output	*y*					

Use the function table for exercises 4–6.

4. Complete the function table. Find the rule.

Rule: ?						
Input	x	0	1	2	3	4
Output	y	0	3	6	?	?

5. Write the values of x and y as ordered pairs.

6. Graph the ordered pairs on a coordinate grid. Connect the points with a line.

For each equation, complete a function table with 5 values for x and y. Then graph each set of ordered pairs on a coordinate grid.

7. $y = x + 2$ 8. $y = x \div 2$ 9. $y = 2x + 2$

Problem Solving

Make a function table to solve each problem. Then graph the ordered pairs on a coordinate grid.

10. Maria needs 2 pizzas for every 6 people at her party. How many pizzas does she need for 24 people?

11. Tad needs 2 cups of punch for every guest at his party. How many cups of punch does he need for 9 guests?

CHALLENGE

Use the coordinate grid you made for exercise 11.

12. Extend the line you drew on the coordinate grid for 10–14 guests.

13. How many cups of punch would Tad need for 13 guests?

Missing Symbols

The symbol $=$ means "is equal to."	The symbol $\neq$ means "is *not* equal to."

$$8 = 8$$
$$4 + 5 = 9$$
$$15 = 3 \times 5$$
$$6 + 1 = 5 + 2$$

$$7 \neq 9$$
$$13 - 4 \neq 12$$
$$6 \neq 20 \div 5$$
$$4 \times 3 \neq 3 \times 5$$

▶ Which symbol completes this number sentence?
$$8 \times 6 \ \underline{\ ?\ } \ 25 + 25$$

To find the correct symbol:

- Simplify the expression on each side of the missing symbol.

$$8 \times 6 \ \underline{\ ?\ } \ 25 + 25$$
$$48 \quad \underline{\ ?\ } \quad 50$$

- Compare. Write $=$ or $\neq$.

$$48 \neq 50$$

So $8 \times 6 \neq 25 + 25$.

Study these examples.

$$3 \times 15 \ \underline{\ ?\ } \ 39 + 6$$
$$45 \quad \underline{\ ?\ } \quad 45$$
$$45 = 45$$

$$60 \times 9 \ \underline{\ ?\ } \ 720 - 170$$
$$540 \quad \underline{\ ?\ } \quad 550$$
$$540 < 550$$

Practice

Write the letter of the correct answer.

1. $6 + 4 \neq \underline{\ ?\ }$

  a. $13 - 3$
  b. $20 \div 2$
  c. 4×2

2. $7 \times 9 = \underline{\ ?\ }$

  a. $87 - 15$
  b. $39 + 24$
  c. $40 + 16$

3. $100 \div 2 \neq \underline{\ ?\ }$

  a. 2×25
  b. $30 + 30$
  c. $62 - 12$

4. $36 \div 6 = \underline{\ ?\ }$

  a. $30 \div 5$
  b. $36 - 6$
  c. 6×6

Compare. Write = or ≠ .

5. $10 + 8$ _?_ $9 + 6$ **6.** $13 - 5$ _?_ $11 - 3$ **7.** 5×8 _?_ 10×4

8. $54 \div 6$ _?_ $56 \div 8$ **9.** $4 + 5$ _?_ $15 - 6$ **10.** 2×3 _?_ $30 \div 6$

11. 45×3 _?_ $125 + 10$ **12.** $225 \div 25$ _?_ $240 \div 30$

13. $7250 + 100$ _?_ $8450 - 200$ **14.** 75×4 _?_ $900 \div 30$

15. $586 - 139$ _?_ $328 + 160$ **16.** $396 \div 3$ _?_ 12×11

17. $685 \div 5$ _?_ 5×71 **18.** 8×525 _?_ 7×600

19. $\$4.50 + \$1.15$ _?_ $4 \times \$1.25$ **20.** $6 \times \$5.95$ _?_ $7 \times \$6.95$

Compare. Write <, =, or >.

21. $500 \div 2$ _?_ $200 \div 5$ **22.** 50×600 _?_ 40×700

23. $2000 - 1500$ _?_ 50×8 **24.** $850 - 125$ _?_ $525 + 200$

25. 2×550 _?_ 5×250 **26.** $400 \div 5$ _?_ $500 \div 4$

Problem Solving

27. Is the product of 8 and 45 equal to the difference of 500 and 140?

28. Is the sum of 534 and 166 equal to the product of 250 and 3?

TEST PREPARATION

29. Which numbers complete the equation?

$56 \div$ _?_ $= 5 +$ _?_

A 2, 2   **B** 5, 1
C 7, 3   **D** 9, 5

30. Which numbers complete the number sentence?

$8 \times$ _?_ $\neq 6 \times$ _?_

F 3, 4   **G** 3, 5
H 6, 8   **J** 9, 12

Use Parentheses

How would you go about using the order of operations to simplify this problem?

$$40 - 3 \times 5 + (10 \div 2) = a$$

$$40-3\times5+(10\div2)=a$$
$$40-3\times5+5=a$$

To simplify:

- Always do the operations in parentheses first.

$$40 - 3 \times 5 + \underbrace{(10 \div 2)}_{} = a$$

- Next, multiply or divide. Work in order from left to right.

$$40 - \underbrace{3 \times 5}_{} + \quad 5 \quad = a$$

- Then, add or subtract. Work in order from left to right.

$$40 - \underbrace{15 \quad + \quad 5}_{} \quad = a$$

$$\underbrace{25 \qquad + \quad 5}_{} = 30$$

Study these examples.

$$2 \times \underbrace{(4 + 3)}_{} - 10 + \underbrace{(4 \times 4)}_{} = b$$

$$\underbrace{2 \times \quad 7}_{} - 10 + \quad 16 \quad = b$$

$$\underbrace{14 \qquad - 10}_{} + \quad 16 \quad = b$$

$$4 \qquad + \quad 16 \quad = 20$$

$$\underbrace{(4 \times 2)}_{} + \underbrace{(9 \div 3)}_{} - 10 + 1 = u$$

$$\underbrace{8 \quad + \quad 3}_{} - 10 + 1 = u$$

$$\underbrace{11 \qquad - 10}_{} + 1 = u$$

$$1 \qquad + 1 = 2$$

Simplify.

1. $(6 - 2) + (6 \times 2)$

2. $(8 \div 4) \times (9 - 5)$

3. $(56 \div 8) \times (10 + 7)$

4. $(4 \times 12) - (20 - 15)$

5. $9.7 + (6.1 - 5.1)$

6. $20 - (10 - 5.5)$

7. $(8.1 - 8.1) \times (5 + 4)$

8. $(3.2 + 4.6) - (2 \times 2)$

Practice

Use the order of operations to simplify.

9. $(6 \times 2) + (9.3 - 7.5)$

10. $(45 \div 5) + (10.75 - 2.25)$

11. $\frac{2}{5} + \left(\frac{4}{5} - \frac{2}{5}\right)$

12. $\left(\frac{7}{10} - \frac{4}{10}\right) + \frac{6}{10}$

13. $\frac{1}{2} + \left(\frac{1}{2} - \frac{1}{4}\right)$

14. $\frac{3}{4} + \left(\frac{1}{2} + \frac{1}{4}\right)$

15. $\left(\frac{1}{4} + \frac{1}{4}\right) + \left(\frac{1}{8} + \frac{1}{8}\right)$

16. $\left(\frac{2}{6} + \frac{3}{6}\right) - \left(\frac{1}{3} + \frac{1}{3}\right)$

17. $\left(\frac{7}{8} - \frac{1}{4}\right) - \left(\frac{2}{8} + \frac{1}{8}\right)$

18. $\left(\frac{5}{6} + \frac{1}{6}\right) \times \left(\frac{1}{2} + \frac{1}{2}\right)$

Equalities

Equals added to or multiplied by equals are equal.

Addition:

equal

$n + (5 + 4) = 2 + (3 \times 3)$

equal

$n \quad + \quad 9 \quad = 2 \quad + \quad 9$

$n \qquad\qquad = \qquad 2$

> You can use the order of operations to check when equations are true.

Multiplication:

equal

$3 \times (1 + 7) = 3 \times (2 \times a)$

equal

$3 \quad \times \quad 8 \quad = 3 \quad \times \quad 2a$

$8 \qquad\qquad = \qquad 2a$

$8 \div 2 = a \longrightarrow 4 \qquad = \qquad a$

Find the value of each variable.

19. $1 + (3 + 2) = 1 + (1 + a)$

20. $4 + (2 \times 3) = u + (1 \times 6)$

21. $(b \times 7) + 8 = (9 + 5) + 8$

22. $5 \times (6 + n) = 5 \times (3 + 4)$

23. $(4 + 8) \times 10 = (d \times 2) \times 10$

24. $7 \times (7 \times 7) = 7 \times (7 + f)$

Problem-Solving Strategy:
More Than One Way

Kim is making a rectangular sign that is
3 ft wide. She uses 14 ft of edging to go
around the sign. How long is the sign?

Read Visualize the facts of the problem
as you reread it.

Facts: width = 3 ft
perimeter = 14 ft

Question: How long is the sign?

Plan There is more than one way to find
a solution. Here are 2 ways.

Method 1

Draw a picture.

Guess and test to find
the length.

Method 2

Use a formula.
$$P = 2 \times \ell + 2 \times w$$
Guess and test to find
the length.

Solve

First Guess ⟶ 3 ft

3 ft + 3 ft + 3 ft + 3 ft = 12 ft
not large enough

Second Guess ⟶ 4 ft

3 ft + 3 ft + 4 ft + 4 ft = 14 ft
correct sum

The sign is 4 ft long.

Let ℓ = length

$P = 2 \times \ell + 2 \times w$
$14 = 2 \times \ell + (2 \times 3 \text{ ft})$
$14 = 2 \times \ell + 6 \text{ ft}$
$14 = 2 \times \underline{?} \text{ ft} + 6 \text{ ft}$
$14 = 2 \times 4 \text{ ft} + 6 \text{ ft}$

The sign is 4 ft long.

Check Use the formula to
check your answer.

Draw a picture to
check your answer.

Solve each problem and explain the method you used.

1. The temperature at Beal Beach was 32.4°C at dawn. It rose 4.7°C by noon, and then fell 6.1°C by dusk. What was the temperature at dusk?

> **Read** Visualize the facts.
> Focus on the question.
>
> **Facts:** dawn —32.4°C
> noon — 4.7°C higher
> dusk — 6.1°C lower
>
> **Question:** What was the temperature at dusk?

> **Plan** What method will you use?
>
> *Method 1*
> Draw and label a number line.
>
> *Method 2*
> Write an equation.
> $32.4 + 4.7 - 6.1 = n$

> **Solve** ········▶ **Check**

2. Karl has 25 wheels for wagons and scooters. How many of each toy can he make if the wagons have 4 wheels and scooters have 3 wheels?

3. The digits of a two-digit number have a sum of 7 and a difference of 5. The number is less than 70 and greater than 20. What is the number?

4. The Hoopsters scored 35 points in the first half of the game and 18 more than that in the second half. The other team scored 90 points in the game. Did the Hoopsters win?

Problem-Solving Applications: Mixed Review

Read ▸ **Plan** ▸ **Solve** ▸ **Check**

Solve each problem and explain the method you used.

1. I am a whole number. If you add me to 28, the sum is 100. What am I?

2. I am a decimal. If I am added together 5 times, the answer equals 43. What decimal am I?

3. I am a decimal equal to the sum of 2.8, 3.2 and 7.4. What decimal am I?

4. What number should you add to complete this sentence? $8\frac{1}{4} + 2\frac{1}{4} + n = 11\frac{1}{2}$

5. Use = or ≠ to complete this number sentence.
$3 \times 4 - 2 \underline{\ ?\ } 18 \div 2 + 4$

6. In which equation does $n = 25$?
   a. $5 + 10 \times 4 \div 2 = n$
   b. $35 - 10 \div 5 + 5 = n$

7. What is the number halfway between 40 and 70?

8. What is the greatest number less than 65 that is divisible by 3?

9. In a contest, players scored 4 points for each correct answer. How many correct answers did the winner give? the player in 3rd place? (Use the bar graph to the right.)

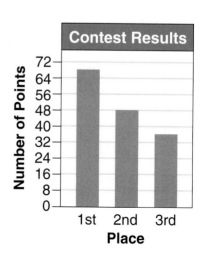

Choose a strategy from the list or use another strategy you know to solve each problem.

Strategy File

Use These Strategies
Use More Than One Step
Guess and Test
Write a Number Sentence
Logical Reasoning
Work Backward

10. The winner of a contest may choose from 2 prizes: a dime a day for a year or a dollar a day during March. Which amount is greater?

11. Mel, Rob, and Carmen were in a contest. Mel did not win, but he scored more points than Rob. Did Carmen win?

12. A program began at 6:30 P.M. and ended at 7:00 P.M. There were two 4.5-minute commercial breaks. How long was the program itself?

13. The winner of a competition received a T-shirt that said, "I'm Number $5 - 2 \times 2$." What does this mean? Create a number sentence for a shirt for the second-place winner.

14. Arrange the numbers in the box so their sum, product, difference, and quotient are equal.
   $\underline{?} + \underline{?} = \underline{?} - \underline{?} = \underline{?} \div \underline{?} = \underline{?} \times \underline{?}$

> 40 19 3 16
> 4 72 6 5

15. *Math Facts* auditioned students. In the first round, $\frac{1}{2}$ were eliminated. In the second round, 30 more were eliminated. There were 10 students left for the third round. How many students came to the audition?

Write Your Own

16. Write a problem modeled on problem 10. Have a classmate solve it.

Write the number that *n* stands for in each equation. *(See pp. 444–445.)*

1. $28 - n = 4 \times 6$

2. $11 \times 12 = 100 + n$

3. $n \div 4 = 12 \times 2$

4. $32 + 20 + n = 52 \times 4$

Complete each function table. *(See pp. 446–447.)*

5.

Rule: ×3	
Input	Output
5	?
9	?
33	?
46	?

6.

Rule: ?	
Input	Output
24	4
36	6
48	8
60	10

7.

n	*n* + 39
15	?
67	?
85	?
92	?
98	?

Use each equation to complete a function table for five values of *x* and *y*. Then graph each equation on a coordinate grid. *(See pp. 448–449.)*

8. $y = x + 4$

9. $y = 2x + 3$

10. $y = x \div 4$

Compare. Write = or ≠. *(See pp. 450–451.)*

11. $36 \times 3 \ \underline{\ ?\ } \ 24 + 24$

12. $25 - 5 \ \underline{\ ?\ } \ 60 - 40$

13. $76 + 2 \ \underline{\ ?\ } \ 92 - 31$

Use the order of operations to solve. *(See pp. 452–453.)*

14. $15 + 8 - 2 \times 9$

15. $9 \times 10 \div 5 + 6$

16. $30 + 4 \times 4 + 20$

17. $49 - 3 \times 7$

18. $(54 \div 6) \times (2 + 10)$

19. $\frac{1}{5} + \frac{3}{5} - \frac{2}{5}$

Problem Solving

Write an equation to solve each problem.

20. Mrs. Lam bought 720 yards of material to make curtains. If 8 yards of material are needed for each pair of curtains, how many windows can she decorate?

21. The school auditorium has 25 rows of seats. Each row has 15 seats. How many seats are in the auditorium?

(See Still More Practice, p. 472.)

Negative Numbers

Numbers that are written with a minus sign, such as ⁻6, ⁻25, and ⁻247, are called negative numbers. Negative numbers are less than zero.

You already know how to use negative numbers to write temperatures below zero.
⁻15°F   ⁻3°C

You can also use negative numbers to show distances below sea level.

⁻5 ft means "5 feet below sea level."

The scale at the right shows the location of different sites in Crystal Caverns.

Solve. Use the scale of Crystal Caverns.

1. Which site is located at ⁻90 ft?

2. About how many feet below sea level is Stalagmite Garden?

3. Which site is farthest below sea level? About how many feet below sea level is it?

4. How many feet difference is there between Bottomless Pool and Stalactite Chamber?

5. Which site is halfway between sea level and Pirate's Rest? How many feet below sea level is it?

6. Suppose there was a site at ⁻150 ft. How much lower than sea level would it be than Bottomless Pool?

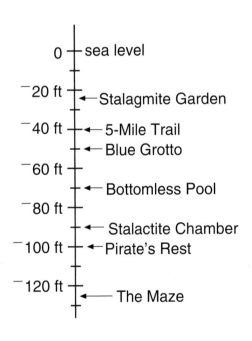

0 — sea level

⁻20 ft ← Stalagmite Garden

⁻40 ft ← 5-Mile Trail
← Blue Grotto

⁻60 ft

← Bottomless Pool

⁻80 ft

← Stalactite Chamber
⁻100 ft ← Pirate's Rest

⁻120 ft
← The Maze

Chapter 14 Test

Find the value of *n*.

1. $6 + 8 = n - 5$
2. $27 \times n = 112 - 4$
3. $n \div 20 = 17 - 12$

Use each equation to complete a function table for five values of *x* and *y*. Then graph each equation on a coordinate grid.

4. $y = x - 4$
5. $y = 3x - 5$
6. $y = x + 4$

Compare. Write = or ≠.

7. $65 \div 5 \underline{\ ?\ } 8 + 5$
8. $7 \times 8 \underline{\ ?\ } 66 - 9$
9. $3 \times 36 \underline{\ ?\ } 6 \times 18$

Use the order of operations to solve.

10. $16 \div 4 + 8$
11. $9 + 8 - 7 + 5$
12. $8 \times (25 + 6) - 7$

13. $12 + (2 \times 9) = \underline{\ ?\ } + (3 + 15)$
14. $3 \times (3 \times 4) = 3 \times (3 + \underline{\ ?\ })$

Problem Solving

Use a strategy you have learned.

15. Brian has 87 stamps in his collecton. Sue has 127 stamps, and Judy has 95 stamps. How many stamps do they have altogether?

16. Paul used 1 mile of fencing to fence in a square field. How many yards long is one side of the field?

Tell About It

Explain how you use equalities to find the value of *n*.

17. $4 \times (8 \times 4) = 4 \times (8 + n)$

18. $(n \times 9) + 7 = (27 + 9) + 7$

Performance Assessment

19. What is the rule for the function table?

20. Make up a function table for each rule.

   a. Rule: $\div 3$ **b.** Rule: $n - 8$

Rule: ?	
Input	Output
5	40
8	64
10	80
12	96

CHAPTER 1

Practice 1-1

Write the number in standard form.

1a. 8 thousands 2 tens   **b.** twenty-two thousand

2a. four hundred seventy-three million   **b.** 700,000,000 + 400,000 + 10,000 + 7000 + 200 + 1

Write the word name for each number.

3a. 1,020,140   **b.** 80,000 + 4000 + 500

Write each number in expanded form.

4a. 668,850,201   **b.** 5,884,901

Write the place and value of the underlined digit.

5a. 2,300,400   **b.** 608,721   **c.** 2,300,400

Compare. Write <, =, or >.

6a. 3983 ? 3892   **b.** 2,120,121 ? 2,102,101

7. Write the amounts $45.15, $38.06, and $37.05 in order from greatest to least.

8. Write the numbers 15,403; 13,405; 14,340; 13,450; and 15,430 in order from least to greatest.

Problem Solving

9. What number is 100 more than 4,506,722?

10. What number is 1000 less than 439,800?

11. What number is 1000 more than 9,829,432?

12. What is the greatest even four-digit number?

13. The Beekman Library has 123,450 books. The Conrad Library has 124,355 books and the Doral Library has 125,320 books. Put the libraries in order from least books to most books.

Practice 1-2

Write each amount.

1a. 2 dollars, 2 quarters, 1 dime, 3 nickels   **b.** 5 quarters, 4 dimes, 8 nickels, 3 pennies

Write the fewest coins and bills you would receive as change. Then write the value of the change.

2a. Cost: $4.20 Amount given: $10.00   **b.** Cost: $18.39 Amount given: $20.00

Round to the nearest hundred or dollar.

3a. 2390   **b.** 821   **c.** 56,472

4a. $3.29   **b.** $12.90   **c.** $35.85

Round to the nearest hundred thousand.

5a. 354,320   **b.** 819,925   **c.** 165,328

About what number is each arrow pointing toward?

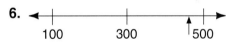

6. (number line: 100, 300, 500)

7. (number line: 4000, 6000, 8000)

8. What is 4809 rounded to the nearest ten?

9. What is $328.59 rounded to the nearest ten dollars?

Problem Solving

10. Suzy has $32.28. Can she buy a fig tree that costs $23.82?

11. Yinka bought a book bag for $15.95. He gave the clerk a twenty-dollar bill. How much change did he receive?

12. What number is halfway between 1000 and 2000?

CHAPTER 2

Practice 2-1

1a. 1 + 0   **b.** 4 + 4   **c.** 0 + 7

2a. 3 + 5 + 4 + 7 + 1   **b.** 6 + 1 + 6 + 1

3a. 3 − 1   **b.** 8 − 0   **c.** 7 − 7

4a. 17¢ − 8¢   **b.** 11¢ − 6¢   **c.** 12¢ − 12¢

Find the value of the variable.

5a. 9 + e = 14   **b.** 9 = 7 + y

6a. 7 − b = 1   **b.** 5 = w − 8

Estimate the sum or difference.

7a. 28 + 22   **b.** 589 + 612   **c.** 825 − 592

8a. $1.28   **b.** $309   **c.** $8.89
      + 1.15   + 194   − 7.20

Find the sum or difference.

9a. 38 + 41   **b.** 211 + 544   **c.** $17 + $32

10a. 85 − 40   **b.** 54 − 43   **c.** $68 − $55

Problem Solving

11. A quilt has 12 blue squares and 24 green squares. How many squares does it have?

12. Max has 48 comic books. He sells 23 of them. How many does he have left?

13. Jan scored 8 points in a basketball game. Ina scored 19 points. How many more points did Ina score than Jan?

14. There are 18 turtles in a pond. There are 7 adult turtles. How many are not adults?

15. Alma needs $14 to buy a compact disc. She has $11. How much more money does she need?

Practice 2-2

Add mentally. Use addition strategies.

1a. 5 + 0   **b.** 7 + 6   **c.** 6 + 7

2a.   6   **b.**   3   **c.**   1
        2   5   2
        5   1   4
      + 4   + 7   + 8

Add mentally.

3a. 14 + 15   **b.** 9 + 9   **c.** 120 + 90

4a.   74   **b.**   8   **c.**   9
         30   5   3
       + 44   8   + 9
                    + 2

Find the value of the variable.

5a. z + 3 = 11   **b.** 15 = 7 + c

6a. 13 − m = 7   **b.** 16 − f = 8

Estimate. Then find the sum or difference.

7a. 253,196 + 546,214   **b.** $82 − $47

8a. $.47   **b.** $9.27   **c.** $191.00
      + .09   − 2.93   − 44.62

Problem Solving

9. Mark has 14 toy trucks in a carrying case. The case can hold 20 trucks. How many more trucks does Mark need to fill the case?

CHAPTER 3

Practice 3-1

1a. 323
+ 679

b. 19
+ 894

c. 695
+ 8126

2a. 94,320
+ 84,002

b. 190,029
+ 870,993

c. $18.26
+ 4.59

3a. 82,302
97,586
+ 73,222

b. 79
500
639
+ 322

c. $ 919
610
8120
+ 1293

4a. 25 + 75 + 50   **b.** $45.99 + $68.20

5a. 8550 + 10,203   **b.** 194,344 + 940,277

Make a rough estimate. Then adjust.

6a. 920
+ 735

b. 2402
+ 5111

c. $79.45
+ 60.99

7a. 382
989
+ 105

b. 277
184
+ 457

c. $18.95
27.72
+ 11.08

Problem Solving

8. A message board has 190 notes in English and 120 in Spanish. How many notes are on the board?

9. Find the total number of pencils in a box of 24 red, 12 blue, 30 green, and 23 yellow pencils.

10. Mr. Kanin has 1940 postcards from the United States and 2430 from other countries. How many postcards are in his collection?

11. Add 19,200 to the sum of 394 and 377.

12. Mitch uses tiles to cover a floor. He uses 287 black tiles, 78 white tiles, and 118 blue tiles. How many tiles does he use?

13. The sum is 54,000. One addend is 28,250. What is the other addend?

14. A necklace has 26 glass beads, 48 metal beads, and 82 tiny wooden beads. How many beads are in the necklace?

Practice 3-2

1a. 894
− 190

b. 300
− 28

c. 738
− 592

2a. 5493
− 2500

b. 7000
− 429

c. 69,504
− 18,366

3a. $9.29
− 1.63

b. $43.50
− 25.70

c. $50.22
− 8.99

4a. 2280 − 2223   **b.** 29,302 − 10,233

5a. $35.98 − $7.23   **b.** $600.75 − $240.80

Estimate the difference. Use front-end estimation.

6a. 849
− 290

b. 8394
− 2011

c. 73,382
− 14,006

7a. $51.20
− 10.75

b. $757
− 522

c. $98.35
− 52.20

Problem Solving

8. How much greater than 427 is 549?

9. Ms. Brownell has 1327 marbles. There are 272 white marbles; the rest are multicolored. How many multicolored marbles does she have?

10. Ruth is reading a 178-page book. She is on page 67. How many pages does she still have to read?

11. Angie sells seed packs. She starts with a carton of 250 packs. She has 117 packs left. How many has she sold?

12. An adult's T-shirt costs $8.99 and a child's T-shirt costs $5.50. How much more expensive is the adult's T-shirt?

13. Subtract 3405 from the sum of 2847 and 5032.

REINFORCEMENT

CHAPTER 4 ....

Practice 4-1

1a. 3×0 **b.** 1×5 **c.** 0×8

2a. 7×6 **b.** 6×7 **c.** 9×1

3a. 3×21 **b.** 5×18 **c.** 6×94

4a. 7×100 **b.** 4×805 **c.** 2×4500

5a. $8 \times \$1.05$ **b.** $9 \times \$31.59$ **c.** $3 \times \$82.80$

Use front-end digits to estimate the product.

6a. 2×148 **b.** 5×822 **c.** 9×704

Find the value of the variable.

7a. $2 \times s = 18$ **b.** $21 = 7 \times x$

8a. $45 = 5 \times u$ **b.** $27 \times y = 27$

9. What is the product of 78 and 7?

10. What is 459 multiplied by 5?

11. The product is 81. One factor is 9. What is the other factor?

12. Which is greater: 7×1 or 0×7?

Problem Solving

13. What is the product of 472 and zero?

14. Joel bought 3 boxes of peaches. There were 6 peaches in each box. How many peaches did he buy?

15. There are 8 shelves of books. Each shelf holds 45 books. How many books are there?

16. What is the product of $19.95 and one?

17. Meg bought 6 CDs. Each CD cost $9.98. How much did she spend?

Practice 4-2

1a. 10×34 **b.** 10×58 **c.** 10×985

2a. 20×12 **b.** 40×42 **c.** 50×50

3a. $\begin{array}{r} 24 \\ \times 18 \end{array}$ **b.** $\begin{array}{r} 57 \\ \times 21 \end{array}$ **c.** $\begin{array}{r} 6123 \\ \times \quad 6 \end{array}$

4a. 96×17 **b.** 7×7931 **c.** 63×403

5a. $12 \times \$1.02$ **b.** $41 \times \$3.40$ **c.** $35 \times \$6.50$

Use rounding to estimate. Then multiply.

6a. 32×41 **b.** 29×491 **c.** 47×307

7a. $12 \times \$1.25$ **b.** $22 \times \$4.59$ **c.** $84 \times \$8.82$

Problem Solving

8. What is the product of 748 and 10?

9. A theater has 24 rows of seats. There are 18 seats in each row. How many seats are there?

10. A compact disc is on sale for $7.99. How much would it cost to buy 11 of the discs?

11. Zenia earns $10.05 an hour. She works 9 hours a week. How much does she earn in one week?

12. Each volume of an encyclopedia has 568 pages. There are 24 volumes. How many pages are in the entire encyclopedia?

13. What is the product of 409 and 89?

14. A pillowcase costs $4.25. How much would cases for 15 pillows cost?

15. A toy store has 52 bags of marbles. There are 35 marbles in each bag. How many marbles does the store have?

16. There are 115 windows on each floor of an office building. The building has 48 floors. How many windows does the building have?

Practice 5-1

1a. $9\overline{)0}$ **b.** $1\overline{)8}$ **c.** $7\overline{)7}$

2a. $5 \div 5$ **b.** $0 \div 4$ **c.** $2 \div 1$

Find the value of the variable.

3a. $42 \div g = 6$ **b.** $i \div 9 = 6$

Estimate the quotient.

4a. $8\overline{)82}$ **b.** $4\overline{)51}$ **c.** $3\overline{)621}$

5a. $2\overline{)6905}$ **b.** $5\overline{)\$5.25}$ **c.** $7\overline{)\$34.89}$

Divide.

6a. $7\overline{)49}$ **b.** $5\overline{)48}$ **c.** $3\overline{)29}$

7a. $4\overline{)84}$ **b.** $9\overline{)90}$ **c.** $6\overline{)73}$

8a. $2\overline{)868}$ **b.** $8\overline{)969}$ **c.** $7\overline{)865}$

9. Is 3892 divisible by 2?

10. Is 193 divisible by 5?

11. Is 711 divisible by 3?

12. Is 3,225,570 divisible by 10?

Problem Solving

13. Elena has 98 inches of ribbon. How many 6-inch pieces can she cut? Will there be any ribbon left over? how much?

14. If 3634 is divided by 7, what are the quotient and the remainder?

15. What is the next number in this pattern: 3645, 1215, 405, 135, . . . ?

16. An album has 164 photos. Each full page holds 8 pictures. At most, how many pages are full? How many pages are partly filled?

17. What numbers between 107 and 125 are divisible by 2?

Practice 5-2

1a. $9\overline{)819}$ **b.** $4\overline{)110}$ **c.** $8\overline{)209}$

2a. $3\overline{)621}$ **b.** $6\overline{)650}$ **c.** $2\overline{)811}$

3a. $5\overline{)515}$ **b.** $7\overline{)745}$ **c.** $4\overline{)839}$

4a. $8\overline{)8968}$ **b.** $5\overline{)1005}$ **c.** $7\overline{)7325}$

5a. $4\overline{)\$31.20}$ **b.** $9\overline{)\$9.36}$ **c.** $8\overline{)\$7.52}$

Write four related facts for each set of numbers.

6a. 6, 9, 54   **b.** 4, 8, 32   **c.** 3, 7, 21

Use the order of operations to solve.

7a. $9 - 2 \times 3$ **b.** $16 \div 2 + 3$

8a. $5 \times 10 \div 2$ **b.** $360 \div 4 \times 2$

9a. $15 - 5 \times 2 + 1$ **b.** $21 \div 7 + 9 \times 3$

Problem Solving

10. There are 3727 flyers. What is the greatest number of flyers there could be in each of 8 equal stacks?

11. Michael bought 8 oak saplings for $48.40. How much did each sapling cost?

12. Leila makes 850 muffins for a bake sale. She places them in bags of 8. How many bags can she fill? How many muffins are left over?

13. Zack spent $200.35 during a 5-day vacation. How much did he spend each day if he spent an equal amount daily?

14. What is the mean of 104, 205, 47, and 36?

15. In their games this season, the Hoops scored 64, 68, 42, 70, 92, and 54 points. What is their mean score per game?

16. A train travels 600 miles in 9 hours. About how many miles per hour does the train travel?

CHAPTER 6

Practice 6-1

Write *in., ft, mi, c, gal,* or *lb* for the unit you would use to measure each.

1a. the length of a finger **b.** the weight of a bowling ball

2a. the capacity of a juice glass **b.** the distance from San Diego to Las Vegas

3a. the height of a door **b.** the capacity of an oil barrel

Add.

4a. 8 ft 5 in. **b.** 6 ft 8 in.
   + 4 ft 7 in.   − 3 ft 5 in.

Rename each unit of measure.

5a. 36 in. = _?_ ft **b.** 4 gal = _?_ qt

6a. 3 lb = _?_ oz **b.** 32 c = _?_ pt

7. Is a shoelace for a pair of sneakers about 3 in., 3 ft, 3 yd, or 3 mi long?

8. Would you need 2 fl oz, 2 c, 2 pt, or 2 gal of water to fill a large bucket?

Problem Solving

9. Does a wild rabbit probably weigh 3 oz, 3 lb, or 33 lb?

10. A recipe calls for 3 c of milk. Janet has 1 qt of milk. Does she have enough for the recipe?

11. There are 5 apples in a bag. Each apple weighs 5 oz. Does the bag weigh more than 2 lb?

Rename the units of time.

12a. 33 min = _?_ s **b.** 2 y 65 d = _?_ d

13. How many inches are there in 12 ft?

14. Is a 5-lb box heavier than a 90-oz box?

Practice 6-2

Write *cm, m, km, mL, L,* or *g* for the unit you would use to measure each.

1a. the mass of a goldfish **b.** the thickness of a book

2a. the distance from Rome to Madrid **b.** the capacity of a fish tank

3a. the capacity of a teaspoon **b.** the length of a large rug

Compare. Write <, =, or >.

4a. 200 cm _?_ 20 m **b.** 7 L _?_ 6000 mL

5a. 6000 g _?_ 5 kg **b.** 4 km _?_ 5000 m

Write how much time has passed.

6. from 12:30 A.M. to 4:00 A.M.

7. from 10:20 P.M. to 11:15 P.M.

8. Is a room comfortable when it is 68°F or 68°C?

9. Will ice melt at 2°F or 2°C?

10. What time is it when it is 12 minutes before noon?

11. Does a postcard have a mass of 1 g or 1 kg?

12. Is a pencil about 15 mm, 15 cm, or 15 m long?

Problem Solving

Use the map to solve.

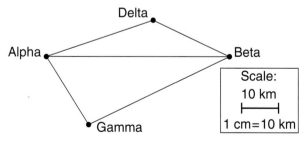

13. How far is it from Alpha to Beta in kilometers?

14. Is Beta closer to Alpha or Delta?

CHAPTER 7

Practice 7-1

Problem Solving

Use the survey results to solve problems 1–3.

Favorite Numbers of Mr. Porter's Class
7, 5, 7, 11, 2, 3, 13, 5, 7, 11, 2, 8, 8, 7, 7, 5

1. Make a tally chart and a line plot from the survey data.

2. Which was the most popular number?

3. Which numbers were equally popular?

Use the line graph to solve.

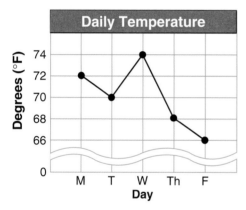

4. Which day was the warmest?

5. On which day was the temperature 70°F?

Use the chart to solve.

Type of Boat	Number
Motor Boat	45
Sail Boat	80
Canoe	60
Row Boat	35

6. Make a pictograph from the data in the chart.

7. What type of boat was second most popular?

Use the bar graph to solve.

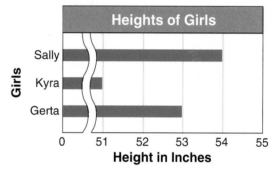

8. Which girl is 2 in. taller than Kyra?

9. How much taller is Sally than Gerta?

Practice 7-2

Problem Solving

Use the circle graph to solve.

Cards at Holly's Card Shop

1. Does the shop have more *thank you* or *get well* cards?

2. How many cards in all does the shop have?

3. Molly must wear a blue, red, or white shirt with either black, brown, or blue pants to work. How many combinations of shirt and pants can she wear?

4. A computer picks a random number between 1 and 100. Is it more or less likely to pick a number above 20?

5. Is the computer more likely, less likely, or equally likely to pick an odd number?

6. On a 1–6 number cube, what is the probability of rolling an even number?

7. Irene tosses a nickel. It lands tails up. What is the probability that it will land tails up on her next toss?

CHAPTER 8

Practice 8-1

Write each as a fraction.

1a. two fifths   **b.** three sevenths

Write each fraction in words.

2a. $\frac{3}{4}$ **b.** $\frac{5}{6}$ **c.** $\frac{1}{3}$ **d.** $\frac{2}{8}$

About what fraction of the region is shaded?

3.

Write the equivalent fraction.

4a. $\frac{1}{2} = \frac{d}{12}$ **b.** $\frac{3}{4} = \frac{r}{8}$

5a. $\frac{2}{3} = \frac{v}{9}$ **b.** $\frac{8}{10} = \frac{16}{f}$

Problem Solving

6. A carnival wheel is divided into 10 equal parts. Three of the parts are red. Write a fraction to show what part is red.

7. An orange has 9 equal sections. Rose ate 6 sections. Write a fraction to tell what part was eaten.

8. Eight out of 32 students are honor students. What fraction shows how many are honor students?

Tell whether the fraction is closer to 0, $\frac{1}{2}$, or 1.

9. $\frac{1}{5}$ **10.** $\frac{3}{4}$ **11.** $\frac{5}{8}$

12. How many sixths are equal to one half?

Practice 8-2

List all the common factors of each set of numbers. Then circle the GCF.

1a. 8 and 10   **b.** 20 and 30   **c.** 6, 12, and 42

Write each fraction in simplest form.

2a. $\frac{5}{25}$ **b.** $\frac{3}{9}$ **c.** $\frac{6}{18}$

3a. $\frac{20}{100}$ **b.** $\frac{2}{14}$ **c.** $\frac{8}{12}$

Compare. Write <, =, or >.

4a. $\frac{1}{2} \, ? \, \frac{3}{4}$ **b.** $\frac{1}{10} \, ? \, \frac{2}{20}$

5a. $\frac{1}{6} \, ? \, \frac{1}{12}$ **b.** $\frac{5}{8} \, ? \, \frac{1}{8}$

6a. $\frac{4}{5} \, ? \, \frac{4}{6}$ **b.** $\frac{7}{8} \, ? \, \frac{6}{12}$

Write in order from least to greatest.

7a. $\frac{3}{8}, \frac{5}{8}, \frac{1}{8}$ **b.** $\frac{2}{3}, \frac{7}{12}, \frac{1}{12}$

8. What is the greatest common factor of 8, 12, 20, and 40?

Name the fraction for letter A.

9.

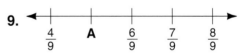

10. Write nine and two ninths as a mixed number.

11. What whole number is equivalent to $\frac{16}{1}$?

12. What whole number is equivalent to $\frac{22}{22}$?

Problem Solving

13. A flag shows 15 equal sections, 5 of which are blue. What fraction tells the part of the flag that is blue? Write the fraction in simplest form.

14. EFEF is to GHGH as FEEF is to ___?___

REINFORCEMENT

CHAPTER 9

Practice 9-1

Solve. Write the answer in lowest terms.

1a. $\frac{6}{8} + \frac{1}{8}$ **b.** $\frac{4}{10} - \frac{2}{10}$

2a. $3\frac{3}{5} + 2\frac{1}{5}$ **b.** $9\frac{7}{8} - 4\frac{3}{8}$

3a. $\frac{2}{3} + \frac{4}{6}$ **b.** $\frac{8}{10} + \frac{3}{5}$

4a. $\frac{1}{2} - \frac{1}{4}$ **b.** $\frac{2}{5} + \frac{3}{10}$

List the first six common multiples for each. Circle the least common multiple.

5a. 4, 10   **b.** 2, 6   **c.** 3, 6, and 9

Write as a whole number or mixed number in simplest form.

6a. $\frac{12}{10}$ **b.** $\frac{16}{4}$ **c.** $\frac{22}{4}$

7. Len eats $\frac{1}{8}$ of a pizza and Mia eats $\frac{3}{8}$ of the pizza. What part of the pizza did they eat?

8. A recipe calls for $\frac{3}{4}$ cup of milk. Rachel has $\frac{1}{8}$ cup of milk. How much more does she need?

9. There are 6 red marbles and 3 blue marbles in a bag. Lou picks one without looking. What is the probability that Lou picks a red marble?

10. What is one fourth of 40?

11. What is $\frac{2}{5}$ of 25?

12. Alan makes 20 brownies. He sells $\frac{3}{4}$ of them at a bake sale. How many does he sell?

13. There are 35 horses. One fifth of them are brown. How many of the horses are brown?

CHAPTER 10

Practice 10-1

Name each figure.

1a. $\overset{\bullet}{T}$ **b.**    **c.**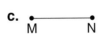

2a.   **b.**   **c.**

3. Which lines are parallel?

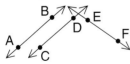

4. Which lines are *not* perpendicular?

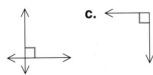

a.   **b.**   **c.**

5. What shape is formed when two rays share a common endpoint?

6. How many sides does a triangle have? a pentagon? a hexagon?

7. How many vertices does a quadrilateral have? an octagon?

8. Name this figure.

9. Name the diameter and two radii.

10. Is this a simple closed curve?

11. How is a square different from a rectangle?

12. A sign has 4 straight sides and 4 vertices. No 2 sides are the same length. What shape is the sign?

13. Is a circle a simple closed curve? Explain.

Practice 10-2

Write *triangle*, *right triangle*, or *equilateral triangle* to describe each figure.

1a.   **b.**   **c.**

How is the pattern made? Write *translation* or *reflection*.

2a.

2b.

3. Are these figures congruent?

4. Are these figures similar?

5. Which figure is symmetrical?

6. Which figure has half-turn symmetry?

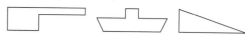

Use the grid to answer each question.

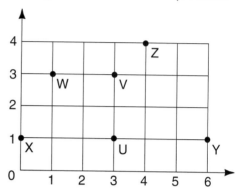

7. What point is located at (1, 3)?

8. What ordered pair gives the location of point *X*?

CHAPTER 11

Practice 11-1

Find the perimeter of each figure.

1a.  23 ft

b.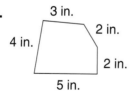
3 in.
2 in.
4 in.
2 in.
5 in.

Find the area of each figure.

2a.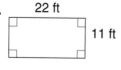

b. 22 ft 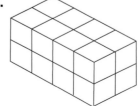 11 ft

3. A tabletop is 4 feet long and 5 feet wide. What is the perimeter of the tabletop?

4. A solid figure has no faces and a curved surface. What is it?

5. How many faces, edges, and vertices does a cube have?

6. Name the shape of the new flat surface made by the cut.

Find the volume of each figure.

7a.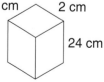

b. 2 cm, 2 cm, 24 cm

CHAPTER 12

Practice 12-1

1a. $8 \div 1$ **b.** $80 \div 10$ **c.** $800 \div 10$

2a. $420 \div 70$ **b.** $500 \div 50$ **c.** $210 \div 30$

3a. $20\overline{)4000}$ **b.** $80\overline{)640}$ **c.** $90\overline{)54{,}000}$

Estimate the quotient. Use compatible numbers.

4a. $56 \div 11$ **b.** $249 \div 32$ **c.** $109 \div 48$

5a. $62\overline{)142}$ **b.** $74\overline{)657}$ **c.** $52\overline{)\$4.80}$

Divide and check.

6a. $21\overline{)88}$ **b.** $31\overline{)94}$ **c.** $33\overline{)\$.99}$

7a. $35\overline{)73}$ **b.** $72\overline{)360}$ **c.** $91\overline{)\$5.46}$

Problem Solving

8. How many dozens are there in 48?

9. A factory can make 21 toy trains in one hour. How long will it take to make 147 trains?

10. Roger worked 30 hours a week at summer camp. He worked a total of 240 hours. How many weeks did he work?

11. A box can hold 52 cans. How many boxes are needed to hold 260 cans?

12. There are 682 baseball cards and 31 children. If each child takes the same number of cards, what is the greatest number each child will get?

13. Avi buys 11 marbles for $.99. How much does each marble cost?

14. The dividend is 549. The divisor is 61. What is the quotient?

15. Amy earns $44 in 11 hours. How much does she earn in 1 hour?

16. A ship travels 29 miles an hour. How long will it take the ship to travel 87 miles?

Practice 12-2

1a. $28\overline{)100}$ **b.** $12\overline{)90{,}000}$ **c.** $14\overline{)234}$

2a. $79\overline{)229}$ **b.** $98\overline{)877}$ **c.** $38\overline{)279}$

3a. $65\overline{)541}$ **b.** $72\overline{)630}$ **c.** $63\overline{)371}$

4a. $86\overline{)\$20.64}$ **b.** $92\overline{)5060}$ **c.** $54\overline{)2920}$

5a. $62\overline{)3000}$ **b.** $47\overline{)\$9.40}$ **c.** $24\overline{)23{,}600}$

6a. $8\overline{)832}$ **b.** $16\overline{)\$32.16}$ **c.** $25\overline{)\$50.75}$

Problem Solving

7. A carton can hold 24 cans of soup. A diner uses 627 cans in a month. How many full cartons does the diner use?

8. The diner has 576 drinking glasses stored on shelves. Each shelf holds 48 glasses. At most, how many shelves are there?

9. Rita buys 25 postcards for $8.75. How much does each postcard cost?

10. A paper company donates 774 packs of paper to 18 schools. If the packs are shared equally, how many does each school receive? How many are left over?

11. The dividend is 46,460. The divisor is 23. What is the quotient?

12. A train travels 68 miles per hour. How long will it take the train to travel 748 miles?

13. Trudy buys a newspaper every day for 14 days. She spends $4.90. How much does each newspaper cost?

14. Glen's dog eats 14 oz of dry food every day. Will a 400-oz bag of dog food last four weeks?

15. Ruth buys 18 yards of ribbon for $18.90. How much does one yard of ribbon cost?

16. What is the remainder when 824,402 is divided by 42?

CHAPTER 13

Practice 13-1

Write the value of the underlined digit.

1a. 5.<u>2</u>   **b.** 0.6<u>1</u>   **c.** <u>2</u>5.83

Write as a decimal.

2a. eight hundredths   **b.** 30 + 6 + 0.4 + 0.02

3a. $\frac{72}{100}$ **b.** $3\frac{5}{10}$

Compare. Write <, =, or >.

4a. 5.54 _?_ 5.45   **b.** 7.12 _?_ 7.1

5a. 21.98 _?_ 22   **b.** 0.80 _?_ 0.8

Compute.

6a. 2.4 + 4.5   **b.** 3.6 + 5.89 + 4

7a.   7.2   **b.**   5   **c.**   0.57
        − 2.7   4.2   0.75
                    + 6.81   + 0.22

8. Write 25.89 in expanded form.

9. What is 3.28 rounded to the nearest tenth?

10. What is 45.92 rounded to the nearest one?

11. Write 0.1, 1.1, 1.11, and 1 in order from least to greatest.

Problem Solving

12. Joel swam 89.71 m. Kate swam 93.2 m. About how many more meters did Kate swim than Joel?

13. Ben's cat is 28.8 cm tall. Gil's cat is 32 cm tall. How much taller is Gil's cat?

14. Which is a better buy: 18 crayons for $6.12 or 25 crayons for $8?

15. A bean plant is 46.3 cm tall at the end of May. It grows 10.45 cm in June. How tall is it at the end of June?

16. Write 6.5, 65.5, 65.6, and 60.5 in order from greatest to least.

CHAPTER 14

Practice 14-1

Find each value for n.

1a. $32 + n = 50$ **b.** $100 − n = 19$

2a. $21 \times n = 105$ **b.** $693 \div n = 63$

Complete the function table.

3.

10	8	17	25	64	3	92
60	48	102	?	?	?	?

Rule: Multiply by 6.

Compare. Write = or ≠.

4a. 140×5 _?_ $600 + 20$
b. $210 \div 15$ _?_ $16 − 2$

5a. $2.2 + 1.7$ _?_ 39
b. 7×7 _?_ $55 − 2 \times 3$

Problem Solving

6. There are 8 boxes of books. Each box holds 16 books. Which number sentence will help you find how many books in all: $8 \times 16 = n$ or $16 \div 8 = n$?

7. Which is greater: $100 \div (2 + 3)$ or $100 \div 2 + 3$?

8. Which is equal to zero: $10 − 2 \times 5$ or $(10 − 2) \times 5$?

For each equation, complete a function table with 5 values for x and y. Then graph each set of ordered pairs on a coordinate grid.

9a. $y = x + 4$ **9b.** $y = x \div 3$

Brain Builders

SET 1

Compare. Write $<$, $=$, or $>$.
1. $8 + 4$? $18 - 9$ 2. $16 - 8$? $7 + 6$

Compute.
3. $(3 \times 7) + 1$ 4. $(5 \times 8) - 7$
5a. $63 \div 7$ b. $8\overline{)48}$

Give the place and the value of the underlined digits.
6. $5\underline{2}8,\underline{3}47,10\underline{6}$

Give 4 related facts for:
7a. 9, 8, 17 b. 5, 7, 35

Write in standard form.
8. eighty thousand, forty-nine

9. Stickers cost $.06 each. How much will 9 stickers cost?

10. Joan has 356 stickers in her collection. Diane has 365. Which girl has more stickers?
11. Round the sum of $350 + 23 + 126$ to the nearest hundred.
12. At $.96 a yard, what is the cost of 8 yards of material?
13. A bookcase has 8 shelves. There are 6 books on each shelf. How many books are in the bookcase?
14. Forty strawberries were divided equally among 5 children. How many did each child receive?
15. How much greater is the product of 6 and 7 than the product of 5 and 8?

SET 2

Order from least to greatest.
1. 304, 340, 356, 324

Round to the place of the underlined digit.
2a. $\underline{9}2,315$ b. $\underline{3}87,082$

Write in standard form.
3a. one hundred four thousand, three hundred seventy
 b. $100,000 + 20,000 + 300 + 4$

Compute.
4a. $n - 8 = 5$ b. $15 = 6 + b$

5. $\begin{array}{r} 23 \\ + 34 \\ \hline \end{array}$ 6. $\begin{array}{r} 651 \\ + 728 \\ \hline \end{array}$ 7. $\begin{array}{r} 59 \\ - 24 \\ \hline \end{array}$ 8. $\begin{array}{r} 738 \\ - 216 \\ \hline \end{array}$

9. $21.50 + $7.25 10. $33.95 - $1.84

11. Helen buys a toothbrush for $.96 and soap for $.45. How much change will she receive from $2.00?
12. What four coins have the same value as one quarter?
13. How many odd numbers are there between 132 and 180? Name them.
14. Write 4,305,060 in expanded form.
15. Jack gave the clerk $1.00 to pay for a $.32 item. The clerk then gave him 2 quarters, 1 dime, 1 nickel, and 2 pennies. Did he receive the correct change? Explain.

SET 3

Compute.
1. $3 + 6 + 4 + 5$
2. Double 8 and add 3.

Round to estimate.
3. $\begin{array}{r} 46 \\ + 22 \\ \hline \end{array}$ 4. $\begin{array}{r} 371 \\ + 119 \\ \hline \end{array}$ 5. $\begin{array}{r} 68 \\ - 37 \\ \hline \end{array}$ 6. $\begin{array}{r} 482 \\ - 245 \\ \hline \end{array}$

Compute.
7. $\begin{array}{r} 163 \\ + 257 \\ \hline \end{array}$ 8. $\begin{array}{r} 572 \\ + 388 \\ \hline \end{array}$ 9. $\begin{array}{r} 429 \\ - 194 \\ \hline \end{array}$ 10. $\begin{array}{r} 2610 \\ - 1436 \\ \hline \end{array}$

11. Add mentally.
$75 + 60 + 50 + 40 + 25$

12. Jan, Sue-ling, and Tanya scored 86, 80, and 100 on the math test. Jan's score was the lowest. Sue-ling had hoped to do better. Give each child's score.
13. Julio bought a sweater for $15.40 and shoes for $22.90. How much change will he receive from $40?
14. Find the total number of days in June, February, December, and July.
15. Mr. Doyle is traveling 682 km from Pensacola to St. Augustine. If he has already traveled 495 km, how much farther must he travel?

SET 4

Compute.

1.
```
  3475
    63
+ 8468
```

2.
```
  $ 6.95
   15.47
+  38.56
```

3.
```
  40,000
-    960
```

4.
```
  306,058
-  98,738
```

5.
```
  4060
×    8
```

6.
```
   143
×    7
```

7.
```
   809
×   76
```

8.
```
  $2.56
×    10
```

Use front-end digits to estimate. Then multiply.

9. 4×18

10. 22×631

11. Patrick is 18 years old and is 6 ft tall. Bud is 23 years old. How much older is Bud?

12. How long will it take Traci to read a book of 168 pages if she reads 8 pages each day?

13. If a jet travels 300 miles an hour, how far will it go in 13 hours?

14. Each of the 136 students in the graduating class will be inviting 4 guests to the ceremonies. How many guests will be invited in all?

15. If Phillipe earns $4.50 an hour, how much will he earn if he works 20 hours?

SET 5

Estimate each product by rounding.

1. 403×7

2. 3×242

Discover the pattern and complete.

3. 6, 8, 10, 7, 9, 11, 8, 10, _?_ , _?_ .

Complete.

4. $6 \times 7 = 42$ is to $42 \div 6 = 7$ as $4 \times 9 = 36$ is to _?_ .

Estimate the quotient.

5. $5)\overline{38}$

6. $7)\overline{\$48.75}$

Divide.

7. $6)\overline{900}$

8. $4)\overline{8608}$

Which are divisible by 3?

9. 75

10. 82

11. The Kane family drove 1800 miles in five days. How many miles did they average each day?

12. Patsy gave 8 stickers to her sister, and double that amount to each of her 4 friends. She still has 14 stickers left. How many stickers did Patsy start with?

13. Estimate the cost of 7 CDs if each one costs $8.98.

14. A notepad costs $.89 and a pen costs $.59. What is the total cost of six notepads and six pens?

15. If 466 apples are to be put equally into 9 baskets, how many apples will there be in each basket? How many apples will be left over?

SET 6

Rename each unit.

1. 30 in. = _?_ ft

2. 6 yd = _?_ ft

Compute.

3.
```
  2 ft 8 in.
+ 3 ft 9 in.
```

4.
```
  4 yd 2 ft
- 3 yd 1 ft
```

Compare. Write <, =, or >.

5. 6 qt _?_ 2 gal

6. 3 pt _?_ 6 c

Rename each unit.

7. 24 oz = _?_ lb _?_ oz

8. 6500 lb = _?_ T _?_ lb

Choose the best estimate.

9. length of a paper clip: 30 cm or 30 mm?

10. capacity of a swimming pool: 2000 L or 2000 mL?

11. Which is the longer distance: 1800 m or 2 km?

12. There were 936 library books. If an equal number were placed on each of 9 shelves, how many books were on each shelf?

13. Find the mean of Rashon's 4 math test scores: 86, 80, 93, 93.

14. Dad needs 95 nails to make a doghouse. If they come packaged 10 nails to a bag, how many bags will Dad need to buy?

15. If the temperature starts at 0°C and drops 4°, what is the temperature? If it then rises 6°, what will the temperature be? If it rises another 3°, what will the temperature be then?

SET 7

Rename the unit of time.
1. 3 h = ? min   **2.** 96 h = ? days

Compute.

3. 3658
    + 2793

4. 9657
    − 2985

5. 3841
    × 52

6. $3\overline{)1063}$

Use the graph to answer questions 7 and 8.

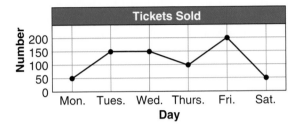

Tickets Sold

(Number / Day: Mon. Tues. Wed. Thurs. Fri. Sat.)

7. How many tickets were sold altogether?
8. How many more tickets were sold on Tues. and Wed. than on Mon. and Thurs.?
9. What is the mass in grams of a 5-kg bag of flour?
10. Find the date of the 40th day after March 8.
11. Two books cost $1.65 and $2.25. What would be the change from $10.00?
12. A point halfway between 20 and 30 on a graph stands for what number?

In a jar with 10 red marbles, 5 each of green and blue, and 1 yellow marble, are you equally, more, or less likely to select:
13. a yellow marble?
14. a green or blue marble?
15. a red marble?

SET 8

Closer to 0, $\frac{1}{2}$, or 1?
1. $\frac{3}{6}$ **2.** $\frac{7}{8}$ **3.** $\frac{1}{9}$

Give the equivalent fraction.
4. $\frac{2}{3} = \frac{v}{12}$ **5.** $\frac{4}{5} = \frac{r}{15}$ **6.** $\frac{2}{9} = \frac{p}{27}$

Find the GCF.
7. 12 and 36   **8.** 28 and 42

Write each fraction in simplest form.
9. $\frac{15}{40}$ **10.** $\frac{20}{38}$
11. Latisha has 4 apples. She wants to share them equally with a friend. How many apples does each child get?

12. Make up a question. Maria baby-sat for 3 hours. She was paid $5.00 an hour. Then she spent $12.00.
13. The box holds $\frac{3}{4}$ cup of raisins. The recipe calls for $\frac{2}{3}$ cup of raisins. Will there be enough raisins for the recipe?
14. Cindy is $4\frac{2}{4}$ ft tall, Desiree is $4\frac{1}{4}$ ft tall, and Emile is $4\frac{3}{4}$ ft tall. Who is the tallest? Who is the shortest?
15. Eight-tenths of the building is above ground level and $\frac{2}{10}$ is below ground level. Write these fractions in simplest form.

SET 9

Find the pattern and complete.
1. $\frac{1}{12}, \frac{4}{12}, \frac{2}{12}, \frac{5}{12}, \frac{3}{12}, \frac{?}{?}, \frac{?}{?}$

Compute. Write the answer in simplest form.
2. $\frac{1}{8} + \frac{1}{8} + \frac{5}{8}$ **3.** $\frac{12}{5} + \frac{8}{5}$
4. $\frac{1}{8} + \frac{3}{4}$ **5.** $\frac{5}{6} - \frac{1}{2}$

Find the LCM.
6. 8 and 10   **7.** 4 and 7
8. To $\frac{1}{3}$ of 36 add 4.
9. Subtract 5 from $\frac{2}{5}$ of 40.
10. A piece of wood measures $4\frac{3}{8}$ ft in length. Another piece is $6\frac{1}{8}$ ft. What is the combined length?

11. On a fair spinner with the numbers 1, 2, and 3, what is the probability of spinning either a 1, a 2, or a 3?
12. Bill had 63 marbles. He gave $\frac{1}{9}$ of them to Chung. How many did Bill have left?
13. At $309 each, what will a store pay for 85 television sets?
14. Julie has 3 quarters, 4 dimes, 3 nickels, and 7 pennies in her pocket. Does she have enough to buy a toy that costs $1.29?
15. Daryll did $\frac{3}{8}$ of a project, and Dana did $\frac{1}{4}$ of it. How much of the project is completed? How much still needs to be completed?

SET 10

Identify each.

1. 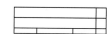 A⟷B **2.** •C **3.** D•——•E

Draw 3 angles:
4a. a right angle   **b.** acute   **c.** obtuse

5. The rungs of a ladder form ___?___ lines.
6. Trace a penny. Then draw a diameter and a radius. Label these line segments.
7. Draw a hexagon. How many angles are there?
8. Draw 2 special quadrilaterals. Label them.
9. Is the figure a reflection or a translation?   **a.** ▲▲   **b.** ▲▲
10. Write *congruent* or *similar figures.*   **a.** ◆◆   **b.** ∞ ∞

11. How many rectangles?
12. Find the perimeter of a pentagon whose sides measure: $1\frac{1}{8}$ in., 2 in., $1\frac{5}{8}$ in., 2 in., and $2\frac{1}{8}$ in.
13. The baseball field measures 125 yd long and 75 yd wide. Find the area.
14. Which solid figure has 8 edges and 5 faces?
15. A box measures 2 m long, 1 m wide, and 2 m high. Find the volume of the box. Then decide whether you can fit a television that measures 150 cm long, 75 cm wide, and 120 cm high into the box.

SET 11

1a. $83 + 74 + 36$ **b.** $80 + 24 + 65$
2a. $651 - 289$ **b.** $708 - 498$
3a. $7\overline{)749}$ **b.** $20\overline{)180}$
4a. $30\overline{)241}$ **b.** $23\overline{)7432}$
5a. $52\overline{)67,652}$ **b.** $13\overline{)11,726}$
6. How many 8s are in: 26; 37; 43; 57?

Estimate the quotient.
7a. $36\overline{)82}$ **b.** $41\overline{)211}$

Write the number.
8. $7 + 0.2 + 0.09$

9. 2.59
      $.09$
   $+ 3.84$

10. 23.50
      $- 7.65$

11. Vince puts a border around his room, which measures 8 ft by 11 ft. How many feet of border does he need?
12. Mrs. Taylor spent $86.40 to buy 27 identical pairs of scissors. How much did each pair cost?
13. There are 1902 people in line for the roller coaster. Each ride holds 28 people. How many times will the roller coaster need to run so that everyone in line has one ride?
14. Tom's ski run was 61.45 s. Carol's time was 61.39 s. Whose time was faster?
15. How many feet are in a spool of cotton that contains 30 yards?

SET 12

Round to the nearest one; then to the nearest tenth.
1a. 36.18   **b.** 12.96   **c.** 44.50

Write +, −, ×, or ÷ to make each sentence true.
2a. 48 _?_ 3 = 9 _?_ 7   **b.** 6 _?_ 8 = 59 _?_ 11

Solve.
3. $0.7 + 0.6 - (2 \times 0.3) \div (1.9 - 0.9)$

Order from least to greatest.
4. 1.3, 1.36, 0.3, 1.63   **5.** 2.4, 2.43, 2.423

Estimate.
6. $8.6 + 2.9$ **7.** $15.3 - 10.4$

Find the value of the variable.
8. $t \times 15 = 25 \times 3$ **9.** $w \div 4 = 120 \div 6$

Compute.
10. $1 + 7 - 2 + 3 + 4 - n = 5$
11. Mrs. Riso bought 1 dozen donuts at $.30 each and $\frac{1}{2}$ dozen muffins at $.65 each. How much change will she receive from $10?
12. Complete the pattern.
   0.1, 0.5, 0.7, 0.2, 0.6, 0.8, _?_, _?_
13. If a ship travels 409 miles in one day, how far will it travel in six days?
14. After Greg paid $40.00 for shoes and $3.50 for socks, he had $20.50 left. How much money did Greg have at first?
15. Maggie had 2 dozen eggs. She used $\frac{2}{3}$ of them for baking. How many eggs were left?

CHALLENGE

Mental Math

Listen to your teacher read the directions. You do not need paper and pencil.

SET 1

1.
$$3 \quad 2 \quad 5 \quad 3 \quad 4 \quad 7$$
$$+7 \quad +9 \quad +2 \quad +6 \quad +8 \quad +7$$

2.
$$7 \quad 10 \quad 9 \quad 16 \quad 14 \quad 8$$
$$-3 \quad -2 \quad -4 \quad -8 \quad -9 \quad -3$$

3. Give related facts. $8 + 2$, $6 + 5$, $7 + 4$, $5 + 3$, $6 + 7$, $9 + 7$, $1 + 9$

4. $2 \times 3 \quad 2 \times 5 \quad 3 \times 6 \quad 3 \times 8$
$2 \times 9 \quad 3 \times 9 \quad 2 \times 7 \quad 3 \times 4$

5. $4 \times 2 \quad 4 \times 6 \quad 5 \times 9 \quad 5 \times 6$
$4 \times 8 \quad 5 \times 2 \quad 4 \times 7 \quad 5 \times 7$

6. Don is 9 years old. How old will he be 6 years from now?

7. A farmer had 11 cows. He sold 8 of them. How many cows did he have left?

8. Crackers are 9¢ each. How much will Joey pay for 3 crackers?

9. How many nickels are worth 50 cents?

10. Anna picked 9 flowers. Laura picked 3. How many flowers did they pick in all?

SET 2

1.
$$9 \quad 8 \quad 7 \quad 5 \quad 6 \quad 7$$
$$+9 \quad +6 \quad +9 \quad +8 \quad +9 \quad +8$$

2.
$$16 \quad 17 \quad 15 \quad 18 \quad 14 \quad 13$$
$$-7 \quad -9 \quad -6 \quad -9 \quad -7 \quad -7$$

3. $7 \times 3 \quad 6 \times 4 \quad 7 \times 7 \quad 6 \times 9$
$7 \times 5 \quad 7 \times 6 \quad 6 \times 8 \quad 6 \times 6$

4. $8 \times 4 \quad 8 \times 8 \quad 9 \times 4 \quad 9 \times 7$
$8 \times 6 \quad 9 \times 8 \quad 8 \times 5 \quad 9 \times 3$

5. $8 \div 2 \quad 10 \div 2 \quad 12 \div 3 \quad 18 \div 3$
$15 \div 3 \quad 4 \div 2 \quad 21 \div 3 \quad 14 \div 2$

6. Josh has 8¢. Therese has twice as much. How much money does she have?

7. At 9¢ each, what will 7 pencils cost?

8. Thirty-five cents is divided equally among 5 students. How much will each student receive?

9. Tom paid 24¢ for 3 balloons. How much did each balloon cost?

10. The dividend is 42. The divisor is 7. What is the quotient?

SET 3

1. Give related facts. $6 \div 2$, $9 \div 3$, $10 \div 2$, $3 \div 3$, $8 \div 4$, $6 \div 3$

2. Subtract 3 from: 21, 18, 15, 12, 9, 6, 3, 24, 27, 30

3. $28 \div 7 \quad 24 \div 4 \quad 30 \div 5 \quad 48 \div 6$
$49 \div 7 \quad 32 \div 4 \quad 40 \div 5 \quad 36 \div 6$

4. 10 more than: 58, 14, 82, 95, 103, 191

5. Give the value of the underlined digit: 5̲63; 721̲; 34̲5; 2̲,976,588; 3,1̲26,908

6. When 67 is divided by 9, what is the quotient? the remainder?

7. What is 78 in words?

8. What is $5000 + 100 + 60$ in standard form?

9. What number is ten thousand less than 56,201?

10. There are 3189 adults and 3819 children at the fair. Are there more adults or children?

SET 4

1. Order from least to greatest:
   3,601,432; 3,562,620; 3,563,634;
   3,610,981
2. Round to the nearest ten: 57, 111,
   363, 288, 435, 519, 604, 792
3. Divide by 4: 24, 16, 36, 28, 32,
   8, 12
4. Multiply by 7, by 8, by 9: 3, 5, 6, 4,
   8, 2, 9, 0, 1, 7
5. Round to the nearest hundred
   thousand: 659,752; 348,796;
   789,214; 204,046

6. What is one hundred and twelve in
   standard form?
7. What is 4,000,000 + 500,000 +
   30,000 + 2000 + 10 + 8?
8. There are 18 caps. Six are red.
   How many caps are not red?
9. What number comes between
   613,725 and 613,727?
10. A DVD costs $17.99. How much
    change will you receive from a
    twenty-dollar bill?

SET 5

1. Round to the nearest hundred
   dollars: $275.10; $316.05; $760.13;
   $440.44; $859.77
2. Name the period of the underlined
   digits: 74,<u>118</u>; <u>25</u>,308,433; 8,<u>065</u>,243;
   117,<u>589</u>; <u>608</u>,145; <u>3</u>,698,572
3. Add 7 to: 8, 18, 28, 38, 58, 78, 48, 68
4. Subtract 8 from: 15, 25, 45, 65,
   85, 35
5. Count back by 10 from: 200–150,
   390–210, 510–380, 220–90,
   165–15, 605–505, 412–342,
   1110–890

6. How much money: 1 ten-dollar
   bill, 2 quarters, 3 dimes, 1 nickel?
7. Which is less? by how much?
   183,575 or 183,775
8. What is the value of 3 in 630,241?
9. Tony scored 5 points in the 1st
   quarter, 6 in the 2nd, and 4 each
   in the 3rd and 4th quarters. How
   many points did he score?
10. What must be added to 9 to make
    a sum of 17?

SET 6

1. $8 + 0 + 4$ $7 + 2 + 3$ $6 + 4 + 1$
   $5 + 6 + 0$ $8 + 9 + 2$ $1 + 9 + 5$
2. Double each and add 2: 4, 2, 6, 5,
   7, 3, 8, 1, 9
3. $u + 8 = 11$ $4 + p = 13$
   $12 - a = 7$ $9 = 16 - t$
   $z - 3 = 9$ $12 = 6 + r$
4. Add 9 to: 5, 15, 45, 35, 55, 75, 37,
   87, 17, 57, 43, 63, 73, 23
5. Estimate. $46 + 21$ $52 + 38$
   $12 + 17$ $29 + 33$ $13 + 76$
   $42 - 22$ $38 - 11$ $59 - 18$
   $15 - 11$ $67 - 45$

6. Is the sum reasonable? Check by
   estimation. $524 + 46 = 984$
7. Complete the pattern.
   9, 18, 27, _?_, _?_, 54, _?_, 72
8. Nora had $10.68 and spent
   $10.35. How much money did she
   have left?
9. Grace is 23 years old. Mary is 11
   years older than Grace. How old
   is Mary?
10. Ned needs $17. He has $8.
    How much more money does
    he need?

(478)

SET 7

1. Add 110 to: 34, 134, 244, 354, 424, 564, 634, 714, 844
2. Add 8 to: 7, 17, 57, 37, 47, 27, 67, 77
3. Subtract 9 from: 13, 43, 73, 25, 55, 85, 14, 74, 34, 12, 92, 62, 82, 52
4. Estimate. 123 + 164 185 + 216 351 + 435 694 − 375 716 − 297
5. 4000 + 1200 2300 + 6000 6100 + 3400 5300 + 2400 7500 + 1300

6. Bob's coat cost $67. Ted's coat cost $8 more than Bob's. How much did Ted's coat cost?
7. Gina is 47 in. tall. Don is 5 in. shorter. How tall is Don?
8. Add. 138 + 22 + 19
9. Ramon has $17.30 and Joe has $8.70. How much do the boys have altogether?
10. Rosa had 24 cookies. She gave 7 to Jane. How many cookies did Rosa have left?

SET 8

1. Subtract 5 from: 13, 43, 73, 33, 53
2. $10.00 − $4.00 $12.00 − $6.00 $25.00 − $20.00 $36.00 − $24.00
3. Multiply by 3, then add 4: 4, 8, 0, 9, 1, 5, 3, 6, 2, 7
4. Estimate. 584 − 126 431 − 279 1842 − 1256 3421 − 1538 7186 − 4515
5. Multiply by 7: 2, 4, 5, 7, 9, 1, 0, 3, 6, 8

6. How much greater than 150 is 220?
7. Frank is 7 years old. His sister is 5 years older than Frank. How old is Frank's sister?
8. What is 4 more than the product of 9 times 7?
9. Add 2300 + 3200 + 132.
10. Pedro is 42 in. tall. Dave is 9 in. taller. How tall is Dave?

SET 9

1. 1×6 4×6 7×6 9×6 6×1 6×4 6×7 6×9
2. 3×0 5×1 4×0 6×0 1×7 8×0 9×1 2×0
3. $8 \times b = 24$ $5 \times w = 45$ $n \times 2 = 12$ $d \times 6 = 48$ $7 \times m = 35$ $p \times 4 = 36$
4. Multiply by 2: 10, 20, 30, 40, 50, 70, 90, 60, 80
5. $3 \times (2 + 5)$ $(1 + 4) \times 4$ $2 \times (1 + 3)$ $6 \times (2 + 2)$ $(3 + 2) \times 5$ $(3 + 3) \times 1$

6. Myra pulled out fourteen white socks from the laundry basket. How many pairs of socks can she make?
7. Which is the greater product? 3 times 40 or 4 times 20
8. Paul is 20 years old. Jack is 3 times as old as Paul. How old is Jack?
9. About how much will 5 toys cost if each toy costs $1.98?
10. There are 24 stickers on a sheet. How many stickers are on 2 sheets?

SET 10

1. Multiply by 6, then add 2: 0, 8, 6, 2, 4, 10, 1, 3, 5, 9, 7
2. Multiply by 8, then add 5: 2, 4, 0, 3, 7, 1, 9, 10, 5, 8, 6
3. Estimate. $3 \times \$.48$ $2 \times \$.12$
   $4 \times \$.23$ $5 \times \$.36$ $6 \times \$.38$
4. Estimate. 28×21 39×12
   13×17 43×36 51×22
   14×67
5. 20×100 30×100 20×300
   40×200 30×300 20×200

6. Mr. Lass sold 52 tickets on each of the 4 days before the dance. How many tickets did he sell?
7. Tanya bought 2 kites that cost $18 each. How much did she pay for the kites?
8. Velvet costs $8 a yard. How much do 4 yards cost?
9. Complete the pattern.
   0, 4, 3, 7, 6, __?__, __?__
10. How much greater is the product of 7 and 6 than the product of 0 and 6?

SET 11

1. 30×60 90×20 30×31
   10×210 10×880 40×31
2. $8\overline{)8}$ $1\overline{)7}$ $6\overline{)0}$ $5\overline{)5}$
   $1\overline{)4}$ $3\overline{)0}$ $9\overline{)0}$ $4\overline{)4}$
3. $2\overline{)14}$ $5\overline{)30}$ $7\overline{)28}$ $6\overline{)36}$
   $8\overline{)64}$ $9\overline{)72}$ $4\overline{)36}$ $8\overline{)40}$
4. Divide by 4: 25, 17, 37, 29, 33, 9, 13, 21, 26, 18, 38, 30, 34, 10, 22
5. $g \times 4 = 32$ $6 \times c = 24$
   $h \times 2 = 18$ $e \times 7 = 21$
   $8 \times i = 56$ $f \times 8 = 72$

6. The factors are 23 and 68. Estimate the product.
7. The product is 42. One factor is 6. What is the other factor?
8. What is the remainder when 20 is divided by 9?
9. It took Sam 6 hours to pack 325 cartons. About how many cartons did he pack each hour?
10. Five ties cost $60. Each tie costs the same. How much does 1 tie cost?

SET 12

1. Divide by 9: 29, 11, 46, 20, 38, 40, 31, 15, 48, 33, 14, 49, 19, 42, 44
2. Which are divisible by 2? by 5? by 10? 12, 25, 42, 90, 63, 75, 110, 68, 130
3. $2\overline{)222}$ $5\overline{)555}$ $3\overline{)363}$ $4\overline{)484}$
   $4\overline{)888}$ $2\overline{)462}$ $3\overline{)393}$ $2\overline{)846}$
4. Divide by 8: 73, 74, 78, 79, 69, 71, 65, 12, 19, 21, 30, 31, 35, 38, 37, 59, 61, 57, 63, 49, 52, 55, 53
5. $12 + 4 - 3$ $16 - 9 + 5$
   $8 + 7 - 4$ $12 \div 4 \times 5$
   $5 \times 6 \div 2$ $40 \div 5 \div 2$

6. Sue has $12.72 to share equally with Meg. How much money will each girl receive?
7. Jim spent $1.40 for 2 feet of wire. How much did each foot cost?
8. A farmer plants 800 corn plants in 4 equal rows. How many plants are in each row?
9. Which is greater? by how much? 12,626 or 12,662
10. What number comes next after 124,169?

SET 13

1. Rename as feet: 12 in. 36 in. 24 in. 48 in. 72 in. 60 in. 84 in.
2. Name the time a half hour later. 8:15, 10:30, 12:00, 3:45, 5:20, 6:10, 4:05, 7:15, 9:25
3. Compare. Use $<$, $=$, $>$. 3 c _?_ 2 pt 3 pt _?_ 6 c   1 gal _?_ 6 qt 8 pt _?_ 4 qt
4. Name the date 1 week later. Jan. 8, Mar. 12, Aug. 23, Oct. 2, Nov. 18, Dec. 20
5. Divide by 9: 27, 29, 81, 84, 72, 75, 9, 13, 45, 49, 53, 63, 64, 69

6. Mr. Jones spends $25 every work week on tolls. He works 5 days a week. How much does he spend each workday on tolls?
7. Which is longer, 1 meter or 98 centimeters?
8. Pete's pet weighs 30 oz. How many more ounces does it need to gain to weigh 2 lb?
9. How much longer is 5 feet than 1 yard?
10. Which distance is longer, 10 kilometers or 1000 meters?

SET 14

1. Multiply by 4: 6, 7, 8, 0, 1, 2, 5, 4, 3
2. Count by 1000: 1400–6400; 2300–7300; 5900–10,900; 9700–18,700
3. Divide by 7: 61, 62, 58, 57, 60, 59, 31, 36, 38, 37, 40, 41, 29, 34
4. Subtract 99 from: 109, 239, 479, 658, 918, 338, 525, 865, 785
5. Give the fraction for the shaded part of each region.

6. Lori needs 1 L of water. She has 600 mL. How much more does she need?
7. What is $100,000 + 7$ in standard form?
8. Would you go ice skating at 35°C?
9. Can Jan go skiing at 20°F?
10. Randy worked from 11:30 A.M. to 1:00 P.M. on his bike. How long did Randy work?

SET 15

1. What part of a dollar is: 10¢, 50¢, 25¢, 5¢, 1¢, 75¢, 30¢, 70¢, 20¢
2. $\frac{1}{3} = \frac{k}{6}$ $\frac{1}{4} = \frac{y}{16}$ $\frac{1}{2} = \frac{v}{10}$
   $\frac{2}{5} = \frac{q}{15}$ $\frac{2}{3} = \frac{j}{12}$ $\frac{3}{4} = \frac{x}{20}$
3. $\frac{1 \times 2}{8 \times 2}$ $\frac{3 \times 3}{7 \times 3}$
   $\frac{1 \times 4}{3 \times 4}$ $\frac{4 \times 3}{5 \times 3}$
4. Closer to 0, $\frac{1}{2}$, or 1? $\frac{1}{8}, \frac{4}{7}, \frac{2}{6}, \frac{1}{9}, \frac{8}{10}, \frac{4}{5}, \frac{2}{3}, \frac{2}{4}, \frac{11}{12}$
5. Name the GCF of: 6 and 12; 3 and 15; 8 and 24; 10 and 12; 9 and 12

6. Would you use centimeters or meters to measure the length of a pencil?
7. One paper clip weighs 1 g. How many paper clips do you need to equal 1 kg?
8. Key: Each ▽ = 10 cones. How many cones does ▽ ▽ ▽ ⦚equal?
9. A _?_ graph is used to show change over a period of time.
10. If 1 mi equals 5280 ft, how many feet are there in 2 mi?

SET 16

1. Express in lowest terms: $\frac{3}{6}$, $\frac{6}{8}$, $\frac{5}{10}$, $\frac{2}{4}$, $\frac{7}{21}$, $\frac{4}{12}$, $\frac{6}{18}$, $\frac{5}{20}$, $\frac{9}{18}$, $\frac{2}{10}$

2. Fraction or mixed number? $\frac{5}{6}$, $1\frac{2}{3}$, $2\frac{4}{5}$, $\frac{5}{8}$, $3\frac{1}{9}$, $\frac{6}{7}$, $4\frac{7}{8}$, $\frac{9}{10}$

3. Order from least to greatest: $\frac{2}{3}$, $\frac{1}{3}$, $\frac{3}{3}$. $\frac{2}{5}$, $\frac{4}{5}$, $\frac{1}{5}$. $\frac{3}{6}$, $\frac{5}{6}$, $\frac{2}{6}$

4. Multiply by 6, then add 7: 10, 8, 6, 4, 2, 0, 1, 3, 5, 7, 9

5. Subtract a nickel from: 25¢, 18¢, 50¢, $1.35, $2.05, $1.16, $6.96

6. A jar has 10 red beans, 5 green beans, 5 blue beans, and 1 yellow bean. What is the probability of choosing red? yellow? blue? green?

7. In a survey of 100 people, 30 people chose hot dogs. What part of the people chose hot dogs?

8. At 0°C, water __?__ .

9. Roy rolled a ball 6 yards. Was that more or less than 20 feet?

10. What is 3 more than the product of 9 times 5?

SET 17

1. $\frac{3}{5} + \frac{1}{5}$ $\frac{2}{7} + \frac{3}{7}$ $\frac{1}{6} + \frac{4}{6}$
   $\frac{1}{3} + \frac{1}{3}$ $\frac{3}{9} + \frac{5}{9}$ $\frac{4}{10} + \frac{5}{10}$

2. $\frac{5}{8} - \frac{2}{8}$ $\frac{2}{3} - \frac{1}{3}$ $\frac{6}{7} - \frac{4}{7}$
   $\frac{3}{5} - \frac{2}{5}$ $\frac{8}{9} - \frac{3}{9}$ $\frac{7}{8} - \frac{3}{8}$

3. Express as a mixed number.
   $\frac{15}{2}$, $\frac{7}{4}$, $\frac{11}{3}$, $\frac{17}{5}$, $\frac{9}{2}$, $\frac{13}{6}$, $\frac{15}{4}$

4. $3 + 1\frac{1}{4}$ $2\frac{1}{2} + 4$ $3 + 5\frac{2}{3}$
   $1 + 3\frac{2}{5}$ $4 + 1\frac{3}{4}$ $2\frac{7}{8} + 6$

5. Multiply by 3, then add 4: 4, 8, 0, 9, 5, 6, 7, 10, 2, 3, 1

6. Tom ate $\frac{1}{3}$ of the pizza. Sal ate $\frac{2}{3}$. Who ate more?

7. Six ninths minus four ninths is __?__ .

8. In a pet store $\frac{1}{5}$ of the pets are cats and $\frac{2}{5}$ are dogs. What part of the pets are cats and dogs?

9. Sasha bought $5\frac{3}{4}$ lb of chicken. She cooked $3\frac{1}{4}$ lb. How much is left?

10. Estimate the sum of $2\frac{1}{8} + 3\frac{3}{4} + 4\frac{1}{2}$.

SET 18

1. Subtract 2 from: $3\frac{1}{2}$, $4\frac{1}{5}$, $7\frac{1}{8}$, $8\frac{2}{3}$, $5\frac{2}{5}$, $2\frac{7}{8}$, $2\frac{1}{3}$

2. How many nickels are there in: 25¢, $.20, $.35, $.50, 45¢, 60¢, $.30, $.55, $.40

3. Find $\frac{1}{6}$ of: 6, 18, 42, 54, 24, 36, 12

4. Find half of: 14, 10, 8, 18, 20, 6, 4

5. Add 5 to: 9, 19, 59, 29, 38, 68, 28

6. If 47 is divided by 8, what is the quotient? the remainder?

7. Al did $\frac{1}{6}$ of his homework in school and $\frac{1}{2}$ before dinner. How much of his homework did he do?

8. In a set of 10 pens, 3 are black. What fractional part of the set is black?

9. Of 20 fish, $\frac{3}{4}$ are striped. How many fish are striped?

10. Estimate. $6\frac{5}{10} - 3\frac{1}{3}$

SET 19

1. Double each, then add 3: 10, 20, 30, 40, 50, 60, 70, 80, 90

2. Name the line segments.

3. Compare to a right angle. $<$, $=$, $>$.

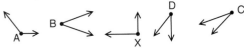

4. Intersecting or parallel?

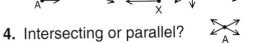

5. Closed or open?

6. An ? is formed by two rays with the same endpoint.

7. Are the sides that meet at each corner of a square frame parallel or perpendicular?

8. Name the radii and the diameter of the circle.

9. How many sides and angles does a pentagon have?

10. Name the parallel sides.

SET 20

1. Congruent or similar? □□
   ○○ ◁◁ □□ ○○

2. Reflection or translation? →←   →→

3. Divide by 9, then add 2: 18, 9, 36, 81, 27, 54, 72, 63, 36, 45

4. 20 × 200   60 × 20   4 × 800
   40 × 600   50 × 300   30 × 700

5. Multiply by 8: 4, 6, 3, 9, 5, 7

6. Which letter has no line of symmetry, G or M?

7. What number comes next after 9999?

8. Ben's calculator costs $25. Ann's costs $19. What is the difference in cost?

9. Find $\frac{1}{3}$ of 27¢, then add 4¢.

10. What is the value of zero in 4,036,645?

SET 21

1. Name the solid figure.

2. Multiply by 9, then add 3: 2, 3, 7, 5, 0, 1, 10, 6, 4, 9, 8

3. 3)666   4)448   2)684
   1)175   5)505   3)906

4. 3 × 5 × 2   4 × 2 × 6   3 × 3 × 5
   7 × 3 × 2   2 × 6 × 5   8 × 5 × 2

5. Find $\frac{1}{5}$ of: 10, 30, 40, 25, 5, 35, 20, 15, 45, 50

6. What is 100,000 + 5000 + 9 in standard form?

7. Find the perimeter of a fenced lot whose sides measure 7 m, 8 m, 5 m, 9 m, and 6 m.

8. What is the perimeter of a square playpen $2\frac{1}{2}$ yd on each side?

9. The bedroom rug measures 10 m by 4 m. What is its area?

10. What solid figure has 2 flat surfaces and 1 curved surface?

SET 22

1. How many tens are in: 370, 420, 550, 600, 780, 190, 830, 240, 960
2. $2\overline{)140}$ $3\overline{)210}$ $4\overline{)160}$ $7\overline{)350}$
   $20\overline{)180}$ $30\overline{)150}$ $40\overline{)200}$ $50\overline{)450}$
3. How many 20s are in: 49, 67, 84, 182, 121, 165, 108, 114, 143
4. How many 7s are in: 45, 66
5. Estimate the quotient. $24\overline{)42}$, $31\overline{)89}$, $47\overline{)99}$, $43\overline{)82}$, $20\overline{)85}$, $34\overline{)69}$, $27\overline{)88}$

6. Find the volume of a dollhouse that is 3 ft long, 2 ft wide, and 2 ft high.
7. Dan put 480 soccer cards on the floor. He put them into 20 equal rows. How many cards were in each row?
8. Bus fare to the zoo was $18. About how much did the driver collect from 19 children?
9. Express 6 feet as yards.
10. Each box holds 28 crayons. How many crayons are in 4 boxes?

SET 23

1. How many 9s are in: 56, 19, 12, 39, 46, 68, 76, 29, 84, 65
2. How many 30s are in: 95, 62, 159, 277, 158, 243, 126, 214, 181
3. $16 = q \times 8$ $56 = b \times 8$
   $40 = h \times 8$ $24 = d \times 8$
   $64 = c \times 8$ $48 = v \times 8$
   $32 = a \times 8$ $72 = m \times 8$
   $80 = z \times 8$
4. Estimate the quotient. $32\overline{)124}$, $51\overline{)98}$, $16\overline{)135}$, $23\overline{)144}$, $49\overline{)152}$, $62\overline{)188}$
5. Multiply by 6: 1, 2, 5, 8, 9, 6, 0, 7, 4, 3, 10

6. A box of cupcakes costs $2.40. If there are 24 cupcakes in a box, how much does each cupcake cost?
7. How many dimes are in $4.00?
8. What is the difference in cents between 1 quarter and 3 nickels?
9. Ramon earns $63 a week. He saves $\frac{1}{7}$ of this amount. How much does he save weekly?
10. What is the sum of 19, 17, and 110?

SET 24

1. $4\overline{)200}$ $5\overline{)300}$ $6\overline{)300}$ $7\overline{)700}$
   $8\overline{)400}$ $2\overline{)100}$ $3\overline{)900}$ $9\overline{)900}$
2. Multiply by 7, then add 4: 6, 3, 4, 1, 9, 2, 0, 5, 7, 8
3. How many tens are in: 85, 62, 77, 43, 38, 22, 15, 94, 51
4. Read. 0.4, 0.9, 0.07, 0.5, 0.03, 0.46, 0.72, 0.01, 0.35, 0.11
5. Read. 1.6, 3.7, 8.6, 4.9, 12.5, 5.03, 8.07, 26.3, 6.18, 35.01

6. A parking garage holds a total of 480 cars with an equal number of cars on 4 levels. How many cars does each level hold?
7. What is one fifth of 20 cents?
8. Dan is 36 years old. David is 9 years old. How much older is Dan than David?
9. Name a decimal between 0.1 and 0.3.
10. What is 0.2 more than 1?

SET 25

1. Give the value. 0.4<u>2</u>, <u>6</u>.23, 14.<u>3</u>, 0.0<u>5</u>, <u>3</u>6.1, 8.0<u>7</u>, 1.4<u>8</u>

2. Compare. $<, =, >$. 0.7 ? 0.3 0.16 ? 0.19 2.36 ? 2.63 6.35 ? 6.3 1.7 ? 1.72

3. Order least to greatest: 0.3, 0.1, 0.6; 0.13, 0.25, 0.20; 3, 0.3, 0.03

4. Complete the pattern. 0.1, 0.4, 0.7, __?__ ; 0.05, 0.15, 0.25, __?__ ; 1.1, 2.1, 3.1, __?__ ; 3.4, 3.6, 3.8 __?__ ; 5.9, 5.6, 5.3, __?__

5. 0.5 + 0.2   0.6 + 0.2   1.3 + 1.4 2.1 + 1.6   0.8 + 0.1   1.7 + 1.2

6. Name two decimals between 3 and 4.

7. Jesse ran 3.25 m and Tim ran 3.55 m. Who ran farther? by how many meters?

8. Round $382.87 to the nearest dollar.

9. Missy spent 2.3 min on the first problem and 3.5 min on the next. How long did she spend on both problems?

10. What is the rule for this pattern? 0.3, 0.1, 0.5, 0.3, 0.7, 0.5, 0.9

SET 26

1. Add 0.2 to: 1.2, 0.3, 2.7, 1.4, 3.9, 2.1, 0.6, 1.5

2. Add 5 cents to the sum of: $.04 + $.06 $.25 + $.50 $.02 + $.03 $.18 + $.02

3. Round to the nearest one: 8.6, 4.9, 6.2, 7.8, 2.3, 3.4, 5.5, 0.7

4. Round to the nearest tenth: 4.18, 5.61, 3.22, 2.73, 7.45, 1.55

5. $w + 2 = 7 - 1$
   $g \div 4 = 3 \times 3$
   $6 \times r = 9 + 9$
   $24 \div y = 10 - 2$

6. The finishing times for the race were 59.1 s for 1st place and 59.6 s for 2nd place. What is the difference in the times?

7. Milk costs $2.89 and bread costs $1.64. About how much money do both items cost in all?

8. Pam bought 2 six-packs of soda. She spent $6.00. What did each can cost?

9. What is 4 + 0.5 in standard form?

10. How much greater than 0.2 is 0.48?

SET 27

1. Subtract 0.1 from: 9.6, 0.4, 6.3, 1.8, 0.6, 5.4, 3.3, 2.7

2. $3 + 4 - 2$
   $10 - 7 + 2$
   $7 + 8 - 9$
   $9 + 9 - 10$

3. Divide by 5, then subtract 2: 35, 20, 45, 15, 25, 40, 30, 10, 50

4. $(3 \times 3) \div 9$ $10 \times (4 - 4)$
   $(6 - 2) \div 1$ $(4 + 4) \times 2$

5. $2 \overline{)\$1.80}$ $3 \overline{)\$2.70}$ $4 \overline{)\$4.00}$
   $5 \overline{)\$4.50}$ $6 \overline{)\$4.80}$ $7 \overline{)\$4.20}$

6. Tom had $21.40. He spent $12.50. Then he found $5.00. How much money does he have now?

7. Multiply 6 and 4, add 2, subtract 5.

8. 1 quarter, 2 dimes, 3 pennies = __?__ ¢

9. Three friends share $1.86 equally. How much does each friend receive?

10. There are 25 cookies in each of 3 bags. Tony eats 2 from each bag. How many cookies are left?

Glossary

also on-line

A

acute angle   An angle that measures less than 90°.

addend   A number that is added to another number or numbers.

angle   The figure formed by two rays that meet at a common endpoint.

area   The number of square units needed to cover a flat surface.

associative (grouping) property   Changing the grouping of the addends (or factors) does not change the sum (or product).

axis   The horizontal or the vertical number line of a graph.

C

capacity   The amount, usually of liquid, that a container can hold.

center   A point from which every point on a circle is the same distance.

centimeter (cm)   A metric unit of length; 10 cm = 1 dm; 100 cm = 1m.

certain   An event that cannot fail to occur, or has a probability of 1.

circle   A simple closed curve; all the points on the circle are the same distance from the center point.

circle graph   A graph that uses sections of a circle to represent data.

clustering   To find addends that are nearly alike in order to estimate their sum.

common factor   A number that is a factor of two or more products.

common multiple   A number that is a multiple of two or more numbers.

commutative (order) property   Changing the order of the addends (or factors) does not change the sum (or product).

compatible numbers   Two numbers, one of which divides the other evenly.

composite number   A whole number greater than 1 that has more than two factors.

cone   A solid figure that has one circular base.

congruent figures   Figures that have the same size and shape.

cube   A solid figure with six congruent square faces.

customary system   The measurement system that uses inch, foot, yard, and mile; cup, pint, quart, and gallon; and ounce and pound.

cylinder   A solid figure that has two congruent circular bases.

D

data   Facts or information.

decimal   A number in base ten that is written with a decimal point.

   2.04 ← decimal

          decimal point

decimeter (dm)   A metric unit of length; 1 dm = 10 cm; 10 dm = 1 m.

degree (°)   A unit used to measure angles.

degree Celsius (°C)   A unit for measuring temperature. The freezing point of water is 0°C.

degree Fahrenheit (°F)   A unit for measuring temperature. The freezing point of water is 32°F.

denominator   The numeral below the bar in a fraction; it names the total number of equal parts.

diameter   A line segment that passes through the center of a circle and has both endpoints on the circle.

difference   The answer in subtraction.

digit   Any one of the numerals 0, 1, 2, 3, 4, 5, 6, 7, 8, or 9.

distributive property Multiplying a number by a sum is the same as multiplying the number by each addend of the sum and then adding the products.

dividend The number to be divided.

$$24 \div 4 \qquad 4\overline{)24}$$
dividend

divisibility rules A rule that tells whether one number is divisible by another.

divisible One number is divisible by another if it can be divided by that number and yield no remainder.

divisor The number by which the dividend is divided.

$$36 \div 9 \qquad 9\overline{)36}$$
divisor

E

edge The line segment where two faces of a solid figure meet.

elapsed time The amount of time between two given times.

endpoint The point at the end of a line segment or ray.

equation (See **number sentence.**)

equilateral triangle A triangle whose three sides are congruent.

equivalent decimals Decimals that name the same amount. $0.4 = 0.40$

equivalent fractions Different fractions that name the same amount. $\frac{1}{2} = \frac{2}{4}$

estimate An approximate answer; to find an answer that is close to an exact answer.

event A set of one or more outcomes.

F

face A flat surface of a solid figure surrounded by line segments.

fact family A set of related addition and subtraction facts or multiplication and division facts that use the same numbers.

factors Two or more numbers that are multiplied to give a product.

flip (reflection) The movement of a figure over a line so that the figure faces in the opposite direction.

fluid ounce (fl oz) A customary unit of capacity; 8 fluid ounces = 1 cup.

formula A rule that is expressed by using symbols.

fraction A number that names part of a whole or part of a set.

front-end estimation A way of estimating by using the front, or greatest, digits to find an approximate answer.

function A quantity whose value depends on another quantity.

G

gram (g) A metric unit of mass; 1000 g = 1 kg.

greatest common factor (GCF) The greatest number that is a factor of two or more products.

H

half-turn symmetry A figure that matches its image when it is turned halfway around has half-turn symmetry.

hexagon A polygon with six sides.

I

identity property (property of one) The product of one and a number is that number.

impossible An event that cannot occur, or has a probability of 0.

improper fraction A fraction whose numerator is greater than or equal to its denominator.

inch (in.) A customary unit of length; 12 in. = 1 ft.

intersecting lines Lines that meet or cross at a common point.

inverse operations Mathematical operations that *undo* each other, such as addition and subtraction or multiplication and division.

isosceles triangle   A triangle with at least two sides that are equal in length.

K

kilogram (kg)   A metric unit of mass; 1 kg = 1000 g.

kilometer (km)   A metric unit of distance; 1 km = 1000 m.

L

least common denominator (LCD)   The least common multiple of two or more denominators.

least common multiple (LCM)   The least number that is a multiple of two or more numbers.

like denominators   Denominators that are the same in one or more fractions; the fractions $\frac{3}{7}$ and $\frac{5}{7}$ have like denominators.

line   A straight set of points that goes on forever in opposite directions.

line graph   A graph that uses points on a grid connected by line segments to represent data.

line plot   A graph of data on a number line.

line segment   The part of a line between two endpoints.

liter (L)   A metric unit of capacity; 1 L = 1000 mL.

lowest terms (simplest form)   A fraction is in lowest terms when its numerator and denominator have no common factor other than 1.

M

mass   The measure of the amount of matter an object contains.

mean (average)   A number derived by dividing a sum by the number of its addends.

median   The middle number of a set of numbers arranged in order.

meter (m)   A metric unit of length; 1 m = 10 dm; 1 m = 100 cm; 1000 m = 1 km.

metric system   The measurement system that uses centimeter, decimeter, meter, and kilometer; milliliter and liter; and gram and kilogram.

mile (mi)   A customary unit of distance; 5280 ft = 1 mi; 1760 yd = 1 mi.

milliliter (mL)   A metric unit of capacity; 1000 mL = 1 L.

millimeter (mm)   A metric unit of length. 10 millimeters = 1 centimeter.

minuend   A number from which another number is subtracted.

mixed number   A number that is made up of a whole number and a fraction.
$$1\frac{1}{2} \longleftarrow \text{mixed number}$$

mode   The number that appears most frequently in a set of numbers.

multiple   The product of a given number and any whole number.

N

negative numbers   Numbers that are less than zero; ⁻4 is a negative number.

net   A flat pattern that folds into a solid figure.

number line   A line that is used to show the order of numbers.

number sentence   An equation or inequality.
$$16 = 9 + 7 \qquad 28 < 52$$

numerator   The numeral above the bar in a fraction; it names the number of parts being considered.

O

obtuse angle   An angle that measures more than 90°, but less than 180°.

octagon   A polygon with eight sides.

one million   The next counting number after 999,999, or 1,000,000.

order of operations   The order in which operations must be computed when more than one operation is involved.

ordered pair   A pair of numbers that is used to locate a point on a grid or coordinate graph.

origin   The point (0, 0) on a coordinate grid where the x-axis and y-axis intersect.

ounce (oz)   A customary unit of weight; 16 oz = 1 lb.

outcome   The result of a probability experiment.

P

parallel lines   Lines in the same plane that never intersect.

parallelogram   A quadrilateral whose opposite sides are parallel and congruent.

partial product   When multiplying numbers with two or more digits, the product of a single digit in one factor and the other factor.

pentagon   A polygon with five sides.

percent (%)   The ratio or comparison of a number to 100.

perimeter   The distance around a figure.

period   A group of three digits set off by commas in a whole number.

perpendicular lines   Intersecting lines in the same plane that form four right angles.

plane   A flat surface that extends indefinitely in all directions.

point   An exact location in space.

polygon   A simple closed flat figure made up of three or more line segments.

prime factorization   The expression of a composite number as the product of prime numbers.

prime number   A whole number other than 0 or 1 that has exactly two factors, itself and 1.

probability   The chance or likelihood of an event occurring.

protractor   The tool used to measure angles.

pyramid   A solid figure that has a polygon for a base and has triangular faces that meet at a point. A square pyramid has a square base.

Q

quadrilateral   Any four-sided polygon.

R

radius   A line segment with endpoints at the center of a circle and on the circle.

range   The difference between the greatest and least numbers in a set of data.

ratio   The comparison of two numbers, often expressed as a fraction.

ray   The part of a line that starts at an endpoint and goes on forever in one direction.

rectangle   A parallelogram with four right angles.

rectangular prism   A solid figure with six rectangular faces.

regrouping   Trading one from a place for ten from the next lower place, or ten from a place for one from the next higher place.

remainder   The number left over after dividing.

$$\begin{array}{r} 7 \quad \text{R}\,2 \\ 3\overline{)23} \\ -\ 21 \\ \hline 2 \end{array} \leftarrow \text{remainder}$$

rhombus   A parallelogram with all sides the same length.

right angle   An angle that measures 90°. It forms a square corner.

right triangle   A triangle that has one right angle.

rounding   Writing a number to the nearest ten or ten cents, hundred or dollar, and so on.

S

scale   The tool used to measure weight.

scalene triangle   A triangle with no sides that are equal in length.

side   A line segment that forms part of a polygon.

similar figures   Figures that have the same shape. They may or may not be the same size.

simple closed curve   A path that begins and ends at the same point and does not cross itself.

slide (translation)   The movement of a figure along a line without changing direction.

solid figure   A figure that is not flat, but that has volume; a solid figure is three-dimensional.

sphere   A solid figure that is shaped like a ball.

square   A parallelogram that has four right angles and four congruent sides.

square pyramid   A pyramid with a square base.

straight angle   An angle that measures 180°.

subtrahend   A number that is subtracted from another number.

survey   A way to collect data to answer a question.

T

temperature   The measure of how cool or warm something is.

thermometer   An instrument used to measure temperature.

ton (T)   A customary unit of weight; 2000 pounds = 1 ton.

trapezoid   A quadrilateral with exactly one pair of parallel sides.

triangle   A polygon with three sides.

triangular prism   A solid figure with two parallel triangular faces.

turn (rotation)   The movement of a figure around a point.

turn image   The result of a turn (or rotation) of a figure.

U

unlike denominators   Denominators that are not the same in one or more fractions; the fractions $\frac{1}{8}$ and $\frac{1}{7}$ have unlike denominators.

V

variable   A letter or other symbol that replaces a number in an expression, equation, or inequality.

vertex   A common endpoint of two rays or line segments. In a solid figure, the point at which three or more edges meet.

volume   The number of cubic units needed to fill a solid figure.

W

whole number   Any of the numbers 0, 1, 2, 3, 4, . . .

X

x-axis (horizontal axis)   The horizontal number line on a coordinate grid.

x-coordinate   The number that tells how many spaces to move horizontally along the x-axis; in the ordered pair (1, 2), 1 is the x-coordinate.

Y

y-axis (vertical axis)   The vertical number line on a coordinate grid.

y-coordinate   The number that tells how many spaces to move vertically along the y-axis; in the ordered pair (1, 2), 2 is the y-coordinate.

Z

zero (identity) property of addition   The sum of zero and a number is that number.

zero property of multiplication   The product of zero and a number is zero.

Mathematical Symbols

=	is equal to	·	decimal point	$\overleftrightarrow{AB}$	line AB
≠	is not equal to	°	degree	$\overline{AB}$	line segment AB
<	is less than	+	plus	$\overrightarrow{AB}$	ray AB
>	is greater than	−	minus	∠ABC	angle ABC
$	dollars	×	times	‖	is parallel to
¢	cents	÷	divided by	⊥	is perpendicular to
				(3, 4)	ordered pair

Table of Measures

Time

60 seconds (s)	= 1 minute (min)
60 minutes	= 1 hour (h)
24 hours	= 1 day (d)
7 days	= 1 week (wk)
12 months (mo)	= 1 year (y)
52 weeks	= 1 year
365 days	= 1 year
366 days	= 1 leap year

Money

1 nickel	=	5¢ or $.05
1 dime	=	10¢ or $.10
1 quarter	=	25¢ or $.25
1 half dollar	=	50¢ or $.50
1 dollar	=	100¢ or $1.00
2 nickels	= 1 dime	
10 dimes	= 1 dollar	
4 quarters	= 1 dollar	
2 half dollars	= 1 dollar	

Metric Units

Length

10 millimeters (mm)	= 1 centimeter (cm)
100 centimeters	= 1 meter (m)
10 centimeters	= 1 decimeter (dm)
10 decimeters	= 1 meter
1000 meters	= 1 kilometer (km)

Capacity

1000 milliliters (mL)	= 1 liter (L)

Mass

1000 grams (g)	= 1 kilogram (kg)

Customary Units

Length

12 inches (in.)	= 1 foot (ft)
3 feet	= 1 yard (yd)
36 inches	= 1 yard
5280 feet	= 1 mile (mi)
1760 yards	= 1 mile

Capacity

8 fluid ounces (fl oz)	= 1 cup (c)
2 cups	= 1 pint (pt)
2 pints	= 1 quart (qt)
4 quarts	= 1 gallon (gal)

Weight

16 ounces (oz)	= 1 pound (lb)
2000 pounds	= 1 ton (T)

FORMULAS / PERCENTS